D1314300

# The State in the American Political Economy

## Public Policy and the Evolution of State-Economy Relations

MARC ALLAN EISNER

Wesleyan University

 PRENTICE HALL, Englewood Cliffs, New Jersey 07632

# CONTENTS

viii Contents

## 2 THE STRUCTURE AND PERFORMANCE OF THE AMERICAN ECONOMY 40

The Structure of the Economy, 40
  The Modern Corporation and the Theory of the Firm, 41
  Strategy, Structure, and the Development of the Modern Corporation, 43
  The Modern Corporation: An Antiquated Institution? 48
The Structure and Role of Finance, 49
Industrial Organization and Governance, 53
The Position of Labor, 61
The State and Economic Organization, 64
Notes, 65

## 3 THE LEGACY OF THE NINETEENTH CENTURY 69

The Constitutional and Legal Framework, 70
Sectional Stress and Political Economies in Conflict, 76
The Transportation Revolution and Economic Growth, 81
  Transatlantic and Inland Shipping, 83
  Turnpikes and Canals, 84
  The Railroad, 85
Capital and Finance, 87
Economic Organization and the Modern Corporation, 92
Notes, 95

## 4 PROGRESSIVISM AND THE POLITICAL ECONOMY 98

The Emergence of the New Corporate Economy, 98
  The Labor Problem, 100
  The Farm Economy, 103
The Progressive Movement and Reform, 104
Progressivism and the Economy, 106
Constructing the Progressive Political Economy, 109
  The Tariff, 110

# 5 FROM THE GREAT WAR TO THE GREAT DEPRESSION

# 6 POLITICAL RESPONSES TO THE GREAT DEPRESSION

# PREFACE

The past few decades have witnessed the publication of an endless number of books with the term "political economy" in the title. Political scientists, sociologists, historians, economists, and anthropologists have contributed to the growing literature in political economy. What explains the rise of this large political-economic literature? A skeptic might respond that the answer is simply one of academic fashion. Academics, like members of any other profession, seek to be in style. While this may be part of the explanation, one cannot dispute the assertion that the interplay between the political and the economic has become increasingly important and politically salient in recent decades. With the weakening of economic growth rates, stagnant family incomes, a rising national debt, growing competition from abroad, and unprecedented trade deficits, the political economy impacts on the welfare of all. It also contributes more than a fair amount of the recent dissatisfaction that many citizens express concerning established public policies and the role of the state in society. Indeed, one could argue that core political-economic questions have been at the heart of each presidential campaign of the past 20 years. The ability or inability to answer these questions successfully through new public policies has contributed to the results of these elections.

This book presents a broad overview of the American political economy, focusing on changing patterns of state-economy relations in the United States over the course of the past century. The book has three related goals. First, the book strives to introduce the reader to key concepts necessary to understanding economic activity and public policies managing this activity. We shall have the opportunity to examine corporate organization, industrial relations, international regimes, regulatory policies, fiscal and monetary management, and a host of institutions involved in implementing public policies affecting the economy. Second, the book seeks to place current political-economic questions in a broader historical and political-institutional context. Recent political debates have obscured the complexity of the political economy through the reference to simply comparisons, such as the relative virtues of planning versus the market or laissez faire versus protectionism. While such distinctions may make for exciting political rhetoric, they obscure more than they reveal and they often hinge on misrepresentations of the history of key public policies. Finally, this book seeks to illustrate some important features of American political development. To be certain, there are a number of constants in the American political system: A strong appreciation for market governance, a cynicism concerning the role of the state in society, and high levels of interest group mobilization in a highly decentralized institutional structure seem to be permanent features of the American system that have an ongoing impact on policymakers. However, political development is not bound by a fixed set of parameters. Rather, policymakers are forced to address a variety of conflicts, crises, and the growing complexity of economic activity. In the process, they have limited the discretion of those that follow. As will become clear in the following chapters, past decisions concerning public policies, institutional design, and patterns of state-economy relations have gone far in limiting the kinds of options that are open to policymakers at any given time. Thus, while political rhetoric may know no bounds, political development is clearly bounded by the past.

This book finds its origins in a course that I have taught for several years at Wesleyan University. My students and my colleagues at Wesleyan and elsewhere have contributed much to my understanding of the political economy, asking questions that I could not answer and pushing me to sharpen my arguments. Similarly, a number of anonymous readers for the press forced me to refine my arguments. My intense interest in the questions addressed in this book reflects, in large part, the influence of those who first taught me of politics, the political economy, and public policy. Leon N. Lindberg, Booth Fowler, Graham Wilson, Ken Meier, James Rhodes, Michael Fleet, Barbara Stallings, Raju Thomas, and Leonard Weiss, among others, introduced me to so many of the issues and controversies addressed in the following chapters during my days as a graduate student. Jack Stacy contributed as well, albeit many years earlier. Their enthusiasm for knowledge was irresistible. Hence, my vocation. The greatest thanks I can offer is to convey some of their excitement to my readers and students.

# The State in the
# American Political
# Economy

text that places distinct constraints on policymakers. The legacy of past policy decisions, a lack of administrative resources and effective policy tools, and established patterns of state-economy relations can place dramatic limits on the ability of policymakers to pursue these goals. Finally, corporations, trade associations, organized labor, and consumers can frustrate the best of policies both through their individual decisions (e.g., decisions concerning investment, labor contracts, consumption) and their use of established channels of political participation to force new policy goals onto the agenda and protect existing policies deemed to be in their favor.

The relationship between politics and economics has been at the heart of political, social, and religious theories for millennia. However, with the professionalization of the social sciences, the interplay between economic and political processes has been frustrated by disciplinary specialization that carries over to methodology and the subjects of analysis. This can create impediments to research. As Martin Staniland explains:

> The fundamental difficulty lies in the radically incompatible perspectives of economics and political science, the first (in its non-Marxian versions) emphasizing markets, the second, power. The assumptions and working logic of economics cannot easily accommodate, except as "externalities," the phenomenon of coercive power, since they rest on the axiom of a freely choosing individual. Equally, political science cannot easily accept the deductive procedures of economics, which seems to insist on exploring an imaginary world of unconstrained rationality instead of the empirically observable world of conflict, misunderstanding, and coercion.[2]

The conflict between the methodologies of economics and political science creates impediments to research only as long as political scientists attempt to address the economy as represented within the highly stylized framework generated by neoclassical economics. As will be discussed in greater detail later, some economists have negotiated this methodological conflict by employing economic theories to explain political phenomena. Other social scientists have pursued a similar strategy by examining the economy through the lens of noneconomic theories. Although the elegant deductive models of neoclassical economics have successfully addressed a host of economic phenomena, the model of the rational utility-maximizer functioning in free markets seems less than compelling as an explanation of how the economy actually functions. And perhaps with good reason. As James Swaney and Robert Premus note: "A common practice in economics is essentially to invert the scientific process by developing fully formulated theoretical structures based on casual empiricism, hunches, and unrealistic assumptions. The 'applications' of theory . . . ignore or represent important aspects of reality, resulting in irrelevant if not destructive policy prescriptions."[3]

Outside of neoclassical economics, heterodox economists, political scientists, historians, and sociologists have examined the economy as a dense network of complex organizations, elites, classes, and interests struggling to acquire and preserve power and wealth. The social process of production and distribution takes place in a context that is structured by public policies which define the limits of property rights, acceptable forms of interorganizational relations, and legitimate transactions.[4] Likewise, fiscal, monetary, and trade policies will go far in shaping the context within which investment decisions are made and growth occurs—or fails to occur. Thus conceived, the methodology of political science appears particularly relevant in explaining economic activity, particularly when combined with organizational theory and historical sociology.

## COMPETING LOGICS OF ANALYSIS

The social sciences offer a number of competing theoretical perspectives that can prove quite useful in analyzing the political economy. Pluralist, elite, and class theories provide a wealth of insights into political organization, collective action, and the tensions inherent in political life. Because these theories adopt somewhat different levels of aggregation, units of analysis, and logics of political action, they produce different explanations and predictions. They are, in turn, commonly understood as competing approaches to political analysis. This said, there is much to justify a synthetic approach which recognizes the contributions of the different political perspectives. The analyst can focus on the ways in which they can be combined fruitfully to direct our analytic efforts toward a somewhat broader range of variables.

### The Pluralist Perspective

The pluralist perspective, long dominant in American political studies, begins with a simple but important empirical observation, namely, that society consists of individuals and voluntary organizations. Individuals are driven by self-interest to engage in political action and they join political organizations (e.g., parties, interest groups) as a means to that end. Individuals and organizations compete in hopes of shaping policy outputs. As one might expect, the key unit of analysis in the pluralist perspective is the individual. Individuals are self-interested and rational actors who participate in politics in hopes of receiving particular benefits. Thus, Sidney Verba, Norman H. Nie, and Jae-Oh Kim present political participation as "largely a goal-oriented activity in which citizens take part in order to obtain some benefit from the government."[5] Because parties are ineffective means of representation and elections "are quite ineffective as indicators of majority preferences," individuals find it necessary to create or join groups and coalitions in pursuit of these benefits.[6] "The individual facing the government is in unequal competition—especially if he has any but the most particularlized goals in mind. Effective political action often depends upon the ability of citizens to work collaboratively."[7] For the pluralist, the system is open to participation. Democratic norms and a market economy allow for continual interaction and place few constraints on participation.

Pluralism presents a vision of the world in which multiple centers of power compete to shape policy. There are no permanent and dominant sources of power; there is no single group, class, or segment with a hegemonic position. Power is diffuse and ever changing: "The fact about American power . . . is that it is plural and fluid. It is many-faceted rather than uniform; it is dispersed among a number of groups; it has shifted geographically and in its class distribution."[8] Moreover, the decentralization of American institutions and the relative openness of the political system promote stability by guaranteeing competing groups access and some degree of power. As Robert Dahl notes with respect to the American system: "With all its defects, it does nonetheless provide a high probability that any active and legitimate group will make itself heard effectively at some stage in the process of decision." This access is critical for "decisions are made by endless bargaining; perhaps in no other national political system in the world is bargaining so basic a component of the political process."[9]

With high levels of participation, multiple bases of organization, and ongoing competition over policy, one must ask: How is stable competition possible? For the pluralist, stability is, in part, maintained through a broad value consensus encompassed by the political culture. A political culture, according to Sidney Verba, "consists of the system of empirical beliefs, expressive symbols, and values which defines the situation in which political action takes place. It provides the subjective orientation to politics."[10] For pluralists, political culture fulfills an important function. For individuals, it "provides controlling guidelines for effective political behavior, and for the collectivity it gives a systematic structure of values and rational considerations which ensures coherence in the performance of institutions and organizations."[11] There are shared rules of the game that define the parameters of legitimate political action and state activity. As long as such norms are accepted and observed by the competing groups, stability will be possible even in the midst of change.

However, stability is also maintained through a self-equilibrating political process that results in a certain balancing of interests. As David Truman explains: "Any mutual interest . . . any shared attitude is a potential group. A disturbance in established relationships and expectations anywhere in society may produce new patterns of interaction aimed at restricting or eliminating the disturbance." In short, "serious disequilibrium" can stimulate "the formation of new groups that may function to restore the balance"[12] A pluralist system thus automatically adjusts to crises, conflicts, and change.

Given the key concerns of the pluralist perspective—the rules of participation, the propensity of interest groups to form and affect policy—one should not be surprised that there is little in the way of a pluralist theory of the state. For the pluralist perspective, the state is synonymous with the governmental decision-making process. The concern is whether citizen participation (policy inputs) affect what elected officials do (i.e., policy outputs). To put things more simply, the question is whether officials are responsive to the demands of participants in the political system. When the state is synonymous with the political process and the process is understood as a set of representative mechanisms that transform inputs into outputs, the state remains unconceptualized.[13] A simplified portrayal of the pluralist interpretation of the policy process is presented schematically in Figure 1–1.

There is nothing in the pluralist perspective that mandates a small state. Conceivably, the citizenry could share a consensus favoring large-scale government intervention. Yet, many pluralists suggest that a minimalist state is somehow necessary. If decentralization of decision making is necessary for pluralism, one

**Figure 1–1**  The Pluralist Perspective

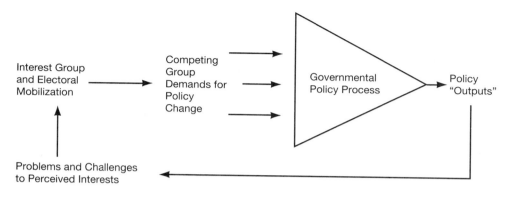

can understand why the state's role in the economy is so often presented in these terms. Milton Friedman presents the clearest defense of the minimalist state, one which fits well with the general worldview of the pluralist perspective. He notes that "a good society requires that its members agree on the general conditions that will govern relations among them, on some means of arbitrating different interpretations of these conditions, and on some device for enforcing compliance with the generally accepted rules." The government is to play the role as a "rule-maker and umpire," providing the mechanism necessary for making, modifying, interpreting, and enforcing rules.[14] Since the market is sufficient for governing most economic activities, "the role of the government . . . is to do something that the market cannot do for itself, namely, to determine, arbitrate, and enforce the rules of the game." For Friedman this entails regulating the economy in those limited circumstances where markets fail to function (i.e., monopoly and significant externalities or "neighborhood effects").[15]

Despite the common portrayals of the pluralist perspective as simplistic, naive, and relevant to a limited number of political systems, one cannot examine serious contributions to the perspective without arriving at a strong appreciation for the careful empirical analyses of public opinion and participation. Moreover, while a simplified presentation of the perspective may leave the impression that pluralists fail to acknowledge the biases inherent in a political system, this would be a significant distortion of the truth. Take, for example, Sidney Verba and Norman H. Nie's *Participation in America*. They carefully distinguish between the right to participate, which is available to all, and the reality of participation, which carries a distinct upper-class bias. They conclude that "a major force leading to participation . . . is associated with social status and civic attitudes that accompany it. This skews the participant population in the direction of the more affluent, the better educated, those with higher-status occupations."[16] They continue: "Participation helps those who are already better off. In general, lower-status citizens participate less than do upper-status ones. And even when some of them become active, their preferences are not communicated to leaders as adequately as are those of the upper-status activities, because they are such a small minority of the activist population."[17] In the memorable words of E.E. Schattschneider, "the flaw in the pluralist heaven is that the heavenly chorus sings with a strong upper-class accent."[18]

This insight—that economic status can create the basis for the overrepresentation of wealthy interests—has been extended by so-called neopluralists like Charles Lindblom, Theodore Lowi, and Grant McConnell, whose presentations challenge the pluralist notion that power is diffuse and that no single interest dominates the political system.[19] In *Politics and Markets*, Charles E. Lindblom explains that corporate officials exist as a set of policymakers parallel to elected officials but not subject to the same kinds of controls: "Corporate executives in all private enterprise systems . . . decide a nation's industrial technology, the pattern of work organization, location of industry, market structure, resource allocation, and, of course, executive compensation and status."[20] In short, "a large category of major decisions is turned over to businessmen, both small and larger. . . . Businessmen thus become a kind of public official and exercise what, on a broad view of their role, are public functions."[21] Not only are corporate officials free from the constraints placed on public decision makers, but because of the importance of the functions they execute, government officials must accommodate them on a regular basis. "Government exercises broad control over business activities. But the exercise of that authority is curbed and shaped by the concern of government officials for its possible adverse effects [on] business, since adverse effects can cause unemployment and other consequences that government officials are unwilling to accept." Corporate officials understand this situation and use it to actively place demands on government. In turn, "government has to meet business needs as a condition of inducing business performance."[22] The biases within the system and the privileged position of business—the core concerns of the neopluralists—provide the basis for those working in the elite perspective.

## The Elite Perspective

The elite perspective differs in many ways from the pluralist perspective, even if neopluralists and elite theorists share a number of points of agreement. The elite perspective begins with a simple empirical observation: Despite the discussion of cross-cutting cleavages, open competition, and the plural and fluid nature of power in America, the reality is quite different. Power is concentrated in elites drawn from the government, large corporations, and the military. Competition within the political and economic spheres is very limited. Where it exists, competition is subject to institutional management.

As one might expect, the key unit of analysis is not the individual or the pressure group but the relatively small stratum of elites who are in control of large bureaucratic organizations: the government, military, and corporations. Rather than competing in an open political system to translate policy inputs into policy outputs, the key dynamic is one of dominance. Elites use the resources of their respective organizations to manage and impose order on society. This is often criticized as a concerted attempt to maintain the status quo—one which represents the interests of elites. Stability rests, then, not on a common political culture and set of values—as suggested by pluralist scholars—but on a forced consensus created and reinforced by the elite. Elite in government and the media structure the debate to turn real issues into nonissues or to depoliticize problems that threaten the existing distribution of power.

As one might expect, the state is not understood as the open and neutral institutional system envisioned by the pluralist perspective. Rather, it too is controlled by elites who exercise power in their own best interest. As C. Wright Mills explains, this governmental elite is not synonymous with the corporate elite.

> We should . . . be quite mistaken to believe that the political apparatus is merely an extension of the corporate world, or that it has been taken over by the representatives of the corporate rich. The American government is not, in any simple way nor as a structural fact, a committee of the "ruling class." It is a network of "committees," and other men from other hierarchies besides the corporate rich sit in these committees. Of these, the professional politician himself is the most complicated, but the high military, the warlords of Washington, are the newest.[23]

The image of a network of elites managing society is pervasive in the elite analyses. However, the acceptance of such a network does not preclude the existence of pluralist politics. Rather, pluralist politics do exist and are quite common. Elite theorists like Mills do not lose sight of campaigns, elections, interest group competition, and the often dramatic legislative debates in Congress that result in the passage of legislation. The key point, however, is that these political actors are commonly involved in addressing issues that are not at all central to the welfare of society. As Mills explains: Pluralism "confuses, indeed it does not even distinguish between the top, the middle, and the bottom levels of power." He goes on to note: "Undue attention to the middle level of power obscures the structure of power as a whole, especially the top and the bottom. American politics, as discussed and voted and campaigned for, have largely to do with these middle levels, and often only with them."[24] Thus, key decisions regarding economic policy and the use of nuclear weapons are made at the top level of power by elites, insulated from the countervailing forces and open interest group politics that are the subject of pluralist analyses. Thus, the open pluralist system obscures a policy process best characterized by elite bargaining and management within the confines of the bureaucratic organizations. Popular and electoral politics are, for the most part, symbolic. The most important issues are not addressed within the electoral arena but resolved through elite interaction. The elite interpretation of the policy process is presented schematically in Figure 1–2.

While C. Wright Mills, the father of elite theory in the United States, presented a vision of a society dominated by corporate, governmental, and military elites manipulating public authority in their own interests, more contemporary debates have departed somewhat from this vision to devote relatively greater attention to elites working within governmental agencies and the possibilities for broad elite agreements as a means of managing some of the more perplexing problems that are encountered by the advanced industrial state.

**Figure 1–2**   The Elite Perspective

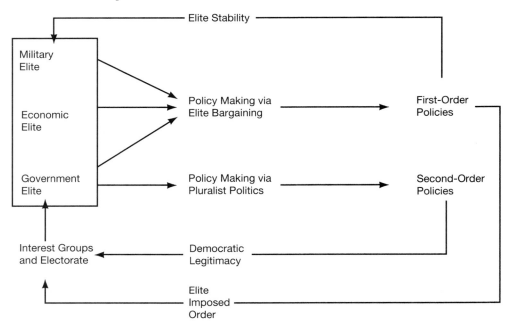

Several analysts working in the elite perspective claim that power has been transferred over time from society and pluralist interest associations to bureaucratic structures. The specialized expertise of bureaucrats, when combined with the complexity of core public policies, has driven this centralization of power, both in the polity and the economy.[25] The elite need not be seen as somehow monolithic. Some, like Ralf Dahrendorf argue that conflicts between competing bureaucratic elites have replaced economic class conflicts in importance.[26] Others, like Daniel Bell, argue that the core conflict is not among competing elites but between the bureaucratic and democratic institutions in the state.[27] The existence of bureaucratic decision rules can frustrate the expression of political interests, thus placing limits on democracy. Similarly, many have argued that bureaucrats constitute a new class, characterized by their possession of advanced training and specialized expertise. Working through bureaucratic organizations, it is argued, they engage in social engineering to impose a particular vision on society.[28]

Although some use elite theory to identify sources of conflict and competition within society, others have identified forms of elite intermediation that allow for the management of conflict and the economy. In the late 1970s and early 1980s, many analysts looked to the example of a number of northern European nations that adopted corporatist arrangements which brought together representatives of the public sector, business associations, and labor organizations to forge macroeconomic policies. While some claimed that corporatism was essentially an extension of pluralism by virtue of the role of groups, this interpretation was not widely accepted. Elites representing the state, corporations, and labor organizations—all large bureaucratic organizations in their own right—arrived at agreements to manage society.[29] Through such arrangements, unstructured conflicts usually fought out in the market or on the shop floor were managed through broad social contracts which promoted price stability *and* full employment.[30] Corporatism was thus seen by many as an effective means of managing class struggle to the end of stabilizing the economic and political system.

## The Class Perspective

The class or Marxist perspective is derived from an empirical observation which sets it apart from both the pluralist and the elite perspectives. Scholars working in the class perspective acknowledge that there are multiple bases of organization in society and that there are often significant differences in the demands of competing coalitions and elites. However, it is argued, actors can be separated into distinct classes when considered in reference to their relationship to the means of production. The key unit of analysis is the class. However, it is critical to be clear that class is used as an analytical category. Both pluralist and elite theorists will invoke class as a descriptive category. That is, they will freely place individuals into classes (e.g., lower class, middle class, upper class) based on a particular socioeconomic indicator (e.g., annual income). They may ascribe particular opinions or behaviors to members of the class. For Marxists, however, class is not a descriptive category but an expression of an organic relationship to the means of production. Capitalists are simply those who own capital, are in control of capital, or profit through the creation of surplus value. Labor, in contrast, has nothing to sell but itself. It is, as a result, completely dependent on the decisions made by those who possess control over the means of production.

As noted above, the key dynamics in the pluralist and institutional frameworks are, respectively, group competition and elite dominance. For the class theorist, the key dynamic is class conflict and struggle. To maintain the capital accumulation process, capitalists must maximize surplus value or profit. Workers seek to maximize their wages. In the end, the system is driven by the struggle over national product. While Marxists see the foundations for conflict expressed in the divergent interests of capital and labor, they also recognize a fair amount of stability. This stability is maintained through the capitalist's control over key social institutions. Traditional Marxists maintain a distinction between structure and superstructure. The key argument is that all social institutions and culture are, at any given time, a reflection of the dominant set of class relations. These institutions are used to exercise societal hegemony, that is, to force workers to adopt the values of capitalism as their own. Thus, in their analysis of public education, Samuel Bowles and Herbert Gintis argue that "the educational system . . . reproduces and legitimizes the preexisting pattern in the process of training and stratifying the work force." It reproduces the "social relations of dominance, subordination, and motivation in the economic sphere."[31] Similarly, workers may give in to the demands for wage concessions out of fear that their corporations will not realize sufficient profits to remain open. They may conceptualize unemployment as an individual moral issue rather than questioning the right of the corporation to displace work-

through taxation. The state is structurally dependent on the ongoing health of the capitalist economy. Unfortunately—or fortunately, depending on your perspective—the demands of legitimation and accumulation are not necessarily compatible. Democratic institutions may provide policies that erode growth and profitability; the demands of accumulation may require limiting the extent of democracy. Public managers are thus forced to walk a tight rope of types when seeking to accommodate the two sets of demands.

A second response to this interesting question addresses the nature of the state and the conditions under which the state has been able to exercise autonomy from capitalists. Following Fred Block, one can cite the example of the Great Depression.[35] During the crisis of the Great Depression, Roosevelt and his advisers were able to promote policies that furthered the interests of labor relative to capital (i.e., the National Industrial Recovery Act of 1935) and reduced the dependency of citizens on the capitalist production process (i.e., the passage of critical welfare state legislation, such as the Social Security Act of 1935). Under normal conditions, such efforts would have been impossible due to the likelihood of a capital strike— that is, the refusal to reinvest under conditions of extreme uncertainty or the expectation of reduced profitability. Such a capital strike, under normal conditions. would force higher levels of unemployment and a reduction in state revenues. However, this threat declined dramatically during the depression while popular demands for recovery loomed large. Hence, state managers had far greater autonomy to introduce innovations that might have been impossible only a few years earlier. The policy process as portrayed by the class perspective is presented in Figure 1–3.

## Integrating Competing Logics of Political Action

The pluralist, elite, and class theories of politics—combined with the analogous economic perspectives—provide a rather diverse set of assumptions concerning the appropriate focus of analysis and the dominant logic of political-economic action. Each perspective has its strengths within its particular "home domain."[36] The pluralist perspective functions well when addressing the politics surrounding policies in which group access is assured. The elite perspective provides a clearer understanding of the kinds of forces at play in a political economy dominated by large bureaucratic organizations. This elite position focuses our attention on the ways in which elites in complex organizations attempt to manage competition and uncertainty both in the economic and political spheres and the ways in which organizational factors both empower actors and place limitations on the kinds of things they can accomplish. Finally, the class perspective alerts us to the larger societal context of political-economic life. While elite and group forces may draw a good deal of analytical attention, there remain a number of conflicts inherent in the capitalist production process. The tension between democratic legitimation and capital accumulation, for example, suggests an explanation for the limitations of pluralist politics. The key features of the competing theoretical perspectives are presented in Table 1–1.

The competing perspectives thus provide different visions of political action, albeit at different levels of analysis. They can be employed usefully to fully explore key episodes in the evolution of the political economy. Before developing

**Figure 1–3**  The Class Perspective

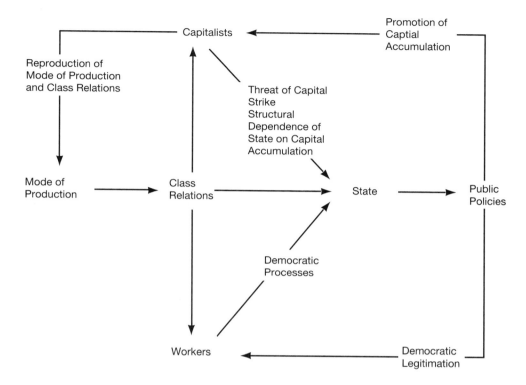

this point in greater detail, it is necessary to turn to the status of institutions and the tension between structure and human agency. As will be argued below, institutions can provide a critical focal point of assessing the interplay of group, elite, and class forces.

## STRUCTURE, AGENCY, AND INSTITUTIONS

As suggested above, political economy addresses a substantive area of intellectual inquiry. Political economists examine changing patterns of state-economy relations and their impact on economic and political performance. However, it is important to note that political economy describes a method of analysis as well as a substantive field of study. For many economists, political economy is the use of economic models and theories to explain political action and public policy decisions.[37] A growing body of public-choice literature aspires to this form of political economy, describing it as the "new" political economy. Dennis C. Mueller explains: "Public choice can be defined as the economic study of nonmarket decision making, or simply the application of economics to political science. The subject matter of public choice is the same as that of political science: the theory of the state, voting rules, voter behavior, party politics, the bureaucracy, and so on. The methodology of public choice is that of economics, however. The basic behavioral postulate of public choice, as for economics, is that man is an egoistic, rational, utility maximizer."[38] The public choice variant of political economy adopts the same behavioral assumptions as applied in economics. Individual actors are presented as rational utility maximizers who will make political decisions based on a narrow calculus of self-interest. The most interesting questions address the issues of how individuals gain information, aggregate preferences, or identify equilibria or points where preferences coincide.

Public-choice political economy adopts the position of methodological individualism. That is, "the basic units are choosing, acting, behaving persons rather than organic units such as parties, provinces, or nations."[39] For methodological individualists, all political phenomena can be reduced to individual goals and decisions as aggregated. The methodological individualism of public-choice political economy reflects the economics training of most of its practitioners. *Homo economicus* is the rational, utility maximizer making decisions in the context of free markets. Even after *homo economicus* becomes *homo politicus*, the basic approach to decision making is retained. While this approach to the study of political economy has been fruitful, it is limited by virtue of its limited appreciation of institutions. Institutions are presented in the most minimal sense, either as mechanisms for aggregating the decisions and actions of individual actors and resolving disputes between competing claims, or alternatively, as unitary actors with the same attributes as a rational individual actor.[40]

**TABLE 1–1**   Competing Theoretical Perspectives

|  | *Pluralist* | *Elite* | *Class* |
|---|---|---|---|
| Primary unit of analysis | Individuals and interest groups | Elites and bureaucracies | Classes |
| Power | Diffuse | Concentrated in elite and organizations | Concentrated in capitalist class |
| Logic of action | Group competition | Elite control | Class conflict |
| The state | Neutral set of procedures that integrate group demands | Set of bureaucratic organizations with various levels of integration | Apparatus structurally dependent on capital accumulation |
| Economy | Businesses competing in the market | Organizational network dense in interorganizational relations | Class relations of production associated with capitalism |
| Source of stability | Value consensus Multiple group membership | Imposed order; insulated policy-making | False consciousness and fear of repression |
| Source of instability | Concentration of power in groups that represent monied interests | Failure of bureaucratic planning and elite competition | Inherent contradictions of capitalism; the conflicts between capital accumulation and legitimation |

The claim that political economy describes a particular methodology of analysis is not unique to public choice. Let us return to Marixian political economy. Marx adopted a political-economic methodology that was diametrically opposed to the approach embraced by contemporary public-choice theorists. One of the main differences is the understanding of economic laws as being somehow transcendent. As Marx argued, the standard economic theories present economic activity "as encased in eternal natural laws independent of history, at which opportunity bourgeois relations are then quietly smuggled in as the inviolable natural laws on which society in the abstract is founded."[41] Marx claimed repeatedly that "every form of production creates its own legal relations, form of government, etc."[42] The laws that appeared inviolable were, in fact, historical artifacts that reflected the relations of production and configuration of class forces at a given time.

Marx's materialist interpretation of the political economy began with the assumption that humans must be understood first and foremost in their productive existence: "Men can be distinguished from animals by consciousness, by religion, or anything else you like. They themselves begin to distinguish themselves from animals as soon as they begin to produce their means of subsistence, a step which is conditioned by their physical organization. By producing their means of subsistence men are indirectly producing their actual material life."[43] By starting with this premise, Marx ties human activity into existing relations of production. This, in turn, provides a basis for a distinctive political economic methodology that places a central emphasis on structure. Marx approached political economy through the lens of class relations inherent in the production process and the political, cultural, and legal institutions that reflect and reproduce these class relations. In this vein, consider Marx's portrayal of the political economy: "In the social production of their life, men enter into definite relations that are indispensable and independent of their will, relations of production which correspond to a definite stage of development of their material productive forces. The sum total of these relations of production constitutes the economic structure of society, the real foundation, on which rises a legal and political superstructure and to which correspond definite forms of social consciousness."[44] Marxian political economy focuses on the relations of production—a structure against which human agency fades from view. Although contemporary class theorists have departed from the more deterministic elements of Marxian political economy, there remains a strong element of structural analysis that limits the role of human agency.

The juxtaposition of public choice and Marxian class analysis strongly suggests, firstly, that the approach one adopts to studying political economy is more than a trivial question. One would not expect class and choice-theoretical analysts to arrive at remotely similar analyses of common political-economic phenomena. Whereas the former would seek to discover the connection between the particular phenomena and the prevailing class relations of production, the former would interpret them as the products of individuals acting rationally to maximize their utility. Structure and agency—each perspective emphasizes one, often to the exclusion of the other. Interestingly, the most sophisticated class analysts have labored to develop an approach that is more sensitive to the autonomy of government decision makers. While it is convenient to present the state as "a committee for managing the common affairs of the whole bourgeoisie"[45] that single-mindedly promotes capital accumulation and manages the class struggle, there are simply too many examples of policy-makers acting against the immediate and/or long-term interests of the dominant class. Likewise, many working in the public choice perspective are rethinking the role of structure and the factors that may limit the relevance of methodological individualism in response to state actions that seem to frustrate the logic of utility maximization.

The tension between structure and agency is critically important and deserves some attention. To facilitate this examination, it is useful to consider state institutions and their impact on shaping the power of public officials and addressing conflicts and crises in society. The state is best understood as a set of complex organizations that exercises a legitimate monopoly of coercive power both within the boundaries of a nation and in a nation's relations with other nations.[46] The complex organizations that constitute the state are more-or-less differentiated along functional lines. They may be engaged in extracting resources from the economy and citizenry; making authoritative and binding rules for social interaction; allocating resources to public works and various clientele groups; adjudicating disputes among citizens and between citizens and the state; or maintaining internal or external order. Institutions are best conceived as the roles, rules, and decision-making procedures that define the internal workings of an organization and the relationships between a given organization and other organizations. In anticipation of a more detailed examination of the American state in the following pages, it is useful to identify some of the ways in which institutions condition the range of actions available to individual decision makers. The rules that make up an institution determine how authoritative decision makers are to be selected (e.g., through elections, appointments, completion of civil service exams) and define the mechanisms for making and implementing authoritative decisions (e.g., statutes must be passed by a majority in two chambers of Congress and signed by the president). These features of institutions have been recognized by public-choice theorists and provide a basis for the assumption that electorally selected officials will use their authority to maximize the support of voters.

When we consider institutions, it is critical to go beyond the formal rules that determine how authoritative decision makers are selected and how their individual preferences are aggregated in the policy process. Institutions determine what kinds of analytical and administrative resources decision makers can draw on in formulating and implementing policies. However, institutions are not determinantive. Rather, the effects of institutions on government capabilities are contingent. As R. Kent Weaver and Bert A. Rockman note:

> Specific institutional arrangements are insufficient to guarantee a high or low level of a specific capability, but they may exacerbate failures of governance or help to make societies more manageable. Even where institutional arrangements do contribute to overall differences in specific capabilities, moreover, these effects usually are strongly mediated by other institutional and noninstitutional factors. Thus, instead of speaking of the sufficiency of certain institutional arrangements, it is more appropriate to

speak of opportunities they provide for strong capabilities when other conditions are present to facilitate those opportunities.[47]

Thus, as Weaver and Rockman point out, "the risk that separation of powers will lead to unclear policy priorities and big budget deficits is likely to be greatest when there is divided partisan control of government and the public holds inconsistent preferences on taxing and spending."[48] Institutional design creates particular biases that find their clearest impact on policy and performance when combined with other factors.

Ideas are critical to the policy process in several senses. At the broadest level, ideas concerning the appropriate role of the state in civil society condition the determination of what sort of governmental actions will be deemed legitimate, absent an emergency situation. At a much more specific level, ideas or theories are central to designing and implementing particular policies. The kinds of ideas integrated into the policy process will shape the way problems are defined and addressed, the linkages among a broader range of problems and policies, and the ultimate success of policy. To a great extent, institutions affect whether ideas are available to policymakers. This is true in two senses. First, the more decentralized or fragmented the institutional structure, the greater the capacity of private-sector actors to present ideas that may be integrated into the policy process. In highly centralized institutions, the universe of ideas available to policymakers may be limited to those presented by individuals occupying leadership positions (e.g., department secretaries) or official advisory positions (e.g., a member of the Council of Economic Advisers). Second, even if a diverse universe of ideas is presented in the policy debates, the capacity of officials to make use of these ideas will be contingent on the analytical resources available to administrators. Professionalized bureaucracies are necessary if policies that embody complex theories are to be administered effectively. Indeed, as the following chapters will reveal, the bureaucracy is often a source of the ideas that provide a basis for policy.

Public policy is not synonymous with rhetoric or statements of intent. Rather public policy must describe an authoritative pattern of actions taken by public officials in pursuit of predefined goals. If we are concerned with patterns of action, then we must focus on implementation as well as authorization. The success of legislative mandates and executive orders will depend, in large part, on the existence of administrative resources and existing patterns of state–interest group relations. Administration agencies are highly specialized organizations. The expertise of administrators, the agency's analytical resources, and the collection of available policy tools are not static but evolve in response to prior decisions about policy and resources. Agencies that lack large professional staffs and planning and evaluation offices may simply be incapable of implementing technically complex policies unless, of course, legislative mandates are combined with efforts to professionalize the agency and institute new procedures.

While there are examples of successful agency reorganizations and professionalization processes that overpower existing routines and bureaucratic biases, they are rare and occur largely in response to significant crises. More often than not, administrators seek to redirect existing bureaucratic resources to meet new demands. The practical importance is quite clear: Past policy and budgetary decisions place boundaries on the opportunity set available to policymakers. Because policy and administrative capacities are clearly linked, significant constraints are placed on the universe of policy options open to decision makers. Policy evolution is bounded by the existing trajectory of institutional development.

Institutions also shape interest aggregation and articulation. That is, they shape the way in which societal interests organize, the extent to which various social groups have access to policymakers, and how their interests are integrated into the decision-making process. Are legislative bodies relatively permeable to interest group demands? Are there effective peak associations and political parties that can articulate a comprehensive agenda and promote consistency across an otherwise fragmented set of institutions? These are critical questions. In many complex policy areas, interest groups play a central role in implementation. In several regulatory policy areas (e.g., finance, agriculture, transportation), economic associations serve a certain self-regulatory function under the direction and supervision of administrators. These self-regulatory organizations can facilitate policy implementation by regulating the behavior of their own members, serving essentially as quasi-public institutions. Of course, interest group aggregation and articulation also affect policymaking. If power is fragmented along vertical and horizontal dimensions and interest groups have unlimited access to sites of policymaking, it may make sense for interests to organize at relatively low levels of aggregation. Moreover, in this environment of vigorous interest group competition, it may prove very difficult for public officials to construct effective policies. They may be forced by electoral pressures and majoritarian decision rules to define policy in the broadest possible sense in order to build a broad coalition in support of the policy.

Institutions, interests, and ideas all impact on the ability of policymakers to effectively formulate and implement policies addressing the economy. We will address each in greater detail, with special reference to the American state. However, it is important to preface this discussion by emphasizing once again that we are not looking at a stable set of relationships. Rather, institutions evolve over time in response to a host of factors. Political development is, in many ways, path dependent. Decisions at a given point in time effectively foreclose certain options at a subsequent point in time. What a policymaker can do is thus contingent on earlier decisions. The key point is not merely that a historical perspective is useful. Rather, it is essential for one to understand the evolution of the state and patterns of state-economy relations.

## INSTITUTIONS, INTEREST, AND IDEAS IN THE AMERICAN STATE

Institutional design, interest articulation, and ideas provide important focal points for examining the key dimensions of the American state. First, one must address the high levels of institutional fragmentation. By design, the American state is highly decentralized. Power is fragmented along horizontal and vertical dimensions.[49] This has significant implications for the coherence of policy and the success of implementing public policies. Second, one must address political representation in the American system. A strong party system with class-based programmatic parties could, in theory, provide a means of bridging the fragmented organizational structure. However, parties in the United States are remarkably weak, thus expanding the role of interest groups. They provide a key means for mobilizing economic interests and are more important than parties when examining the political representation of business and labor. Because interest groups are organized at a low level of aggregation (i.e., on an issue-specific or industry-specific basis), their central role in politics only reinforces the above mentioned fragmentation. Finally, we turn to the way in which policy-relevant expertise is integrated into the policy process. The high levels of fragmentation, both in institutional design and interest representation, affect the context in which ideas are integrated into the policy process.

## Institutional Design: Fragmentation and the American State

The institutional fragmentation that characterizes the American state finds its origins in constitutional design. In response to prevailing treatises on institutions and the negative experience with colonial rule, the framers of the Constitution consciously sought to create a decentralized governmental system in which power was assigned to separate legislative, executive, and judicial branches. In *The Federalist*, No. 9, Alexander Hamilton listed the key features of the new system: "The regular distribution of power into distinct departments; the introduction of legislative balances and checks; the institution of courts composed of judges holding their offices during good behavior; the representation of the people in the legislature by deputies of their own election: these are wholly new discoveries, or have made their principal progress towards perfection in modern times. They are means, and powerful means, by which the excellences of republican government may be retained and its imperfections lessened or avoided."[50]

This "government of separated institutions *sharing* powers" was designed to impede the concentration of power.[51] As James Madison explained in *The Federalist*, No. 51, this institutional separation provided "great security against a gradual concentration of powers in the same department." "Ambition must be made to counteract ambition" so that each branch would jealously guard its mandate from the infringement of the others.[52] Moreover, such a system would insulate public policy from the riotous interplay of factions that dominated politics. If institutions could be designed to retard the policy process and provide a series of checks and balances, there would be a greater chance that reason would triumph over passion and the limited government would not exceed its legitimate bounds.

Outside the key structural features—the separation of powers, checks and balances—the system created under the Constitution bears little resemblance to the system which exists today. The limited prebureaucratic state has been replaced by an expansive, if relatively uncoordinated, network of government agencies executing a wide range of public policies. However, the decentralization of the system, over two centuries after the ratification of the Constitution, attests to the remarkable permanence of the original tenets of institutional design. The executive branch consists of hundreds of agencies, advisory structures, and planning offices with virtually no central power capable of coordinating their efforts. Likewise, Congress consists of hundreds of committees and subcommittees with overlapping jurisdictions and yet few means exist for integrating or reconciling their activities. With the erosion of seniority, the weakening of party leadership, and the rise of subcommittee autonomy, Congress continues to churn out legislation without direction. To be certain, there was greater party cohesion in Congress in response to the decentralizing reforms of the post-Watergate years, divided government, and growing fiscal restraints, yet the structural decentralization continues to frustrate the definition of clear priorities in congressional policymaking.[53] While district courts, appellate courts, and the Supreme Court are nominally structured in a hierarchical fashion and, in theory, all courts are subject to Supreme Court decisions, the reality is quite different. Vastly different decisions can emerge from parallel courts, thus providing ample opportunity for "district shopping." Lower courts commonly ignore, reinterpret, or consciously misapply Supreme Court decisions. To make matters worse, the Supreme Court's docket simply cannot accommodate all the controversies that are addressed at the lower levels. The result of this extraordinary fragmentation seems less the rational application of the "new science of politics" than an evolutionary process run amok.

This horizontal fragmentation carries important implications for economic policymaking. Efforts to make comprehensive policies governing the economy can be thwarted by the independent powers and competing policies of a large number of executive branch and independent agencies, as well as committees and subcommittees in two houses of Congress and the courts. Because the agencies and committees have well-established relationships with organized interests, there is a great capacity on the part of each to impede change. Consider the example of finance. Comprehensive policies governing finance would require the coordination of the Commodity Futures Trading Commission, the Comptroller of the Currency, the Federal Deposit Insurance Corporation, the Federal Home Loan Bank Board, the Federal Reserve Board and Federal Reserve Banks, the National Credit Union Administration, the Resolution Trust Corporation, the Securities and Exchange Commission, the Finance Committees and subcommittees in both chambers of Congress, and a number of trade associations (e.g., the National Association of Securities Dealers) that have been delegated certain self-regulatory functions. The impediments to working with so large a number of agencies are so great that usually each entity will function with relative independence. Whether the policies of the above mentioned agencies work at the same ends is at all times an open question.

The institutional fragmentation also has a strong vertical dimension. The Constitution created a federal system in hopes of establishing a workable national authority while retaining relatively autonomous states. The Articles of Confederation created, according to Hamilton in *The Federalist,* No. 15, a system "destitute of energy" by maintaining "the political monster of an *imperium in imperio.*"[54] The Constitution addressed this situation by carving out relatively distinct spheres of national and state authority. While the Federalists themselves seemed to disagree as to the precise relationship between the national and state governments, both Madison and Hamilton presented visions of federalism that placed far greater power in the states than would exist even a few decades after the ratification of the Constitution. As the federal government moved to address commerce, economic development, and successive crises of war and depression, it extended its authority beyond what was initially envisioned.

The result of this evolution, however, has not been the complete diminution of authority at the state and local levels. Rather, in many policy areas the past two centuries have witnessed the evolution of parallel systems. Thus, in our dual banking system, federal regulations executed by multiple agencies are combined with regulations in 50 states. A similar state of affairs exists with antitrust, environmental protection, occupational safety and health, consumer protection, and a host of industries, including insurance, electricity generation, telecommunications, and transportation. Moreover, in a host of policy areas, federal authorities define rules and regulations and delegate authority to state officials through a system of proxy administration. With 50 parallel jurisdictions regulating a common set of activities with little coordination and ongoing conflicts with the federal government, the results are often incoherence.

The incoherence is often combined with a good deal of competition. This is true in two senses. First, states compete with each other in hopes of attracting commerce and new investment. Thus, they may play an entrepreneurial role by suspending state regulations and providing special incentives such as tax exemptions, loan guarantees, and direct subsidies.[55] Second, because American economic development created distinct regional economies with competing and diverse interests, there has been competition to shape national legislation (e.g., regulations, tariffs, taxes) to affect the economic balance of power. Historically, a core manufacturing and financial economy in the Northeast and industrial Midwest competed with an agricultural and extractive economy in the rest of the nation. Because of well-established norms of congressional localism, these sectional conflicts have shaped a good deal of national economic policy, as revealed by Richard Franklin Bensel.[56]

## Interest Articulation: Fragmented Parties in a Fragmented System

Parties play a critical role in a democratic polity. By providing a label such as Democrat or Republican to a slate of candidates, parties reduce the information required of voters. In this capacity, parties facilitate elections as a means of channeling popular demands. As Benjamin Ginsberg notes: "Elections . . . substitute an institutional mechanism for the informal sanctions, including riot and insurrection, that might otherwise be available to a mass public. Elections transform citizens' capacity to influence their rulers' behavior from a matter of purely private activities and resources to a result of mass participation in a routine public function."[57] The party can also serve an important role in linking elites in government institutions and orienting them to a common policy agenda. Institutional fragmentation need not be debilitating. A strong programmatic party, for example, could forge an important bridge between officials in different branches and at different levels of government, giving them shared objectives and providing a means of forcing discipline. However, as Richard Neustadt correctly notes: "What the Constitution separates our political parties do not combine. The parties are themselves composed of separated organizations sharing public authority."[58] To understand the failure of American political parties to fulfill this function, it is necessary to con-

sider the key features of American political parties and their evolution in historical and comparative perspective.

The first thing one must recognize about American political parties is their
extreme decentralization. Their chief existence has been as state and local organizations. As E.E. Schattschneider observed, this is an essential starting point for understanding U.S. political parties: "Decentralization of power is by all odds the most
important single characteristic of the American major party; more than anything else
this trait distinguishes it from all others. Indeed, once this truth is understood, nearly
everything about American parties is illuminated."[59] National party conventions were
created to provide a means of aggregating the decisions of state and local party elites.
Even in the late nineteenth and early twentieth centuries, when the national parties
became much stronger than they had been earlier, they retained their confederative
structure. Both parties have attempted to federalize their organizations in recent years
through the provision of financial resources and in-kind services, or, as in the case of
the Democrats, by imposing regulations governing the composition and selection of
state delegations to the national convention. However, the national parties remain
composites of state parties concerned, in large part, with state and local issues.

The localism of the two parties must be combined with some understanding of the parties' concern with elections. In past decades, it was common to accept
the thesis that the programmatic, mass-based parties so common in Western Europe marked something of an end point in party development.[60] However, as Leon
Epstein has argued, one must view party type—mass programmatic or electorally
based—as being the product of a particular historical sequence of events.[61] In nations like the United States with an early extension of suffrage, a large, relatively
unorganized electorate existed and only needed to be mobilized to the polls. In this
environment, parties were created to wage elections. Large electorally based parties had to make ideological and programmatic concessions on a regular basis in
order to mobilize a large electorate to the polls and forge national coalitions of party
elites. This was a rational response to a distinct political environment. In contrast,
in nations which lagged in the extension of suffrage, preexisting organization altered their activities to fill this new void. Thus, class based organizations with preexisting programs moved to mobilize a new electorate, albeit without sacrificing
their existing mandates.

The existence of electorally based parties in the United States is only part
of the answer, however. One must also note the significance of the single-member,
simple-plurality electoral system. In a proportional representation system—common in many European nations—even parties with a small electoral showing (e.g.,
5 to 7 percent) receive representation in the parliament. A single-member simple
plurality system is a winner-take-all system in which the party with a simple plurality in a district claims the seat, regardless of its overall proportion of the vote or
the support shown for second or third parties. This type of system promotes a two-
party system. As Larry Sabato notes: "Placing second, even by a smidgen, doesn't
count, and this condition obviously encourages the aggregation of interests into as
few parties as possible."[62]

With two parties competing for the vote, centrism is the rule. Both parties
function as catchall parties competing for the middle of the ideological spectrum.

To be certain, at various times in the nation's history the two parties were successful in mobilizing the electorate and maintaining distinctive policy positions backed by disciplined members. This was possible because of the dominance of party elites, the availability of patronage, and an ongoing influx of immigrants settling in urban centers.[63] However, the reduction or elimination of patronage, the introduction of social welfare services as a right rather than a product of party support, and a number of electoral reforms reduced the power of parties and the role of elites. Most important, in this context, was the introduction of nonpartisan elections at the municipal level and the introduction of the Australian ballot. With the Australian ballot, government provided secret ballots to replace those provided by the parties. In the process, they required compliance with state electoral regulations to gain access to the ballot. This entailed replacing the party's selection of candidates with the use of primaries and caucuses which transferred power away from the party organization to the electorate.[64]

In the words of Leon Epstein, electoral reforms of the early twentieth century transformed political parties into "public utilities." Epstein explains: "American states began to regulate parties—without regulatory commissions to be sure—at about the same time and in more or less the same progressive reform spirit that they, and in some areas the national government too, began to regulate businesses performing special public services. Like many of these enterprises, political parties were perceived in monopolistic terms; only two parties, so technically duopolies, or in many places only one party, actually elected public officeholders and exerted control over governmental policymaking."[65] The results were two. First, electoral regulations protected existing parties and impeded new parties' access to the ballot. Second, and more important, because selection of candidates occurred through legally defined processes, parties could no longer control their own label. Democrat and Republican now described the collection of candidates officials selected by the electorate to run under the banners of the two parties—regardless of their ideology or their support for a party platform. Moreover, they could not effectively force discipline by "de-selecting" party candidates. Thus, adherence to the party platform was not supported by some sanction.

At the same time that so many forces have worked against effective parties, the United States has witnessed a series of realigning elections over the course of the past two centuries. Critical elections emerge as a response to structural crises (e.g., depressions) or salient issues (e.g., slavery) that cannot be accommodated within existing party coalitions. At these junctures, new coalitions of interests unite under the banners of the two parties. The majority party, complete with a new ruling coalition, possesses the power and opportunity to pursue a relatively coherent policy agenda that often entails changing the role of the state in society. As Walter Dean Burnham notes, since critical realignments "involve constitutional readjustments in the broadest sense of the term, they are intimately associated with and followed by transformations in large clusters of policy. This produces correspondingly profound alterations in policy and influences the grand institutional structures of American government. . . . they result in significant transformations in the general shape of policy; and they have relatively profound aftereffects on the roles played by institutional elites. They are involved with redefinitions of the universe of voters, political parties, and the broad boundaries of the politically possible."[66] Of course, as the central issues that were responsible for the realignment are addressed with policies or fade from relevance, the ruling coalition begins to decompose and all of the decentralizing forces addressed above take their toll. Thus, the New Deal coalition that emerged following the realignment of 1932 provided sufficient support for a host of welfare state and regulatory reforms before falling, in the postwar period, into a process of gradual decomposition.

In a two-party system composed of electorally based parties that function as public utilities, representation tends to occur at the most general level. Interest groups play an important role in compensating for the lack of specific representation. All individuals and social groups have interests that are affected by economic policies and threatened by economic change. To protect or advance their interests more effectively, they commonly form organizations or associations. The importance of organization varies by group. Corporations, for example, exist both as organizations with economic resources which they can contribute to candidates or use to maintain their own staff of lobbyists, and as members of larger trade associations. Workers, in contrast, are simply voters, absent a labor organization to represent their interests in the political arena.

When compared with other industrialized democracies, the American interest group system is large and remarkably decentralized. Although there are some active business peak associations, which represent firms from a wide range of industries (e.g., the National Association of Manufacturers, the U.S. Chamber of Commerce), they play a limited role by comparison with trade associations organized on an industry-specific basis. Reflecting the limited role of peak associations in the United States, there are almost 1,200 business associations functioning at the national level. More than 400 additional groups represent foreign commerce and corporations. Moreover, individual corporations are political actors in their own right: More than 3,000 corporations have Washington representatives. There are, in addition, almost 500 professional associations and more than 100 labor organizations.[67]

Several factors can be seen to explain why peak associations are weak in the United States relative to trade associations. For example, it might be suggested that peak associations have been weak precisely because business has been so strong. Historically, the lack of a credible political threat to business interests in the form of a powerful labor or socialist party, the broad ideological support for capitalism, and unlimited access to sites of policymaking have made the formation of strong peak associations unnecessary. In other nations, in contrast, class-based programmatic parties and strong labor movements force businesses to rely more heavily on their peak associations.[68] Ideological and cultural explanations are attractive. However, one can gain much by returning to the structure of the American state. As previously noted, the United States has an institutional structure characterized by high levels of horizontal and vertical fragmentation. This fragmentation contributes to a decentralized interest group system. When legislation is written at the subcommittee level and regulations addressing economic activities are drafted by agencies exercising industry-specific mandates, political organization at the level of the industry is efficient and sufficient for participation in regulatory politics. In short, the specialization of interest groups closely parallels the specialization that characterizes the governmental structures.

This is, of course, a descriptive representation of the contemporary interest group system—a system which has evolved over the course of the past century. In the early decades of the century, the national system consisted of a small number of peak business associations, labor unions, and agricultural commodity groups. Since then, the interest group system has grown both in size and diversity. The ever-growing importance of public policy and budgetary decisions for corporate profitability and the incomes of many social groups (e.g., retired pensioners, public employees) undoubtedly contributed to that growth. As the profitability of many industries has become highly dependent on public policy, decisions concerning taxation, tariffs, regulatory standards, research and development subsidies, and government procurement, the propensity of corporations to organize and mobilize has increased.

A vibrant and active interest group system functioning in an open and relatively decentralized political system provides the basis for a working pluralist system and the core assumptions adopted by pluralist theory. As noted above, the decentralization of the American system is remarkable. Access is largely guaranteed to those groups that mobilize. However, representational asymmetries are significant, due in large part to the disparity in financial resources. When one considers the representation of economic interests, one cannot escape the conclusion that the interest group system overrepresents certain groups, particularly business. Although individuals occupying managerial and administrative positions make up 7 percent of the population, business associations and corporations with Washington representatives account for 71 percent of the interest groups. In contrast, nonfarm workers comprise 41 percent of the population but are represented by 4 percent of the interest groups.[69] As noted above, one must note that corporations are represented at different levels of aggregation. Large corporations commonly have their own Washington representatives and are also represented both by multiple trade associations and by peak associations. In contrast, industrial workers find representation—assuming they are unionized—in their union locals, which are seldom involved in national politics and in labor peak associations such as the AFL-CIO.[70]

In the study of interest group politics, it is almost axiomatic that there will be a direct relationship between the salience of a given policy (defined in terms of the mix of costs and benefits) and the level of mobilization. Moreover, the distribution of costs and benefits will play a critical role in determining which groups will mobilize in an attempt to shape policy. The relationship between costs and benefits will likewise affect the form of politics—conflictive or consensual, pluralistic or elite—which will emerge to characterize the policy subsystem.[71] Salience is of critical importance when attempting to understand the propensity of groups to mobilize and the politics within a given policy subsystem. However, an equally important factor is complexity.[72] When we use the term complexity, we are referring in part to the nature of the policy problem itself. Some policy problems will be more complicated and intricate than others. However, complexity must be understood as a subjective rather than an objective attribute. Thus, it is more useful to state that complex problems are problems that are difficult to analyze without specialized expertise or training. This specialized knowledge is necessary to translate one's understanding of a problem into a critique of existing policies and the formation of a coherent policy response.

Complexity has important implications both for group mobilization and the effects of participation. Certain problems are rather easy to understand. Interest groups and citizens can clearly identify the relevant dimensions of a problem and evaluate the costs and benefits associated with alternative responses. If the effects of policy are immediate and the benefits of participation are clearly evident, there may be few significant nonfinancial impediments to mobilization. However, many policies address rather puzzling problems. Actors require specialized knowledge if they are to evaluate the magnitude of the problem, the causal factors at work, and the costs and benefits of various possible remedies. In highly complex policy areas, groups with concrete interests may fail to mobilize simply because they find the policy debates impenetrable.

Even when complexity does not prevent mobilization, it may limit the influence of some parties. Complex policies commonly evolve within issue networks or policy communities. Parties within these communities (i.e., experts drawn from congressional committees, agencies, interest groups, and the relevant disciplines at universities) are united by a highly specialized discourse. They actively debate the various dimensions of policy and existing practices.[73] Without the competence to engage in this technical intercourse, groups may mobilize without exerting influence, despite their real stakes in the success of policy. Public advocacy groups, for example, may be concerned that existing regulations do not provide adequate protection from toxic chemicals in the workplace. However, without the capacity to assess the risks and compare the effectiveness of competing regulatory remedies, it is difficult to translate the concern into a coherent critique and specific policy proposals. Likewise, without sufficient training in nuclear engineering, it may be impossible for environmental groups to assess nuclear power plant design or siting decisions. The complexity of certain policy issues limits the extent to which mobilization can be translated into influence. Groups which possess the resources to maintain professional staffs or consultants will have a far greater capacity to influence policy debates in complex policy areas. Most economic policies are accurately described as complex due to the high reliance on specialized theory and data analysis.

## Policy Expertise: The Integration of Ideas in the Policy Process

State structures are of critical importance when attempting to explain the success and failure of economic policy. As explained above, the fragmentation of American institutions along vertical and horizontal dimensions places distinct limitations on the coherence of policy and the speed with which new policies can be introduced and implemented. However, one must also address the role of ideas. Economic policy is strongly influenced by the quality of the ideas that are used to formulate policy goals and appropriate policy tools. As a result, it is important to address both the quality of the ideas that bear upon policy and the means by which ideas are integrated into the policy processes.

In recent years, a good deal of attention has been directed toward *issue networks* and *policy communities* when attempting to identify the sources of policy ideas and the ways they are brought to bear on the policy process. The complexity of many policy problems requires the active participation of policy specialists drawn from the bureaucracy, congressional committees, interest groups, think tanks, and universities. The institutional fragmentation addressed earlier provides a clear opportunity for a greater number of participants and thus simultaneously provides policymakers with access to a far greater number of policy ideas. Although the participants may have different agendas and institutional concerns, they are linked through a shared body of knowledge and a concern over the evolution of a related set of policies. While experts are not disinterested analysts attempting to interpret a complex reality for their elected patrons, it would be too skeptical to present specialized knowledge as merely a means of rationalizing self-interested policy goals. Commonly, expertise and advocacy are joined. Experts attempt to solve complex problems through the application of scientific or social scientific knowledge. At the same time, they are seeking to further a specific policy agenda or idea. Ultimately, their influence in the policy debates will reflect both the expertise they possess and the extent to which the ideas they promote can be linked to persistent problems or larger political agendas. In the end, the roles of expert and advocate may be difficult to untangle.[74]

Much of the work on policy communities falls squarely in the pluralist tradition, stressing the importance of advocacy and group mobilization, while providing minimal attention to the role played by specialized knowledge in shaping the evolution of policies and administrative change. It is widely understood that policy-relevant ideas evolve within the communities of specialists that surround most policy areas. While it is often correct to view these networks or communities as unstructured and open to new participants, this cannot simply be assumed. Rather, the permeability of policy communities depends in large part on the complexity of the policies in question. As William Gormley suggests, it is useful to consider policies along two dimensions: salience and complexity.[75] For decades, policy analysts and political scientists have acknowledged the importance of salience in structuring the politics in a particular policy arena. The salience of a given policy problem—often presented as an expression of the costs and benefits associated with the problem—will shape group mobilization. We should not be surprised that income tax increases stimulate higher levels of mobilization than minor alterations in patent law. The former can have a tremendous impact on the lives of a large percentage of the population whereas the latter is limited in impact.

In addition to salience, one must address the importance of complexity in structuring politics in a given policy area. In complex policy areas, specialized expertise may be necessary to decipher the complicated language in which policy is framed. Even if a given policy has a potentially significant impact on a large portion of the population, the complexity of the policy may be such to limit levels of mobilization. Take, for example, the case of monetary policy. The Federal Reserve's policies can have a monumental impact on growth, prices, and employment levels. As discussed in Chapter 10, in the early 1980s the Federal Reserve played a central role in inducing higher levels of unemployment in pursuit of price stability.

The interesting question, of course, is: Why does this extraordinary power fail to stimulate high levels of mobilization? In part, one may attribute this state of affairs to the political insulation of the Federal Reserve. The Fed is, arguably, the least democratic portion of the American state.[76] The open access that is so common in Congress and regulatory agencies is entirely absent at the Federal Reserve. The Federal Open Market Committee, the chief decision-making body concerned with determining government policies on buying and selling securities, is not subject to open meeting regulations common in other regulatory bodies. However, one must also address the complexity of monetary policy. The vast majority of those affected by the Federal Reserve's open market activities lack the expertise in monetary economics to understand or contribute to the policy debates. Similar conclusions can be reached with respect to fiscal policy.

In policy areas characterized by high levels of complexity, an interesting pattern of politics may be observed. In areas characterized by a combination of complexity and salience, groups may mobilize and elected officials may enter the fray in hopes of capitalizing on the political controversies. However, the political discourse may have few connections to the more rarified policy debates taking place within the policy communities. As a result, one may discover dual discourses—one explicitly political, one more technical in nature. The tension between these two discourses may undermine the quality of the ultimate decisions. In general, one can predict that when a policy is characterized by a combination of low salience and high complexity, deliberations will be dominated by the small community of experts who possess the necessary training to address the key features of policy. In high-salience, high-complexity policies, experts may be forced to compete with mobilized constituencies and elected officials.

Elsewhere, I have argued that in policy areas characterized by high levels of complexity, one discovers communities of expertise that are much more structured than the policy communities or issue networks that one discovers in less complex policy areas.[77] A *community of expertise* consists of specialists drawn from government, interest groups, think tanks, and universities. The members of the community are engaged in the ongoing examination of problems in light of existing policies and administrative procedures, and the identification of possible alternatives. The term community of expertise can also be used to refer to the body of knowledge and analytic tools which unite members of the community in a common discourse. The shared expertise often carries distinct biases. It may present certain options as legitimate while portraying others as unworkable or beyond serious consideration. In complex policy areas expertise may be necessary to influence the evolution of policy. It provides a specialized language that is the medium of communication The common expertise provides a basis for community cohesion and differentiates the community from the larger set of actors. Often, disciplinary norms also insulate core policy debates from popular political struggles that dominate electoral institutions.

Despite the common discourse, communities of expertise are seldom monolithic. Competing groups within the community promote different visions of policy and administration. However, subsets of community actors differ with respect to their ability to affect public policy. Oftentimes, the analytical tools, schools of thought, and disciplinary orientations that are recognized as authoritative in the academic disciplines will carry their status of orthodoxy into the policy debates. Thus, in the postwar period, Keynesians, post- and neo-Keynesians, supply-side and rational-expectation economists, monetarists, Marxists, and institutionalists addressed the problems of macroeconomic management and offered competing arguments as to the optimal mix of policies. However, the debates were dominated by mainstream Keynesianism, reflecting the dominance of Keynes's ideas in the academic discipline of economics. This continued to be the case until the 1970s, when serious problems of managing the dual problems of inflation and unemployment discredited Keynesian theory.

It is important to recognize that the influence of various groups is not fixed. The understanding of policy problems may evolve, shifts may occur within the academic disciplines, or broader political agendas may be linked to particular theories, thus increasing their influence on policy. In the process, new actors may become central to the definition of public policy. Thus, in the late 1970s and early 1980s, supply-side economic theories were linked to the Reagan agenda and the popular revolt against the Keynesian welfare state, despite the ongoing questions about the theoretical and empirical support for supply-side models.

As this discussion suggests, the significance of communities of expertise is tied to their practical impact on policy and administration. The debates within the communities can provide a justification for particular policy options and strategies of institutional change. The connections between the communities and policy are many. The list of potential presidential appointees is developed, in part, on the basis of community reactions. Thus, the chairman of the Federal Reserve is selected after close consultation with the financial community and monetary economists yields a short-list of potentially suitable candidates. Secondly, peer review provides another means of translating community deliberations into policy. After appointment, agency officials are at all times subject to the scrutiny of community members. The chairman of the Federal Reserve must be concerned with whether the financial community will support his policies. The determination will be made, oftentimes, on the basis of criteria developed within the community or the formal discipline.

There are, however, indirect means of affecting policy. The most important means is simply the structuring of policy discourse. As noted above, community members are engaged in the ongoing examination of policy problems and alternatives. As they construct explanations of policy problems, they employ certain metaphors, models, and forms of argumentation. As policy discourse is structured, certain policy alternatives are favored while others are removed from informed debate. The community debates determine the epistemological, disciplinary, and normative boundaries within which all serious policy options must fall. Simultaneously, they determine which members of the community are best suited to addressing a problem. If changes in policy and administration fail to fall within the boundaries established through the debates, they risk the opposition of those considered expert.[78] This broad intellectual context may find many expressions. Ideas become the basis of political coalition formation. Legislators may apply prevailing theories when writing legislation. Attorneys may apply economic or social scientific theories when arguing their cases; judges may write decisions that are embedded with prevailing theoretical assumptions. Congress may assess the performance of an agency or political executive on the basis of criteria developed through community interaction.

While this discussion has focused on the community of expertise and its effects on defining the activities of a given agency, it is important to note that the orthodoxy that emerges from community deliberations may play an important role in linking multiple institutions and promoting a greater coordination of policy and administration across a policy subsystem. Insofar as actors from multiple institutions are involved in a common community of expertise and subject to a common set of community generated norms, their activities will reveal a degree of consistency. Broad-based interest coalitions are often necessary to create coherent public policy in systems characterized by high levels of institutional fragmentation. In highly complex issue areas, communities of expertise serve a similar function.

As suggested above, the complexity of economic policy places distinct limits on the universe of potential participants. At the same time, because participants are so closely linked to the discipline of economics, trends within the academy may be translated directly into the community. Those who work within the consensus will have far greater emphasis than those who depart from that consensus.[79] Economic ideas are integrated into the policy process in the ways discussed above and through agency professionalization. Public sector economists in the United States do not receive specialized training. Rather, they are trained in the same fashion as academic economists and often approach public service as a form of apprenticeship or postdoctoral training. Professionals in government agencies pose some interesting challenges for students of organization. Unlike other bureaucrats, professionals commonly look outside their agencies to sources of influence within their disciplines. As a result, they simultaneously operate according to a set of professional and organizational norms. The existence of dual sources of authority creates problems of bureaucratic control that are beyond the focus of this discussion. What is important in the current context is that the professionals within an agency may be highly receptive to changes within their discipline. The key question is whether the ideas that are transmitted into economic policymaking agencies are suited to politically defined policy goals. Or, alternatively, will intellectual advance developed for an academic audience have any connections to policy in an empirical setting?

## THE EVOLUTION OF THE AMERICAN STATE

As suggested in the above discussion, the core features of the American state have evolved over time. The contemporary American state is significantly different from that which existed at earlier points in U.S. history. To understand the key features of this evolutionary process, it is important to address the factors that cause significant changes in the state, the impact on institutions, and the ways in which changes at one point in time impact the decisions open to officials at subsequent points. Finally, it is important to address the cumulative impact of the evolution of the state and its relationship to civil society. Let us address these factors serially.

Following Stephen Skowronek, one must acknowledge at least three broad sources of institutional change: complexity, crisis, and conflict.[80] As public officials attempt to manage the pressures associated with complexity, crisis, and conflict, they *may* dramatically alter existing patterns of state-economy relations and the administrative capacities of the state. Complexity has been a particularly important factor in forging the changes in policy and administration in this century. The rise of a large-scale corporate economy at the turn of the century provides a particularly useful example. The large corporations adopted new productive technologies which fundamentally altered the relationship between capital and labor. They threatened to replace a formerly decentralized market system with national distributional networks and market governance with various forms of interorganizational planning. These changes, which will be explored in some detail in Chapter 4, forced Progressive Era policymakers to consider a host of new regulatory policies that would direct the evolution of an increasingly complex economy while preserving markets and responding to concerns over a loss of individual and group autonomy.[81] Similarly, the complexity of economic production in the postwar period when combined with political mobilization forced policymakers to create new policies and agencies to regulate environmental quality and the exposure to toxins in the workplace.[82]

Crises are also important in stimulating institutional change.[83] During crises, established constitutional relations can be renegotiated. What constitutes a crisis is largely a political question. Does a sequence of events mobilize a significant portion of society demanding a governmental response? Is the mobilization sufficient to force a realignment of the party system? At the turn of this century, the rise of the large-scale corporate economy was interpreted by many as a crisis. Farmers, workers, small businesses, and social reformers portrayed the trusts as threatening the traditional values and social organization. In many ways, the realigning election of 1896 was a referendum on whether the federal government should continue to promote industrial development or strike a position in support of agrarian interests. Some events appear to nearly all to constitute a crisis and thus to justify tremendous changes in the state-economy interface. In the 1930s, the Great Depression provided the clearest example of a crisis that created an opportunity for policymakers to act autonomously and experiment with policies that may have been defeated under other circumstances. With business incapacitated and the Democrats strengthened through the New Deal realignment, Roosevelt was provided the opportunity to promote a wealth of policies and innovations in institutions and groups relations.[84] Similarly, as Chapter 9 will reveal, the rapid decline in economic performance in the late 1960s and 1970s provided policymakers with the opportunity to introduce measures that well exceeded existing definitions of legitimate state activity. President Nixon's application of economywide price and wage controls stands as a case in point. Prior to Nixon's New Economic Policy, incomes policy had been, at best, a necessary expedient of wartime economic management.

Military conflicts also provide the opportunity for dramatic changes in the state and its role in society. Charles Tilly, for example, has argued that state formation and development have been chiefly a byproduct of the preparation for, and waging of, war.[85] To be certain, the Civil War, World War I, and World War II allowed for the creation of new patterns of state-economy relations. Presidents used the emergency of war to justify the redefinition of the constitutional balance of power and a greater concentration of authority in the presidency. One of the long-term legacies of war has been the centralization of power in the executive. At the same time, war has provided the opportunity for constructing new patterns of state-corporate relations. Thus, the state-corporate relations developed during World War I provided the basis for greater cooperation in the 1920s.[86] The central role of the state in funding the expansion of munitions production during World War II resulted in the creation of a close financial and organizational relationship between the military and the defense sector in the postwar period. Within the confines of the military-industrial complex, forms of planning and state financing have been common, despite the allegiance to market norms in other parts of the economy.[87]

Complexity, crises, and conflicts *may* force officials to alter existing patterns of state-economy relations. While they create opportunities, however, they are not determinative. The nature of the crisis does not determine the nature of the response. To understand the way in which such challenges are managed, it is necessary, firstly, to acknowledge the power of existing roles, routines, and relationships. The decision to depart significantly from prevailing practices may be heavily constrained by the existing administrative capacities available to policymakers. Take the example of World War I's War Industries Board, the agency responsible for mobilizing the domestic economy to meet the needs of the war. Because President Wilson could not draw on the bureaucracy for the needed expertise to coordinate planning, it was necessary to staff the board with corporate officials, the so-called dollar-a-year men and draw on the administrative capacities of businesses and trade associations. A similar pattern was evident in the New Deal's National Recovery Administration. Stated somewhat differently, the opportunity set available to policymakers at any given time is bound by past decisions and the related administrative capacities. To be certain, enormous crises or conflicts that threaten the existence of the state can create the opportunities for establishing new patterns of state-economy relations. However, the long-term impact of these departures will depend on the success of officials in creating the needed administrative resources.

Political development is path dependent. Once the decision is made to pursue a certain strategy and muster the needed administrative resources, other options are foreclosed. Policymakers often address new challenges through analogy. They consider a new crisis in light of earlier crises and deploy existing models of state-economy relations. Take the example presented above. As will be shown in Chapter 6, Roosevelt looked explicitly to the War Industries Board and the crisis of World War I when attempting to address the depression. Of course, this tendency to draw analogies to past crises and responses reflects the existence of a core of bureaucrats and politicians who can draw on their experiences and existing administrative capacities. Thus, while crises and conflicts may create a window of opportunity for departures from existing patterns of state-economy relations, there remains a strong incentive to extend past experiences into the future. When seen as a process, political development is inherently conservative.

Despite the conservatism of institutional change, significant changes do occur. Often this takes place when the opportunities for change are paired with new ideas, intellectual innovations that recast the role of the state in a new and imaginative fashion. Ideas play a critical role in the policy process, particularly in complex policy areas in which access to a particular body of expertise is critical to the formulation, implementation, and evaluation of policy. Ideas are also critical in structuring a given problem and drawing connections between the problem in question and other problems and/or policies. Thus, Keynesian theory provided a means of linking aggregate demand policy, welfare state policies, and manpower policies—albeit unsuccessfully due to the unique circumstances of the postwar period and the failure of the Roosevelt administration to establish long-term planning mechanisms that could survive the assaults waged by an increasingly conservative Congress.[88] Similarly, supply-side economics provided a simple means of conceptualizing the causes and remedies of economic decline while simultaneously justifying a conservative agenda for institutional change. If high marginal tax rates—a legacy of state expansion—could be eliminated, economic growth would eliminate the stagnant economy while providing a source of ever greater revenues.[89]

As this discussion suggests, ideas may be particularly attractive and influential if they provide intellectual justification for state-building strategies that have already received the support of officials. To quote Deborah Stone: "Policymakers often create problems (in the artistic sense) as a context for the actions they want to take. . . . they represent the world in such a way as to make themselves, their skills, and their favorite course of action necessary."[90] When considering competing policy-relevant ideas, policymakers have the opportunity to select among theories that cast problems in different ways and associate them with different policies and potential strategies of institutional change.

Crisis, conflict, and complexity play a central role in stimulating policy change. As the above discussion suggests, the extent and manner in which such changes will occur is bound, in large part, by past policy decisions, existing administrative resources, and the kinds of policy-relevant ideas available to policymakers. As Robert Higgs explains, however, one must be careful to distinguish between secular growth in government and growth that occurs in response to conflicts and crises.[91] While governmental authority expands in scope in response to crises—and is commonly justified as a short-term deviation to address the crisis at hand—the retrenchment that follows the end of crisis only eliminates some of this expansion. There is something of a ratchet effect. Government authority never returns to its precrisis levels. The reasons for this should be clear. As new policies are created, administrative capacities evolve, bureaucratic units are created, staffs are hired, and new clientele relations are established. Moreover, prevailing understandings of what the government may legitimately do evolve in response to recent experiences, creating new popular expectations. Thus, crises (broadly construed) leave important legacies of expanded state capacities, a larger role for the state in society, and new patterns of state-economy relations.

In the following chapters, we will not be concerned with the rise of Big Government per se. Rather, we will focus on changing patterns of state-economy relations. The critical question, it would seem, is not how much a government governs, but how it governs. What are the goals and the prevailing patterns of relations with economic actors? What kinds of models are being adopted in the policy process and how effectively are they being used to manage economic performance? To what extent is there a mismatch between the goals of policy (and popular expectations about these goals) and the capacity of the state to effectively pursue these goals? The answers to these questions will change depending on the period in question. As the size of government ratchets up and new patterns of state-economy relations are created, the old relations and old expectations continue to exist, both as a challenge to new policies and an artifact of past decisions over how best to structure the political economy.

## OVERVIEW

This chapter has presented a discussion of state institutions and institutional change as a preface of what is to come. To a large extent, this book is an examination of the evolution of the American state and patterns of state-economy relations during the twentieth century. Before we embark on this examination, we must provide the basis. Thus, Chapter 2 addresses the organization of the American economy, focusing on corporate organization and economic governance. Chapter 3 turns to the legacy of the nineteenth century, exploring some of the factors that contributed to the remarkable growth of the period and the creation of an institutional infrastructure upon which the twentieth century political economy was built.

Chapter 4 examines the political economy of the Progressive Era. The growing complexity of the economy forced new policies addressing corporate organization, railroads, and finance. The domestic reform agenda of Progressivism was dissipated once the United State entered World War I. The War Industries Board constituted an experiment in corporatist planning hitherto unprecedented in U.S. history. World War I and the experiments of the 1920s are the topics of Chapter 5. The 1920s were characterized both by the strong record of growth and new forms of state-corporate cooperation. However, the decade ended with the Great Depression which undermined the economic gains and growing incomes of the 1920s and engendered new hostility between the state and corporations. Franklin Roosevelt's New Deal brought together a host of experiments in social welfare, regulation, industrial relations, and economic policymaking. It fostered new patterns of state-economy relations under the claim that experimentation was necessary for the nation to survive the Great Depression. Chapter 7 moves to the final episode of the Roosevelt administration, World War II. As with the War Industries Board of World War I, World War II required close relationships between the state and corporations and a decentralized network of planning agencies to control most facets of economic activity. The legacy of the war was a greater role for the state in the economy and the emergence of defense industries that were dependent on the state as a market for their goods and as a source of capital to fund the expansion of physical facilities and research and development.

World War II forever altered the configuration of powers in the international arena. Following the war, the United States stood as the most powerful industrial economy in the world economy and thus in a key position in defining new international monetary and trade regimes. The experience of the Great Depression and war mobilization also created new expectations as to the role of the state in managing economic fluctuations. Chapter 8 explores the central features of the postwar political economy and the two decades of growth following World War II. During this period, U.S. hegemony in the international economy combined with effective macroeconomic management in the domestic economy to provide a basis for steady growth. These features disintegrated by the late 1960s, however, as inflation resisted existing economic strategies. The inflationary forces were strengthened dramatically in the 1970s when combined with the OPEC oil embargo and high levels of international demand for food. The new high rates of inflation were combined with declining growth rates and high unemployment rates. The war against inflation during the late 1960s and the 1970s is the subject of Chapter 9.

The experience of the 1970s stood in strong contrast with the growth of the previous decades. The optimism in the capacity of the state to manage trying social and economic problems dissipated and was replaced by growing skepticism. These events set the stage for the election of Ronald Reagan in 1980. The Reagan presidency sought, with mixed success, to redefine existing patterns of state-economy relations and the expectations concerning the role of the state in the economy. The events of the Reagan and Bush presidencies are presented and assessed in Chapter 10. The debates over the reconstruction of the American economy following the events of the 1970s are reviewed in Chapter 11. Various factors have been cited as bearing chief responsibility for the decline in American competitiveness and growth rates following 1968. These factors are examined along with the competing visions of industrial policy.

## NOTES

1. John Stuart Mill, *Principles of Political Economy, with Some of Their Applications to Social Philosophy*, 5th ed. (New York: Appleton & Co., 1909), p. 17.
2. Martin Staniland, *What is Political Economy? A Study of Social Theory and Underdevelopment* (New Haven, Conn.: Yale University Press, 1985), p. 4.
3. James A. Swaney and Robert Premus, "Modern Empiricism and Quantum-Leap Theorizing in Economics." In *Why Economics is Not Yet a Science*, ed. Alfred S. Eichner (New York: M.E. Sharpe, 1983), p. 50.
4. See Madeline Barbara Léons and Frances Rothstein, eds. *New Directions in Political Economy: An Approach from Anthropology* (Westport, Conn.: Greenwood Press, 1979), Chapter 1.
5. Sidney Verba, Norman H. Nie, and Jae-Oh Kim, *The Modes of Democratic Participation: A Cross-National Comparison* (Beverly Hills, Calif.: Sage, 1971), p. 11.
6. Robert A. Dahl, *A Preface to Democratic Theory* (Chicago: University of Chicago Press, 1956), p. 131.
7. Ibid., p. 14. Also see Robert A. Dahl, *Dilemmas of Pluralist Democracy: Autonomy versus Control* (New Haven, Conn.: Yale University Press, 1982).
8. Max Lerner, *America as a Civilization: Life and Thought in the United States Today* (New York: Simon & Schuster, 1957), pp. 397–98.
9. Dahl, *A Preface to Democratic Theory*, p. 150.
10. Sidney Verba "Comparative Political Cultures." In *Political Culture and Political Development*, ed. Lucien W. Pye and Sidney Verba (Princeton, N.J.: Princeton University Press, 1965), p. 513.
11. Lucien W. Pye, "Introduction: Political Culture and Political Development." In *Political Culture and Political Development*, ed. Lucien W. Pye and Sidney Verba (Princeton, N.J.: Princeton University Press, 1965), p. 7.
12. David Truman, *The Governmental Process: Political Interests and Public Opinion* (New York: Alfred A. Knopf, 1955), pp. 511, 31.

making. This, in turn, has increased the autonomy of management. As Adolf Berle explains:

> The rise of the corporate system, with attendant separation of ownership from management due to concentration of industry in the corporate form, was the first great twentieth-century change. In three decades it led to the rise of autonomous corporation management. The second tendency, pooling of savings, voluntary or forced, in fiduciary institutions now is steadily separating the owner (if the stockholder can properly be called an "owner") from his residual ultimate power—that of voting for management. In effect this is gradually removing power of selecting boards of directors and managements from these managements themselves . . . to a different and rising group of interests—pension trustees, mutual fund managers and (less importantly) insurance company managers.[19]

Large institutional investors (e.g., mutual funds, insurance companies) have the capacity, by virtue of their large investments, to exercise greater control over management than individual stockholders. However, because these investors are required to invest to maximize returns to their pensioners and fund members and because secondary stock markets are both well developed and relatively costless, they will be far more likely to sell the stock of companies involved in poor management decisions than invest resources in forcing managers to adopt a different strategy. This is an important point that will be addressed in greater detail later.

There seems to be little question that the vast majority of large U.S. firms are run by managers rather than owners. Edward S. Herman's analysis of the top corporations provided results that were even more striking than those provided five decades earlier by Berle and Means. Herman found that "ultimate management control accounted for 82.5 percent the number and 85.4 percent of the assets of the 200 largest nonfinancials and 78 percent of the number and 80 percent of the assets of the 100 largest industrials in the mid-1970s."[20] Herman also compares these figures to estimates of managerial control in earlier periods. In 1900 to 1901, 23.8 percent of very large corporations were management controlled—a figure which increased to 40.5 percent by 1929.

The separation of ownership and control and the rise of a managerial capitalism should not be surprising. They are, in many ways, the inevitable result of a corporate expansion and the attendant need for expertise and investment capital. A key question, however, is whether this separation has any practical significance. Berle and Means postulated that the separation would result in the emergence of different goals than those that drove decision making when ownership and control were combined. Although they never precisely determined what management goals might be, they noted that there were "opposing groups, ownership on the one side, control on the other—a control which tends to move further and further away from ownership and ultimately to lie in the hand of the management itself, a management capable of perpetuating its own position."[21] If, as Berle and Means suggested, owners are primarily concerned with corporate profitability, then there is very little evidence that opposition exists. As Herman notes: "The triumph of management control in many large corporations has both left them in the hands of neutral technocrats. The control groups of these organizations seem as devoted to profitable growth as are the leaders of entrepreneurial and owner-dominated companies, past and present. The frequently assumed decline in managerial interest in profits, which supposedly should result from the decreased importance of direct owner control, has not, in fact, been proved." Rather, there has been "an internalization of profitable growth criteria in corporate psyches and in the rules of large managerial corporations."[22] As Michael Useem notes, one finds "a comparatively low stress on corporate priorities other than returns on investment . . . regardless of the locus of control."[23]

The separation of ownership and control resulted in the displacement of owner-entrepreneurs and the establishment of a distinct managerial class. While there is little question that this has occurred, it is, perhaps, equally significant to note that the origins of corporate mangers has changed overtime. Although members of corporate management reflect a common educational and class background, there have been changes in the composition of the leadership in the 100 largest U.S. corporations in this century.[24] These changes in the origins of corporate presidents reflect changes in dominant corporate strategies and structures.[25] During the period 1900 to 1919, corporate presidents were commonly entrepreneurs who controlled the firms they created, with a growing percentage being drawn from manufacturing subunits within the firm. From 1919 to 1939, in contrast, the presidents of the top 100 firms were most commonly drawn from manufacturing, reflecting the need for manufacturing expertise in the coordination of the large firm engaged in mass production. During the period 1939 to 1959, however, the dominant strategy began to change in light of the experience of the Great Depression and the 1950 revisions in the antitrust laws (the Celler-Kafauver Act of 1950) which strengthened the legal prohibition of horizontal mergers. Responding to a desire for stability and concerns over antitrust prosecution, corporations moved away from large scale manufacturing for a single market to diversify into related products and thus serve multiple markets simultaneously. Although manufacturing remained the dominant source of corporate presidents, there was a growing tendency to select presidents with backgrounds in sales and marketing.

In the period after 1959, there was another significant change in the origin of corporate presidents reflecting, once again, changes in strategy and structure. In hopes of maximizing growth, corporations increasingly diversified into unrelated product lines through conglomerate mergers. Reflecting this financial strategy, financial backgrounds became decisive in the selection of corporate presidents. As Fligstein explains: "Since the firm was no longer involved in a few product lines, manufacturing expertise proved too narrow and sales and marketing strategy applied only to growth in market share of related products. Once firms started investing in products too dissimilar to consider related, the only criterion that could be used to evaluate product lines was financial."[26] As Chapter 11 will reveal, this latest shift in corporate strategy and leadership may have important implications for the willingness and capacity of firms to embark on the kinds of long-term investments that may erode short-term profits in the hopes of creating a basis for long-term growth. Managers with expertise in finance may find it very difficult to formulate long-term strategies that involve production rather than acquisitions.

## The Modern Corporation: An Antiquated Institution?

The multiunit corporation engaged in mass standardized production of one or multiple product lines has provided an organizational and technological foundation for American economic performance for much of the twentieth century. A large domestic market and, following World War II, unfettered access to foreign markets, allowed for extraordinary growth and economies of scale. However, the same combination of productive technology and hierarchical management, many suggest, limited corporate adaptability and created perverse incentives for managers. These problems became strikingly evident in the 1970s and 1980s as the U.S. economy faced growing challenges from an unstable international economic environment and competition from foreign-based producers.

One of the key problems was organizational rigidity. When a corporation seeks to function in dynamic international markets, it must possess the capacity to adjust rapidly to changes in the kinds of goods demanded in foreign markets. While the large corporate structure and mass production technologies could produce at historically unprecedented levels, they were rigid and terribly slow to respond to changes in demand. The time required to introduce new product features was significant in comparison with smaller corporations. At the same time that U.S. firms were finding it difficult to respond to rapidly changing market conditions, they were discovering new sources of competition. Mass standardized production technologies were widely available for foreign-based firms. Because the cost of production would be determined, in large part, by the cost of labor, the United States began to lose its competitive advantage. Foreign competitors were entering the market with new and more efficient capital and access to far cheaper sources of labor than that which was available in the United States.

The competing responses to the changing economic conditions of the 1970s and 1980s will be explored in some detail in Chapter 11. It is important to note, however, that corporations in many industries (e.g., steel, automobiles) responded by demanding the creation of tariff and nontariff barriers to limit access to the U.S. market. Even if international markets remained highly contested, it was believed, the domestic economy could provide something of a safe harbor. Another response was the attempt to adopt what Robert Reich has referred to as "paper entrepreneurial" strategies. American corporations tend to adopt short-term profit horizons. As noted above, the separation of ownership and control and the diffusion of stock ownership are characteristic of the modern firm. Because it is relatively costless to sell corporate securities in well-developed secondary markets, individual stockholders and institutional investors commonly choose this strategy in response to downturns in corporate earnings. Even if it is clear that a corporation is investing heavily in a growth-oriented strategy that could reduce current profits while providing the basis for even greater profitability in the long term, it is rational for investors to sell the company's stocks and reinvest at a later date. To maintain higher profit margins in the face of an increasingly hostile environment, many managers became paper entrepreneurs. This strategy entails acquiring undervalued assets via acquisition and engaging in a wide array of accounting and tax-avoidance strategies to show short-term profits. The rise of financiers in the corporate hierarchy made U.S. firms particularly suited for such a strategy. Unfortunately, it neither creates wealth nor allows for the kinds of investments that would be necessary for productive activity in the future.[27]

During the industrial policy debates of the 1980s, many argued that one response to this state of affairs was to recognize that the United States no longer exercised distinct advantages in mass-standardized production. Rather than attempting to preserve a productive technology that could not be applied successfully under existing conditions, Robert Reich, Michael Piore, and Charles Sabel, and others called for a movement to flexible specialization.[28] As Piore and Sabel present it, "flexible specialization is a strategy of permanent innovation . . . based on flexible—multi-use—equipment; skilled workers; and the creation, through politics, of an industrial community that restricts the forms of competition to those favoring innovation."[29] Flexible specialization would rely on a more skilled workforce and an integration of production and computerization. By focusing on the high end of production and maintaining flexibility, it was argued, this strategy would allow for the maintenance of high wage levels and a far greater capacity to respond to changes in foreign markets. Others called for more flexible forms of corporate organization to replace rigid hierarchies and thus enhance the transmission of innovations into the production process.[30]

We will have the opportunity to address flexible specialization in Chapter 11. For the present, it is important to note that even though the giant mass-standardized production firm is popularly associated with U.S. economic success, some 75 percent of manufacturing production (by value) is produced via small batches. Electrification, small electric motors, innovations in transportation and communications, and microelectronics have allowed for a greater decentralization of production than Reich might suggest is descriptively accurate of the U.S. economy.[31] Although it is convenient to portray U.S. corporations as top-heavy, rigid, managerial hierarchies responding slowly to changes in their environment, this description is accurate for only the largest manufacturing firms. Small corporations with more flexible systems of management and labor relations are responsible for the majority of production and employment, even if they are relatively invisible to many analysts.

## THE STRUCTURE AND ROLE OF FINANCE

The financial structure of a nation plays an important role in shaping economic performance. Financial intermediaries execute a number of very important functions, albeit with variable success. Through the system of fractional-reserve banking, financial intermediaries actually create money. This, in turn, provides an important lever whereby monetary policy authorities such as the Federal Reserve in the United States can manipulate the money supply and thus attempt to manage fluctuations in the business cycle. Moreover, by aggregating the deposits of small investors, intermediaries can make larger pools of capital available for investment.

markets and the justification for adopting the market as a norm for assessing the performance of all forms of industrial organization, we must ask new questions: How do corporations adapt to an environment characterized by information complexity and resource scarcity, particularly when markets fail as effective coordinating mechanisms? What kinds of internal mechanisms and/or institutional arrangements can corporations develop to manage complexity and minimize their own vulnerability?

To answer these questions, it is useful, once again, to return to transaction-cost economics. Following Williamson, transaction-cost economics is concerned with the factors that lead corporations to organize transactions in one way rather than another.[48] Some of the principal factors that shape the decision include asset specificity and the frequency of transactions. Let us explore each briefly. Asset specificity is, perhaps, the most important factor. Corporations often have the opportunity to chose between "special-purpose" and "general-purpose" components when designing products. The decision to acquire special-purpose components such as a custom microchip may reduce costs of production and service while introducing special design features that make the end product superior to competing goods and what might have been possible via a reliance on a general-purpose component. However, this decision carries inherent risks for both the supplier and the purchaser. Since the assets in question are not general purpose and thus cannot be easily redeployed for alternative uses, the party responsible for producing the goods may be left with costs that cannot be recovered should the transaction fail to occur as anticipated. Likewise, the purchasing party may discover that a failure to deliver on the contract may undermine the product design and leave it without immediate access to substitutes.

Williamson distinguishes among several types of asset specificity: site specificity, physical asset specificity, human asset specificity, and dedicated assets.[49] Site specificity exists when assets cannot be relocated economically. For example, a facility may be built close to another with the expectation that the facilities will be involved in successive stages of production for the productive life of the facility in question. Physical asset specificity describes a situation where the assets may not suffer from the immobility of site specificity, but they may be specialized to meet the needs of a given product. Human asset specificity addresses the situation that exists when workers involved in a given production process possess highly specialized skills by virtue of their education, experience with a given technology, or experience working as a team. Finally, dedicated assets exist when a corporation expands existing facilities to meet the demands of a specific buyer. The assets are dedicated in the sense that they were created in response to anticipated demand on the part of a particular party. As Williamson notes "The importance of asset specificity to transaction cost economics is difficult to exaggerate. . . . Absent this condition, the world of contract is vastly simplified; enter asset specificity, and nonstandard contracting practices quickly appear."[50]

Of course, the full significance of asset specificity is difficult to gauge until the condition of uncertainty is introduced. In contrast with neoclassical economists who commonly assume for convenience sake the existence of complete and costless information, transaction-cost economics acknowledges the scarcity and complexity of information. The resulting uncertainty may hamper adaptation to environmental disturbances. The problem of information scarcity imposes limits on actor rationality (i.e., bounded rationality) and thus limits the capacity to assess alternative strategies for adapting to change. This is often combined with the problems that arise in any principle-agent relationship. Transactions often entail delegation of authority from the purchaser to the supplier. The greater the specificity of the order, the greater the problems of monitoring compliance. Problems of shirking, opportunism, and miscommunication may abound and become more severe as the complexity of the goods increases. The costs of monitoring compliance may be prohibitive, forcing corporations to rely on general-purpose components and thus sacrificing some of the most important product features.

There is, then, a positive relationship between asset specificity and uncertainty. The uncertainty can be managed and the costs of monitoring reduced dramatically through a reliance on specialized governance structures (i.e., nonmarket forms of interfirm relations). However, the costs of such governance structures may be prohibitive if transactions are not frequent and recurrent. Thus, Williamson presents the frequency of transactions as being one of the factors, along with asset specificity, that one must address when seeking to understand the emergence of specialized governance structures.

On the basis of the frequency of transactions and the characteristics of the investments made by the supplier (i.e., asset specificity, characterized as nonspecific, mixed, or idiosyncratic), Williamson identifies various forms of efficient governance.[51] As one might expect, transactions for goods requiring nonspecific investments fall under *market governance*, regardless of the frequency of transactions. Because goods are general purpose (i.e., not customized to meet specific and unique design specifications), markets can give buyers access to competing sources of supply without sacrificing critical design features. Parties are not extremely vulnerable to the unanticipated end of a commercial relationship because the goods can be sold to others and the assets can be redeployed.

When addressing cases where transactions are occasional and require high levels of investment specificity, Williamson suggests that *trilateral governance* will be common. Examples of such transactions may include the purchase of highly specialized equipment or the construction of a new plant. Given the high degree of asset specificity (and commonly the large devotion of resources), both parties will be vulnerable to poor performance and both will have incentives to preserve the relationship to the final stages of execution. Thus, the purchasers and suppliers may contract with a third party such as an architectural or an industrial design firm to resolve conflicts between parties, communicate technical needs, and assess performance.

Given that transactions are not frequent, trilateral governance is relatively rare when compared with bilateral and unified governance, both of which exist when transactions are frequent and the investments required are characterized by higher levels of asset specificity. Under *bilateral governance*, parties to the transaction retain their organizational autonomy. However, contracts are bilateral in the sense that they commonly observe norms of reciprocity. Thus, one firm can be assured a supply of a specialized component only after it has agreed to invest in the

zation will develop a clan." While self-interest does not disappear, it is placed in a different context—one which recognizes the importance of sacrifice in the short term and can rely on the existence of a "social memory" to guarantee compensation in the long term. Ouchi continues: "In a clan . . . equity is achieved serially rather than on the spot. That is, one clan member may be unfairly underpaid for three years before his true contribution is known, but everyone knows that his contribution will ultimately be recognized, that he will still be there, and that equity will be achieved in the end."[56]

Finally, Campbell, Hollingsworth, and Lindberg present *associations* as a common governance mechanism under conditions of high levels of organizational integration and a multiplicity of actors. Trade associations and cooperatives are common forms of association that play an important political and economic role. Associations allow for the coordination of economic decision making. They are critical for the exchange of information, the development of technical standards, and the creation of rules of conduct or fair competition. As Campbell, Hollingsworth, and Lindberg explain, associations differ from markets, hierarchies, and informal networks in that they are organized along a horizontal dimension: They coordinate actors involved in a common form of activity (e.g., steel producers, retail grocers).[57]

From time to time, associations have played an important role in managing competition within an industry—a point to be explored in greater detail below. Outside of wartime emergencies and the New Deal innovations, however, associations have been chiefly involved in the policy process as interest associations. As one might expect, 71 percent of all private organized interests involved in national politics represent business or professional interests.[58] Because most associations are organized on the sectoral level, when they enter national politics it is chiefly to lobby for legislation that would promote the profitability of industry actors (e.g., changes in the tax code, tariff and nontariff barriers).

The kinds of governance mechanisms adopted by actors in an industry are not determined by technology or the transaction costs inherent in a given sector in the economy. Rather, the search for new governance mechanisms reflects changing economic and political circumstances. Changes in transaction and production costs, demand, international competition, and technology are combined with changes in public policy to alter the environment in which business acts. In response to such uncertainty, corporations engage in a search process where they seek to discover a means of managing their environment.[59] While transaction-cost economics often present the transformation as being instantaneous and relatively costless, firms react to changes in their environment in an environment of scarce and costly information. As a result, there is always something of a lag between changing environmental factors and changes in governance regimes that may, in turn, create a tension that forces additional search. The product is an ongoing evolutionary process in economic governance and the organization of the economy.

Three important points need to be made about governance mechanisms. First, an industry may pass through multiple governance regimes as it evolves in historical time. As noted above, the modern corporate hierarchy emerged as an alternative to market governance as the scale of production and the complexities of coordinating activities in geographically dispersed markets exceeded the limits of existing corporate organization. Likewise, when dealing with complex technologies such as computers, clans may prevail at an early stage, being replaced by corporate hierarchies at a latter stage when managers gain greater experience with the technologies in question. Second, the governance mechanisms are not mutually exclusive. Clanlike and associational mechanisms may exist side-by-side in a given industry. Certain transactions may be governed by markets while others are governed by alternative mechanisms. Finally, adjustment lags behind changes in the production process, technology, and the broader economic environment. This lag in adjustment is of some importance. Patterns of economic relations do not adjust instantly to changing economic conditions. Indeed, they may be locked in place through established organizations and routines. Many of the difficulties experienced by the economy may be traced, at one time or another, to the failure of firms to change existing governance arrangements in keeping with changes in competitive pressures and new technologies. As Chapter 11 will show, some analysts attribute many of the problems faced by the American economy in recent years to a failure to dispose of established forms of corporate and interorganizational governance.

## THE POSITION OF LABOR

Up to this point, the discussion has focused almost exclusively on corporations and various forms of intercorporate relations. Much in keeping with the key features of the elite and institutional frameworks, the corporate economy appears to be a complicated network of elites and organizations seeking to maximize stability and minimize uncertainty in an environment of technical complexity and information scarcity. The rather simple Marxian characterization of a unified bloc of capital is difficult to reconcile with this reality. Nevertheless, the class framework is quite revealing when considering the relationship between capital and labor.

This chapter began, quite consciously, with the examination of the corporate economy. The rationale of beginning with a discussion of corporations is quite simple: The organization of capital determines, in the first instance, the organization of labor. Workers are brought into a preexisting production process; the kind of work they do will be dependent on earlier decisions concerning capital investment and productive technologies. Thus, the mass production worker became part of the political economy precisely because of the earlier decision to employ mass production technologies and to invest in the appropriate capital. Thus, as Marx and others acknowledged, labor cannot be understood separate from the broader set of class relations, the relations of production.

The organization of work—when combined with situational factors such as waves of immigration and prevailing political ideologies—has had a significant impact on the political mobilization of labor. In 1886, the American Federation of Labor (AFL) was formed to represent some 25 different labor unions including the bakers, carpenters, cigar makers, granite cutters, iron molders, journeymen furniture workers, journeymen tailors, metal workers, miners and mine laborers, and typographers. As this list reflects, these organizations, with some 15,000 members,

## THE STATE AND ECONOMIC ORGANIZATION

Neoclassical economics is concerned, primarily, with market behavior and economic performance coordinated by the price system. Yet, as the above discussion suggests, markets function well as mechanisms of exchange and coordination only under specific conditions. When the goods to be exchanged are more or less standardized and of limited complexity, markets are appropriate in coordinating the actions of diffuse buyers and producers. When these conditions fail to obtain, corporations have reason to adopt other means of coordinating. While Williamson and Campbell, Hollingsworth, and Lindberg, among others, present a host of factors that can shape the search for effective nonmarket governance structures, we are concerned primarily with the role of the government in shaping the decision. A quick survey of American economic history suggests that policy has played a crucial role in affecting the choice of governance structures and thus shaped the capacity of corporations to adjust to changes in their economic environment.

As is well documented, public policy is biased toward market governance in the United States. The antitrust laws place limits on certain forms of corporate behavior and intercorporate strategies. More important, for present purposes, they restrict the nature and ends of intercorporate relations. Under the antitrust laws, corporations cannot form associations to fix prices, manage output, or divide markets. Likewise, they cannot adopt a host of strategies designed to establish market control.[66] Although the enforcement of antitrust has focused on horizontal restraints in recent years due to the growing reliance on Chicago School economic doctrines which question the value of policy and the long-term impact of other strategies and intercorporate relations, the provision for private litigation and treble damages constitutes a significant threat and limits corporate autonomy.[67]

Associational governance became widespread in the United States as a response to the destabilizing forces inherent in the transition from a decentralized market system to a national market system that occurred at the turn of the century. As noted above, associations of one kind or another were created in the decades surrounding the turn of the century as a means of preventing overexpansion and unrestrained price competition. While antitrust was initially used to impede the formation of associations, associations were fostered by policymakers during World War I. With the need to gather information on economic performance and coordinate wartime production, wartime managers placed great reliance on trade associations and granted them what amounted to a grant of public authority. Thus, for example, in World War I, the War Industries Board relied on the information provided by war service committees made up of trade association personnel and certified by the U.S. Chamber of Commerce (see Chapter 5). During the New Deal, a host of policies established government-supervised self-regulation through economic associations that exercised quasi-public power (see Chapter 6). These associations were integrated into new regulatory structures where they determined rates of return and managed legal barriers to entry designed to retain a stable industrial structure.[68]

The associational structure that was locked into place during the New Deal was strengthened through World War II mobilization (see Chapter 7). As during

World War I, economic associations were forced to exercise quasi-public authority in coordinating the allotment of resources and the production of goods for the war effort. When Roosevelt expanded the associational system of government-supervised self-regulation, he did so under the belief that such structural reforms were necessary to maintain economic stability. An administrative corporatist system, it was believed, would provide a means of cooperative planning.[69] At the end of the war, policymakers increasingly relied on macroeconomic policy to promote stability. The associational structure was left in place, however, and was reinforced by the New Deal public policies, a prolonged period of economic growth in a postwar world economy dominated by the United States, and a capital-labor accord that provided growth-based wage increases in exchange for stability in industrial relations (see Chapter 8). Indeed, the system would not be challenged effectively until the 1970s and 1980s, when growing international competition, persistent inflation, and sluggish growth forced policymakers to reassess the core elements of the New Deal state (see Chapters 9 and 10). Deregulation and growing antitrust prosecutions against economic associations were partially successful in dismantling the associational system. More important, however, was the declining viability of mass standardized production. Increasingly, the keys to American economic success early in the century appeared to be contributing to its economic demise. This realization has forced a search for new policies and patterns of state-economy relations that can increase American competitiveness and facilitate the emergence of high-wage, technologically sophisticated industries. This may require a movement to alternative forms of corporate organization and economic governance.

As with governance structures, there is something of an institutional lag in public policies addressing the economy.[70] Given the fragmentation of American institutions and the permeability to interest group lobbying, this lag can be significant. By the time policymakers address one set of problems, conditions have changed to limit the impact of their initiatives. Moreover, because existing administrative capacities, ideas, and policy tools limit the range of options open to policymakers, past decisions commonly impact on the way in which new problems are addressed. There are ongoing efforts to conserve resources already devoted, policies already designed and implemented, regardless of their ultimate applicability to the problems at hand. These features of the American policy process and political-economic management will become clear as we turn to the history of state-economy relations in the twentieth century. Before we do this, however, it is necessary to address briefly the legacy of the nineteenth century. This is the subject of Chapter 3.

## NOTES

1. Neil Fligstein, "The Interorganizational Power Struggle: Rise of Finance Personnel to Top Leadership in Large Corporations, 1919–1979." *American Sociological Review* 52 (1987): 44–58.
2. See Alfred D. Chandler, Jr., *Strategy and Structure: Chapters in the History of the Industrial Enterprise* (Cambridge: M.I.T. Press, 1962).
3. Fligstein, "The Interorganizational Power Struggle," p. 45.
4. Yoram Barzel, *Economic Analysis of Property Rights* (Cambridge: Cambridge University Press, 1989), p. 43.
5. Ibid.

6. Ronald H. Coase, "The Nature of the Firm." *Economica* 4 (1937): 386–405.

7. Oliver E. Williamson, *Markets and Hierarchies: Analysis and Antitrust Implications* (New York: Free Press, 1975), p. 255.

8. Thráinn Eggertsson, *Economic Behavior and Institutions* (Cambridge: Cambridge University Press, 1990), p. 15.

9. Chandler, *Strategy and Structure*, and Alfred D. Chandler, Jr., *The Visible Hand: The Managerial Revolution in American Business* (Cambridge, Mass.: Harvard University Press, 1977).

10. Chandler, *Strategy and Structure*, pp. 13–14.

11. Ibid., p. 13, 14.

12. Alfred D. Chandler, Jr., "The United States: Seedbed of Managerial Capitalism." In *Managerial Hierarchies*, ed., Alfred D. Chandler Jr. and Herman Daems (Cambridge, Mass.: Harvard University Press, 1979), pp. 16–24.

13. See David F. Noble, *America by Design: Science, Technology, and the Rise of Corporate Capitalism* (Oxford: Oxford University Press, 1977).

14. Chandler, "The United States: Seedbed of Managerial Capitalism," p. 11.

15. Harry N. Scheiber, Harold G. Vatter, and Harold Underwood Faulkner, *American Economic History* (New York: Harper & Row, 1976), p. 233.

16. Thorstein Veblen, *The Theory of Business Enterprise* (New York: Charles Scribner, 1904).

17. Adolf A. Berle, Jr., and Gardiner C. Means, *The Modern Corporation and Private Property* (New York: Commerce Clearing House, 1932), p. 121.

18. See Edward S. Herman, *Corporate Control, Corporate Power* ( Cambridge: Cambridge University Press, 1981), pp. 5–14.

19. Adolf A. Berle, Jr., *Power without Property: A New Development in American Political Economy* (New York: Harcourt, Brace and Co., 1959), p. 59.

20. Herman, *Corporate Control, Corporate Power*, p. 66.

21. Berle and Means, *The Modern Corporation and Private Property*, p. 124.

22. Herman, *Corporate Control, Corporate Power*, pp. 112–13.

23. Michael Useem, *The Inner Circle: Large Corporations and the Rise of Business Political Activity in the U.S. and U.K.* (New York: Oxford University Press, 1984), p. 32.

24. Michael Useem and Jerome Karabel, "Pathways to Corporate Management." *American Sociological Review* 51 (1986): 184–200.

25. Fligstein, "The Interorganizational Power Struggle."

26. Ibid., p. 50.

27. Robert B. Reich, *The Next American Frontier* (New York: Times Books, 1983).

28. See Ibid.; and Michael J. Piore and Charles F. Sabel, *The Second Industrial Divide: Possibilities for Prosperity* (New York: Basic Books, 1984).

29. Piore and Sabel, *The Second Industrial Divide*, p. 17.

30. See William G. Ouchi, *The M-Form Society* (Reading, Mass.: Addison-Wesley, 1984).

31. Mark H. Lazerson, "Organizational Growth of Small Firms: An Outcome of Markets and Hierarchies?" *American Sociological Review* 53 ( 1988): 330–42. See Craig Littler, "Taylorism, Fordism and Job Design." In *Job Redesign: Critical Perspectives on the Labor Process*, ed. David Knights, Hugh Willmott, and David Collinson (Aldershot, England: Gower, 1985); and Mark Granovetter, "Small is Bountiful: Labor Markets and Establishment Size." *American Sociological Review* 49 (1984): 303–34.

32. John Zysman, *Governments, Markets, and Growth: Financial Systems and the Politics of Industrial Change* (Ithaca, N.Y.: Cornell University Press, 1983).

33. See John E. Owens, "The Regulation and Deregulation of Financial Institutions in the United States." In *State, Finance and Industry: A Comparative Analysis of Post-War Trends in Six Advanced Industrial Economies*, ed. Andrew Cox (New York: St. Martin's Press, 1986).

34. Kenneth J. Meier, *Regulation: Politics, Bureaucracy, and Economics* (New York: St. Martin's Press, 1985), pp. 37–76.

35. See Marc Allen Eisner, *Regulatory Politics in Transition* (Baltimore, Md.: Johns Hopkins University Press, 1993), pp. 103–12.

36. See Arthur F. Burns, "The Ongoing Revolution in American Banking." In *Capital, Technology, and Labor in the New Global Economy*, ed. James H. Cassing and Steven L. Husted (Washington, D.C.: American Enterprise Institute, 1988).

37. Ibid.

38. See Anne M. Khademian, *The SEC and Capital Market Regulation: The Politics of Expertise* (Pittsburgh: University of Pittsburgh Press, 1992), pp. 151–57; Joseph Auerbach and Samuel L. Hayes III, *Investment Banking and Diligence: What Price Deregulation?* (Boston: Harvard Business School Press, 1986), pp. 108–19; Joel Seligman, *The SEC and the Future of Finance* (New York: Praeger, 1985), pp. 195–280.

39. See Marc Allen Eisner, "Economic Regulatory Policies: Regulation and Deregulation in Historical Context." In *Handbook of Regulation and Administrative Law*, ed. David H. Rosenbloom and Richard D. Schwartz (New York: Marcel Dekker, 1994), pp. 111–12; Kenneth J. Meier and Jeff Worsham, "Deregulation, Competition, and Economic Changes: Assessing the Responsibility for Bank Failure." *Policy Studies Journal* 16, 3 (Spring 1988): 427–39; and Edward J. Kane, *The S&L Insurance Mess: How Did It Happen?* (Washington, D.C.: The Urban Institute, 1989).

40. Joe S. Bain, *Industrial Organization*, 2nd ed. (New York: John Wiley, 1968), p. 120.

41. See Bain, *Industrial Organization*, p.182; F.M. Sherer, "Economies of Scale and Industrial Concentration." In *Industrial Concentration: The New Learning*, ed. Harvey J. Goldschmid, H. Michael Mann, and J. Fred Weston (Boston: Little, Brown, 1974).

42. See Joe S. Bain, *Barriers to New Competition: Their Character and Consequences in American Manufacturing Industries* (Cambridge, Mass.: Harvard University Press, 1956).

43. See Ralph L. Nelson, *Merger Movements in American Industry, 1895–1956* (Princeton, N.J.: Princeton University Press, 1959); Carl Eis, "The 1919–1930 Merger Movement in American Industry." *Journal of Law and Economics* 12 (October 1969): 267–96; F.M. Scherer and David Ross, *Industrial Market Structure and Economic Performance*, 3rd. ed. (Boston: Houghton Mifflin, 1990), pp. 153–98; Marc Allen Eisner, *Antitrust and the Triumph of Economics: Institutions, Expertise, and Policy Change* (Chapel Hill: University of North Carolina Press, 1991), pp. 184–223.

44. See Scherer and Ross, *Industrial Market Structure and Economic Performance*, pp. 86–89; and F.M. Scherer, Alan Beckenstein, Erich Kaufer, and R.D. Murphy, *The Economics of Multi-Plant Operation* (Cambridge, Mass.: Harvard University Press, 1975).

45. See Richard A. Posner, "The Chicago School of Antitrust Analysis." *University of Pennsylvania Law Review* 127 (April 1979): 925–48; and Harold Demsetz, "Two Systems of Belief about Monopoly." In *Industrial Concentration: The New Learning*, ed. Harvey J. Goldschmid, H. Michael Mann, and J. Fred Weston (Boston: Little, Brown, 1974).

46. See Eisner, *Antitrust and the Triumph of Economics*.

47. See Coase, "The Nature of the Firm."

48. Oliver E. Williamson, *The Economic Institutions of Capitalism: Firms, Markets, Relational Contracting* (New York: Free Press, 1985), pp. 52–63.

49. Williamson, *The Economic Institutions of Capitalism*, pp. 55–56, 95–96.

50. Ibid., p. 56.

51. Ibid., pp. 72–84.

52. See Charles Perrow, "Markets, Hierarchies and Hegemony." In *Perspectives on Organization, Design, and Behavior*, ed. Andrew Van de Ven and William Joyce (New York: Wiley, 1981); and Charles Perrow, *Complex Organizations: A Critical Essay*, 3rd. ed. (New York: Random House, 1986).

53. Lazerson, "Organizational Growth of Small Firms," p. 333.

54. See John L. Campbell, J. Rogers Hollingsworth, and Leon N. Lindberg, eds., *Governance of the American Economy* (Cambridge: Cambridge University Press, 1991).

55. See Michael Patrick Allen, "The Structure of Interorganizational Elite Cooptation: Interlocking Corporate Directorates." *American Sociological Review* 39 (1974): 393–406; Useem, *The Inner Circle*.

56. Ouchi, *The M-Form Society*, p. 27.

57. Campbell, Hollingsworth, and Lindberg, *Governance of the American Economy*, p. 27.

58. See Kay Schlozman and John T. Tierney, *Organized Interests and American Democracy* (New York: Harper & Row, 1986).

59. See Richard R. Nelson and Sidney G. Winter, *An Evolutionary Theory of Economic Change* (Cambridge, Mass.: Harvard University Press, 1982).

60. Foster Rhea Dulles and Melvyn Dubofsky, *Labor in America: A History*, 4th ed. (Arlington Heights, Ill.: Harlan Davidson, 1984), pp. 211–16.

61. See Christopher L. Tomlins, *The State and the Unions: Labor Relations, Law, and the Organized Labor Movement in America, 1880–1960* (Cambridge: Cambridge University Press, 1985); and Chapter 6 of this book.

62. Claus Offe and Helmut Wiesenthal, "Two Logics of Collective Action." In *Disorganized Capitalism: Contemporary Transformation of Work and Politics*, ed. John Keane (Cambridge, Mass.: MIT Press, 1985), p. 211.

63. See Barry Bluestone and Bennet Harrison, *The Deindustrialization of America: Plant Closings, Community Abandonment, and the Dismantling of Basic Industry* (New York: Basic Books, 1982).

64. Nelson Lichtenstein, "From Corporatism to Collective Bargaining: Organized Labor and the Eclipse of Social Democracy in the Postwar Era." In *The Rise and Fall of the New Deal Order, 1930–1980*, ed. Steve Fraser and Gary Gerstle (Princeton, N.J.: Princeton University Press, 1989), p. 145

65. See Roy B. Helfgott, "America's Third Industrial Revolution." *Challenge* 29, 5: 41–46.

66. See A.D. Neale and D.G. Goyder, *The Antitrust Laws of the U.S.A.: A Study of Competition Enforced by Law* (Cambridge: Cambridge University Press, 1980).

67. See Marc Allen Eisner, *Antitrust and the Triumph of Economics: Institutions, Expertise, and Policy Change* (Chapel Hill: University of North Carolina Press, 1991).

68. Eisner, *Regulatory Politics in Transition*, Chapters 4 and 5.

69. See Donald Brand, *Corporatism and the Rule of Law: A Study of the National Recovery Administration* (Ithaca, N.Y.: Cornell University Press, 1988).

70. See John E. Elliot, "The Institutionalist School of Political Economy." In *What is Political Economy?* ed. David K. Whynes (Oxford: Basil Blackwell, 1984).

# THE LEGACY OF THE NINETEENTH CENTURY

When considering the political economy of the nineteenth century, Americans share a common myth of a land ruled by rugged individualism and a state that was either insignificant or completely invisible with respect to the economy. To be certain, the size and scope of the nineteenth-century American state can seem very limited from the perspective of the late twentieth century. It would take the advent of rapid industrialization, the Great Depression, and two world wars to give birth to the modern American state and the modern political economy. Yet, the record of government involvement in the economy during the nineteenth century is rather impressive. Through the basic tenets of constitutional design, investment in transportation innovations, and a legal framework promoting capital accumulation, the state created a context that promoted growth. This said, it is important to note that the state is only part of the story. A full account of the nineteenth-century political economy must address competing regional economies, successive technological innovations, particularly in transportation, and the rise of modern forms of corporate organization. The legacy of the nineteenth century is an economic structure and set of public policies and institutions that were strongly oriented toward growth.

By any measure, growth during the nineteenth century was significant. During the period 1800 to 1855, real gross national product grew at a rate of 4.2 percent per year. Between 1855 and 1905, real product growth equaled 3.9 percent. Growth rates of this magnitude would not be seen again in the twentieth century, when the average annual rate was 3.3 percent in 1905 to 1927, and 3.2 percent from 1927 to 1967. The abundant growth of the nineteenth century could support a large and growing population. During the period 1800 to 1860, the total labor force grew from approximately 1.7 million to over 11 million, an average annual growth rate of 3.2 percent. Despite the rapid population growth, the broader economic expansion promised a higher standard of living for most Americans. Thus, per capita Gross Domestic Product (GDP), expressed in 1840 prices, increased from $77.61 in 1800 to $134.61 in 1860. In essence, during the first six decades of the nineteenth century, per capita GDP almost doubled in real terms. As a result, per capita growth in real product averaged 1.1 percent per year from 1800 to 1855, increasing to 1.6 percent per year during the subsequent half century.[1]

To explain the growth of the period, it is convenient to focus on the tremendous endowment of mineral resources, land, navigatable internal rivers, and a coastline with natural harbors. However, the natural endowment of resources was not determinative. The colonial economy was rich in its endowment of natural resources but simultaneously faced serious shortages of capital and labor.[2] What was decisive was the legal and constitutional framework that defined property rights and the role of the federal government and states in regulating economic activity and facilitating growth.

## THE CONSTITUTIONAL AND LEGAL FRAMEWORK

To take the word of many neoclassical economists and economic liberals, markets are prepolitical institutions that function optimally according to the principle of laissez faire. Milton Friedman thus states with little hesitation: "Fundamentally, there are only two ways of co-ordinating the economic activities of millions. One is central direction involving the use of coercion—the technique of the army and of the modern totalitarian state. The other is voluntary co-operation of individuals—the technique of the market place."[3] Such simple distinctions rest on a conception of the market as being, at least in its ideal state, completely free from the effects of public policy. However, even Friedman is forced to concede that "the role of the government . . . is to do something that the market cannot do for itself, namely, to determine, arbitrate, and enforce the rules of the game."[4] Of course, determining the rules of the game—that is, defining and assigning property rights, the terms of legitimate transactions, and the rights of the parties and the state when disputes arise—is essentially creating the legal or institutional infrastructure for markets. In the words of Karl Polyani: "There was nothing natural about *laissez faire*; free markets could never have come into being merely by allowing things to take their course."[5] He continues: "The road to the free market was opened and kept open by an enormous increase in continuous, centrally organized and controlled interventionism. . . . even those who wished most ardently to free the state from all unnecessary duties, and whose whole philosophy demanded the restriction of state activities, could not but entrust the self-same state with the new powers, organs, and instruments required for the establishment of *laissez faire*."[6]

Polyani's study *The Great Transformation* is largely a study of the creation of the market in Europe. However, his insights are easily applicable in the American context. The market economy of the nineteenth century—so often presented as a stateless alternative to the interventionist economy of the post–New Deal decades—functioned on the basis of a set of well-articulated public policies. When one considers the factors promoting growth in the new republic, it is essential that one begins by addressing the importance of the basic constitutional and legal framework established in the few first decades of the nation's existence. The Constitution, major statutes, and early court decisions established a set of property rights and a division between national and state authority that facilitated growth. To be certain, laws and policies cannot guarantee high rates of growth. They must be combined with ongoing technological innovations, capital formation, and organizational advances—factors that will be examined later in this chapter. However, a nation's basic legal framework is important insofar as it creates a system of incentives that can promote growth and risk taking.

For decades constitutional scholars and historians have addressed the thesis presented by Charles A. Beard, namely, that the Constitution must be understood as an economic document written by economic elites to promote their narrow economic interests, particularly the interests of financiers, slave owners, holders of the war debt, manufacturers, and those involved in trade. Unlike those interests that were well represented at the constitutional convention, the large mass of citizens lacking property were not given the opportunity to contribute to or vote on the ratification of the new Constitution.[7] The Beard thesis—an interesting synthesis of elite and class analyses—continues to animate discussions over the nature of the Constitution. While the Beard thesis remains a source of controversy, there are at least three points that must be considered whenever one wishes to view the Constitution as an economic document. First, the mere fact that economic and social elites dominated the convention does not lead one inexorably to the conclusion that the results of the convention were somehow tainted. Indeed, the same generalization about the background of participants could be made at virtually any period in U.S. history. When has it not been the case that economic and social elites have been more involved in national policymaking than farmers, laborers, or small merchants? If we wish to accept the conclusion that at all times and under all circumstances public policy reflects the goals and interests of the most powerful, it becomes something of a meaningless generalization. Second, there is little evidence that anyone was made worse off by the elimination of the defective Articles of Confederation. This is not to say that the provisions of the Constitution were optimal. The preservation of slavery, for example, would continue to plague the republic, leading ultimately to the crises of the Civil War, Reconstruction, and efforts to promote civil rights that continue to this day. Finally, the most salient economically oriented provisions of the Constitution did not provide for the preservation of the existing distribution of wealth and economic power. Rather, they facilitated trade and the evolution of national markets and thus promoted the ongoing generation of wealth.

If we wish to understand the Constitution as an economic document, there are several provisions in which its most lasting impact on economic performance can be found. The Constitution established taxation powers to provide for the defense and the common welfare; power to borrow money on the credit of the United States; power to regulate interstate and international commerce; power to establish uniform immigration and naturalization laws; power to establish laws for bankruptcy; power to establish uniform weights and measures for trade; power to coin money and regulate the value of the money; power to establish a postal system with postal roads; and power to maintain and protect intellectual property through copyrights. The impressive list of powers enumerated in the Constitution provided the national government with the authority to create a framework for a national market.

As Forest McDonald explains, however, one should not be too anxious to portray the Constitution as a document which transformed the economy whole-sale: "The merest glance at the Constitution is enough to show that the document did not, in a stroke, terminate existing conditions and usher in the age of capital-ism. A somewhat closer look indicates that the Constitution did make the trans-formation possible."[8] By creating a flexible framework that preserved a significant role for commerce and private property rights while granting to the government the authority to maintain these rights and facilitate transactions, the Constitution enabled economic growth to occur at a rapid pace. James Willard Hurst expands on this notion in presenting "the release of energy" as a goal of the legal system. He thus identifies one of the working principles that guided constitutional design and the use of law in the early republic: "The legal order should protect and pro-mote the release of individual creative energy to the greatest extent compatible with the broad sharing of opportunity for such expression. In pursuit of this end, law might be used both (a) to secure a man a chance to be let alone, free of arbitrary public or private interference, while he showed what he could do, and (b) to pro-vide instruments or procedures to lend the support of the organized community to the effecting of man's creative talents, even where this involved using the law's compulsion to enforce individual arrangements."[9]

A brief survey of early federal legislation suggests that Congress was never truly wedded to the principles of laissez faire but used its powers, where possible, to promote domestic commerce and economic growth. In 1787, Congress (working under the Articles of Confederation) enacted the Northwest Ordinance to create an orderly system for distributing land, the most important factor in establishing American wealth. The new policy defined the process for settlement and gaining political representation. It also provided a basis for public support for education: The proceeds from the sale of one portion of each township were reserved for the support of schools. Most important for present purposes, however, was the fact that the ordinance established the policy of selling land at a minimum price in rel-atively small plots to reduce speculation and meet the claims of the landless and the pressures on the new republic. Land rights were fixed and perpetual. Property could thus be transferred perpetually through sale or inheritance (albeit barring the system of primogeniture) and could be reclaimed by the state only for failure to pay taxes or under eminent domain. The basic principles established through the Northwest Ordinance were revolutionary. As Jonathan R. T. Hughes explains: "A feat of self-government as remarkable as the Constitution itself, these ordinances were also something of a revolution in human affairs; men were vested with secure property ownership by purchase from governments elected by themselves. That the lands had to be purchased established land-owning capitalism in the new ter-ritories, and also determined that the land would be distributed by settled law and not by force of arms, Indian lands being the exception."[10]

The support for commercial expansion continued in the first Congress, following the ratification of the Constitution. In 1789, Congress passed the Tariff Act. Although the act had some mild protectionist features, it was chiefly designed to raise revenues through tariff duties paid in specie. In 1791, Treasury Secretary Alexander Hamilton presented Congress with his *Report on Manufactures* which, among other things, called for a system of protectionist tariffs to stimulate the growth of particular infant industries. Despite congressional resistance to a Hamiltonian industrial policy, the tariff was used increasingly as an important means of discriminating against imports and thus protecting certain domestic goods. In addition to the Tariff Act, Congress passed the Tonnage Act in 1789. The act provided for the registry under a U.S. flag of only those ships that were built in the United States and owned by Americans. These ships would receive a 10 percent reduction in custom duties when involved in the export-import trade and would be exempt from a discriminatory tonnage tax affecting coastwise shipping. By 1817, foreign ships were prohibited altogether from coastal shipping, thus reserving this lucrative business for American ships.[11]

In addition to promoting domestic industry and shipping, Congress was concerned with addressing the problem of the war debt. In his *Report on the Public Credit*, Alexander Hamilton argued that the new government must assume the foreign and domestic debt assumed by the Continental Congress and the Confederation, as well as the debts incurred by the state during the Revolution. Moreover, Hamilton argued, the new government must assume responsibility for principal and interest, bringing the total obligation to $77,124,465. Hamilton argued that assumption of the debt would create greater support for the new government, secure the credit of the United States for future borrowing, and reduce the shortage of currency in that federal bonds could circulate as a surrogate for specie. Despite the objections of some who argued that much of the debt was now in the hands of foreigners and speculators, Hamilton convinced the Congress which moved quickly to pass the Funding Act of 1790. The repayment plan dramatically increased the value of old war bonds and foreign willingness to assume debt. As foreign holdings of the debt increased from $3 million to $33 million (of $52 million total), domestic capital was freed for domestic investment, thus further reducing the liquidity problems.[12] In 1791, Congress created the Bank of the United States to broaden the market for bonds and serve as the fiscal agent of the government. It could transfer money between regions, engage in national branching, and accept private business.

The expansion of state authority in the early republic provided a means of establishing greater opportunities for economic action. In this institutional milieu, the courts played a significant role in adjudicating individual property rights and maintaining the boundaries of state authority in the economy and in relation to the individual states. As Gordon S. Wood explains: "The result was paradoxical: As the public power of the state grew in the early Republic, so too did the private rights of individuals—with the courts mediating and balancing the claims of each."[13] It is useful to consider briefly some of the early Supreme Court decisions that affected economic development. Although it is impossible to provide an exhaustive overview of key decisions, it is useful to address the broad thrust of the Court in addressing the authority of the national government relative to the states as expressed in the commerce clause and the Court's interpretation of the contract clause.

Article I, Section 9, of the Constitution grants Congress the power to "regulate Commerce with foreign Nations, and among the several States, and with the Indian Tribes." In *Gibbons* v. *Ogden* (1824), the Supreme Court addressed a dispute involving New York's authority to grant a steamboat monopoly in state waters. The state monopoly came into conflict with federal licensing of ships involved in coastal transportation. The conflict between state and federal practices was resolved by the Marshall Court through an appeal to the interstate commerce clause of the Constitution. The decision cast national authority broadly, to encompass navigation and commerce with foreign nations, even if that commerce terminates well within a state's jurisdiction. Moreover, unlike taxation which is a concurrent power (i.e., exercised by both state and national governments), the power to regulate commerce with foreign nations and among the states was vested solely in the national government.

Another early decision—perhaps even more important than *Gibbons* v. *Ogden*—was *McCulloch* v. *Maryland* (1819). The dispute involved a $15,000 tax that had been imposed on banks doing business in Maryland without holding a Maryland state charter. Of course, the only bank that fell into this category was the Bank of the United States. Marshall's decision moved well beyond what was required to resolve the controversy, reflecting his tendency to exploit such opportunities to establish broader constitutional points and thus flesh out the vague definition of national authority in the Constitution. Marshall found, firstly, that although the Constitution did not enumerate the power to incorporate a national bank, such a power was "necessary and proper" given the other powers explicitly assigned to the national government. The powers to lay and collect taxes, borrow funds, regulate commerce, and maintain a defensive capacity were enumerated in the Constitution and depended for their execution on the existence of an appropriate administrative apparatus—in this case, a bank. Congress was granted the power to make "all laws which shall be necessary and proper" for executing constitutionally vested powers. Hence, the bank was deemed constitutional.

Marshall's interpretation of the "necessary and proper" clause of the Constitution was crucial given the fact that the national government would need to employ new administrative agencies and policies to execute its basic mandate. Equally important, however, was Marshall's determination of Maryland's power over the Bank of the United States. Marshall correctly noted that "If the States may tax one instrument, employed by the government in the execution of its powers, they may tax any and every other instrument. They may tax the mail; they may tax the mint; they may tax patent rights; they may tax the papers of the custom-house; they may tax the judicial process; they may tax all the means employed by the government, to an excess which would defeat all the ends of government." In essence, this would make the national government dependent on the constitutionally inferior state governments. This decision would limit the constitutionality of state policies that might frustrate the national government's efforts to execute its mandate—much of which was economic in nature.

Article I, Section 10, of the Constitution contains the commerce clause, another source of judicial decision making during the early nineteenth century. Section 10 proclaims that states shall not pass any "Law impairing the Obligation of Contracts." In *Fletcher* v. *Peck* (1810), the first significant case decided under the contract clause, the Marshall Court determined that the clause prohibited the states from rescinding on their own contractual obligations. In *New Jersey* v. *Wilson* (1812), the Court found that a tax exemption granted by the legislature conveyed a contractual obligation on the part of the state which could not be revoked through legislation. The most important of the Marshall Court decisions addressing the contract clause came in *Dartmouth College* v. *Woodward* (1819). In this case, the dispute addressed the attempts of the New Hampshire legislature to place the college on a state charter, despite the existence of a royal charter that established it as a private institution. The Marshall Court decided that the corporate charter constituted a "contract for the security and disposition of property." Hence, the legislature's efforts were clearly in conflict with the contract clause of the Constitution. Corporate charters were constitutionally protected contracts.[14]

The impact of the *Dartmouth* decision was limited by the adoption of general incorporation laws at the state level which reserved the right to repeal or alter the terms of incorporation. However, the key point, namely that corporate charters were constitutionally protected from state laws was an important principle in establishing the stability necessary to promote risk taking and long-term investment. While stability is important, it is also easily translated into rigidity in the face of rapid technological change. It is thus important to address, briefly, the decision in *Charles River Bridge* v. *Warren Bridge* (1837). The decision addressed the Charles River Bridge Company's assertion that the Massachusetts legislature's decision to charter a second company, the Warren Bridge Company, to build a second bridge over the Charles River impaired the obligation of contract in the original charter. Because the Charles River Bridge Company's charter did not explicitly grant it exclusive rights, the majority decision rejected that such rights existed. As a result, states had far greater opportunities to charter new projects except in those cases where the language in the charters explicitly granted monopoly rights. It is important to note that Chief Justice Roger Taney argued that implied corporate privileges should not be allowed to serve as an impediment to technological advances. Otherwise, the established property rights of companies applying old technologies (e.g., turnpike companies) could effectively stop the investment in new technologies (e.g., railroads and canals). While corporate charters were still protected from legislative assaults, they were not interpreted as granting implied monopoly rights that could limit progress.[15] As James Willard Hurst notes, Taney's decision revealed "the preference for dynamic rather than static property, or for property put to creative new use rather than property content with what it is." In so doing, it "expressed the dominant mid-century preference for property as an institution of growth rather than merely of security."[16]

Debtor-creditor relations are critical in shaping the decision to invest resources and incur risks. Bankruptcy laws provide an important source of protection for debtors and promote innovation by limiting the costs of commercial failure. As a result of bankruptcy laws, failed entrepreneurs are given a heightened opportunity to reenter the stream of commerce and take risks on new ventures. Under the Constitution, Congress had the authority to pass uniform bankruptcy laws. In practice, however, the task of shaping bankruptcy laws fell to the states. Thus, in *Sturges* v. *Crowninshield* (1819) and *Ogden* v. *Saunders* (1827), the Supreme Court recognized the validity of state bankruptcy laws, absent the uniform national bankruptcy laws authorized in the Constitution. In keeping with the contract clause of the Constitution, bankruptcy laws could not alter debtor-creditor relations that predated the passage of the bankruptcy laws since this would entail an effort on the part of states to alter the terms of contract retroactively.[17]

If the courts took great care in addressing the rights of corporations and the constitutional protections associated with the corporate charter, far less attention was devoted to labor. In part, this reflects the fact that the economy was largely agrarian and a large industrial labor force would not emerge until the last decades of the century when combined with mass production technologies. The key questions involving labor addressed, first, labor organization and, secondly, the limits of employer liability for workplace accidents. Collective action directed against employers was commonly portrayed as criminal conspiracy and thus subject to prosecution. However, an important exception was *Commonwealth* v. *Hunt* (1842), decided by the Massachusetts Supreme Court. The decision established that association was not per se illegal: "The manifest intent of association is, to induce all those engaged in the same occupation to become members of it. Such a purpose is not unlawful. If would give them a power which might be exerted for useful and honorable purposes, or for dangerous and pernicious ones."[18] Thus, the organization of a union was not deemed an illegal conspiracy. Rather, the association had to be involved in illegal activities. This did not prevent employers from seeking injunctions in response to strikes or boycotts—a common and effective recourse in the latter half of the nineteenth century. With respect to employer liability, the state courts tended to embrace the "fellow servant rule" which essentially rejected employer liability for injuries that resulted from the negligence of another employee. This doctrine, when combined with the argument that employees in dangerous occupations, assumed responsibility for occupational risks, essentially protected employers from liability.[19]

## SECTIONAL STRESS AND POLITICAL ECONOMIES IN CONFLICT

While it is convenient to speak of the growth of the nation's economy, there was, in reality, nothing resembling a national economy. Rather, there were relatively distinct regional economies engaged in different forms of production, each with a unique set of interests and stakes in public policy. Richard Bensel has provided a useful framework for understanding the resulting political conflicts which draws on the world system theory of Immanuel Wallerstein that presents world politics as a struggle between a capitalist metropole and nations on the periphery of the world capitalist economy.[20] Bensel explains:

> The bipolar structure of sectional stress in American politics is a reflection
> of the internal core-periphery continuum around which the economic life

of the country is organized. At one end of the continuum, the oldest and largest industrial centers and seaports in the nation are concentrated. In American economic history, these regions have dominated the national political economy through control of the state apparatus and the domestic financial community. As the nation developed, the policy imperatives of the industrial-commercial core—policies viewed by the political representatives of the section as necessary for the maintenance or advancement of its interests in the national political economy—have often changed. However, whenever the implementation of those policy imperatives has provoked a high level of sectional stress, the industrial-commercial core has been opposed by the interior-hinterland periphery.[21]

Although Bensel's insightful analysis focuses on the period after 1880, the basic tension he identifies was clearly a driving force in the definition of the American political economy for the whole nineteenth century. In essence, there were three distinct economies. The Northeast constituted the industrial-commercial core, to use Bensel's terminology. It was closely integrated through trade and political coalitions with the agricultural West. The South, in contrast, was dependent on the North and West for manufactured goods, capital, mercantile services, and foodstuffs. The policies designed to promote development in the Northeast and West were, in large part, in conflict with the interests of the South, thus introducing a distinct tension into the process of American political development.

In the Northeast (i.e., New England and the Mid-Atlantic states), the economy evolved from agriculture to manufacturing, finance, and trade during the first half of the nineteenth century. Ironically, while much of the economic growth of the period 1800 to 1861 was driven by foreign demands for southern cotton, the main impact of cotton receipts were felt in the Northeast. The South was dependent on northern manufacturers for a host of goods that were not produced in its monoculture economy. Likewise, the southern economy depended on the North for capital, insurance, and shipping associated with the cotton trade. The heavy demand for manufactured goods combined with technological innovations in production (e.g., standardized products) reduced transportation costs and the demands associated with expanding the transportation infrastructure to promote rapid industrialization. As one might expect, this industrialization was concentrated in the North, which accounted for three-quarters of the nation's manufacturing workforce in 1850. Of course, the Northeast's preeminence in manufacturing was, in part, a product of history. Early settlement and trade patterns resulted in a more developed transportation infrastructure and the nation's largest urban centers which provided both a manufacturing workforce and a powerful source of demand in its own right.[22]

The western economy (i.e., the settled West and the current Midwest) was engaged primarily in agricultural production and mining. Wheat and flour, corn and meal, livestock and meat products (e.g., ham, salt pork, bacon), and whisky (an economical means of shipping grains) were the key commodities produced in the highly decentralized farm economy. Following the adoption of steamboat river transportation in 1816, western farmers increasingly produced for markets in the

South and Northeast. The growing demand for western grains drove the major waves of western expansion. As new lands were brought under cultivation to meet the high demands, surplus commodities drove down prices, thus creating excess capacity that was gradually absorbed. While demand was a critical factor in stimulating expansion, one must not lose sight of the importance of transportation innovations. Without expenditures in river improvement, canal construction, and railroads, large-scale farming in interior regions would not have been feasible.

With the growing efficiency of transportation (see the later discussion) the West forged a direct link with the Northeastern cities. Reductions in transportation costs allowed for greater specialization and production for more expansive markets. Hence, foodstuffs were traded east for consumption in the urban centers and export. Capital equipment, textiles, and manufactured goods were shipped west. While the South remained an important source of demand, it was overshadowed by the eastern trade by the 1840s, reflecting the combination of eastern industrialization, urbanization, and growing demands for exports to Europe. This trade proved increasingly profitable as reductions in transportation costs and innovations in production made manufactured goods less expensive relative to foodstuffs.[23]

The growing interdependence of the northeastern and western economies was accompanied by a convenient political agreement. Western legislators exchanged support for the Northeast's high tariff rates in exchange for land policies that provided low cost or free homestead lands for further western expansion and internal improvements. These tariffs, in turn, provided some protection for northeastern manufacturers—allowing for import substitution industrialization—and thus stimulated further development while serving as a source of government revenues. Despite real questions over whether the tariff actually promoted development, the tariff had been a source of controversy since the Tariff Act of 1789. However, as rates were increased and extended to a host of northern manufactured goods at the expense of a southern economy that was dependent on manufactured items produced in the North or abroad, the conflicts escalated. The controversies over the tariff reached new heights with the Tariff Act of 1828, the so-called Black Tariff or Tariff of Abominations which imposed high rates to protect woolen manufactures and iron products. With an average ad valorem rate on dutible goods of 49 percent, the Tariff Act met with the near-unified opposition of the South and resulted in calls for secession or nullification. While the controversies surrounding the Black Tariff of 1828 quickly subsided, the tariff stood as an important symbol of the political alliance between the West and the Northeast.[24]

In contrast to the northeastern and western economies, the southern economy was strictly agricultural, export oriented, and dependent on a completely different mode of production. The large southern plantations were largely devoted to growing cotton for export markets, although they also serviced northern textile industries. Of course, tobacco, sugar, and rice were also grown, albeit in limited quantities due to the special conditions required for their cultivation. Plantations in the Old South also raised some foodstuffs for consumption whereas plantations in the Southwest (e.g., Mississippi, Arkansas, Louisiana) were able to specialize in cotton production due to the availability of inexpensive foodstuffs produced in the West.

While it is convenient to think of the South as dominated by the plantation, it remains the case that the majority of the white population was engaged in subsistence agriculture. The growth in manufacturing and urbanization that characterized the other regions were absent in the South. Until the time of the Civil War, the economy relied on slave labor and there was little capital available for diversifying or promoting domestic manufacturing. With a large portion of the southern population consisting of black slaves (4 million of a population of 12 million) and poor white farmers, there was little incentive to produce manufactured goods for a market that didn't exist. The lack of domestic industry, low levels of urbanization, and low literacy rates among the white population were additional products of the dominance of the cotton monoculture. Outside of the capital invested in new lands and slaves, plantation owners simply failed to reinvest the income from cotton production in the region. Rather, the income was transferred to the North and West—the sources of many of the manufactured goods, services, and foodstuffs consumed in the South.

While the northeastern and western economies were increasingly integrated, the southern economy remained externally oriented and dependent on the North. Merchant houses, financial institutions, and insurance companies that had grown in the Northeast in response to the transatlantic trade provided the southern economy with its links to export markets. Southern cotton was transported by northern coastwise shipping services to New York for export to Liverpool or other markets. The cotton shipments were insured by northern insurance companies and shipped to meet commercial agreements arranged by northern merchants. Likewise, the imported manufactured goods were shipped South, often by the same shipping services that collected the cotton. Finally, the southern economy depended heavily on the North for capital to expand cotton production westward. Finance was necessary to buy new lands, transport slaves, and prepare the lands for cultivation.[25]

The issue of slavery had distinct moral implications in the North as a growing abolitionist movement called for an end to the pernicious institution. In the South, the issue of slavery had strong economic features due to the impact that an elimination of slavery could have on production via gang labor and southern wealth. However, it also had a salient political dimension for those who resented the intrusion of the North and Washington on what were understood as state issues and local concerns. The issue of slavery, when taken by itself, may be insufficient to explain the decision to leave the union. Of the 8 million whites living in the slave states, only 400,000 actually owned slaves; only 300 families had plantations with over 200 slaves.[26] As Richard Bensel notes: "Slavery had no discernible impact on the economic interest of most nonslaveholding southerners because their subsistence existence was almost entirely detached from the national and world economies. For other poor whites, the dependence of slave plantations on cash crops provided a vast market for the production of foodstuffs that otherwise might not have existed. For another group, perhaps the smallest in number, the hostility of the plantation economy to industrialization retarded the development of comparatively attractive wage-labor opportunities."[27]

While the uncertainty and financial losses associated with emancipation were undoubtedly great, the core problem for many remained the perceived de-

The expansion of land devoted to agriculture continued throughout the nineteenth century. However, it drew to a close more than a half century ago. Since then, the land devoted to agricultural production has declined rapidly. Despite the declines, the key problem in agriculture in this century has been overproduction. Public policies regulating agriculture have been designed to create artificial scarcity of supplies, thereby raising prices and farm incomes. This has been possible because of the role that technological advances can play in mitigating the problem of limited resources. Scarcity forces technological innovations that allow for advances in extraction, better ways of economizing on resources, and diversification into substitute goods. If economic history provides any lessons as to the impact of natural resource constraints, it is that they promote technological innovation and prove highly responsive to these innovations. Although a scarcity of agricultural lands was not a driving force in the nineteenth century, the period provides an excellent example of the role of technology—in this case, transportation technology—in converting abundant natural resources into growth.

When we consider the importance of transportation in the nineteenth century, we immediately think of the railroads. As will be discussed later, the railroads made a significant contribution to development. However, one must first address the role of other transportation innovations, including turnpikes, canals, and steamboats. In each case, the introduction and dissemination of new transportation technologies resulted in significant reductions in the costs of production, thus stimulating more rapid development. In each case, public policy facilitated the dissemination of new transportation technologies.

The availability of land and other resources created the potential for an expansive national economy. The greatest barrier to the realization of this potential was the lack of cheap transportation. In 1800, the cost of transporting 1 ton across ocean was approximately the same as transporting the same ton 40 miles across land. The high costs of land transportation promoted a distinctive settlement pattern along coasts and rivers. At the same time, it promoted an ongoing reliance on imports, even where domestic producers existed. Transportation innovations were critical in altering this state of affairs. Between 1815 and 1860, the nation underwent something of a transportation revolution resulting in dramatic reductions in the costs of shipping goods and allowing for the rapid economic development of the interior. The role of transportation in economic development is self-evident once we realize that the largest single factor in the costs of most goods was transportation expenses. A lack of reliable and rapid transportation forced businesses to incur higher costs for shipping, financing, and insuring goods such that in many cases economic development was simply prohibitively expensive. Innovations in transportation allowed for access to markets, promoted the development of domestic industries, facilitated specialization, and increased land values, thus stimulating westward expansion. Beyond the commercial interests, however, one must recognize the political importance of transportation innovations. An efficient transportation infrastructure enhanced the capacity of the federal government to penetrate the interior, imposing laws, provisioning troops, and enhancing communications. Moreover, transportation allowed for a greater sense of national unity in a nation characterized from the beginning by strong norms of localism and regional divisions.[33]

Despite the contributions of transportation to nation building, we are concerned primarily with the impact on commercial development. The transportation revolution promoted development in a number of ways. Building new turnpikes, canals, ships, and railroads resulted in a greater demand for resources. These backward linkages were combined with forward linkages, as the transportation advances provided lower prices in the economy as a whole. Finally, the transportation revolution reduced the costs of inputs to the economy, thus making it possible for the nation to substitute domestically produced goods for imports while expanding exports as well.

## Transatlantic and Inland Shipping

Because of differences in technology and the timing of innovations, it is useful to address shipping separate from land transportation. Significant advances in ocean transportation were important to development. With respect to ocean transportation, we can identify innovations in the organization of shipping, the design of vessels, and the introduction of steam power. In the area of organization, the creation of packet services—the regular and guaranteed service between Europe and the United States—resulted in a reduction of transaction costs relative to the transient traders who were highly irregular in their routes, schedules, and shipments. Rather than booking a vessel, arranging for insurance, and negotiating schedules on a shipment-by-shipment basis, it was possible to rely on a growing shipping industry that combined the various services, used larger ships, and sailed on fixed schedules between predetermined ports. The transatlantic packet lines were accompanied by a thriving coastwise shipping trade that distributed goods between New York and other coastal cities. More important, however, were changes in the design of sail-driven ocean vessels. Between the 1820s and the 1850s, vessels nearly tripled in size, from an average of 361 tons to an average of 1,087 tons. At the same time, design improvements allowed for a 15 percent reduction in shipping time and a parallel reduction in costs.[34]

The innovations in sailing ships were combined in 1838 with transatlantic steamship services. Because of the bulkiness of the fuel, steamships had to be much larger and stronger than sailing ships in order to carry a profitable load. Ongoing technical and managerial problems with transatlantic steamship services were reduced significantly in 1848. Between 1848 and 1860, the total registered tonnage of steamships in the nation increased from 5,631 to 97,296 tons. The new ships were larger and faster: A steamship could cross the ocean in 10 days, compared with 33 days for a comparable sailing ship. Moreover, the gradual adoption of iron hulls and screw drives allowed for improved safety and lower insurance costs than available in the wooden-hulled, paddle wheel ships. Despite the difference in speed, before 1860 the cost of steamship transportation was three to four times greater than the costs of passage on a comparable sailing ship, due in large part to the costs of maintenance and fuel. As a result, steamships focused on transporting passengers and more expensive goods whereas the sailing ships concentrated on the low end, shipping poor immigrants and raw materials.[35]

Steam power was also important in domestic shipping, particularly on the Missouri, Ohio, and Mississippi rivers. During the period 1815 to 1860, the number of steamboats operating on Western rivers increased from 7 to 817, with tonnage growing from 1,516 tons to 195,022 tons. Steamboats were particularly important in upstream travel. Between 1815 and 1860, real freight rates for upstream transportation fell by 90 percent, compared with 40 percent reductions in downstream rates. Productivity of steamboats increased by a factor of nine during the period due to innovations in boat design, innovations in steam engines, and enhanced docking facilities. Paradoxically, the short life of steamboats (approximately 5 ½ years) promoted greater efficiency insofar as new boats embodying new technology were needed to replace boats lost due to fires, explosions, and accidents. The average practice at any given time was close to the best practice. There was a rapid diffusion of technical innovations as a result of the short life of the ships. The federal government subsidized the industry by assuming the responsibility for river maintenance, thus reducing the risks.[36] The growing reliance on steamboats during the decades preceding the Civil War is striking. In 1810, less than one-tenth of one percent of ship tonnage was steam driven. The remainder of vessels were sailing ships. By 1835, 6.7 percent of vessel tonnage was steam driven. By 1860, over 16 percent of the ships were steam ships. Of course, the reliance on steam would continue to grow over the course of the century.[37]

## Turnpikes and Canals

The significant efficiency gains in shipping in transatlantic and coastal routes were combined with similar gains in turnpikes and canals. Turnpikes provided great advantages over common roads due to the better quality surfaces (e.g., gravel or planks rather than dirt). However, they were expensive to construct, costing some $3 to $5 thousand per mile for roads averaging 20 miles. Typically, a state-chartered corporation constructed and operated a turnpike, raising funds through the sale of shares. In New England and many of the Middle Atlantic states, turnpikes were financed through private funds available by virtue of the greater population density. Investors hoped to realize returns on their funds through tolls. In other regions, a good deal of financing came from state funds. Regardless of the funding sources, states usually supported turnpike companies by allowing them to exercise eminent domain and imposing legal penalties for the avoidance of tolls. By 1830, near the end of the boom in turnpike construction, some 27,800 miles of turnpikes had been built. However, turnpikes were rarely profitable due to state regulation of tolls and the high costs of maintenance. By 1819, companies began abandoning their roads. By 1838, a majority of turnpikes were completely or partially abandoned as turnpike companies were falling into bankruptcy.[38]

The decline of turnpikes was contemporaneous with the rise of canals, arguably the most effective part of the transportation system at the time. Depending on the quality of the roads, canals allowed a horse to pull 20 to 50 times the load that it could pull on land. The first major canals were completed early in the century: the Santee Canal in South Carolina was completed in 1800 and the Middlesex Canal in Massachusetts was finished in 1808. However, the period of intensive canal building began in 1825, following the completion of the Erie Canal connecting Albany and Buffalo led many to consider the potential impact of canal construction on local and regional development. The reduction in transportation costs led the state governments to devote a good deal of the capital necessary for canal construction. Depending on the year in question, the share of public funds ranged from 66.2 percent to 79.4 percent. The wave of canal construction continued until 1845, declining rapidly thereafter as competition with the railroads and escalating costs of maintenance reduced the incentives for further investments. In the end, over $188 million was invested, creating more than 4,000 miles of canals.[39]

Canals provided a source of extremely cheap transportation. While the cost of transportation on a turnpike averaged 15¢ per ton-mile in 1853, the rates on canals ranged from a low of 25¢ on the Chesapeake and Ohio Canal, to a high of 2.4¢ per ton-mile on the Pennsylvania Main Line Canal. While canals brought great efficiencies when compared with existing land transportation, there were limitations to the use of canals. First, because canals used relatively shallow, stagnant water, there were effectively closed once the temperature fell below freezing. Second, they were expensive to build because of the need for locks to compensate for changes in elevation—a common problem in New England and the Middle Atlantic states As a result, most canals cost $20,000 to $30,000 per mile to construct. Moreover, canals were expensive to repair and required repair on a regular basis to maintain the integrity of their banks and the proper water depth. Finally, as a mode of transportation, canals were remarkably slow. These features of canals limited their appeal to private investors, particularly with the emergence of the railroads which, in some instances, made canals obsolete before they were even fully operational.[40]

## The Railroad

The major transportation innovation—one which was virtually synonymous with the transportation revolution—was the railroad. Railroad expansion began in earnest, following the inauguration of the Baltimore and Ohio Railroad in 1830, with rapid increases in mileage and investment thereafter. In 1840, there were 2,818 miles of road. This more than tripled to 9,021 miles by 1850, more than tripling again to reach 30,626 miles by 1860. By 1890, 166,703 miles of road were in operation. The expansion of the railroad was rapid, and it came at a very high price. Railroad investment reached $1.15 billion in 1860, compared with $318 million a decade earlier. By 1890, there would be more than $10 billion invested in the rail system.[41] These unprecedented sums of money were raised through stock and bond markets. The demand for capital stimulated the development of capital markets that would be of great value in funding industrial expansion later in the century—a point that will be addressed in greater detail later.

The railroads promoted further reductions in transportation expenses despite the fact that tracks were often laid parallel to existing river routes and charged a higher rate per ton-mile than the canals. Even if canals that directly competed with railroads could provide a cheaper rate per ton-mile, railroads could provide delivery in one-third the time and often provided more points at which goods could be loaded for transportation. Moreover, the railroads usually operated with complete disregard for the weather that left many canals impassable for months per year. Albert Fishlow estimates that the direct benefits from shipping on the railroad rather than the next best alternative form of transportation were $175 million in 1859, or about 4 percent of GNP, although some economic historians have discounted such estimates of direct benefits.[42]

Despite the benefits of rail transportation, one must note the disadvantages. First, the rapid expansion of the rail system resulted in a failure to devote sufficient time and resources to maintenance and safety. At times, the results could be disastrous. Thus, in 1853, over 100 major rail accidents resulted in 234 deaths and 496 serious injuries. Moreover, because the individual rails were rarely linked and often used different gauges of rail, transportation along the rail system would require changing cars and lines and moving goods between terminals by other means of transportation. These problems would be addressed after the Civil War with the consolidation of the railroads through merger and acquisition.[43]

The federal government played a truly decisive role in promoting the expansion of the railroads. Because of the large and risky investment and the potentially great impact on economic development, state charters provided railroads with a host of special privileges. The charters granted the railroads special action franchises allowing them to exercise the right of eminent domain when laying track. In addition, some charters provided monopoly provisions, tax exemptions, and state land grants. Although Pennsylvania, Georgia, Michigan, Illinois, and Indiana experimented with direct state construction, this was the exception. However, states and municipalities provided a good deal of capital through the direct purchase of stock and loans secured through tax-secured bond issues. The federal government provided assistance as well. Possible routes were surveyed by army engineers and construction was promoted through preferential tariffs on the importation of iron in the 1830s and 1840s. Most important, however, were the extensive land grants. In the end, federal land grants to the railroads amounted to 6.93 percent of the continental United States, more than the combined area of Indiana, Illinois, Michigan, and Wisconsin. Federal and state land grants accounted for more than one-quarter of total railroad investment.[44]

The economic impact of the railroads was significant, even if the direct benefits are less than often assumed.[45] As with other transportation innovations, the railroads reduced the overall costs of transportation, thus contributing to lower production costs. Moreover, one must acknowledge the backward linkages: The demand for rails and coal resulted in the expansion of the mining industry, even if a majority of rail iron was imported as late as 1860. However, the most important factor was the tremendous impact of the railroads on the overall organization of the American economy. By opening mass markets for grain, they stimulated the creation of sophisticated systems of distribution and centralized storage facilities. Moreover, because railroads demanded an incredible amount of investment (beginning at $10 million), they stimulated the rapid growth of stock and bond markets. Once these markets were in place, they provided corporations with greater access to capital, thus stimulating growth on an economywide scale. Finally, as will be discussed in greater detail below, the railroads forced a revolution in corporate organization as well. Due to the complexity of managing and maintaining a rail system and an unprecedented number of employees, the lines had to develop a complex organizational structure with multiple divisions and layers of accountability. To manage the high levels of investment in a variety of inputs, the railroads brought about innovations in cost accounting. The railroads were the first large-scale bureaucratic structures to emerge in the nation; the models they developed were rapidly diffused through the economy to provide the basis for modern corporate organization. Before we address this legacy of the railroads, we must consider another factor that contributed to growth in the nineteenth century: the availability of capital and capital markets.

## CAPITAL AND FINANCE

Natural resources provided a sound foundation for American economic growth during the nineteenth century, particularly when combined with ongoing innovations in transportation. These innovations and others throughout the economy were contingent on the existence of capital and capital markets. The potential for technical progress can be exploited if and only if there is an increase in the stock of machinery and equipment in which the technology is embodied and the infrastructure in which they operate. Financial intermediaries such as banks, insurance companies, and stock markets are important because they aggregate the savings of individuals and make it available to large commercial borrowers. The greater the supply of capital, the lower the costs of borrowing funds, and hence the greater the incentives to expand existing facilities and/or replace labor-intensive production processes with capital-intensive production processes. Finally, financial intermediaries can determine the allocation of capital among channels of commerce, thus shaping development over time.

The nineteenth century was a period of rapid change in financial institutions and capital markets. As noted in Chapter 2, the United States has a capital market-based system of industrial finance. That is, corporations sell securities in primary and secondary stock and bond markets to finance expansion. While this is certainly true in the twentieth century, stock and bond markets were relatively undeveloped until the final decades of the nineteenth century. Indeed, the financial system consisted of a highly decentralized system of commercial banks and non-bank intermediaries operating under very limited government supervision. For most of the period in question, there was no national bank capable of influencing financial decisions or policies.

The Bank of the United States was created in 1791, chartered for 20 years to serve as the fiscal agent of the United States. A quasi-public institution, the bank served some central banking functions. The bank was embroiled in political disputes throughout its brief and troubled history. While 20 percent of the bank's stock was held by the U.S. Treasury, the remainder was in the hands of private investors, including some foreign investors. Jefferson, Madison, and many of the old anti-Federalists objected to the bank because it was created without an explicit constitutional mandate (see the earlier discussion of *McCulloch* vs. *Maryland*) and the fact that some of the bank stock was held by foreigners. In 1811, anti-Federalist opposition was sufficient to prevent the rechartering of the bank. Such an institution was seen as a monument to big government and the concentration of economic power. Following the cancellation of the bank charter, the number of state-chartered banks and the circulation of bank notes increased significantly.

Following the War of 1812 and a financial panic in 1814, the Second Bank of the United States was chartered in 1816. This bank performed well, particularly after 1823 when placed under the direction of Nicholas Biddle. It served as the fiscal agent of the U.S. government and, at the same time, it served a regulatory function by limiting the issuance of state bank notes and thus the expansion of the money supply. Although the second bank did not have authorization to regulate the financial system in this fashion, it assumed the power by remaining a net creditor and holding a deposit of state bank notes. In response to evidence that the banks were expanding at too fast a rate, the second bank would demand that some of the notes in its portfolio be redeemed for specie, thus contracting the money supply in what was essentially an early form of the open market activities that the Federal Reserve would rely on more than a century later.[46]

With the 1828 election of Andrew Jackson as president, the second bank was on unsure footing, despite the quality of its performance. President Jackson was an advocate of hard money and a proponent of the view that banks were closely linked to urban-industrial interests and against the farmers and small businesses in the agrarian regions he claimed to personify. Following a run on the banks in 1814, many hard money advocates like Jackson were hesitant to support an institution that promoted the broad reliance on bank notes. Moreover, Jackson shared the concerns about monopoly and the wealthy and foreign investors who capitalized the Bank, as well as the fear that the bank constituted a concentration of federal powers that was both unconstitutional and a threat to state powers. In short, Jackson was motivated by many of the same forces that marked the demise of the first bank of the United States. Thus, Jackson took his first opportunity, an address before Congress in 1829, to question the constitutionality and performance of the bank and announced his plan to veto the recharter of the bank unless its powers were significantly reduced. Over the course of the next few years, Jackson began to consider other means of constituting the government's fiscal agent—for example, placing a bank with lesser powers into the Treasury Department. He received his chance to address the second bank in 1832, after Biddle and others forced an early recharter on the theory that Jackson's decision to veto the charter would cost him dearly in his reelection bid. The anti-Jackson forces believed, incorrectly, that the population supported the bank with such vigor that they would vote for Henry Clay in reaction to a veto.[47]

The veto of the bank charter came early, leaving some time for proponents of a new charter to pass more acceptable legislation or hope for enough Whigs in midterm elections to override Jackson's veto. Neither hope bore fruit. Biddle, for his part, began exerting the power of the bank in hopes of forcing a recharter. By the summer of 1833, Biddle was attempting to contract the money supply by redeeming bank notes and hoarding specie. He hoped that this could provide evidence of the fragility of the economy and the consequent need for a central bank. However, this strategy only hardened Jackson's resolve and revealed what many had suspected: The bank had too much power and could be used in a capricious manner to further the agenda of a single man. In September 1833, Jackson decided that the federal government would exhaust its deposits in the second bank and deposit new funds in 29 state banks. In essence, the second bank would cease to be the fiscal agent of the state until the charter lapsed.

Although the decision to have the Treasury deposit its funds in the so-called pet banks effectively eliminated the second bank, it simultaneously created a new problem in its impact on the money supply. In 1835 and 1836 in particular, depositing the large Treasury surpluses provided a basis for concerns over credit expansion as banks sought to lend out a multiple of reserves. Land speculation provided a major channel for the expanded credit base. It was feared that this speculation was destabilizing. Moreover, it was feared that the balance of payments deficit with Britain would force an outflow of specie. The long-term solution addressed both problems. The Specie Circular, issued July 16, 1836, essentially required that land sales occur in specie, gold or silver, rather than state bank notes. As a result, western banks called on eastern banks to meet the demand for specie which, in the end, flowed westward rather than across the Atlantic. The Species Circular ended the credit expansion. However, it precipitated a panic, forcing banks to suspend specie payments. This panic ended the speculative land purchases and investments. It also marked the beginning of heightened economic instability from 1837 to 1843.[48]

The period separating the 1837 Specie Circular and the beginning of the Civil War is commonly referred to as the Era of Free Banking. A wave of state bank failures during the depression of 1837 forced a resurgence of the popular dislike of bankers—a sentiment never far below the surface in the United States. As with the Second Bank of the United States, popular concerns focused on the power of the banks which, under the protection of special charters, functioned as monopolies. In response, states passed free banking statutes that allowed a group to form a bank without a special charter, assuming that they met capitalization or other requirements which varied widely on a state-by-state basis.

State charters provided by state legislatures commonly restricted the types of loans that the banks could make as well as the maximum interest rates and the geographical market. State-chartered banks were created when private investors provided specie that would serve as the bank's capital, receiving stock in the bank in return. Subsequently, the banks would solicit deposits and issue bank notes at three to five times the reserve level. From one-third to one-half of the bank loans were made to members of the bank's board of directors and used to finance commercial ventures. In essence, these banks provided a vital means of channeling consumer savings into capital formation.

While the steady growth in bank notes (approximately 5 percent growth per year) suggested growing confidence in the banking system, there were persistent problems. First, banks regularly lent money well beyond what could be supported by their reserves. Absent a lender of last resort and regulatory agencies capable of controlling bank reserve ratios and the quality of the loans, panics and failures were relatively common. Second, the availability of credit was, at best, spotty. In larger cities, bank competition would allow for credit at far lower rates than in the countryside where monopolies and high interest rates were the rule. Moreover, because the rural banks were distant and information traveled slowly, notes were commonly discounted to compensate for the risk of potential failure. The lack of financial intermediaries on the frontier was partially addressed with the creation of wildcat banks which commenced operations with low levels of reserves and hence high levels of risk. While these banks failed at a high rate, they were necessary.

In antebellum America, capital was not restricted to the commercial banks but was also made available by savings banks and insurance companies. The first savings bank was incorporated in Philadelphia in 1816 to promote savings among the poor and thus limit the need for community relief. The savings banks combined small deposits and invested them in the safest of all investments: state and local bonds and real estate mortgages. Savings banks proliferated in the Northeast during the antebellum period, particularly in New York and Massachusetts. The total deposits of the nation's 278 savings banks reached $150 million by 1860. Insurance companies were also important as financial intermediaries. Fire and marine insurance companies claimed almost $3 billion by the eve of the Civil War, with another $160 million in life insurance companies. As with commercial banks, the funds aggregated in savings banks and insurance companies were available for investment in commercial ventures.[49]

The Civil War brought significant changes in the financial system. On the eve of the war, the nation had a highly decentralized financial system of some 1,562 state banks. There was no uniform currency. Rather, a complicated collection of some 10,000 different kinds of paper money—the vast majority bank notes—provided the basis for transactions. Determining the present value of the notes complicated transactions and forced those holding bank notes to accept a lower exchange rate or value in return for the risk incurred by a merchant whose knowledge of the bank issuing the note might be fragmentary and dated.[50] To complicate matters more, there was no lender of last resort and thus no way to prevent panics from occurring. This latter problem would not be addressed until the creation of the Federal Reserve in 1914. However, the complicated system of bank notes was addressed, in large part, through the Civil War banking legislation.

To meet the fiscal needs of the Union's war effort, Congress passed the National Banking Act in 1864. The act created national bank charters and allowed national banks to use government bonds as reserves to back the issuance of bank notes. Indeed, the national banks were chartered as a means of placing the federal debt. The nationally chartered banks could purchase union debt and use it to back the issuance of national bank notes. The National Banking Act established minimum capitalization (based on the population of the host city) and reserve requirements for national banks while limiting branching and regulating the composition of bank portfolios. National banks would be subject to the oversight of the Comptroller of the Currency in the Treasury Department. Given the laxity of regulations at the state level, there should be little surprise that few banks initially opted to sacrifice their state charters for national charters. The importance of a national charter was magnified in 1865, when revisions in the internal revenue schedule placed a

10 percent tax on state bank notes. The tax forced many state banks to adopt national charters. However, state banks adapted to the challenge by developing demand deposits (i.e., checking) to substitute for bank notes while, in some cases, reducing requirements on member banks. As a result, state-chartered banks were common in marginal markets where assets were relatively scarce. By 1900, there were 4,369 state banks with assets of $1. 756 billion, compared with 3,731 national banks with assets of $4.944 billion.[51]

While many corporations relied on banks for access to funds, the nineteenth century witnessed the emergence of the stock markets as a primary source of railroad and industrial finance. Stock exchanges provided another important source of capital in the nineteenth century. Early in the century, markets were poorly developed and the funds for commercial investment would come through individual savings or reinvested profits. While exchanges emerged in the 1790s in Philadelphia and New York, they were small and largely concerned with trading federal bonds and shares in banks or insurance companies. Things had changed significantly by the 1860s, when over $2 billion worth of corporate securities were in circulation. Shares in banks, canals, and railroads constituted an important part of this pool of securities. Although exchanges were operating in several cities, concerns seeking to sell stock issues gravitated to New York, which quickly became the nation's financial center. Investment banks and brokerage agencies had developed in New York to place larger issues with savings banks, insurance companies, and wealthy investors and tap into sources of European capital. Telegraph linkages increasingly gave capitalists throughout the country access to New York financial markets. While the secondary markets expanded rapidly, the primary markets remained relatively underdeveloped. As late as the 1860s, many of the largest corporations and railroads created their own underwriting syndicates and marketed their own security issues.[52]

The railroads played a critical role in the development of capital markets in the United States due to the unprecedented financial demands. In the 1850s, few manufacturing companies demanded as much as $1 million to finance, compared with the railroads, many of which were capitalized at $10 to $20 million. Some of the capital for the railroads was raised through bond sales to those living along the proposed routes who expected to benefit from construction. However, the financial demands of railroad construction were so great that they required access to organized capital markets. Thus, in the 1850s, railroad securities from all parts of the country began to be listed and traded in the New York Stock Exchange. Large commercial banks and investment bankers also worked to place railroad bonds with wealthy investors in the United States and Europe. Since the investment bankers played such an important role as middlemen in placing railroad issues, they gained increasing prominence in engineering railroad consolidations and guarding against the overextension of existing lines. J. Pierpont Morgan, the most influential of the investment bankers, applied his experience in engineering railroad consolidations to the manufacturing economy when he helped organize some of the giant firms (e.g., General Electric, International Harvester, United States Steel) that became synonymous with the industrial and organizational revolution in the American economy.[53]

# ECONOMIC ORGANIZATION AND THE MODERN CORPORATION

By the end of the nineteenth century, the United States had a dual system of banking, a network of smaller intermediaries, and a growing stock market. There can be little question that the availability of capital promoted growth and innovation during the nineteenth century. However, one must note the importance of organizational factors as well. The period following the Civil War witnessed something of a revolution in corporate organization and the emergence of the modern form of corporate organization. The new complex managerial structures provided an important means of administering growth in what was quickly becoming a national economy.

One should not be surprised that the modern form of corporate organization evolved out of administrative innovations in the railroads. At the middle of the nineteenth century, most corporations functioned at a relatively small scale and were involved in a single chief function (e.g., manufacturing a particular product). As a result of the scale and form of production, most functions could be directed by a single president or general superintendent. While the smaller railroads (e.g., those with lines of 50 to 100 miles) followed this example, the great trunk lines (e.g., the Erie, the Pennsylvania, the Baltimore and Ohio) were forced to adopt a different form of management due to the scale of activity. Thus, operating divisions were established for lengths of road and managed by division superintendents whose activities were overseen and coordinated by general superintendents. An exhaustive flow of information and reports from the divisions proved critical in managing traffic, maintenance, and investment. While the general superintendents were involved in operating decisions, the presidents and boards of directors were able to focus on strategic issues such as expanding lines, raising capital, and managing competition between the railroads. By the 1880s, this organizational model had been refined further, to create a line-and-staff organization wherein the lines of communication and authority linking the general manager, the general superintendent, and the division superintendents were clearly defined. The division superintendents exercised authority over day-to-day operations and personnel issues.[54]

The sophisticated managerial innovations in the railroads facilitated administration and an expansion of individual lines. Moreover, it allowed for greater cooperation among the railroads and thus the movement toward an integrated national rail network. Middle managers within the railroads worked through railroad associations to develop uniform operating procedures, standardize equipment, and limit competition and overexpansion of the rail system. While the agreements to adopt standardized equipment and procedures were relatively successful, railroad managers honored pricing agreements only so long as they retained a necessary level of demand. When traffic declined, they commonly responded by reducing rates (and thus violating agreements) or providing rebates that were less visible to their competitors. Pooling worked imperfectly prior to the passage of the Interstate Commerce Act in 1887. Once it was explicitly prohibited and maximum rates were determined administratively by the Interstate Commerce Commission, control over rate making was compromised significantly.[55]

The basic tasks addressed by the railroad were relatively simple when compared with the larger integrated industrial enterprises that emerged in the final decades of the nineteenth century. The railroads provided a basic service—transportation—and operated geographically linked segments over a single line of road. The new industrial enterprises, in contrast, engaged in several distinct lines of business, combined production with the extraction of inputs or marketing, and operated in geographically dispersed markets. As a result, multiple departments competed for resources and had to be coordinated. The diversity of corporate activities required a diversity of managerial and technical skills. Thus, as the organizational innovations developed in the larger railroads were disseminated to manufacturing corporations, they were simultaneously refined and extended to meet the challenges specific to the form of production in question. While some corporations were successful in integrating their activities and creating an effective form of administration, others failed to make an effective transition and thus failed to employ their resources effectively.[56]

The new models of corporate organization were rapidly disseminated during the period because their introduction coincided roughly with the great merger wave that began after the depression of 1883 and ended in 1904. During the merger wave, thousands of corporations simply disappeared as they were engulfed by larger firms or became the basic building blocks of new industrial giants. The most famous of the firms created during the period was U.S. Steel, which was formed in 1901 out of a consolidation of 785 plants to create the first American corporation capitalized at over $1 billion. Its control of 65 percent of the nation's steel-ingot pouring capacity was not striking but not unprecedented. Indeed, because the merger wave of the period was largely horizontal in nature, the result was the creation of monopolies in some 71 industries. The greatest changes in market structure came in critical industries including copper, lead, explosives, tin cans, railroad cars, electrical equipment, rubber, paper, chemicals, farm machinery, business machinery, tobacco products, bricks, leather, photographic supplies, and shoe machinery.[57] Consolidation increased the complexity of production, given the new scale of activity and the extreme geographical dispersion of facilities. The new managerial models proved critical to coordinating the activities of the new industrial giants.

One cannot address the rise of the new corporate economy without returning, briefly, to the tariff. As noted above, American tariff policy in the antebellum period was oriented to the interests of the North and West while operating to the disadvantage of the slave South. Although tariff rates began to fall after the 1846 Walker Tariff Act, rates drifted upward during and following the Civil War. Prior to the war, tariff rates had fallen to an average of 26 percent on dutiable imports, and 24 percent on all imports. The wartime tariff increases brought the average rates up to 34 percent and 28 percent, respectively. A series of tariff acts passed in the subsequent decades won the support of northern Republicans and raised rates sharply. Thus, the Dingley Tariff Act of 1897, supported by President McKinley and the Republican party machine, raised the average rate on dutiable goods to 52 percent, while raising the rate on free and dutiable goods to an average of 30 percent.[58]

The tariff was one of the core issues separating the Democratic and Republican parties during the late nineteenth century. Advocates of high tariffs attributed the rapid growth of industrial and agricultural production to protection whereas the opponents argued that the mercantilist policies of the Republicans placed limits on growth and effectively closed some foreign markets to U.S. food and fiber exports. Despite the heated rhetoric and central role of the tariff in defining the political divisions of the period, the evidence over the impact of the tariff is, at best, contradictory and ambiguous.[59] In part, the problem may be tied to the fact that the effects of the tariff were themselves contradictory. Thus, Samuel P. Hays notes: "Although the tariff stimulated some lines of production, it retarded others. Congress found it especially difficult to protect both manufactured items and raw materials; industries which demanded protection for their finished products insisted equally on free entry for their supplies."[60] However, the potential impact of the tariff must be kept in perspective. As Morton Keller explains: "It is doubtful whether the ups and downs of tariff policy had major consequences for the economy. Both exports and imports remained well under 7 percent of the gross national product; comparable figures for Great Britain ranged from 20 to 40 percent."[61]

Whether or not the tariff was a significant factor in industrial development, two points are clear. First, contemporaries operated on the assumption that support for, or opposition to, the tariff reflected one's vision of appropriate state-economy relations. The tariff was understood as a means of using public policy to subsidize the rapid development of northern industry, complete with large-scale corporate entities, urbanization, and immigrant laborers. Opposition to the tariff was simultaneously support for a more decentralized market system with a very limited role for the state. Second, the tariff was an important tool of coalition building. As Tom E. Terrill notes:

> the political uses of the tariff were infinite. Both major parties employed the tariff issue to unify an increasingly discordant society and to construct broader political coalitions to break the political equipoise. . . . By emphasizing the tariff issue, both parties tried to avoid more divisive or less attractive issues such as currency, civil service reform, and temperance. This emphasis also gave the parties some basis for distinguishing themselves . . . Tariff positions became the litmus paper test for political affiliation, while intraparty divisions over the tariff were forgotten for the sake of party unity.[62]

Of course, the political utility of the tariff was not limited to its symbolic importance. The tariff provided a major source of government revenues: Between 1886 and 1890, over 57 percent of federal revenues were raised through custom duties. These funds were used, increasingly, to fund a Civil War pension system for Northern veterans which created popular support for the tariff among populations which could not benefit directly from economic growth. By 1893, the military pensions cost the federal government $159 million per year. As Richard Bensel explains, the tariff and pension systems should be seen as central to a regional coalition that linked the North and the West at the expense of the South: "Elites, labor, and pensioners, were located in the North and, thus, this section retrieved the 'taxes' it paid through imposition of the tariff. The tax imposed by the higher costs of manufactured goods was recaptured by regionally repatriated profits and customs duties were recaptured by the payment of military pensions. The development engine left the southern periphery to shoulder almost the entire cost of industrialization; Confederate veterans were not eligible for federal pensions and no indigenous product (save sugar) was protected by the tariff."[63]

The pension system expanded in the decades following the war, absorbing and justifying the continued increases in the tariff. Over time, the Civil War pensions "were changed into de facto old-age and disability pensions that provided coverage for some one million elderly Americans, reaching about one half of all elderly, native-born men in the North around the turn of the century."[64] As Progressive tariff reformers turned to address the "mother of trusts" and the population of eligible recipients declined, the tariff-pension system fell from prominence. A comparable system of social pensions would not come into existence until the New Deal. However, while in existence, the connection allowed for the existence of a coalition between western interests and the northeastern commercial core promoting ongoing industrial development under the protection of the tariff.

The nineteenth century is often presented as an age of laissez faire, when the spheres of the state and market were clearly demarcated. As this chapter suggests, public policy played a very important role in promoting the rapid growth of the century. Of course, the Constitution, early statutes, and a series of important court decisions created an environment that facilitated, in James Willard Hurst's words, "the release of energy."[65] However, the role of the state and public policy did not end with these foundations. Enormous financial support for new transportation technologies, tariffs designed to promote development, and financial regulations were some of the most explicit areas in which public policy promoted economic development in the nineteenth century. Public policy provided an important basis for economic growth and facilitated the emergence of a new corporate economy. However, the modern corporation, the growing reliance on mass production technologies, and the new scale of economic activity created demands for new policies—policies to restrain the unleashed giant. The questions of whether and how new public policies and institutions could reconcile further economic development and particular political values would be answered during the Progressive Era. We turn now to a discussion of this period.

## NOTES

1. Thomas Weiss, "U.S. Labor Force Estimates and Economic Growth, 1800–1860." In *American Economic Growth and Standards of Living Before the Civil War*, ed. Robert E. Gallman and John Joseph Wallis (Chicago: University of Chicago Press, 1992), pp. 22–31; Stanely Lebergott, *The Americans: An Economic Record* (New York: W. W. Norton, 1984), p. 61.

2. Gary M. Walton and James F. Shepherd, *The Economic Rise of Early America* (Cambridge: Cambridge University Press, 1979), p. 5.

3. Milton Friedman, *Capitalism and Freedom* (Chicago: University of Chicago Press, 1962), p. 13.

4. Ibid., p. 27.

5. Karl Polyani, *The Great Transformation* (New York: Rinehart & Co., 1944), p. 139.

6. Ibid., pp. 140–41.

7. See Charles A. Beard, *An Economic Interpretation of the Constitution* (New York: Macmillan, 1913).

8. Forest McDonald, "The Constitution and Hamiltonian Capitalism." In *How Capitalistic Is the Constitution?*, ed. Robert A. Goldwin and William A. Schambra (Washington, D.C.: American Enterprise Institute, 1982), p. 57.

9. James Willard Hurst, *Law and the Conditions of Freedom in the Nineteenth-Century United States* (Madison: University of Wisconsin Press, 1956), p. 6.

10. Jonathan R. T. Hughes, *The Governmental Habit Redux: Economic Controls from Colonial Times to the Present* (Princeton, N.J.: Princeton University Press, 1991), pp. 56–57.

11. See Frank Bourgin, *The Great Challenge: The Myth of Laissez-Faire in the Early Republic* (New York: Harper & Row, 1989); Merle Fainsod, Lincoln Gordon, and Joseph C. Palamountain, Jr., *Government and the American Economy*, 3rd ed. (New York: W. W. Norton, 1959), pp. 97–99; 105–07.

12. William J. Shultz and M. R. Caine, *Financial Development of the United States* (New York: Prentice Hall, 1937), pp. 96–103.

13. Gordon S. Wood, *The Radicalism of the American Revolution* (New York: Random House, 1991), p. 325.

14. James W. Ely, Jr., *The Guardian of Every Other Right: A Constitutional History of Property Rights* (New York: Oxford University Press, 1992), pp. 63–65.

15. Ibid., pp. 68–70.

16. Hurst, *Law and the Conditions of Freedom in the Nineteenth-Century United States*, p. 28.

17. Ely, *The Guardian of Every Other Right*, pp. 66–67; Hurst, *Law and the Conditions of Freedom in the Nineteenth-Century United States*, pp. 26–27.

18. *Commonwealth* v. *Hunt* 4 Met. (45 Mass.) 111 (1842) in *American Legal History: Cases and Materials*, ed. Kermit L. Hall, William M. Wiecek, and Paul Finkelman. (New York: Oxford University Press, 1991) p. 153.

19. Kermit L. Hall, William M. Wiecek, and Paul Finkelman, *American Legal History: Cases and Materials* (New York: Oxford University Press, 1991), pp. 153, 156.

20. See Immanuel Wallerstein, *The Modern World System: Capitalist Agriculture and the Origins of the European World-Economy in the Sixteenth Century* (New York: Academic Press, 1976).

21. Richard Franklin Bensel, *Sectionalism and American Political Development, 1880–1980* (Madison: University of Wisconsin Press, 1984), p. 35.

22. Douglass C. North, *The Economic Growth of the United States, 1790–1860* (New York: W. W. Norton, 1966), pp. 159–76.

23. Ibid., pp. 135–55.

24. See Sidney Ratner, *The Tariff in American History* (New York: Van Nostrand, 1972), pp. 15–18; Richard Franklin Bensel, *Yankee Leviathan: The Origins of Central State Authority in America, 1859–1877* (Cambridge: Cambridge University Press, 1990), pp. 66–68; Edward Pessen, *Jacksonian America: Society, Personality, and Politics* (Homewood, Ill.: Dorsey Press, 1978), p. 136.

25. North, *The Economic Growth of the United States*, pp. 122–34; Harry N. Scheiber, Harold G. Vatter, and Harold Underwood Faulkner, *American Economic History* (New York: Harper & Row, 1976), p. 176.

26. Scheiber, Vatter, and Faulkner, *American Economic History*, pp. 178–79.

27. Bensel, *Yankee Leviathan*, p. 34.

28. Ibid., pp. 233–34.

29. Jonathan R. T. Hughes, *American Economic History*, 3rd ed. (Glenview, Ill.: Scott, Foresman, 1990), pp. 247–49.

30. Ibid., p. 255.

31. Lebergott, *The Americans*, p. 79.

32. See Angus Maddison, *Phases of Capitalist Development* (Oxford: Oxford University Press, 1982), pp. 16–17.

33. See Lebergott, *The Americans*, pp. 91–94.

34. George Rogers Taylor, *The Transportation Revolution, 1815–1860* (New York: Holt, Rinehart and Winston, 1951), pp. 104–12.

35. Ibid., pp. 116–19.

36. Hughes, *American Economic History*, pp. 169–70.

37. Calculated from statistics provided in *Statistical History of the United States*, Series Q-154, 155.

38. Taylor, *The Transportation Revolution*, pp. 22–28; Hughes, *American Economic History*, p. 163; Scheiber, Vatter, and Faulkner, *American Economic History*, p. 147.

39. Russell Bourne, *Floating West: The Erie and Other American Canals* (New York: W. W. Norton, 1992), p. 186; Scheiber, Vatter, and Faulkner, *American Economic History*, p. 150.

40. Taylor, *The Transportation Revolution*, pp. 52–55, 442.

41. *Statistical History of the United States*, Series Q-15, 34.

42. Albert Fishlow, *American Railroads and the Transformation of the Ante-Bellum Economy* (Cambridge, Mass.: Harvard University Press, 1965), p. 52. See, for example, Robert William Fogel, *Railroads and American Economic Growth* (Baltimore, Md.: Johns Hopkins University Press, 1964).

43. John F. Stover, *American Railroads* (Chicago: University of Chicago Press, 1961), pp. 34–35, 50.

44. Ibid., pp. 30–31; Lloyd J. Mercer, *Railroads and Land Grant Policy: A Study in Government Intervention* (New York: Academic Press, 1982), p. 7; Morton Keller, *Affairs of State: Public Life in Nineteenth Century America* (Cambridge, Mass.: Harvard University Press, 1977), pp. 165–67.

45. See Albert Fishlow, "Internal Transportation." In *American Economic Growth: An Economist's History of the United States*, ed. Lance E. Davis (New York: Harper & Row, 1972).

46. See Paul Studenski and Herman E. Krooss, *Financial History of the United States* (New York: McGraw-Hill, 1952), pp. 97–110; Pessen, *Jacksonian America*, pp. 141–44.

47. Studenski and Krooss, *Financial History of the United States*, pp. 104–106.

48. Reginald C. McGrane, *The Panic of 1827: Some Financial Problems of the Jackson Era* (Chicago: University of Chicago Press, 1924); Studenski and Krooss, *Financial History of the United States*, pp. 109–11.

49. Shultz and Caine, *Financial Development of the United States*, pp. 239–40; Taylor, *The Transportation Revolution*, pp. 231–23.

50. Hughes, *American Economic History*, p. 204.

51. Bensel, *Yankee Leviathan*, p. 172; Eugene Nelson White, *The Regulation and Reform of the American Banking System, 1900–1929* (Princeton, N.J.: Princeton University Press, 1983), pp. 10–62.

52. Shultz and Caine, *Financial Development of the United States*, pp. 132, 239, 361.

53. Alfred D. Chandler, Jr., *The Railroads: The Nation's First Big Business* (New York: Harcourt, Brace & World, 1965), pp. 43–45.

54. Alfred D. Chandler, Jr., *Strategy and Structure: Chapters in the History of the Industrial Enterprise* (Cambridge, Mass.: M.I.T. Press, 1962), pp. 21–23, 38.

55. Alfred D. Chandler, Jr., *The Visible Hand: The Managerial Revolution in American Business* (Cambridge, Mass.: Harvard University Press, 1977), pp. 143–44.

56. Chandler, *Strategy and Structure*, pp. 39–40

57. F. M. Scherer and David Ross, *Industrial Market Structure and Economic Performance*, 3rd. ed. (Boston: Houghton Mifflin, 1990), pp. 153–55.

58. Ratner, *The Tariff in American History*, pp. 39–41; Thomas K. McCraw, "Mercantilism and the Market: Antecedents of American Industrial Policy." In *The Politics of Industrial Policy*, ed. Claude E. Barfield and William A. Schambra (Washington: American Enterprise Institute, 1986), p. 38.

59. McCraw, "Mercantilism and the Market."

60. Samuel P. Hays, *The Response to Industrialism: 1885–1914* (Chicago: University of Chicago Press, 1957), p. 19.

61. Keller, *Affairs of State*, pp. 376–77.

62. Tom E. Terrill, *The Tariff, Politics, and American Foreign Policy, 1874–1901* (Westport, Conn. : Greenwood Press, 1973), p. 32.

63. Bensel, *Sectionalism and American Political Development*, p. 70.

64. Ann Shola Orloff, "The Political Origins of America's Belated Welfare State." In *The Politics of Social Policy in the United States*, ed. Margaret Weir, Ann Shola Orloff, and Theda Skocpol (Princeton, N.J.: Princeton University Press, 1988), p. 38.

65. Hurst, *Law and the Conditions of Freedom in the Nineteenth-Century United States*, Chapter 1.

# 4

# PROGRESSIVISM AND THE POLITICAL ECONOMY

The late nineteenth century was torn by tensions between a decentralized market system and a burgeoning corporate-based economy. The two were characterized by different levels of investment, different patterns of ownership and labor relations, and different implications for the role of the state in the economy. The conflict between these two systems reflected the rapid transformation of the American political economy. Virtually no segment of American society was free from this transformation and the calls for remedial public policies. Rapid economic consolidation, the growing size of corporations, waves of immigration, conflictive industrial relations, urban poverty, and political corruption stimulated the demands for reform and institutional change. Progressives reformers approached the problems of their day with a strong sense of mission and a faith in the role of scientific and social scientific knowledge in solving the problems of the period. In this chapter, we examine the factors that contributed to the period's rapid transformation, the key features of Progressivism, the debates over the political economy, and a number of key economic policies initiated or extended during the period.

## THE EMERGENCE OF THE NEW CORPORATE ECONOMY

As shown in Chapter 3, in the decades following the Civil War the United States entered a period of rapid economic growth which coincided with significant changes in the organization of production, thus facilitating the emergence of a new corporate economy. The period's growth was substantial. In current dollars, Gross

National Product increased from an annual average of $6.71 billion (1869 to 1873) to $17.3 billion (1897 to 1901). On a per capita basis, current dollar income increased from $165 to $231 during the period.[1] Growth was accompanied by wild fluctuations in the business cycle, including recessions in 1887 to 1888, and 1899 to 1900, and a deep depression in 1893 to 1896. The higher incomes translated into higher levels of savings and thus a larger pool of capital available for commercial investments. As a result, the growth of the capital stock surpassed the growth of the population: In three decades the capital stock per worker increased by 80 percent. The resulting efficiency gains allowed for a rapid increase in manufacturing output relative to other segments of the economy, despite the fact that the manufacturing labor force remained quite stable.[2] The record of growth continued across the Progressive Era. In current prices, Gross National Product increased from an annual average of $17.3 billion (1897 to 1901) to $88.9 billion in 1920. However, these increases were partially eroded by the inflation rate which accelerated as the U.S. economy felt the effects of the World War I. Nonetheless, when adjusted for inflation and expressed in 1929 dollars, per capita income increased from $496 (average in 1897 to 1901) to $688 in 1920, an increase of more than 38 percent in two decades.[3]

Changes in the organization of production and the structure of industry drove much of the period's growth. The dissemination of mass production technologies resulted in higher levels of production and the potential for larger markets than might otherwise have been possible. Corporations increasingly employed hierarchical multidivisional organization to manage production and distribution. Improvements in communications and transportation provided access to new and larger markets. Corporate consolidation brought new economies of scale. With the growing productive and distributive capacities of American corporations, problems of overproduction and consequent bouts of destructive price competition were inevitable. In hopes of coordinating expansion and pricing to promote stability, some corporations relied on the trust. Although the term trust was popularly employed to describe and condemn any large firm, a trust was a specific form of intercorporate arrangement whereby separate companies gave their stock to a board of trustees in exchange for trust certificates. The trustees could then manage the various concerns as a single enterprise.[4] The 1880s brought the formation of the Standard Oil Trust, the American Cotton Oil Trust, the National Linseed Oil Trust, and the Distillers and Cattle Feeders Trust. Consolidations of formerly independent corporations provided an alternative to the trust. Between 1897 and 1904, an unprecedented merger wave combined 4,227 businesses to create 257 corporations, including United States Steel and International Harvester. As a result of this merger wave, 1 percent of the companies claimed control over some 45 percent of manufactured goods.[5]

While the largest corporations engaged in more capital-intensive production frequently sought to manage competition through trusts, consolidations, and price-fixing agreements, peripheral firms were forced to adopt different strategies. Increasingly, small producers, distributors, and retailers formed trade associations to exchange information and devise joint strategies to manage competition. Associations also provided a defense against the aggression of larger corporations and became active proponents of much state and national regulatory legislation designed to limit the power of the industrial core.[6]

The economic changes of the period were combined with equally significant demographic changes. Reductions in the cost of ocean transportation and the growth of the American economy during the latter half of the nineteenth century attracted a growing number of immigrants. Between 1885 and 1900, over 6.35 million immigrants entered the United States. Between 1901 and 1914, immigration increased to bring an additional 12.93 million immigrants to the nation's shores. After 1914, the influx of immigrants fell to less than a third of the previous levels as war consumed Europe and isolationism again dominated U.S. immigration policy.[7] The high levels of immigration altered the composition of the population. For example, in areas like the Northeast, over one-quarter of the population was foreign-born by 1910—a figure that would decline to 22.9 percent by 1920 as a result of restrictions on immigration.[8] New immigrants often settled in urban areas despite the fact that many had worked on farms prior to coming to the United States. The pattern of urban settlement was in part determined by the existence of ethnic communities and the opportunities they presented for securing employment. Thus, successive waves of immigration accelerated the urbanization of American society. In 1900, 39.7 percent of the population lived in urban areas, a figure that would grow to 45.7 percent by 1910 and over 51.1 percent by 1920.[9] Immigration and urbanization were important symbols of changing circumstances that threatened the traditional composition and organization of American society.[10]

The interplay of immigration and urbanization exacerbated the problems of the period. The rapid urban growth exhausted the urban infrastructure and undermined the ability of municipal governments and private charitable groups to ameliorate urban poverty, particularly during downturns in the business cycle when the magnitude of the need simply outpaced the available resources. While voluntary efforts such as the Salvation Army, the urban settlement houses, and a host of charitable associations played an ever greater role in attenuating the devastation of poverty, the impact was quite limited. In addition, the influx of immigrants constituted a dramatic expansion of the largely unskilled industrial labor force. This created barriers to wage increases and undermined the incentive of many businesses to substitute capital for labor.[11] Finally, the influx of immigrants created a situation in which demands for new goods, services, and public works were combined with a rapidly growing but unorganized electorate. The power to assign construction contracts and employment fueled the urban political machines and provided an effective means of mobilizing the electorate. In the end, the persistence of urban poverty and governmental corruption gave rise to calls for municipal reforms and new policies.

## The Labor Problem

The labor problem of the Progressive Era was a source of concern for politicians and intellectuals. The key questions were: What role would labor occupy in the new corporate economy? Secondly, how should policymakers respond to the claims of labor rights and the expressions of labor militancy? Workers reacted to changes in the production process and the growing concentration of capital by forming new and stronger labor organizations. Initially, workers were represented by the short-lived National Labor Union, a number of industry-specific unions, and the Knights of Labor. The Knights had membership rolls of some 700,000 crafts and industrial workers by 1886, before falling into rapid decline following the Haymarket Square riot in Chicago and concerted employer resistance.[12] The gap left by the Knights' demise was almost completely filled by the newly formed American Federation of Labor which had been created to unite union locals in a national organization. Unlike the earlier Knights, the AFL represented a narrower constituency of skilled and semiskilled craft workers. The low-skilled industrial workers who would play a growing role in the mass production economy were, for the time being at least, without the services of a national organization. Samuel Gompers, head of the AFL, suspended his own socialism and promoted a pragmatic strategy of business unionism. This entailed eschewing class politics and emphasizing the improvement of wages and working conditions. Although this approach was firmly rejected by many radical labor leaders as overly conciliatory, the role of the AFL and overall levels of union membership increased dramatically under Gompers's direction (see Figure 4–1). The AFL's membership increased from 265,000 in 1897, to over 1.5 million in 1910, and over 4 million by 1920.[13]

Rising levels of unionization were combined with growing workplace militancy. Strikes occurred with growing frequency during the period in question. The 1,839 work stoppages in 1900 increased to between 3,353 and 4,450 per year for the period 1916 to 1920, when the demands of war created opportunities for labor advances.[14] Some of the industrial conflicts enraged a nation concerned with the grow-

**Figure 4–1**  Union Membership, 1900–1920

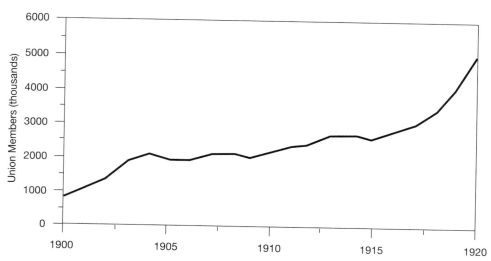

Source: *Statistical History of the United States*, Series D-735.

everyday life. They were successful in forcing new state railroad regulations and antitrust laws in 17 states. In 1888, they won a victory with the Interstate Commerce Act which authorized national rail regulation, In 1890, they won passage of the Sherman Act creating national antitrust prohibitions (see the discussion below). In the 1880s and 1890s, Populists formed parties at the state and local levels, demanded the nationalization of railroads and banks, and called for an inflation of the economy (and farm incomes) through the coinage of silver.[20]

In 1892, agrarian groups entered national partisan politics. The People's party backed James B. Weaver in the presidential campaign and presented a harsh critique of the existing order that demanded nothing short of systemwide reform. As the People's Platform of 1892 declared:

> The conditions which surround us best justify our co-operation; we meet in the midst of a nation brought to the verge of moral, political, and material ruin. Corruption dominates the ballot-box, the Legislatures, the Congress, and touches even the ermine of the bench. The people are demoralized; most of the States have been compelled to isolate the voters at the polling places to prevent universal intimidation and bribery. . . . The urban workmen are denied the right to organize for self-protection; imported pauperized labor beats down their wages, a hireling standing army, unrecognized by our laws, is established to shoot them down, and they are rapidly degenerating into European conditions. The fruits of the toils of millions are boldly stolen to build up colossal fortunes for a few, unprecedented in the history of mankind; and the possessors of these, in turn despise the Republic and endanger liberty. For the same prolific womb of governmental injustice we breed the two great classes—tramps and millionaires.[21]

In 1896, the Populists joined the Democrats to support William Jennings Bryan, a fusion candidate for President. The election, which may interpreted as a referendum on whether the nation should pursue an agrarian or industrial path of development, resulted in a realignment and established a Republican hegemony which would continue until the New Deal realignment. It stripped the Populists of what little influence they had gained in national partisan politics. Nonetheless, agrarian activists in the Midwest remained a key source of support for the Progressives.[22]

## THE PROGRESSIVE MOVEMENT AND REFORM

The reform movements that proliferated in the final decades of the nineteenth century set the stage for the political accomplishments of the Progressive Era. The problems of urban poverty, violent industrial relations, the growing concentration of industrial power, and political corruption demanded a response from those who rejected the Social Darwinist explanations for the era's crises and the attendant willingness to sacrifice the less fit as an inevitable price of progress. Muckraking journalists delivered news of social degeneration and economic conflicts in serial for a middle-class mass audience. Agrarian populists successfully mobilized in the South and West to demand reforms to limit the power of the trusts, railroads, and financiers who allegedly used their economic power to exploit farmers and workers and to establish a relationship of dependency where individual opportunities used to exist. The Social Gospel movement mobilized protestant clergy to present social reform as a necessary extension of the Christian faith and individual conversion as a certain pathway to self-improvement and economic betterment. The settlement house movement sought to create a new set of institutions and services to allow the poor working class populations to elevate themselves through community-based educational and cultural opportunities. The strong protestantism, the focus on the community's responsibility to the individual, and the belief that reform of individual and institutions could lead the way to human perfectibility were inherited by the Progressives. Their mission, as they understood it, had moral, political, and scientific dimensions.

While the various reform movements multiplied in the late nineteenth century, the concerted use of policy and institutional reforms to address the most striking problems of the times did not come until the turn of the century and the period commonly referred to as the Progressive Era. In part, this timing can be attributed to changes in the political context. During the last quarter of the century, the intense partisan competition created a formidable barrier to initiatives that might have stressed fragile party coalitions. The realignment of 1896 ended the tenuous balance of partisan forces and thus opened greater opportunities for reform.[23] However, the realignment was not the only factor that facilitated change. One must also consider the uniqueness of Progressivism as a reform movement. The Progressives synthesized their reform agenda with a firm belief that scientific and social scientific knowledge could provide the key to solving society's problems. Through reason and careful analysis, institutions could be designed scientifically to control or direct social and economic forces, thus reclaiming the individuals who had fallen victim to the new social environment.

During the Progressive Era, the nation's system of higher education expanded rapidly. Thus, between 1900 and 1920, the annual number of college degrees conferred increased from 29,375 to 53,516 while the number of faculty members in the same institutions increased from 23,868 to 48,615.[24] At the same time, the nation witnessed the dissemination of the German model of higher education, with its focus on the application of experimentation and scientific methodology to social questions. The expansion and reorientation of higher education were combined with efforts to organize the academic disciplines and define their missions, broadly construed. The American Historical Association, the American Economic Association, the American Political Science Association, and the American Sociological Society were founded between 1884 and 1903. The American Economic Association provides a good example of how a discipline, traditionally associated with laissez-faire doctrines and abstract reasoning, was recast in light of the reform sentiments of the era. The founders and leading members of the association were involved in the Social Gospel movement and viewed the connection between social scientific research and reform as providing a necessary foundation for true advances in social organization. Thus, when they composed the founding platform of the American Economic Association, they presented the state as "an educational and ethical agency whose positive aid is an indispensable condition of human progress." The platform proclaimed "the conflict of labor and capital has brought to the front a vast number of social problems whose solution is impossible without the united efforts of church, state, and science."[25]

While the Progressive movement was unified by the strong reform agenda and the faith in scientific knowledge as an aid to reform, there were internal tensions. One of the chief tensions was between the elitism that naturally emerged from the intellectual features of Progressivism and the populism that many inherited from earlier reform movements. The vision of scientific management was difficult to reconcile with the alternative vision of a raging conflict between the people and a corporate elite, or the protestant reformism that stressed self-improvement and individual conversion. The former sought to engage in some form of social engineering to bring greater efficiency to the economy and to manage scientifically the evolution of the new industrial order. Scientific knowledge of economics and organization, it was hoped, could allow one to preserve valued traditions by directing social and economic progress. The latter strand of Progressivism, in contrast, hoped only to restrain the power of large corporations and impede the emergence of a national economy in hopes of returning to the decentralized system of the past, albeit one with sufficient safeguards to protect individual liberties and opportunities. This tension between the elitist and populist strands of progressivism was never resolved and appeared, most clearly, in the debates over the reformation of the political economy.

## PROGRESSIVISM AND THE ECONOMY

The monumental changes in the economy during the half century following the Civil War forced many to alter their understanding of economics and the appropriate role of the state. Almost universally, the Progressives recognized that the decentralized market economy of the nineteenth century was being displaced by a new system of corporate-based planning in which complex business organizations used a host of complicated strategies to restrain competition and coordinate pricing and expansion. Some were convinced that the application of scientific knowledge and experiments in institutional design could provide a key to managing the changes of the period while providing greater social welfare. Others saw such efforts as contributing to the loss of individual liberty that so concerned many advocates of reform.

Large corporate hierarchies were constructed to integrate activities in geographically dispersed markets, internalize and systematize innovation, and manage expansion; corporations increasingly coordinated their activities in hopes of minimizing overexpansion and destructive competition.[26] The emergence of organized capitalism stimulated lively debates over political organization and the potential for corporate self-governance. For many members of the business community, the traditional liberal focus on the individual was supplemented with a growing role for voluntary organizations. Business associations grew dramatically during the Progressive Era and challenged prevailing notions of competition and industrial structure. Books like Arthur Jerome Eddy's *The New Competition* and Edward N. Hurley's *Awakening of Business* called for greater business cooperation to enhance efficiency and manage competition.[27] As Hurley explained: "Trade associations are the machinery of cooperation. Through them ignorant competition can be destroyed to a large extent merely by throwing light upon it, and the basis upon which business is conducted can be generally made more intelligent." He concluded that "Trade associations are . . . the means of salvation for American business. In a thousand ways they can help to lift American business to a higher plane of efficiency."[28]

The trust problem and labor question forced policymakers to reconsider the role of the state in the economy. The prevailing positions on the appropriate role of the state were articulated with surprising clarity in the 1912 presidential campaign. Incumbent Republican President William Taft presented a classical liberal argument for a limited state. A strong advocate of liberty of contract and individual property rights, Taft rejected administrative control over corporate affairs. He believed that while the Sherman Act could impede rational business agreements and intercorporate relations, this threat was limited in the wake of the Supreme Court's adoption of the rule of reason in 1911—a rule for judicial decision making whereby the courts would exercise discretion in determining whether certain restraints on trade were reasonable and thus not subject to prosecutions under the antitrust statute. Under the common law construction of antitrust, the courts could exhibit flexibility in determining whether restraints of trade were "reasonable" and thus free from Sherman Act prosecutions. For Taft, this was quite fortuitous. Following the adoption of the rule of reason, "the law could be enforced with renewed vigor without threatening the existence of large corporations or reasonable agreements among them; it could strike at practices that were unfair or against the public interest, and from time to time even dissolve or reorganize a specific corporate combination."[29]

Republican insurgent Theodore Roosevelt struck a position far to the left of Taft under the banner of the New Nationalism. Roosevelt shared the faith of Herbert Croly in the potential for policy and institutional change to bring about a new political economic order. As Croly explained in his influential book *The Promise of American Life*: "Democracy must stand or fall on a platform of possible human perfectibility. If human nature cannot be improved by institutions, democracy is at best a more than usually safe form of political organization . . . if it is to work better as well as merely longer, it must have some leavening effect on human nature; and the sincere democrat is obliged to assume the power of the leaven. For him the practical questions are: How can the improvement be brought about? and, How much may it amount to?"[30]

Roosevelt witnessed the rise of a large-scale corporate economy and believed this evolutionary process could, if managed intelligently, result in great gains for society. However, the correct response could not be an appeal to the antiquated policy of antitrust. "Combinations in industry are the result of an imperative economic law which cannot be repealed by political legislation. . . . The way out lies, not in attempting to prevent such combinations, but in completely controlling them in the interest of the public welfare."[31] For this purpose, Roosevelt called for the creation of a federal agency like the Bureau of Corporations that could apply its specialized expertise to separate the good trusts from the bad. It would "put a stop to abuses of big corporations and small corporations alike" by focusing "on conduct and not on size." However, "dissolution is neither control nor regulation, but is purely negative; and negative remedies are of little permanent avail."[32] Roosevelt's commission would form a partnership with corporations to supervise corporate transactions, capitalization, and competition. As the Progressive party platform proclaimed, this "system of constructive regulation" would allow legitimate businesses to "develop normally in response to the energy and enterprise of the American business man."[33]

Roosevelt's position on the trust question was part of a broader vision of the organization of the economy. Roosevelt noted: "Where capital is organized, as it must be organized under modern industrial conditions, the only way to secure proper freedom—proper treatment—for the individual laborer is to have labor organize also."[34] In a similar note, Roosevelt explained:

> A simple and poor society can exist as a democracy on a basis of sheer individualism. But a rich and complex industrial society cannot so exist; for some individuals, and especially those artificial individuals called corporations, become so very big that the ordinary individual . . . cannot deal with them on terms of equality. It therefore becomes necessary for these ordinary individuals to combine in their turn, first in order to act in their collective capacity through that biggest of all combinations called the government, and second, to act, also in their own self-defense, through private combinations, such as farmers' associations and trade unions.[35]

Once labor was organized, the state could claim "the right to regulate the terms and conditions of labor" through the activities of a commission or a cabinet-level Labor Department.[36] Explicitly adopting the AFL's position, he stated: "Our ideal should be a rate of wages sufficiently high to enable workmen to live in a manner conformable to American ideals and standards, to educate their children, and to provide for sickness and old age; the abolition of child labor; safety device legislation to prevent industrial accidents; and automatic compensation for losses caused by these industrial accidents."[37] Roosevelt also supported a number of additional progressive goals, including female suffrage, direct primaries, direct election of senators, the eight-hour work day, the prohibition of injunctions in labor disputes, and a system of social insurance.

Woodrow Wilson presented his New Freedom to occupy a position midway between Taft's juridical liberalism and Roosevelt's corporatism. Wilson differed sharply with Roosevelt over the role of the state in the evolving corporate order. He agreed with Roosevelt on the basic question of good versus bad trusts, proclaiming: "I am for big business, and I am against the trusts." "I admit that any large corporation built up by legitimate processes of business, by economy, by efficiency, is natural and I am not afraid of it, no matter how big it grows."[38] However, one could contrast the large efficient firms (i.e., "the good trusts" in Roosevelt's lexicon) with those that "pass the limit of efficiency and get into the region of clumsiness and unwieldiness."[39] These "giants staggering along under an almost intolerable weight of artificial burdens" eliminate competition by dividing markets with others and de-vote their resources to buying up or destroying potential competitors.[40]

For Wilson, the trust question did not demand a radical restructuring of public institutions: "Any decently equipped lawyer can suggest to you statutes by which the whole business can be stopped."[41] New legislation could prohibit, item by item, the practices that some corporations used to create monopoly power. This could be effective in ending the trend toward monopoly at an early stage. Accord-ing to Wilson, the New Nationalism would create such a concentration of political and economic power that people would have to rely on the benevolence of the cor-porations to receive what should be theirs as the just rewards of their labor. Wil-son warned: "How unassailable would be the majesty and the tyranny of monopoly if it could thus get sanction of law and the authority of government! By what means, except open revolt, could we ever break the crust of our life again and become free men, breathing an air of our own, living lives that we wrought out for ourselves?"[42] Wilson emphasized that his New Freedom could avoid the most troublesome con-sequences of Roosevelt's program.

At first glance, Roosevelt's New Nationalism appeared to call for a more statist solution to economic governance than did Wilson's regulatory state. How-ever, first appearances can be remarkably deceptive. Roosevelt's New Nationalism called for a form of planning completely dependent on corporate cooperation. Cor-porations would be compelled to cooperate in addressing common problems sub-ject to government supervision. While such a system could compensate for the underdevelopment of the American state, it did so by appending the administra-tive capacities and expertise of corporations and trade associations to those of the state. The new entity would be a mixture of public and private power. Its survival would depend on the incentives the state could offer participants (e.g., profitabil-ity, a reduction of competition) or the coercion it could bring to bear (e.g., antitrust prosecutions). Wilson's model, in contrast, would embody a more adversarial re-lationship between the state and corporations and would thus rely more on legal prohibitions backed by state coercion than the provision of benefits.

## CONSTRUCTING THE PROGRESSIVE POLITICAL ECONOMY

Economists commonly argue that public policies regulating the economy are justi-fied if and only if they constitute a response to market failure. Perfect markets are characterized by a number of features. First, information must be exhaustive and shared. Rational, self-interested market action can occur only if individuals have sufficient information. Second, exchanging goods must be a costless process, free from transaction costs. Third, actors must be price-takers; there must be a sufficient level of deconcentration so that buyers and sellers will have to accept the existing market prices. Fourth, markets must exist for any goods that one might want to buy or sell. Fifth, there can be no externalities. In other words, the costs and benefits as-sociated with a given commodity must be represented in the price and consump-tion or production of a given good cannot affect those who are not subject to the transaction. Finally, there can be no collective goods (i.e., goods that can be con-sumed only if everyone consumes them).[43] When one or more of these conditions

sponse to the Commerce Court's dismal performance, Congress eliminated it in 1913.[59]

Even with the failure of the Commerce Court, the ICC was strengthened during the Progressive Era and became a highly effective regulator. Following the passage of the Hepburn Act in 1906, secured in large part with the support of the farming and shipping interests that supported railroad regulation, the ICC exercised its rate-making powers with great skill and became, by most accounts, a success. As Samuel Huntington explains: "The decade which followed the passage of [the Hepburn] Act was the peak of the Commission's power while still dependent upon consumer, public and presidential support."[60] However, after the experience of centralized rail management in World War I, Congress passed the Transportation Act of 1920 which gave the ICC the power to set minimum rates based on a reasonable rate of return. Henceforth, the agency would be far more concerned with guaranteeing stable profits for the industry than advocating lower charges. This shift in focus occurred in many policy areas and will be explored in some detail in Chapter 5.

## Antitrust

The Interstate Commerce Commission provided one model of controlling the concentration of economic power. This model of regulating corporations as public utilities through the issuance of certificates of public convenience and necessity would be extended in later years to other forms of transportation (e.g., trucking, airlines) and communications. It would also be quite important at the state level as applied by state public utility commissions. However, an alternative approach could be found in antitrust, a policy which more than any other policy reflected the American faith in the role of the competitive market as a regulatory tool. As Walter Adams and James W. Brock explain: "Antitrust . . . is a regulatory system that functions through prohibitory rules. It sets the limits within which individuals are free to do as they please." They continue: "Its objectives are the same as any regulatory system's, but its techniques are different. . . . It relies not on the visible hand of the central planner, but on an autonomous, objective, and impersonal market process. It exercises compulsion, not through direct governmental decision-making, but through rules that guide, limit, and discipline private decision-makers."[61]

Antitrust policy, like railroad regulation, finds its origins before the Progressive Era. The Sherman Antitrust Act of 1890 established broad prohibitions on certain forms of corporate behavior. Under section 1 of the Sherman Act, "Every contract, combination in the form of trust or otherwise, or conspiracy in restraint of trade of commerce among the several States, or with foreign nations, is hereby declared to be illegal." Section 2 states: "Every person who shall monopolize, or attempt to monopolize, or combine or conspire with any other person or persons, to monopolize in any part of the trade or commerce among the several States, or with foreign nations, shall be deemed guilty of a misdemeanor." The new antitrust law was to be administered by the Justice Department which could file suit in court. Provisions were also made for private antitrust cases resulting in treble damages.

The limitations of the Sherman Act became evident in its enforcement, or lack thereof. The young Justice Department lacked the resources to actively enforce the Sherman Act and attorneys general were wary to devote their precious resources to the enforcement of a law of questionable constitutionality.[62] In 1890, Congress passed the Sherman Act without providing funds for enforcement. The ten attorneys in the Justice Department and the additional eight in the field were simply overburdened by existing matters. The low levels of enforcement (an average of 1.5 cases per year during the first decade) convinced Congress that the department could not effectively bring antitrust cases without additional resources. Thus, in 1903 Congress authorized a special antitrust staff (five salaried attorneys and four stenographers) and a budget of $100,000 per year. Yet, when one considers the resources devoted to the enforcement of antitrust in comparison to the resources of the largest corporations, these additions appear little more than anemic.[63]

The first major antitrust case to reach the Supreme Court, *United States* v. *E.C. Knight Co.* (1895), created immediate problems for prosecutors and sent a strong message to corporations. The Supreme Court decided that the manufacturing activities of the Sugar Trust did not constitute commerce, even if the products were to be sold in interstate commerce. Following *E.C. Knight*, the nation entered into a tremendous wave of consolidations: Some three thousand mergers between 1897 and 1904 led to the creation of monopolies and oligopolies in over 70 industries.[64] The merger wave came to a close in 1904, following the *Northern Securities* decision in which the Supreme Court broke up a holding company that combined two potentially competitive railroads. In the wake of *Northern Securities* and decisions like *United States* v. *Addyston Pipe and Steel Co.* (1899) which established the per se illegality of agreements between competitors to fix prices, output, and markets, it appeared that antitrust might finally play a central role in regulating the corporate economy.

In 1911, the Court placed antitrust in question once again. In *Standard Oil Co. of New Jersey* v. *United States*, the Court introduced what would become its methodology in antitrust decision making. Collusion to fix prices, limit output, and divide markets would remain per se illegal—that is, illegal regardless of the ultimate impact or intent of the participants. However, Section 1 Sherman Act cases would henceforth be addressed under the "rule of reason." All contracts and economic transactions restrain trade to some extent, the Court argued. The key question is not whether a restraint exists, but whether it is reasonable. The Court would examine the intent of the party, the nature of the restraint, and the competitive impact before arriving at a conclusion as to whether a violation of the Sherman Act had occurred.

While the rule of reason may have seemed justified given the tendency of many to conclude that size was itself an offense, it nonetheless contributed to growing dissatisfaction over the administration and specificity of antitrust. Advocates of active antitrust enforcement feared that the growing concentration of power in the courts would result in a pattern of conservative decisions that would strip away the core of the Sherman Act. Businesses were concerned that a common law construction of the Sherman Act could produce a maze of complicated and irreconcilable doctrines that would fail to provide clear instructions to corporations as to what forms of activities were permissible under the law. While some, like then President Howard Taft, celebrated the rule of reason because it could bring greater flexibility to antitrust and prevent a movement to administrative control over the economy, others were far less celebratory. As noted above, Theodore Roosevelt and Woodrow Wilson devoted a good deal of attention to this very question in the 1912 presidential campaign. Both were convinced that the complexity of the corporate economy necessitated a response. Roosevelt embraced the idea of a new agency that would work closely with business to supervise their activities and ensure that growth through efficiency gains would not be punished. Wilson, in contrast, championed an extension of antitrust through new legislation and the creation of an administrative commission as the chief implementing agency.

Wilson's victory in the 1912 presidential election resulted in a rapid drive for new legislation. One result was the Clayton Act of 1914, enumerating the corporate activities that would constitute violations of the antitrust laws. The act prohibited various forms of discrimination (e.g., discriminatory prices, exclusive dealing, and tying contracts), the acquisition of "the stock or other share capital or another corporation," and interlocking directorates that lessened competition or contributed to monopoly. Like the Sherman Act, the Clayton Act provided for private antitrust litigation and treble damages. Unlike the Sherman Act, it sought to free labor from the threat of antitrust prosecutions by noting that labor was not an object of commerce. The Clayton Act was combined with a second important piece of legislation, the Federal Trade Commission Act of 1914, which created the Federal Trade Commission (FTC), an independent regulatory commission with broad regulatory powers. Under §5 of the act, the FTC could initiate proceedings against corporations that engaged in "unfair methods of competition in commerce," a catchall provision designed to allow the commission the flexibility to address activities that were not explicitly enumerated by the Clayton and Sherman Acts.[65]

Section 5 of the Federal Trade Commission Act delegated significant authority to the new agency. This catchall prohibition was less a product of congressional oversight than an expression of the Progressive faith in expertise. The FTC was designed to be an expert commission staffed by highly professional members. The commission staff would be required to conduct analyses of economic activity pursuant to FTC enforcement activities and at the request of the president and Congress. The staff could use its expertise in the law, economics, and accountancy to regulate the corporate economy only if they were granted a broad mandate and greater procedural flexibility. To this end, Congress provided the broad provisions of §5 and established a process by which the FTC could promulgate rules, initiate complaints against violations, and determine the guilt or innocence of the party in question. This combination of legislative, executive, and judicial powers, when combined with the broad provisions of §5, gave the commission unprecedented powers. It also created the potential for conflicts with the courts which effectively used a series of early decisions to narrow the FTC's authority.

## The Federal Reserve

Tariff reform, rate regulation, and antitrust prosecutions provided three means of eliminating or managing the concentration of business power. All of these had roots in the nineteenth century and were adapted to the new economy of the Progressive Era through new legislation and administrative devices. The Federal Reserve departed from these earlier initiatives both in its model of regulation and in the fact that it was distinctly and completely a product of the period in question.

The last half of the nineteenth century was one of financial instability. Financial crises struck in 1861, 1873, 1884, and 1893. The panic of 1893, combined with a stock market crash and a wave of business failures (including the Erie Railroad) and bank suspensions, contributed to the depression and the Republican realignment of 1896. In each case, financial crises contributed, in some quarters, to the strong opposition to the concentrated power of banks and the persistent fear on the part of many that the banks used their control of credit to promote the interests of the industrial core in the Northeast at the expense of the farmers and small businesses elsewhere in the country. Thus, during the final decades of the century, agrarian radicals proposed any number of schemes for limiting the power of banks and inflating the money supply through the coinage of silver, the movement to a strict paper currency, and the use of farm lands as collateral on loans. While these policy alternatives were politically popular among large segments of the population, they failed to have much of an impact on policymakers whose chief concern was whether the financial system could support commercial expansion.[66]

The financial crises stimulated serious consideration of financial reform, particularly after the crisis of 1907 which was accompanied by a 11 percent reduction of net national product and the suspension of specie convertibility. Although Congress began serious consideration of reform following the crisis, the resulting Aldrich plan failed to pass through Congress due to the lack of consensus over the appropriate combination of public and private power and the need for a decentralized system to thwart the potential dominance of Wall Street. The political environment changed, however, following the election of 1912. Representative Carter Glass, chairman of the House Banking subcommittee responsible for composing new financial legislation, strongly advocated a decentralized system of 15 to 20 independent reserve banks. While the decentralization was a reform measure designed to create a counterbalance to the financial power of Wall Street, Glass's distaste for government controls led him to advocate a privately directed system under the leadership of a 36-member national board dominated by finance. As one might expect, Glass's revision of the Aldrich plan won the support of the banking community. However, reformers within the administration and progressive members of Congress strongly opposed the privately controlled system and demanded, instead, government control over the entire reserve system. Wilson's Treasury Secretary William McAdoo went as far as to recommend that the system be placed within the Treasury Department. After consulting with his adviser Louis Brandeis, Wilson decided that the decentralization promoted by Aldrich and Glass was acceptable. However, it had to be combined with exclusive government control of the executive board and on government issued currency.[67]

After a year of negotiations between various wings of the Democratic party, a host of party elites, and the financial community, Wilson successfully maneuvered the Federal Reserve Act through Congress in December 1913. The Pujo Committee hearings in the Senate, revealing a long list of abuses in investment banking, forced those supporting a private system to accept Wilson's demands out of the fear that procrastination could result in more direct government controls. The Federal Reserve Act created a decentralized system of 12 regional banks, headed by an independent Federal Reserve Board consisting of presidential appointees. As John Woolley notes, "The 'independent' governing board was intended to be a public coordinator of private regulation banks but to remain separate from any larger system of public power. The System was conceived in the spirit of other Progressive reforms that stressed faith in expertise, faith in the effectiveness of tinkering with the machinery of government, and distrust of politicians."[68]

The Federal Reserve was created to bring greater stability to the financial system by discounting (and thus serving as a lender of last resort for member banks) and imposing reserve requirements on its members. Moreover, the Fed was directed to maintain an elastic currency to meet the needs of commerce, agriculture, and industry. It was not, however, given any broad macroeconomic policy responsibilities.[69] While the legislation addressed some of the problems that had troubled finance over the course of the past century, it did not clearly identify where the central power of the system would be vested. At least initially, the system was dominated by the New York Federal Reserve Bank rather than the board of governors. Likewise, there was no mechanism created for coordinating the actions of the various banks. The impact of the Federal Reserve System on the economy would be the unintended product of 12 relatively independent actors.

The role that the Federal Reserve plays today in the management of the economy through the manipulation of the money supply was not envisioned by the framers of the Federal Reserve Act. However, the advent of war and the expansion of the Federal Reserve's selling and purchasing of securities created a need for coordination and ultimately suggested a potential role for the agency in managing the business cycle. Over time, the Federal Reserve Board would assume clear leadership in the system and new mechanisms for coordinating market activities would be developed, thus allowing the Fed to exert a unified will that is relatively rare in the U.S. political economy. The expanded duties of the Federal Reserve will be addressed in greater detail in subsequent chapters.

## PROGRESSIVISM AND THE PROGRESSIVE ERA

Perhaps as a reflection of the label attached to the period, it is often assumed that the Progressive Era contributed a number of progressive policies that limited the power of the growing corporate economy relative to workers, consumers, farmers, and small business. Moreover, popular accounts of the period attribute change to the power of democratic politics. We might, for example, understand the changes through the lens of pluralist theory. In response to changes in the economic and social environment, a variety of groups mobilized and demanded new policies. Electorally vulnerable officials reacted, quite appropriately, by introducing new public policies. They even promoted ever greater levels of mobilization through their frequent praise for "the people" and their role as a counterforce to the growing power of the corporate economy. In this interpretation, Progressive advances were nothing short of a triumph of democracy.

However, one can question the radicalism of the Progressive Era initiatives and even the extent to which they were the products of democratic politics. Although the regulatory policies of the Progressive Era entailed a greater role for the state in the economy, they never seriously challenged the legitimacy of the corporation or the existing distribution of wealth and economic power. Indeed, the new regulations, in many instances, cannot be seen as attempts to restrain corporations on behalf of consumers or small entrepreneurs. The politically expedient promotion of the people must not veil the fact that many of the regulatory initiatives of the period were supported, and in some cases suggested, by the regulated themselves. As Gabriel Kolko reveals in his studies of Progressive politics, representatives of the regulated industries commonly played a significant role in drafting the regulatory legislation.[70] This may, at first glance, appear counterintuitive. However, recall that the corporate expansion of the second half of the nineteenth century created problems of overproduction and bouts of intense competition that often hurt the businesses involved. Corporations needed to discover some means of managing corporate expansion and competition without sacrificing profitability. One response was private. Corporations created trusts, holding companies, and consolidations, albeit with mixed success. The political reaction to these strategies was significant at the state level, particularly in those regions where agrarian radicals and small businesses exercised political power. Because state regulations were rarely coordinated and often reflected Populist interests, the prospect of a single set of national regulations carried a certain appeal—particularly, if the businesses involved could play some role in shaping the basic features of the new regulations. In essence, revisionist historians argue, public policies were created to rationalize production and promote profitability.

Work conducted since Kolko introduced his thesis suggests that the politics surrounding the passage of key regulatory initiatives are not easily captured through this elite framework. Rather, the politics surrounding the passage of regulatory legislation will be shaped by the distribution and concentration of costs and benefits. Moreover, where multiple interests are mobilized, Congress may simply pass relatively vague legislation, thus delegating authority and displacing conflicts to newly created administrative agencies. Kolko's portrayal overemphasizes the dominance of business and thus glosses over the complicated politics surrounding many of the policy debates.[71] Nonetheless, there is little question that the system of political capitalism or corporate liberalism forged during the Progressive Era was one in which public policies were designed with the assistance of socially conscious business leaders to stabilize the economy, thus allowing corporations and finance to function free of the destabilizing forces of competition and local policies that could truly challenge their power. As David Vogel suggests, the Progressive Era was unique and represented "American businessmen's finest hour." As Vogel explains: "The enlightened business leadership of the Progressive Era was made possible by an unusual centralization of authority within the business community. . . . Not only were most major industries dominated by a single entrepreneur, but at the apex of the system stood a few individuals whose personal stature and economic power fully enabled them to understand and represent the interests of business as a whole." Thus, despite a lack of true class consciousness among capitalists, "the individual interests of many of the most powerful capitalists were themselves coincidental with that of the larger industrial system."[72]

Even if the Progressive Era was relatively unique by virtue of its concentration of economic power and the realization, on the part of many executives, that the state could play a central role in guaranteeing stability, we should not lose sight of the piecemeal nature of the system. Even Gabriel Kolko, the most prominent revisionist historian addressing the Progressive Era, suggests that one of the limits on this new "political capitalism" was a lack of coherence. Kolko explains:

> There is a quite low level of conceptualization among business reformers, and what counts most are their functional actions and proposals. These proposals were invariably the concoctions of sick industries seeking help, and their definitions of desirable federal regulation rarely touched other industries content with their own lots. No one, in any case, ever advocated national regulation until they saw that their own interests were directly involved, and until then they often opposed regulation for others on principle. Consistency is a quality all too rare among specific businessmen favoring national political intervention. Political capitalism—the merger of the economic and political structures on behalf of the greater interests of capitalism—was incremental rather than comprehensive during its origins, and one misses the texture of the American experience in both implying excess rationality, efficacy, and coherence to it as well as denying its importance.[73]

If the Progressive Era did not leave a coherent and expansive network of policies designed to support corporate expansion, it did provide a number of important regulatory experiments that would continue to shape the political economy in subsequent decades. Finance, corporate organization, and transportation were each transformed through the policies initiated during the period. World War I is commonly cited as the end of the Progressive Era, or at least the single event that drew the domestic activism of the period to an end. Yet, in many ways, the relationship between the new corporate economy and the state was strengthened during the war. As Chapter 5 will reveal, the war brought new patterns of state-corporate relations that built upon those established during the Progressive Era and affected the evolution of the political economy for decades to come.

## NOTES

1. *Statistical History of the United States*, Series F-1 and F-2.
2. See Robert Higgs, *Crisis and Leviathan: Critical Episodes in the Growth of American Government* (New York: Oxford University Press, 1987), pp. 79–80.
3. *Statistical History of the United States*, Series F-1. Changes in per capita income adjusted for inflation calculated from data in Series F-4.
4. Alfred D. Chandler, Jr., *The Visible Hand: The Managerial Revolution in American Business* (Cambridge, Mass.: Harvard University Press, 1977), p. 319.
5. See Alfred D. Chandler, Jr., "The United States: Seedbed of Managerial Capitalism." In *Managerial Hierarchies*, ed., Alfred D. Chandler, Jr., and Herman Daems (Cambridge, Mass.: Harvard University Press, 1980); Thomas K. McCraw, "Rethinking the Trust Question." In *Regulation in Perspective: Historical Essays*, ed. Thomas K. McCraw (Cambridge, Mass.: Harvard University Press, 1981), p. 32; and Lewis L. Gould, *The Progressive Era* (Syracuse, N.Y.: Syracuse University Press, 1974), p. 2.
6. Samuel P. Hays, *The Response to Industrialism: 1885–1914* (Chicago: University of Chicago Press, 1957), pp. 54–57.
7. *Statistical History of the United States*, Series C-88.
8. *Statistical History of the United States*, Series A-95, 98.

9. *Statistical History of the United States,* Series A-195.

10. See Stanely Lebergott, *The Americans: An Economic Record* (New York: W.W. Norton, 1984), pp. 337–44; Richard Hofstadter, *The Age of Reform: From Bryan to F.D.R.* (New York, Knopf, 1955), p. 174.

11. Lebergott, *The Americans,* pp. 341–43.

12. See Kim Voss, "Disposition Is Not Action: The Rise and Demise of the Knights of Labor." *Studies in American Political Development* 6 (Fall 1992): 272–321.

13. *Statistical History of the United States,* Series D-738.

14. *Statistical History of the United States,* Series D-770.

15. Foster Rhea Dulles and Melvyn Dubofsky, *Labor in America: A History,* 4th ed. (Arlington Heights, Ill.: Harlan Davidson, 1984), pp. 186–87.

16. Christopher L. Tomlins, *The State and the Unions: Labor Relations, Law, and the Organized Labor Movement in America, 1880–1960* (Cambridge: Cambridge University Press, 1985), pp. 60–95.

17. Ibid., pp. 60–95.

18. *Statistical History of the United States,* Series K-73.

19. Hayes, *The Response to Industrialism,* pp. 58–63.

20. See Marc Allen Eisner, *Regulatory Politics in Transition* (Baltimore, Md.: Johns Hopkins University Press, 1993), pp. 47–72.

21. Kirk H. Porter and Donald Bruce Johnson, *National Party Platforms, 1840–1960* (Urbana: University of Illinois Press, 1961), pp. 89–90.

22. See Hayes, *The Response to Industrialism,* pp. 27–32; and Walter Dean Burnham, *Critical Elections and the Mainsprings of American Politics* (New York: W.W. Norton, 1965), pp. 71–90.

23. See Stephen Skowronek, *Building a New American State: The Expansion of Administrative Capacities, 1877–1920* (Cambridge: Cambridge University Press, 1982), pp. 168–69.

24. *Statistical History of the United States,* Series H-327, 317.

25. Richard T. Ely, *Ground under Our Feet* (New York, Macmillan, 1938), p. 135.

26. See Louis Galambos, "Technology, Political Economy, and Professionalization: Central Themes of the Organizational Synthesis." *Business History Review* 57 (Winter 1983): 471–93.

27. Edward N. Hurley, *Awakening of Business* (New York: Doubleday, Page & Co., 1916), pp. 207–08. Also see Arthur Jerome Eddy, *The New Competition* (New York: D. Appleton & Co., 1912).

28. Ibid.

29. Martin J. Sklar, *The Corporate Reconstruction of American Capitalism, 1890–1916: The Market, the Law, and Politics* (Cambridge: Cambridge University Press, 1988), p. 374.

30. Herbert Croly, *The Promise of American Life,* ed. Arthur M. Schesinger, Jr. (Cambridge, Mass.: Harvard University Press, 1965), p. 400.

31. Theodore Roosevelt, *The New Nationalism* (Englewood Cliffs, N.J.: Prentice Hall, 1961), p. 29.

32. Theodore Roosevelt, "Theodore Roosevelt Holds to the Rule of Reason." In *The Progressives,* ed. Carl Resek (Indianapolis, Ind.: Bobbs-Merrill Co., 1967), p. 192.

33. "Progressive Platform of 1912," *National Party Platforms, 1840–1960,* compiled by Kirk H. Porter and Donald Bruce Johnson (Urbana IL: University of Illinois Press, 1961), p. 178.

34. Roosevelt, *The New Nationalism,* p. 99.

35. Quoted in Frank K. Kelly, *The Fight for the White House: The Story of 1912* (New York: Thomas Y. Crowell, 1961), p. 237.

36. Roosevelt, *The New Nationalism,* p. 34.

37. Ibid., pp. 107–08.

38. Woodrow Wilson, *The New Freedom: A Call for the Emancipation of the Generous Energies of a People* (New York: Doubleday, Page & Co., 1913), p. 180.

39. Ibid., p. 166.

40. Ibid., p. 169.

41. Ibid., p. 172.

42. Ibid., p. 213.

43. See Edith Stokey and Richard Zeckhauser, *A Primer for Policy Analysis* (New York: W.W. Norton, 1978), pp. 293–319.

44. Sidney Ratner, *The Tariff in American History* (New York: Van Nostrand, 1972), pp. 36–41.

45. Ibid., pp. 42–43.

46. Arthur S. Link, *Woodrow Wilson and the Progressive Era, 1910–1917* (New York: Harper & Brothers, 1954), p. 38.

47. Quoted in Link, *Woodrow Wilson and the Progressive Era,* p. 41.

48. John F. Witte, *The Politics and Development of the Federal Income Tax* (Madison: University of Wisconsin Press, 1985), pp. 67–87; Ratner, *The Tariff in American History,* pp. 44–46.

49. F.W. Taussig, *The Tariff History of the United States* (New York: G.P. Putnam's Sons, 1923), p. 448.

50. F.W. Taussig, *Free Trade, the Tariff and Reciprocity.* (New York: Macmillan, 1924), pp. 450–52; Merle Fainsod, Lincoln Gordon, and Joseph C. Palamountain, Jr., *Government and the American Economy,* 3rd ed. (New York: W.W. Norton, 1959), pp. 100–101.

51. Robert E. Cushman, *The Independent Regulatory Commissions* (New York: Oxford University Press., 1941), p. 41. See the discussion of the Interstate Commerce Act and the ICC's early decades in Eisner, *Regulatory Politics in Transition,* pp. 48–58.

52. *Munn v. Illinois,* 94 U.S. 113 (1877).

53. *Wabash, St. Louis & Pacific Railway Co. v. Illinois,* 118 U.S. 557 (1886).

54. *The Maximum Rate Case,* 167 U.S. 479 (1897).

55. See Cushman, *The Independent Regulatory Commissions,* p. 68.

56. Theodore Roosevelt, "Annual Message, December 5, 1905." In *The Economic Regulation of Business and Industry: A Legislative History of U.S. Regulatory Agencies,* ed. Bernard Schwartz, vol. 1 (New York: Chelsea House Publishers, 1973), p. 613.

57. Joshua Bernhardt, *The Interstate Commerce Commission: Its History, Activities, and Organization* (Baltimore, Md.: Johns Hopkins University Press, 1923), pp. 20–21.

58. Ibid., pp. 26–28.

59. Cushman, *The Independent Regulatory Commissions,* pp. 27–28.

60. Samuel P. Huntington, "The Marasmus of the ICC: The Commission, the Railroads, and the Public Interest." *The Yale Law Journal* 61, 4 (April 1952), p. 467.

61. Walter Adams and James W. Brock, *The Bigness Complex: Industry, Labor, and Government in the American Economy* (New York: Pantheon Books, 1986), p. 113.

62. See Marc Allen Eisner, *Antitrust and the Triumph of Economics: Institutions, Expertise, and Policy Change* (Chapel Hill: University of North Carolina Press, 1991), Chapter 3.

63. William Letwin, *Law and Economic Policy in America: The Evolution of the Sherman Antitrust Act* (New York: Random House, 1965), pp. 103–05; Walton Hamilton and Irene Till, *Antitrust in Action.* TNEC Monograph no. 19 (Washington D.C.: Government Printing Office, 1941), pp. 135–43; and Suzanne Weaver, *Decision to Prosecute: Organization and Public Policy in the Antitrust Division* (Cambridge, Mass.: MIT Press, 1977), p. 24.

64. See Ralph L. Nelson, *Merger Movements in American History, 1895–1956* (Princeton, N.J.: Princeton University Press, 1959); and Carl Eis, "The 1919–1930 Merger Movement in American Industry." *Journal of Law and Economics* 12 (October 1969): 280–84.

65. See Eisner, *Regulatory Politics in Transition,* pp. 60–61, 67.

66. John T. Woolley, *Monetary Politics: The Federal Reserve and the Politics of Monetary Policy* (Cambridge: Cambridge University Press, 1984), pp. 32–33.

67. Link, *Woodrow Wilson and the Progressive Era,* pp. 43–53.

68. Woolley, *Monetary Politics,* p. 40.

69. See E.A. Goldenweiser, *American Monetary Policy* (New York: McGraw-Hill, 1951), p. 110.

70. See Gabriel Kolko, *The Triumph of Conservatism: A Reinterpretation of American History, 1900–1916* (New York: Free Press, 1963); and Gabriel Kolko, *Railroads and Regulation, 1877–1916* (Princeton, N.J.: Princeton University Press, 1965).

71. James Q. Wilson, "The Politics of Regulation." In *The Political Economy,* ed. Thomas Ferguson and Joel Rogers (Armonk, N.Y.: M.E. Sharpe, 1984); and Michael Reagan, *Regulation: The Politics of Policy* (Boston: Little, Brown, 1987), Chapter 3. Also see Skowronek, *Building a New American State,* Chapter 5, for a detailed analysis of the origins of the Interstate Commerce Act and the politics surrounding the passage of the legislation. Skowronek correctly emphasizes the existence of multiple interests in the policy debates.

72. David Vogel, "Why Businessmen Distrust their State: The Political Consciousness of American Corporate Executives." *British Journal of Political Science* 8 (1978): 70.

73. Gabriel Kolko, *Main Currents in Modern American History* (New York: Harper & Row, 1976), p. 12.

# 5

# FROM THE GREAT WAR TO THE GREAT DEPRESSION

At first glance, one might not expect the experience of World War I to have had much of an impact on the evolution of the American political economy. The duration of U.S. involvement in the war was brief, lasting under two years. Moreover, the success of mobilization was mixed. The limited authority granted to the mobilization agencies, the weakness of existing institutions, problems of coordinating policies and activities in multiple sectors of the economy, and ongoing conflicts between agencies involved in the mobilization process all took their toll. However , the experience left some important legacies. First, economic mobilization introduced a generation to the potential benefits of a more expansive state role in the economy. Given the era's broad concerns with domestic reform, faith in scientific and social scientific knowledge, and grave dissatisfaction with many public institutions, the mobilization agencies seemed to provide a model of what was possible. As Ellis Hawley explains, many viewed mobilization "not only as a requirement for survival but as a stepping stone to the social order that a progressive era had envisioned but failed to achieve. A system of war management, they came to believe, could be adapted to the peacetime management of social programs."[1] Many government and corporate officials returned to their peacetime activities with the experiences of war fresh in their memories. The War Industries Board (WIB), the central war mobilization agency, provided policies and models of administration that might be relevant to a host of social and economic problems. Moreover, the experience shaped the interpretation of events a decade later and provided a model of state-economy relations appropriate to the new emergency situation of the Great Depression.

Second, despite rapid demobilization, the war changed the nature of state-economy relations and the political organization of the economy. The WIB's limited financial and administrative resources forced it to delegate authority to commodity sections which, in turn, devolved authority on to business associations. In this fashion, officials compensated for their limited administrative capacities by relying on the capabilities of private sector organizations. The trade associations and war service committees, created and certified by the Chamber of Commerce to work with the commodity sections, exercised public authority and certain policymaking powers. After the war, many of these associations continued to represent the interests of their sectors and actively sought to establish close relationships with policymakers and key agencies. Thus, new models of state-economy relations existed side-by-side with a new universe of industrial organizations and elites experienced in working with the federal government to control and direct production.

This chapter begins with an examination of the history, structure, and powers of the central agency in the mobilization process, the War Industries Board. We will be concerned not only with the activities of the WIB but also with the way it shaped state-corporate relations during the war. The parallel activities of other mobilization agencies are also addressed. The chapter turns to an examination of the short- and long-term consequences for the American political economy. Wartime mobilization shaped activities in a number of policy areas, particularly in the unique model of state-economy relations it offered.

## WARTIME MOBILIZATION: AN EXPERIMENT IN REGULATION

The significance of the mobilization experience is best assessed when placed in context. While a number of new regulatory agencies were created during the Progressive Era as policymakers sought to accommodate the emergence of a new corporate-based economy, the role of the state in the economy remained a highly divisive issue. As explained in Chapter 4, the role of the state in the economy was central to the presidential campaign of 1912. The incumbent President Taft adopted a conservative interpretation of property rights and was highly suspicious of administrative regulation of the economy. He supported an ongoing reliance on the enforcement of the Sherman Act and a system of judicial regulation. Taft's vision of state-economy relations was overshadowed by the conflicts between Theodore Roosevelt and Woodrow Wilson. Roosevelt presented the emergence of the large corporation as a natural and largely beneficial product of economic evolution. Rather than seeking to destroy large corporations through antitrust, Roosevelt's New Nationalism called for the state to play a central role in defining the terms of economic change. More precisely, it envisioned a quasi-corporatist arrangement in which an agency modeled on the Commerce Department's Bureau of Corporations would collect information on production and corporate organization, facilitate corporate agreements, and supervise labor relations and corporate capitalization. Policymakers would employ the Sherman Act against only the "bad trusts" (compared with the "good," efficiency promoting trusts) that expanded through monopolistic practices. Wilson countered this program with his New Freedom. Claiming that Roosevelt's program would render citizens dependent on the benevolence of large corporations and the state, Wilson called for an extension of antitrust and a return to the market. Wilson's New Freedom was much in keeping with the political economic doctrines of the Progressive Era. Yet, by the 1920s, the state-economy relations presented by Roosevelt captured the imagination of New Era economists, policymakers, and business associations.[2]

While Wilson's vision of state-economy relations prevailed in the short term, the concrete demands of war forced a movement toward a New Nationalist posture. The problems of rapid industrial mobilization in an underdeveloped administrative state forced policymakers to place a heavy reliance on business executives, corporations, and trade associations. They possessed a monopoly on information on industrial capacity, production, and pricing. Moreover, they controlled the flow of raw materials and munitions critical to the war effort. In order to take advantage of their expertise, the War Industries Board developed a highly decentralized structure. It was, in large part, integrated with the trade associations that became an integral part of the mobilization process.

## The Preparedness Controversy

When war erupted in Europe in 1914, the United States lacked the military and naval resources necessary to act on a global basis. The lack of preparedness was, in large part, a natural extension of the domestic orientation of Progressivism. The Progressive reform agenda rested on the faith that the nation's social and economic inequities could be eliminated though the application of scientific and social-scientific knowledge and experiments in institutional design. For many, the goal was not one of active involvement with the corrupt powers of the Old World but the elimination of trying domestic problems. America would stand apart from, and as an example to, the world. Moreover, as Arthur Link explains, many Progressives harbored a powerful assumption about the political-economic origins of the war. "Wars were mainly economic in causation and necessarily evil because bankers with money to lend, munition-makers with sordid profits to earn, and industrialists with markets to win were the chief promoters and beneficiaries of war." Link continues: "The path of progressive righteousness led straight to disarmament, an international system based on compulsory arbitration, and an unequivocal repudiation of war."[3]

The lack of popular support for involvement in the war in Europe forced Wilson to strike a position of neutrality, officially proclaimed on August 4, 1914. However, strict neutrality was most difficult to sustain. The British naval presence and the blockade of the North Sea threatened to undermine U.S. foreign trade. Although Wilson objected to the British blockade, he did not challenge it by any effective means. Rather, trade patterns were quickly adjusted away from Germany and Austria and toward the allies, thus revealing the hollowness of U.S. neutrality. Between 1914 and 1916, U.S. trade with Germany and Austria fell from $169.3 million to $1.16 million. During the same period, U.S. trade with the allies increased from $825 million to $3.2 billion. By 1915, shipments of food, raw materials, and munitions were combined with lines of credit to finance allied purchases.[4] Germany responded to the supply lines connecting the United States and the British Isles with a submarine blockade and the sinking of two British liners, the *Falaba* and the

*Lusitania*, which resulted in the loss of American life. Wilson objected to the growing submarine menace and German policy in a series of letters while simultaneously offering a peace initiative in hopes of ending the war before the United States would be forced into the fray. Ultimately, these efforts proved insufficient.

As U.S.-German relations became increasingly tense, it was clear that the United States could not back its demands with military might. While the strong Progressive support for neutrality was ever present, eastern Republicans—including Theodore Roosevelt, Henry Cabot Lodge, and Elihu Root—increasingly raised the issue of national security. They predicted an invasion of the United States and attacked the administration's response to German aggression as cowardly and imprudent. With the 1916 elections on the horizon and the growing threat posed by German submarines, Wilson moved quickly. In July 1915, he called on the secretaries of war and the navy to develop plans for strengthening national security. The ambitious army proposal was drafted by Secretary of War Lindley Garrison and planners at the Army War College. It called for a significant increase in the size of the army, currently authorized at a strength of 100,000 men, and the creation of a 400,000 man Continental Army, a volunteer national reserve. At the same time, it called for the elimination of the National Guard which, due to its falling under state jurisdiction, was of little use in international conflicts. The navy proposed a grand construction program resulting in naval parity with the British by 1925. In the next five years, the proposal called for a $500 million program to build a wide array of battleships, cruisers, and submarines.[5]

The preparedness debate quickly became a highly divisive issue. Midwestern Republicans strongly opposed the administration's plans for preparedness while the eastern Republicans, led by Theodore Roosevelt, remained strong and vociferous advocates of strengthening the nation's defenses. The key problem, however, was within the Democratic party. A coalition of 30 to 50 Democrats in Congress, largely from the South and West, formed a formidable antipreparedness bloc. With the support of the House Majority Leader Claude Kitchen and control of the House Military Affairs Committee, they threatened to prevent passage or seriously modify any preparedness legislation. Indeed, the antipreparedness bloc countered the proposed creation of a Continental Army by calling for an expansion and "federalization" of the National Guard.

Wilson made a number of public addresses in January and February 1916 designed to make the case for preparedness, albeit with little discernible effect. The congressional opposition to the army reorganization plan continued unabated. In the end, the Army Reorganization Act of 1916 was a compromise measure. It increased the army to 11,327 officers and 208,338 enlisted soldiers, compared with the existing peacetime contingent of 5,029 officers and 100,000 men. As a concession to the antipreparedness bloc, it expanded the National Guard and integrated it into the national system of defense, in lieu of the Continental Army. Finally, it authorized the War Department's volunteer camps to provide summer training for civilians. The final naval legislation passed after a strong Senate version received the vigorous support of the president. The act authorized the navy's five year construction program but accelerated its pace so that it would be completed in three years. During the first year alone, the navy was authorized to complete construction on 4 battleships, 8 cruisers, 20 destroyers, and 30 submarines. In addition, Congress passed the Merchant Marine Act of 1916, which authorized the creation of a United States Shipping Board with the power to own and operate a merchant fleet and to regulate rates and services of ships in interstate, coastal, and international routes.[6]

The dramatic expansion of the army and navy forced policymakers to address the politically hazardous question of finance. Wilson and Treasury Secretary McAdoo were united in their commitment that most of the expenditures should be met with revenues rather than debt. To this end, the administration proposed increases in customs receipts and taxes on tobacco and alcohol. Progressives and radicals in the House and Senate objected that this would force the financial burden of preparedness on the lower and middle classes. Arguing that the rich and the large corporations would gain from preparedness as they would from war, they demanded that they bear the costs. Thus, the Emergency Revenue Act of 1916 raised revenue from the wealthiest part of the population. It increased the income tax from 1 to 2 percent without lowering the existing exemptions, thus leaving the majority of the population free from the new taxes. Moreover, the act raised the surcharge on incomes in excess of $20,000 to a maximum of 13 percent, thus creating an effective income tax as high as 15 percent. The inheritance tax was increased to a maximum of 10 percent, subject to a $50,000 income exemption. The act also targeted corporations, expanding a variety of corporate taxes and imposing a tax of 12.5 percent on the net profits of armament producers. The Emergency Revenue Act of 1916 was correctly portrayed as "soak the rich" legislation that appeased the radical and progressive forces in Congress who objected to the costs of preparedness and the apparent conflict between the expansion of the military and domestic social reform.[7]

Although Congress authorized an expansion of the armed forces and the generation of new revenues, it had yet to develop the institutional apparatus for mobilization. The War Department's General Staff was dramatically understaffed with a mere 19 officers serving under 2 major generals. The lack of staff and the organizational disarray had direct implications for the War Department's capacity to direct a war of any magnitude.[8] Grosvenor B. Clarkson explains that the General Staff

> had made no study and, as a body, had no comprehension of the fact that in modern war the whole industrial activity of the National becomes the commissariat of the army. It had no affiliations with the complex and fecund industrial life of the Nation. It understood nothing of the intertwining ramifications for production. It knew nothing of the economic sequences of new demands, so vast as to exceed existing supplies. Its sole experience in business was the placing of orders for comparatively small quantities of goods in a market so well stocked and so voluminously supplied that they had no appreciable effect on reserves or prices.[9]

Thus, the first step in addressing the lack of preparedness was to conduct an inventory of the nation's industrial capacity. In 1916, a committee of the Naval

Consulting Board conducted an ambitious inventory of approximately 18,000 plants. At the same time, the Secretary of War appointed a board to survey munitions resources and determine the need for government production. Most important, however, were the activities of the Council of National Defense, authorized by Congress as part of the Army Appropriations Act of 1916. The council, consisting of six Cabinet members (Navy, War Interior, Agriculture, Commerce, and Labor) was charged with coordinating industry and national resources, and overseeing preparation for the possible entry into the war. The Council's Advisory Commission united representatives of industry, labor, and the railroads to conduct a survey of America's industrial base.[10]

The council's advisory commission was composed of seven commissioners, each assigned to a specific area of concern for mobilization. Thus, commissioners were assigned to transportation, engineering and education, munitions and manufacturing, medicine and surgery, raw materials, supplies, and labor. To facilitate the collection of information, commissioners worked through committees composed of private sector actors drawn from the areas in question. This loose committee structure provided, in the words of Bernard Baruch, "a center of contact between the Government and the industrial life of the Nation. The purpose was to make available . . . the best thought and effort of American industrial and professional life for the successful prosecution of the war." Although the "council had no administrative power . . . [i]t consciously or unconsciously served as a great laboratory devoted to discovering and making articulate the new administrative problems which the war was to involve."[11] As they developed, the committees were transformed into some of the key mobilization agencies (e.g., the Railroad Administration, the Food Administration). Most important, for present purposes, is the chain of events that led to the creation of the War Industries Board.

### The War Industries Board

In March 1917, the Council created a Munitions Standards Board, under the chairmanship of Frank Scott. Although the board was initially responsible for promoting the standardization of munitions, once reconstituted as the General Munitions Board, it also became the clearinghouse for munitions purchase and supply. Due to its unwieldy size and its limited legislative mandate, most areas of war production were left unsupervised. To remedy this situation, the General Munitions Board was replaced by the War Industries Board on July 28, 1917.[12] The WIB, composed of five civilians and representatives of the army and navy, had a smaller executive than the General Munitions Board to reduce the "need for consultation at the expense of action." However, the WIB was not granted any new powers. "Extralegality for the emergency was again invoked to give it powers which were hardly warranted by the act that had created the patron bodies of the Council of National Defense and the Advisory Commission."[13] The new War Industries Board, as the General Munitions Board before it, was designed as a coordinating body, a clearinghouse for the war-industry needs. A lack of executive authority and staffing and the continual attempts of the army and navy to maintain control over purchasing created severe administrative problems and rendered the board impotent.

Mobilization proceeded by trial and error through the winter of 1918, when critical shortages of coal and rail transportation threatened the war effort.[14]

In response to the near collapse of the mobilization effort, the WIB was reorganized and reconstituted. At the urging of William McAdoo, Wilson appointed the respected financier and WIB veteran, Bernard Baruch, as the new chairman. Under the authority granted in the Overman Act, Wilson separated the WIB from the Council of National Defense and increased its power. In the letter offering Baruch the chairmanship of the WIB, Wilson described the board's duties as: "(1). The creation of new facilities and the disclosing, if necessary, the opening up of new or additional sources of supply; (2). The conversion of existing facilities, where necessary, to new uses; (3). The studious conservation of resources and facilities by scientific, commercial and industrial economies; (4). Advice to the several purchasing agencies of the Government with regard to the prices to be paid; (5). The determination, wherever necessary, of priorities of production and of delivery and of the proportions of any given article to be made immediately accessible to the several purchasing agencies when the supply of that article is insufficient, either temporarily or permanently; [and] (6). The making of purchases for the Allies."[15] Wilson gave Baruch final authority in all areas except price fixing. He vested the power to set prices in the WIB's Price Fixing Committee chaired by Robert S. Brookings.

The WIB was largely a product of executive decree. The lack of firm legislative authority in price fixing and the assignment of priorities hampered the board throughout its existence. Indeed, while it could play a critical role in coordinating the demands of the various consuming agencies, it had limited power to assess the validity of service demands or override the purchasing agents of the army and navy. Its real power rested in its expertise. As George Soule notes: "The real basis of the board's authority, aside from its presidential instructions, lay in the detailed knowledge it accumulated concerning the amount and location of the various supplies that could be obtained, and of the demands being placed upon them."[16] Without the WIB's efforts, the war effort would have been hopelessly complicated by the lack of information on the economy.

## The Organization of the War Industries Board

The War Industries Board, under the chairmanship of Bernard Baruch, consisted of a board and a number of functional divisions. The board included the heads of the divisions and representatives of the navy and the army. The functional divisions addressed price fixing, conservation, requirements, and priorities. Additional divisions addressed steel, chemicals, finished products, and labor. Although there was a centralization of authority in Chairman Baruch, two factors hampered the WIB's efforts. First, the WIB was not given the formal sanctions necessary to implement its mandate. It had the power to establish priorities and fix prices, both of which could be used to force some compliance on the part of business and the armed services. It could also commandeer plants and stockpiles. Although the WIB occasionally threatened to commandeer plants and supplies, it was a blunt policy tool. Moreover, any concerted attempt at coercing businesses could result in the questioning of the WIB's lack of direct legislative authority. Because the WIB had limited means of forcing compliance and its authority was tenuous, it was forced to rely on cooperation. In the end, Baruch was most successful when relying on moral suasion and elite negotiations with industrial leaders.

The second problem was more significant and had direct implications for the organization of the agency. The WIB was required to engage in relatively comprehensive planning activities. Although the nation's involvement in the war was brief, the American Expeditionary Force and allied demands claimed about - one-quarter of the nation's economic output—9.4 million workers in an active workforce of 37 million were engaged in wartime production![17] Despite the magnitude and complexity of the tasks involved, the WIB possessed neither the staff nor the technical expertise to coordinate the mobilization process. The WIB compensated for the deficit of administrative capacities by drawing on the expertise of business. Executives from major corporations—the so-called dollar-a-year men—staffed most of the major offices in the WIB. Critical, in this respect, were the 57 commodity sections. The commodity sections were composed of a WIB official, commonly a top executive from a corporation working in a related line of business, and officers from each of the consuming agencies (e.g., the army). The sections provided information to the functional divisions and maintained constant communication with the companies in specific lines of business. This communication was facilitated by the creation of war service committees representing industry by line of business. The members of the war service committees were selected by the heads of corporations and trade associations to act as agents in negotiations with the government. Although the war service committees were originally under the supervision of the Council of National Defense, the task was assigned to the U.S. Chamber of Commerce in the fall of 1917. "Where a national organization already existed, the chamber had it appoint a war service committee with authority to represent it, and where a trade was not organized, the chamber took steps to secure its organization and the appointment of such a committee."[18] The U.S. Chamber of Commerce also certified the committees as being broadly representative of firms within the industry.

The war service committees and the trade associations provided the WIB with access to critical information concerning supplies and resources. Moreover, they provided a context in which firms in an industry could trade information on production, costs, and pricing. When the WIB needed to address problems of supply or develop appropriate conservation measures, it relied heavily on the associations to hold conferences with corporate representatives from the industries. Finally, the associations provided much of the administrative support and staffing for the commodity sections.[19]

This organizational scheme conveyed quasi-official status on the trade associations and war service committees organized by the chamber. This devolution of authority and decentralization gave the WIB access to a new source of expertise and information. However, it also created distinct but predictable problems. As Robert Cuff explains: "Technical skill was concentrated along the outer edges of the WIB, within the commodity sections. This had important consequences for the distribution of authority within the organization, for it meant that much of the daily decision making affecting industry took place here through close consultation between industrial representatives and the various section heads. Decisions occurred, in other words, where the territory of the board and of industry overlapped, beyond the reach of central officials." The opportunities for abuse were obvious: "If the commodity chief became a lobbyist for his industry . . . there was little the board could do about it."[20] Fortunately, the brevity of U.S. involvement and rapid demobilization after the war limited the impact of these problems.

## The Policy Process

The central responsibilities of the War Industries Board included processing requirements and assigning priorities, controlling prices, and promoting conservation and efficiency in industry. The clearance of requirements and the assignment of priority designations to the various orders were the most critical functions. The Requirements Division was staffed by representatives of the WIB, the army and navy, the Emergency Fleet Corporation, the Allied Purchasing Committee, the Red Cross, the Railroad Administration, the Food Administration, and the Marine Corps. Agencies submitted their requirements for raw materials and finished products to the division. These requirements were subsequently turned over to the commodity sections where they were examined in light of the available resources, facilities, and production schedule, often with the consultation of the war service committees. In the end, they were returned to the division with estimates of when the orders could be met. As the war progressed, the process was hampered by the lack of long-term planning. At times, requirements simply exceeded productive capacity. In this context, it became essential for the WIB to develop some means of processing requirements to given immediate attention to emergency war-related demands and free labor, raw materials, energy, and transportation for defense production. To this end, the WIB established the priorities system.[21]

The Priorities Division examined the orders placed by the services and assigned each a priority designation, part of a complicated classification system. Orders that were of immediate military necessity were assigned the status of AA, whereas other orders were given a designation of declining significance (A, B, C, D). These classifications were combined with numbers (e.g., A-1, A-2) to further refine the system. Although the priorities system began with critical industries, by July 1, 1918, all industries were placed under WIB regulation. Firms failing to observe the priorities system could be commandeered and operated by the Secretary of War, under the authority granted in the National Defense Act of 1916. Short of this drastic measure, the WIB and other mobilization agencies could close off access to transportation and raw materials, making continued production impossible. These sanctions were sufficient to force compliance.

With the expansion of the priorities system to cover all industries, the job of the Priorities Division became increasingly complex. The demands placed on the division were addressed in several ways. First, a system of automatic classifications was established whereby class A orders placed by the navy, the War Department, and the Emergency Fleet Corporation would be assigned a rating of A-5 upon the submission of a signed affidavit describing the uses for the materials. Second, an additional organ, the Priorities Board, was created in March 1918. Under the leadership of Priorities Commissioner Edwin Parker, the board brought together representatives of the services and mobilization agencies to coordinate the ordering and delivery of high priority goods. Third, the priorities system was expanded on an economywide basis. In April 1918, the priorities system was expanded on an economywide basis to direct the flow of coal, coke, and transportation. By September 1918, the Priorities Board had placed 73 industries and some 7,000 plants according to a four-part classification. Class I industries and plants were deemed essential to the war effort; industries in lower classifications could not receive energy and transportation until the needs of the Class I installations had been met. The system for controlling the flow of energy and transportation maintained the war industries and created clear incentives for companies to convert to defense production.[22] In essence, a system for prioritizing the orders of the armed services had evolved into an experiment in economic planning and coordination on a much broader scale.

Initially, procurement depended on cost-plus contracting. Contracts were negotiated individually on the basis of the cost of production plus an acceptable rate of return. However, the process involved "endless disputes concerning the calculation of costs" and placed a "premium on inefficiency, because the more efficient a producer was, the lower his costs and the less his absolute profits."[23] Thus, the War Industries Board moved quickly to set prices on a broader scale through its price-fixing committee, chaired by Robert Brookings. Price fixing was perhaps the most sensitive economic issue associated with the mobilization process. It is for this reason, that the authority to fix prices was not concentrated in the hands of Baruch but was assigned to a price-fixing committee that was directly responsible to the president. To limit the conflicts inherent in the process, price fixing, like other activities at the WIB, was consultative. Rather than impose prices on business, the committee worked closely with trade associations and corporations to arrive at mutually acceptable estimates of the costs of production. The Federal Trade Commission facilitated the determination of prices by conducting investigations of production costs in critical sectors. Price schedules were revised every three months, largely to accommodate the increasing costs of labor that accompanied the labor shortage. The prices commonly took account of the smaller, high-cost producer who would not be capable of producing with the efficiency of its larger competitors. This fit well with the goal of setting prices to stimulate sufficient production. To assure that inflation would not run unrestrained in the civilian economy to compensate, President Wilson determined at a very early point that the administered prices would be maximum prices for military and civilian purposes. This decision created broad support for price fixing in the general population. Price fixing and the WIB's system of priorities worked together as critical components of a single system. Once market processes were suspended and thus were no longer sensitive to scarcity, some means had to be found to allocate products and raw materials to their most urgent use. The priorities system provided such a mechanism.

As noted earlier, the priorities system was designed both to meet immediate war needs and to transfer resources out of civilian production and into the war economy. This latter task was facilitated by the activities of the Conservation Division, under the direction of Arch W. Shaw. The Conservation Division, staffed in large part by Commerce Department bureaucrats, sought to free raw materials, labor, energy, and transportation by promoting greater efficiency in production, shipping and distribution. Much of the division's activities focused on reducing the number of styles and varieties of goods produced. Schedules of regulations were promulgated by the division after close consultation with the relevant trade associations which often made suggestions concerning areas for potential conservation. The regulations were distributed to producers for comments before they became legally binding. Subsequently, producers were required to pledge their compliance with conservation regulations or risk the loss of access to raw materials, energy, and transportation.[24]

Some of the most successful conservation measures promoted standardization, thus reducing the variety of goods produced. A number of examples are quite suggestive. Automobile tire producers reduced the styles and sizes of tires from 287 to 9 within two years, saving rubber, labor, and transportation costs. Standardization of farm implements led one manufacturer to reduce the variety of wagon gears from 1,736 to 16. Even seemingly trivial regulations could have a significant impact. A regulation requiring that thread manufacturers place 200 yards of thread on each spool, rather than the standard 100 to 150 yards, resulted in a 25 percent reduction in labor, wood, packing materials, while freeing some 600 freight cars per year for alternative uses. The schedule for regulations in the woman's clothing industry brought a 20 to 25 percent reduction in the yards of fabric. A related regulation requiring that knit goods be shipped in paper covered bales rather than boxes yielded an estimated annual reduction of 17,312 freight cars and 141 million boxes. These and a multitude of additional regulations left virtually no industry untouched.[25]

## Additional Mobilization Agencies

While the WIB was the central mobilization agency, other agencies deserve some mention. The U.S. Food Administration (USFA) was similar to the WIB both in its decentralization and the pattern of state-economy relations it promoted. The USFA was created in August of 1917 and placed under the direction of Herbert Hoover. Its major duty was to maintain the supply of food for the American Expeditionary Force (AEF) and the allies. The war made incredible demands on the agricultural sector. In the three years prior to the war (1914 to 1916) agricultural exports averaged 6,959,055 tons per year. Under Hoover's direction, exports reached an annual level of 18,667,378 tons by 1919. The USFA met the demand of war by promoting maximum production and conservation, limiting speculation, and calling for the substitution of surplus foodstuffs for those that were in high demand. To a limited extent, the administration stabilized prices and promoted production through direct market activity, by buying foodstuffs through the U.S. Grain Corporation and Sugar Equalization Board. However, regulation relied primarily on licenses, decentralized administration, and profit incentives that promised to raise agricultural incomes. Producers, distributors, and associations were provided with licenses upon agreeing to maintain open books, charge "reasonable" prices (i.e., cost plus the prewar average profit), and observe a variety of practices to prevent hording, speculation, waste, and the inefficient use of transportation.[26]

The administration of agricultural controls was highly decentralized. Each state was under the direction of a federal food administrator who supervised county administrators who, in turn, supervised special committees at the town level. To account for local variations in prices, boards were created at the county level where representatives of grocers, retailers, and consumers could negotiate and determine fair prices. These prices were published in local newspapers and used by the county administrators to determine whether licensees were meeting their obligation. Despite the decentralization of the administrative apparatus, new regulations were adopted only after the Food Administration had consulted extensively with the representatives of commodity groups and trade associations. As with the WIB, this consultation was facilitated by the decision to staff the agency with individuals drawn from the sector.[27]

The National War Labor Board (NWLB) was the key agency responsible for regulating industrial relations. During World War I, organized labor was integrated into the policy process through this tripartite board and representation on other bodies. Participation in the agencies reflected a growing consensus concerning labor's place in the political economy. By the time of the war, the leaders of the labor movement "accepted the reality and inevitability of the new corporate political economy" and began "to seek accommodation for the national unions within it." Thus, the AFL leadership envisioned a system in which "varying numbers of legally equivalent institutions established temporary or permanent accommodations with each other through voluntarist action and looked to the state simply for ratification of these bargains."[28] The regulation of labor was necessary to limit strikes, to provide a mechanism to adjust wages to changing prices, and to promote the transfer of labor to critical industries.[29] The Wilson administration sought to win labor support for the war effort by recognizing the right of workers to organize and engage in collective bargaining. Indeed, the NWLB operated on an official principle that anticipated the National Labor Relations Act: "The rights of workers to organize in trade unions and to bargain collectively through chosen representatives is recognized and affirmed. This right shall not be denied, abridged, or interfered with by the employers in any manner whatsoever."[30] The tight wartime labor markets and the administration's pro-labor position resulted in significant gains for labor. Union roles increased dramatically, from 2.77 million in 1916, to 4.125 million in 1919. Moreover, wage rates increased rapidly: The average annual wage for all industrial workers increased from $765 in 1916 to an unprecedented $1,272 by 1919.[31] Even when one accounts for the wartime inflation, the increase in wage levels was significant.

The WIB, USFA, and NWLB adopted decentralized structures and integrated private associations into the policy process. In certain key areas, however, a more authoritative role was necessary, giving rise to a form of state led planning that imposed more intervention than even the New Nationalists could have condoned absent of an emergency. This was particularly the case with the U.S. Railroad Administration, created in December 1917. A voluntary Railroad War Board formed by the railroads failed when it proved incapable of compensating lines that lost revenue as a result of pooling and equally incapable of coordinating its actions with the mobilization agencies. Problems with priority shipments, a failure to co-ordinate rail shipments and merchant marine vessels, and the resulting near collapse of the rail system and supply effort in 1917 necessitated direct government control. Under the direction of Treasury Secretary William G. McAdoo, the Railroad Administration pooled the lines to administer the national railways as an integrated system. Although the railroads were cautious about such a transfer of authority, the administration guaranteed an acceptable rate of return (based on the earnings during the period 1914 to 1917) and proper maintenance. The direct control of the rails was a success. Prior to the creation of the Railroad Administration, mobilization was plagued by a shortage of rail transportation. The pooling of freight and coordination of lines by the administration resulted in an actual surplus of 300,000 freight cars by the end of the war. Following the experience of unified operation, there were many advocates of some form of nationalization. Wilson rejected nationalization and an extension of wartime controls, thereby forcing Congress to pass new legislation. In the end, the Transportation Act of 1920 incorporated some of the features of wartime rail management into the regulatory activities of the Interstate Commerce Commission.[32]

## DEMOBILIZATION AND DEVELOPMENT

At the end of the war, some 9 million workers—approximately 25 percent of the labor force—were engaged in wartime production. Moreover, some 4 million members of the armed forces had to be reintegrated into the economy. To some extent, the returning soldiers displaced women workers who returned to domestic work. However, the rapid cancellation of defense orders created a problem of unemployment that could have been anticipated. Yet, there were no plans for reintegrating soldiers, minimizing displacement, or to reconvert war industries to a peacetime status. While unemployment surged during the winter of 1918 to 1919, the economy quickly entered a brief but rapid period of expansion as a product of pent-up consumer demand and high levels of personal savings, a product of wartime wages.[33]

The brief expansion of consumer spending, absent wartime price controls, resulted in a rapid price increases. Corporations, hoping to profit from the new demand and rising prices, purchased new capital equipment and began to build new facilities. Speculators also entered the fray, borrowing money for stock purchases. The rapid price increases began to erode consumer demand. However, public policy must be cited as the primary cause of the subsequent economic decline. In 1919, following a period of large wartime budget deficits, the federal government maintained the higher levels of taxation and reduced expenditures to produce budget surpluses. The reduction of fiscal stimulation was combined with Federal Reserve's restrictive monetary policy—a policy adopted out of concern over speculation and inflation. The combined effects of these factors resulted in a depression in January 1920. Unemployment reached 11.7 percent and real GNP fell by some 12 percent. The rapid expansion and optimism of 1919 had been dashed.[34] Although the depression was deep, it was also short lived. By mid-1921, recovery had begun, followed by a rapid period of expansion that continued for the next several years.

However, the economic instability of 1920 and the return of such trying economic problems following a period of unprecedented industrial expansion directed by the WIB raised an important question for many. How could the experiences of the war and the new relationship between the government, corporations, farmers, and labor be used to introduce order into the New Era?

In *Crisis and Leviathan*, Robert Higgs argues that crises result in a long-term increase in the size and scope of the federal government. After the cessation of hostilities, the size of the federal government never returns to the precrisis level, suggesting that there is something of a ratcheting effect.[35] This ratchet is certainly evident in the case of World War I. As Figure 5–1 shows, after the large fiscal stimulus of World War I, receipts and expenditures remained remarkably high when compared with their levels prior to the war. Similarly, as Figure 5–2 reveals, the levels of federal civilian employment increased dramatically in the years following the war, despite the period of Republican rule and the common belief that the era of active reform via federal policy had drawn to a close. These measures of the overall size of government are important. However, we are not simply concerned with "Big Government" versus "Small Government." Rather, we need to address the patterns of state-economy relations. To understand how these patterns were affected by the experience of the war, it is necessary to address the process of demobilization with some care.

Demobilization necessarily entails dismantling the wartime apparatus and lifting temporary controls on prices, wages, and production. However, one can also understand demobilization as a more protracted process. The demands of war force experimentation with new administrative models, policy tools, and patterns of state-interest group relations as officials seek to compensate for the limitations of existing institutions. Following war, the lessons may be disseminated through government agencies, altering their primary roles, routines, and relationships with eco-

**Figure 5–1**   Public Expenditures and Revenues, 1900–1930

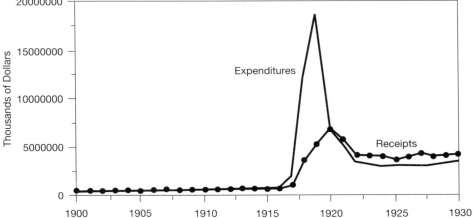

Source: *Statistical History of the United States*, Series Y254, 255.

**Figure 5–2**   Federal Civilian Employment, 1900–1939

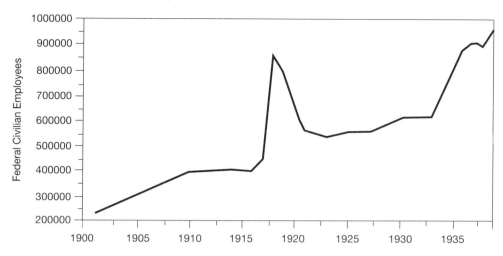

Source: *Statistical History of the United States*, Series Y241.

nomic and social interests. This, in turn, can affect the trajectory of peacetime political development. The impact can be seen through an examination of interwar regulation, economic policymaking, and labor relations.

## ASSOCIATIONALISM AND REGULATION

The WIB had an important impact both on patterns of state-economy relations and the expectations of organized economic actors. In a review of the War Industries Board conducted in 1921, Bernard Baruch addressed the potential role of business associations that emerged during the war:

> These associations, as they stand, are capable of carrying out purposes of greatest public benefit. They can increase the amount of wealth available for the comfort of the people by inaugurating rules designed to eliminate wasteful practices attendant upon multiplicity of styles and types of articles in the various trades; they can assist in cultivating the public taste for rational types of commodities; by exchange of trade information, extravagant methods of production and distribution can be avoided through them, and production will tend to be localized in places best suited economically for it. By acting as centers of information, furnishing lists of sources to purchasers and lists of purchasers to producers, supply and demand can be more economically balanced. From the point of vantage which competent men have at the central bureau of an association, not only can new demands be cultivated, but new sources of unexploited wealth can be indicated.[36]

Baruch's insights were borne out at the Commerce Department and the Federal Trade Commission which began to construct an associational system to promote efficiency, standardization, and "scientific competition." Before examining these agencies, it is useful to consider the vision of an associational order that animated Herbert Hoover's efforts.

Hoover assumed the position of commerce secretary in March 1921, with President Harding's promise that he would be allowed to expand the Department of Commerce and contribute to all aspects of national economic policy.[37] Hoover's wartime experiences reinforced his vision of cooperative planning and contributed to a distinctive model of the state and intercorporate relations. He stated his desire to discover "a plan of individualism and associational activities that will preserve the initiative, the inventiveness, the individuality, the character of man and yet will enable us to synchronize socially and economically this gigantic machine that we have built out of applied science."[38] Hoover's vision of the modern social order found its basis in an individualism that was "only in part an economic creed."[39] The nation "abandoned the laissez faire of the 18th Century" when it infused individualism with "the ideal of equality of opportunity." A new emphasis was placed on "social and economic justice." Hoover continues: "We have learned that the impulse to production can only be maintained at a high pitch if there is a fair division of the product . . . by certain restrictions on the strong and the dominant."[40] If an individualism tempered by equality of opportunity required that constraints be placed on the exercise of economic power, one was forced to ask two questions. First, who would impose the constraints? Second, what safeguards would exist to protect individualism? It was here that Hoover presented the need for an associational order.

Hoover rejected the concentration of political and economic power. In each case, "it necessitates a bureaucracy over the entire population" which "obliterate[s] the economic stimulation of each member." Hoover objected to "the basic foundations of autocracy, whether it be class government or capitalism in the sense that a few men through unrestrained control of property determine the welfare of great numbers." "The will-o'-the-wisp of autocracy in any form is that it supposes that the good Lord endowed a special few with all the divine attributes."[41] Hoover noted that "the American System holds equally that monopoly, group or class advantage, economic domination, Regimentation, Fascism, Socialism, Communism, or any other form of tyranny, small or great, are violations of the basis of Liberty."[42] If equal opportunity and social and economic justice cannot be guaranteed by the state and if bureaucratization threatens to extinguish individualism, Hoover argued, we must look to voluntary associations. These "organizations for advancement of ideas in the community for mutual cooperation and economic objectives" were vitally important for they provided "an opportunity for self-expression and participation in the moulding of ideas, a field for training and the stepping stones for leadership."[43] Moreover, "there are in the cooperative great hopes that we can even gain in individuality, equality of opportunity, and an enlarged field for initiative, and at the same time reduce many of the wastes of over-reckless competition in production and distribution."[44] Hoover was convinced that changes in the production process could yield great benefits: "The only road to further advance in the standard of living is by greater invention, greater elimination of waste, greater production and better distribution of commodities and services, for by increasing their ratio to our numbers and dividing them justly we each will have more of them."[45] A system of voluntary associations provided the best context for the realization of these goals free from the rigidity and control of the much feared bureaucracy.

Hoover was not the only proponent of this model. It should be no surprise that many business leaders adopted this model as well. The National Industrial Conference Board, for example, portrayed the trade association movement as a response to "the historical problem of reconciling freedom and authority." The authors of a volume published by the National Industrial Conference Board identified two economic extremes. First, there was "the individualistic policy of unfettered and unregulated competition" which engendered "much waste and ill-will and . . . such a degree of mastery . . . as to disillusion the most confirmed laissez-faire enthusiasts." In contrast, one could identify "the unpromising alternative of authoritative control of industry under official bureaucratic forms" which involved "such danger of inflexibility and stagnation in economic processes as to deter all but the most venturesome from embracing it." Between these two extremes, the trade association movement was evolving as a "synthesis of freedom and authority in the economic sphere." The authors concluded: "Stimulated by a developing sense of collective responsibility and held in check by the well-established mandates of public policy, the trade association movement may serve to reinvigorate the competitive system and facilitate the fulfillment of its best promise."[46] For Hoover and many of his contemporaries, voluntary association provided the basis for a cooperative social order, a form of "self-government outside of formal government."[47] While cooperative associations provided for economic governance free from the rigidities of bureaucratic control, the state could coordinate, supervise, and facilitate the activities of economic associations, thereby supporting a form of planning without simultaneously dictating the activities of industry or creating a centralized bureaucracy.[48]

## The Commerce Department: An Associational Experiment

Prior to Hoover's appointment, the Commerce Department had not been a powerful agency. However, under his direction Commerce expanded and entered entirely new areas of activity. By 1924, Hoover was actively promoting associationalism through close contacts with the Interior Department, the Labor Department, the Agriculture Department, the Justice Department's Antitrust Division, and the Federal Trade Commission. The goals of the activities at the FTC and other agencies were to promote "progressive organization and practice" and "to reinforce private ordering mechanisms with governmental power or approval."[49] Hoover's experiences as an engineer and his participation in wartime mobilization shaped his understanding of the potential benefits associated with eliminating wasteful practices in industry. Efficiency and an expansion of trade could ameliorate the postwar economic downturn and provide the basis for long-term growth. A 1921 survey of U.S. industry conducted during Hoover's presidency of the American Engineering Council determined that "25 per cent of the costs of production could be eliminated without reduction of wages, increase in hours or strain on workers." Hoover's goal was to "put this plan into voluntary action on a nation-wide scale through the Department of Commerce."[50] The elimination of waste required both the careful survey of existing industrial practices and the cooperative elimination of those deemed wasteful. It required, in short, that the Department of Commerce continue the activities of the WIB's Conservation Division.

Following the war, many of the Commerce Department personnel who had served on the WIB were drawn away into private sector employment. The Commerce Department compensated for this loss through a research associate program which brought researchers from industry, trade, and professional associations into the bureau for a limited term of service, funded by their corporate sponsors. They had full access to department facilities and provided an important link between the agency and corporations. The research associate program, combined with additional full-time staffing, allowed for an expansion of the Bureau of Standards.[51] In 1922, Hoover created a Division of Simplified Practices in the Bureau "to cooperate with American industries in furthering a nation-wide program for eliminating waste in commerce and industry by reducing the number and sizes and types of standard products."[52] The simplification process, established through the joint efforts of the Commerce Department, the U.S. Chamber of Commerce, and the American Engineering Standards Committee, was clearly patterned on the consensual procedures applied by the WIB. After the bureau conducted a survey of an industry and identified wasteful practices, it called a general meeting of producers, distributors, and commercial consumers. During these meetings, participants recommended product variations that could be eliminated without seriously affecting consumers. Once the recommendations were formally accepted by firms responsible for 80 percent of the production, they were disseminated as part of Commerce's *Elimination of Waste* Series. From the creation of the Division of Simplified Practices, in January 1922, to July 31, 1925, the Bureau held some 188 simplification conferences in Washington D.C. covering a variety of industries.[53]

The simplification process, Hoover claimed, yielded tremendous savings for industry: "Manufacturers were able to engage more fully in mass production, as they could produce for stocks instead of filling specific orders; the amount of inventories which must be carried by consumers was greatly reduced, and competition was enhanced in such articles."[54] Despite Hoover's enthusiasm, one could identify clear problems. First, rather than developing technical standards, the process adopted commercial standards and eliminated varieties for which there was little demand. This alienated Commerce engineers who watched their scientific mission sacrificed to commercial calculations. Second, simplification provided a strategic means of eliminating or damaging smaller competitors. Some product varieties which were targeted by the simplification process were the sole products of firms which lacked the resources to effectively mobilize and affect Commerce's decisions.[55] Despite the flaws, it is clear that the Commerce Department gave the wartime conservation efforts a new peacetime footing. Moreover, in this venture as throughout the associational state, cooperation was possible as long as it resulted in greater profitability for participants. While there is little evidence that prices were being fixed, the process narrowed the range of competition (e.g., product competition verses price competition) and standardization resulted in greater economies of scale and profitability. Of course, whether an associational system could be maintained absent the financial benefits remained an open question that would be answered by the end of the decade.

## The Federal Trade Commission: Associationalism as Strategic Adaptation

As noted in Chapter 4, the Federal Trade Commission (FTC) was created in 1914 to bring greater flexibility to antitrust and to eliminate many of the practices that might contribute to monopoly. The new regulatory procedures and the prohibition of "unfair methods of competition in commerce" in §5 of the Federal Trade Commission Act were designed for this purpose. However, the broad prohibition of §5 provided the opportunity to interpret the FTC's mandate in light of prevailing doctrines of state-economy relations and in light of existing political challenges. Although the FTC was an application of Wilson's New Freedom, it evolved in the 1920s to promote associationalism.

Soon after the FTC was created, its economists, accountants, and statisticians were enlisted in the war effort. At the end of the war, the FTC conducted an investigation of the meatpacking industry at Wilson's request. Its report revealed that the big-five meatpackers colluded to create territorial restrictions and inflate the price of livestock and finished products. New competition was impeded through the beef trust's control of stockyards, warehouses, cold storage facilities, and rail cars. The FTC recommended that the government take control of the facilities and administer them as a government monopoly.[56] The congressional reaction was striking: Senator James A. Watson (R-Indiana) successfully introduced a resolution authorizing an investigation of the FTC, arguing "there is reason to believe that a number of employees of the Federal Trade Commission have been, and now are, engaged in socialistic propaganda and in furthering the organization and growth of socialistic organization." The FTC's Chicago office was described as a center "of sedition and anarchy from which radiated the most baleful influence" and "a spawning ground for sovietism" where the FTC staff "plotted for the destruction of the businesses they were charged to investigate and for the confiscation and collective ownership of all the means for the creation and redistribution of wealth." Watson denied that his resolution was "a defense of the packers" but was an effort "to call attention . . . to the socialistic activities of some of the employees of the Federal Trade Commission."[57]

The Senate investigated and exonerated the bureaucrats who executed the study. However, by the end of 1920, all had been fired under the pretense of funding reductions, presumably in an attempt to gain favor from Senator Watson who could exercise great control over FTC appropriations. The scandal also forced one commissioner, W.B. Colver, to decline reappointment. In 1921, Congress transferred jurisdiction over the industry to the Agriculture Department.[58] Despite the concessions to Congress, the FTC's appropriations declined from a wartime high of $1.75 million in 1919, to $974,480 in 1923. While these cuts reflected the movement to a peacetime structure, they occurred in the midst of the conflicts over the alleged politicization of the FTC. For the remainder of the decade, the budget remained relatively stable, increasing slightly to $1.16 million in 1929. The FTC staff (which reached a high of 663 in 1918) fell to 308 in 1923 and increased gradually to 380 in 1929. Congress also limited the FTC's authority by requiring that investigations be initiated only under a concurrent resolution of Congress or evidence of antitrust violations. The effects of the budget cuts and the goal of reducing conflicts with Congress are evident in the enforcement record: The FTC filed 116 cease-and-desist orders in 1921—a number which declined to 44 orders by 1926.[59]

The Supreme Court contributed to the FTC's difficulties in 1920, in its first opportunity to decide on a FTC decision. The dispute in *Federal Trade Commission v. Gratz* was less important than the effects of the decision on commission discretion. The FTC was created to bring flexibility and expertise to antitrust. Yet, when it issued its complaint under the broad prohibition of §5 of the FTC Act, the Court rejected this power. The decision proclaimed: "The words 'unfair methods of competition' are not defined in the statute and their exact meaning is in dispute. It is for the courts and not the Commission ultimately to decide what they include. They are clearly inapplicable to practices never heretofore regarded as opposed to good morals because characterized by deception, bad faith, fraud, or oppression, or against public policy because of their dangerous tendency unduly to hinder competition or create monopoly."[60] With this decision, the Court "reduced the Commission's jurisdiction to a repetition of common-law formulas."[61] The *Gratz* decision came as a blow to supporters of the FTC. Justice Brandeis objected that the decision denied the central mission of the FTC: "The task of the Commission was to protect competition from further inroads by monopoly. . . . [it] was directed to intervene, before any act should be done or conditions arise violative of the Antitrust Act. . . . Its purpose in respect to restraints of trade was prevention of diseased business conditions, not cure." Brandeis believed that inflexible legal standards would leave unfair methods of competition untouched.

Given this hostile environment, the FTC emphasized trade practice conferences to create a cooperative context for the definition of rules. The voluntarism of the new system allowed the FTC to circumvent the courts and avoid further conflicts with Congress. In February 1925, President Coolidge appointed William E. Humphrey, a strong advocate of cooperative regulation, to create a Republican majority on the commission. Speaking before the Chamber of Commerce in 1925, Humphrey made a promise reminiscent of Watson's allegations a few years earlier: "So far as I can prevent it, the Federal Trade Commission is not going to spread socialistic propaganda. In so far as I can prevent it, the commission is not going to be used to advance the political or personal fortunes of any person or party."[62] In March 1925, the FTC announced new procedures which reflected Humphrey's influence. New opportunities were created for informal hearings prior to the issuance of a formal complaint, and businesses were now allowed to settle cases by pledging to end the questionable practices without a formal complaint and the attendant publicity. Most important for present purposes, the FTC placed primary emphasis on trade practice conferences to establish rules of conduct. After the commission created a Trade Practice Conference Division in 1926, "to encourag[e] closer cooperation between business as a whole and the commission," the use of this policy tool increased dramatically.[63] During the next five years, the number of conferences continued to grow, reaching a high of 57 in 1930. In the end, the number of requests for conferences exceeded the capacities of the division.[64] The FTC justified the procedural changes by explaining: "The new policies have principally to do with the idea of self-regulation in business and industry, and it has been possible to progress in these directions without over-stepping the bounds of the commission's powers as laid down by law. 'Helping business to help itself' wherever and whenever it can be done consistently without prejudice to the best interests of the public as a whole is the principle of this new policy." The Chamber of Commerce supported the FTC by urging the formation of "joint trade relations committees" in every line of business to participate in the conferences.[65] This support, however, was not universal. Proponents of active regulation cited 1925 as the end of an effective commission and unsuccessfully called for eliminating the budget of the Harding-Coolidge FTC.[66]

Trade practice conferences were held upon application by a trade association or major corporations. At the conferences, the FTC facilitated a discussion of the practices that were unfair, unethical, or in violation of the antitrust laws. Standards were accepted following a positive affirmation of industry actors. Rules fell into two categories: Group I rules applied the imprecise antitrust prohibitions to specific industries; Group II rules were "expressions of trade" (i.e., activities that were unfair or unethical but legal) and enforced by the trade associations.[67] The conferences integrated trade associations into the regulatory process in the development of new rules, the enforcement of Group II rules, and the initiation of formal complaints. Indeed, by 1928, trade association complaints led to over 400 FTC investigations into rule violations and some 100 formal complaints and/or cease-and-desist orders.[68]

Trade practice conferences allowed the FTC to replace conflict with cooperation while providing a more efficient and equitable process than the traditional case-by-case approach to regulation.[69] As a result, the conferences received the enthusiastic support of business. The National Industrial Conference Board reported that the conferences were "promising signs . . . of a more cordial relationship between coercive and voluntary agencies for the regulation of business conduct." The board surveyed existing government-association activities and noted that they kept alive "the expectation of eventually obtaining legal sanction for unified regulation of supply and control of price, when exercised with moderation and self-restraint."[70] As the codes evolved from the simple application of existing legal prohibitions to particular industries to "practices which had never been recognized as unlawful . . . the interest of the business community increased."[71]

The associational model of state-economy relations ultimately came into conflict with the more traditional model represented in antitrust, claiming the FTC's new practices. In 1929, the FTC decided to condemn as fraudulent actions the secret violation of trade practice rules, thereby actively enforcing Group II rules. Moreover, there were growing concerns that many of the Group II rules restrained competition and were liable to prosecution under the antitrust laws. While Assistant Attorney General John Lord O'Brian testified before Congress that he had found no cases where firms were violating the antitrust laws "on the advice" of the FTC, they commonly "used the rule as a cover of pretext for illegal practices."[72] Under pressure from the Justice Department, the FTC decided unilaterally to reconsider all existing rules. The Chamber of Commerce quickly mobilized corporations and trade associations to preserve the rules. Although this effort was partially successful, the FTC's new posture destroyed business support for the conferences. In 1930, the number of trade practice conferences peaked at 57; the next year, the FTC held 9 conference and revised rules for 62 industries.[73] The unilateral rule revisions purged businesses of the incentive to participate in the conferences.[74]

## LABOR AND WELFARE CAPITALISM

While Hoover promoted associationalism at the Commerce Department and debates over economic policy were addressing the possibility of scientific management of the business cycle, change was also evident in the area of labor. The nation entered into a historically unprecedented period of industrial conflict immediately following the war. More than 4 million workers took part in some 3,630 strikes in 1919 alone. To some extent, the strikes marked an attempt to protect wartime wage gains from the postwar inflation. However, the militancy also reflected the desire to win recognition of labor rights outside of the emergency situation of war. The promise of a new regulatory system and a new relationship between the state and economy was great in the wake of the activities of the NWLB. However, the efforts on the part of Wilson to place the wartime system on peacetime foundations floundered.[75]

The activities of the NWLB drew to a close on June 30, 1919. The failure to extend the key features of the industrial relations system was tied to a number of factors. Major corporations and the National Association of Manufacturers attacked the board's conciliatory posture toward labor; the AFL responded to the board's demise with ambivalence. Although Wilson advocated a continuation of the wartime system, he faced an unsympathetic Congress. Wilson called a tripartite Industrial Conference in 1919 to facilitate the development of proposals for a new peacetime industrial relations system. Ultimately, conflicts over the question of worker representation and the independent powers of a new agency combined with Wilson's ailing health and the Red Scare to create formidable barriers to an extension of the wartime system. Business delegates voted against a critical resolution on the right of workers to bargain through representatives of their own choosing, forcing the AFL to abandon the proceedings. With no regulatory system in place, industrial relations returned to their prewar status, albeit with higher levels of unionization and new labor militancy.[76]

Absent a system for regulating industrial relations, the conflicts between business and labor were resolved in the market with the active intervention of the courts. As in the past, the courts were less than accommodating to the demands of labor. In part, this reflected a commitment to liberty of contract. Under prevailing court doctrine, the employment relationship was understood as a contractual relationship between a worker and a business. The status of the union in this arrangement was less than obvious. Thus, in *Adkins* v. *Children's Hospital* (1923) the Court overturned a minimum wage law on precisely this basis. A minimum wage was portrayed as a legislative effort to fix a price of a commodity (i.e., labor) and thus interfere with the liberty of contract. The Court also protected the use of yellow-dog contracts and injunctions, going as far as to overturn an Arizona law that banned the use of injunctions in labor cases (*Truax* v. *Corrigan*, 1921). In this instance, the ability to appeal for an injunction in labor disputes was considered a necessary protection of property rights; to ban injunctions would be tantamount to depriving the businessman of property without due process of law.[77]

The image of two parties freely contracting over the terms of the wage bargain was difficult to sustain in the 1920s, given the powerful tools at the disposal of corporations intent on limiting the success of organized labor. Injunctions, yellow-dog contracts, black lists, labor spies, and physical violence were used regularly by large corporations. Moreover, organized propaganda campaigns were common, beginning with the Red Scare of 1919 and continuing throughout the decade. These efforts were combined with open shop laws—a key element of the "American Plan." However, managers quickly discovered an even more subtle and effective means of limiting the organization of labor. They could subvert the role of unions by creating company unions and work councils. By assuming the key functions of the unions, it was hoped, unions could be rendered unnecessary and thus would die a natural death.

Welfare capitalism constituted the most important effort to limit the growing power of unions. The efforts of Owen D. Young and Gerald Swope of General Electric were perhaps the best known examples of welfare capitalism. Workers were given nominal representation on workers councils and provided a host of benefits including group insurance, retirement pensions, medical clinics, and stock ownership. The companies sought to construct a social world complete with clubs and recreational activities to increase worker identification with the business enterprise.[78] Fused with norms of scientific management, welfare capitalism constituted an attempt to manage employee relations and create a cooperative system that could promote efficient production. Some 400 company unions were in place by 1926, representing over 1.3 million workers.[79]

Welfare capitalism was successful in several respects. First, it resulted in a dramatic reduction of strike activity. There were 3,630 strikes in 1919, followed by another 3,411 in 1920. By the end of the decade, the number of strikes had fallen significantly. Between 1926 and 1930, there were an average of 780 strikes per year. Moreover, total union membership declined from over 5 million in 1920 to 3.6 million by the end of the decade, suggesting the success of welfare capitalism in undermining the perceived need for unions. This reduction in unionization levels and worker militancy was combined with a 20 percent increase in real wages between 1921 and 1928.[80] The system of welfare capitalism fit nicely into Hooverian associationalism. Large corporations could cooperate with each other to reduce inefficiencies in production. They could cooperate with their workers to promote additional efficiency gains while investing some of the profits into the welfare of their workers. The system promised greater social welfare without the bureaucratic structures that Hoover so feared. However, there was a critical flaw in this system. The resources necessary to maintain worker benefits—the de facto welfare state for many—was dependent on positive economic performance. Economic contraction would increase the incentives to eliminate excess labor and simultaneously the insurance and health programs that provided some hope of security. In the end, the Great Depression revealed both the limits of Hooverian associationalism and welfare capitalism.

## ECONOMIC PLANNING AND THE BUSINESS CYCLE

War presents some difficult economic problems for policymakers. Four problems are immediately apparent. First, there is the problem of prices. The shortages of consumer goods, the pressure on labor markets, and the higher levels of money in the economy due to full employment create strong inflationary pressures. The price system plays an important role in stimulating a movement of resources into different sectors of the economy. High and variable rates of inflation can distort the market signals. Second, policymakers must address the problem of funding the war effort. Wars are accompanied by an expansion of taxation. Rates are increased; taxes are extended to goods and activities previously untaxed. However, the financial demands of modern war limit the extent to which taxation can be used to fulfill the needs. Thus, there has been a great reliance on war debt, incurred through the issuance of new debt instruments such as war bonds. Third, some means has to be discovered for funding industrial expansion. The transformation of a peacetime economy to a war posture can be partially accomplished by converting existing facilities. However, it is also necessary to fund the creation of altogether new factories and plants. Unfortunately, war finance creates shortages of investment capital and thus limits the extent to which, absent direct government investment, such expansion can take place. Finally, the question of trade becomes critical in wartime because of the need to rely on imports to provide critical inputs in the production of munitions.

From a fiscal perspective, the war could not have come at a better time. The Sixteenth Amendment, ratified in February 1913, made the income tax available as a new source of revenues. Before the war, over 90 percent of federal revenues were derived from excise taxes and customs. While there was an increase of the federal government's reliance on the income tax after 1913—income taxes provided 16 percent of federal revenues by 1916—the war was truly a transformative event. During the period 1917 to 1920, a majority of government revenues, an average of 58.6 percent, came from corporate and individual income taxes. This transformation occurred, in large part, through the War Revenue Act of 1917, a highly progressive tax act which lowered exemptions, increased the tax rates, and placed a surcharge on incomes over $1 million. This act alone increased federal revenues from $86 billion in 1917 to $3.76 billion in 1918. Subsequent revenue acts in 1918 and 1919 brought additional increases in marginal rates and imposed a war profits tax based on the change in profits from pre-war levels.[81] While the increase in revenues appears to be astounding, for the vast majority there was no change in the tax code . They remained well below the maximum exemption. The tax acts of 1917 to 1919 were remarkably progressive. Indeed, as John Witte correctly notes: "In effect the income taxes were class legislation—a fact explaining some of their appeal. For 1920, the year in which the most returns were filed, there were only 5.5 million taxable returns for a population of 106 million and a labor force estimated at 41.7 million."[82]

While the income tax provided the government with a new and powerful source of revenue, the demands of war required a movement into the bond market. Despite cautious predictions of the size of the bond market (estimated in 1917 to be some 350,000 people), patriotic appeals, high yields, low denominations, installment plans, and federal income tax exemptions dramatically increased the demand for war bonds. Moreover, the Federal Reserve provided low rates of interest for member banks, increasing their reserves so that they could purchase government bonds for their own portfolios or lend funds to individual buyers. As a result, after four Liberty Loans and a Victory Loan, the Treasury issued bonds worth $21.5 billion in the period 1917 to 1919. Sales were facilitated by investment bankers who marketed the bonds through participation in the War Loan Organization, the National War Savings Committee, and Liberty Loan Committees.[83]

The success of the Liberty Loan drives created some immediate problems for the economy and, ultimately, expanded the government's role in capital markets. The appeal of the war bonds was so great that capital was drawn out of financial institutions and invested in the war. At the same time, the tax exemptions created incentives for wealthy investors to substitute the war bonds for commercial stocks and bonds. The lack of capital for investment was particularly problematic in industries deemed essential for the war effort. To remedy the war-related capital shortage, the War Finance Corporation (WFC) was created in April 1918 to supply $500 million in credit—and in exceptional cases, direct loans—to essential industries, railroads, and savings institutions that might otherwise be forced to sell assets in a highly depressed market.[84]

Beyond the financial activities of the WFC, the government entered the securities markets for the first time, executing duties that presaged the activities of the Securities and Exchange Commission some 15 years later. In 1918, the Federal Reserve created the Capital Issues Committee. It reviewed capital issues over $100,000 to determine whether they were necessary by assessing what percentage of the issue would be devoted to war related activities. Moreover, the committee evaluated the quality of the issue through an examination of the information disclosed in the prospectus. Finally, it manipulated the timing of the release of new securities issues so that they would not coincide with Liberty Loan drives. When the Capital Issues Committee suspended operation in December 1918, it had approved new securities issues worth some $3.7 billion, disapproving of approximately $920 million.[85]

In the area of economic policy, the war left two legacies worth addressing. First, the economic demands of the war forced the federal government to manage money markets actively and to consider the fiscal impact of decisions concerning taxation and spending. For some, these experiences suggested a role for economic policy following the war. To what extent could the Federal Reserve use its control over money markets to manage the business cycle? To what extent could the federal government attempt to design strategies of countercyclical spending to promote growth and limit the pain of recessions? It is often and mistakenly assumed that the debates over the fiscal and monetary role of the state began during the New Deal. The 1920s, according to this account, was a period of laissez-faire economics in which policymakers held fast to classical notions of the economy and flirted with

from others; and, on the other hand, you will find when there is deflation the farmers and others blaming Rockefeller and Morgan and others personifying Wall Street as the cause of their troubles when as a matter of fact the cause is an impersonal one. One of those unjust accusations that the creditor class controls the price level, or the debtor class, you have the evils of distrust and suspicion and ill feeling and class warfare and sometimes bloodshed.[92]

Fisher concluded: "This is not a radical measure, therefore, that is proposed here; it is a way to fight radicalism. It is one of the most conservative measures you have had. It is not a hair-brained dreamer's idea; it is something that will prevent the kind of upset that they had in Russia."[93]

Despite Fisher's active advocacy throughout the 1920s, the independence of the Federal Reserve was deemed too important to permit the political direction of its activities. The central bankers led by Benjamin Strong were skeptical of Fisher's proposals for practical and ideological reasons. They did not believe that one could conduct monetary policy via formula because the price level was driven by a host of forces (e.g., harvests, technological change, events in other nations) over which they could exercise little or no control. Monetary management was considered more an art than a science. Moreover, the notion of requiring the Fed to stabilize prices raised the question of whether that might entail stabilizing incomes at artificially high prices to meet the political demands of strong constituencies (e.g., farmers). Finally, there were concerns that using monetary policy to stabilize domestic prices would require abandoning the maintenance of stability in external exchange rates. Nonetheless, there is evidence that the Fed did engage in some limited open market activities to counter the economic impact of the influx of gold into the American economy during the 1920s with the goal of maintaining. Indeed, there is something of a consensus that Benjamin Strong, the de facto head of the Federal Reserve, was quite successful in acting precisely as Irving Fisher would have required, thus explaining the stability of much of the 1920s.[94]

While Hoover and others believed that monetary policy was important, they placed a far greater emphasis on fiscal policy. In the fall of 1921, the Commerce Department hosted the President's Conference on Unemployment, chaired by Hoover. The conference brought together policymakers, representatives of labor, finance, manufacturing, mining, the railroads, and academic economists. The conference was charged with considering plans to alleviate unemployment, and to provide "a long-view study of the business cycle of booms and slumps and their alleviation."[95] Hoover opened the conference by calling on its members to help identify "the measures that would tend to prevent the acute reaction of economic tides in the future." He presented the task in associational terms: "The Administration has felt that a large degree of solution could be expected through the mobilization of co-operative action of our manufacturers and employers, of our public bodies and local authorities, and that if solution could be found in these directions we would have accomplished even more than the care of our unemployed." As a means to this end, the conference was expanded through state branches and subcommittees at the city and county levels to mobilize public and private resources "to look after the destitute."[96]

The immediate concern of the conference was the existing recession which, by its own estimates, left between 3.5 and 5.5 million unemployed. A number of recommendations were made for creating employment services, expediting private construction and maintenance projects, and promoting public works spending. Manufacturers were asked to contribute to the program by reducing hours and days or work rather than laying off workers and by expanding construction, repair, and production for stocks. Moreover, it was suggested that Congress move quickly to reduce the wartime income and corporate taxes, conclude the readjustment of railway rates, and complete work on the tariff legislation. Finally, the conference called for "definite programs of action that will lead to elimination of waste and more regulator employment in seasonal and intermittent industries . . . in order that the drain upon capital may be lessened and the annual income of workers may be increased."[97]

While the efforts to address the immediate crisis were important, the bulk of the report was devoted to long-term planning in eliminating the impact of the business cycle. To this end, the report carried a number of recommendations for business. The report noted that the "extremes [of the business cycle] are vicious, and the vices of the one beget the vices of the other. It is the wastes, the miscalculations, and the maladjustments grown rampant during booms that make inevitable the painful process of liquidation." As one might expect, the report called on businesses to "check the feverish extremes of prosperity."[98] The federal government, working with trade and commercial associations, should "keep up [the] campaign for simplification of styles and varieties" and "advertise [the] advantages of planning and budgeting." Moreover, during the heights of the business cycle, the government and associations should work together to promote the "advantages of withholding postponable projects." During a recession, the focus would shift to advertising "to business men [the] advantage of undertaking some work for the future, especially work of high labor, low material content." It was hoped that these efforts would be combined with a policy on the part of the Federal Reserve and bankers' associations to grant "preferential treatment to loans for productive purposes."[99]

In terms of public policy, the key problem for the conference was the timing of public investment during the business cycle: "When public works are done in greatest volume during periods of active industry the same men and material are being competed for by both public and private employers. The inevitable result is to raise the height of the crest of the wave of cyclical business inflation and to cause a greater crash when the heightened wave breaks, as it always does."[100] Public works programs are "peculiarly suited for consideration as large undertakings covering a long period and capable of elasticity of execution to synchronize with cycles of business depression." Such countercyclical use of public works spending could provide "a powerful stabilizing influence."[101] It was believed that expanded public works programs during downturns in the business cycle could result in direct and indirect stimulation. The effects of the public spending would reverberate throughout the economy through a "multiplying effect."[102]

The strategy of countercyclical public works spending was strongly advocated by Hoover, who devoted some time to supporting legislation authorizing such a program. The debates over a new economic strategy were combined with changes in the management of the budget. A Bureau of the Budget was created under the Budget and Accounting Act of 1921. By providing the president with budgetary authority, the act constituted a significant transfer of power from the Congress to the executive. The Bureau of the Budget, located in the Treasury but under the direction of the president, provided the president with administrative support in countering agency autonomy and developing appropriations targets. The creation of presidential budgetary authority was the realization of recommendations that dated back to the Taft presidency and the 1912 recommendations of the President's Commission of Economy and Efficiency. Presumably, the bureau could facilitate the use of countercyclical public works spending.[103]

With a new fiscal strategy and new institutions of budgetary control, one might have expected progress toward active fiscal policymaking. However, there were three great impediments to policy change. First, many academic economists continued to view the business cycle as a natural expression of economic change and believed that attempts to control it were misplaced. It would take the Keynesian revolution to change this position and legitimize systematic fiscal management. Second, the economic concerns of the 1920s remained focused on the costs of the war. The war demanded a dramatic expansion of the national debt, which stood at $24.3 billion in 1920, as compared with $1.2 billion four years earlier. The war also forced an increase in taxation beyond what most believed prudent given the limited responsibilities of the national government. Reflecting this fact, debt repayment became a primary concern for Congress and Treasury Secretary Andrew Mellon, followed closely by tax reductions. To this end, the federal government ran a surplus every year from 1920 through 1930, reducing the debt to $16.2 billion.[104] Finally, the government played a relatively small role in the economy during the 1920s. Spending at all levels of government claimed a mere 5.5 percent of Gross National Product—a figure which fell to 3.2 percent by 1929. While the federal government was able to spend at far greater levels at the state and local levels during the war, this emergency violation of federalism could not be justified under conditions of normalcy. Thus, the new strategies of fiscal and monetary management were never fully enacted—a failure with consequences that would become clear only with the onset of the depression.[105]

In the absence of a system of countercyclical spending such as that advocated by Hoover and legal monetary decision rules such as those promoted by Fisher, macroeconomic management rested primarily on the actions of one man—Benjamin Strong, governor of the New York Fed. If the Federal Reserve was relatively successful in managing the economy for extended periods during the 1920s, one must determine why this record broke down at the end of the decade as the nation fell into depression. Although there are several competing positions, most analysts emphasize  untimely death of Benjamin Strong and the change in leadership at the Federal Reserve, combined with changes in the composition of the open market committee. No less an authority than Irving Fisher repeatedly stated that the depression would not have occurred if Benjamin Strong had lived and continued to direct monetary policy through the New York Federal Reserve Bank. As Fisher testified before Congress: "I myself believe very strongly that this depression was almost wholly preventable, and that it would have been prevented if Governor Strong had lived." Fisher explained that Strong "discovered . . . that open-market operations would stabilize . . . and for 7 years he maintained a fairly steady price level in this country, and only a few of us knew what he was doing. His colleagues did not understand it."[106] Similarly, Carl Snyder, who described Strong "as perhaps the most prescient financier this country had produced since Alexander Hamilton," speculated: "Could this man have had twelve months more of vigorous health, we might have ended the depression in 1930, and with this the long drawn out world crisis that so profoundly affected the ensuing political developments."[107]

Strong's leadership was considered particularly important given the structure of the Federal Reserve system. A compelling case can be made for the proposition that the institutional structure and the lack of consensus over the proper objectives for the Fed's policies undermined the Fed's capacity to execute policy. As John Kenneth Galbraith notes: "The idea of a decentralized central bank—twelve central banks, each operating in some measure of undefined independence of its fellows and of Washington—did not yet seem a contradiction in terms. Rather, it looked a spacious and democratic idea, somehow appropriate to the spacious and democratic idea, somehow appropriate to the spacious democracy which the banks would serve."[108] The decentralization of the Federal Reserve system robbed the Board of the influence necessary for coherent policymaking. The 12 district banks—particularly the New York bank—actively affected credit through their open market and loan activities. This decentralization would have been less troublesome if there had been a genuine consensus over policy goals. There were debates over whether the Fed should promote price stability, facilitate business expansion, or seek to curb speculation. When the district banks disagreed with the board, they frequently acted unilaterally, thus cancelling out the impact of monetary policy. In 1929, for example, the Fed's attempt to limit credit by selling securities was partially nullified by an expansion of district bank activities. Without institutional coherence or a common theoretical consensus, the Fed's capacity to manage the economy remained painfully limited.

Fisher's position is echoed by Milton Freidman and Anna Jacobson Schwartz in their *Monetary History of the United States*. Strong was replaced at the New York Federal Reserve Bank by George L. Harrison who, according to Friedman and Schwartz, initially "operated in Strong's legacy and sought to exercise comparable leadership. As time went on, however, he reverted to his natural character, that of an extremely competent lawyer and excellent administrator, who wanted to see all sides of an issue and placed great value on conciliating opposing points of view and achieving harmony." He was "too reasonable to be truly single minded and dominant."[109] Harrison's appointment came at a critical time. With Strong's death, the Federal Reserve Board attempted to assert its authority but was simply too divided to do so effectively. Likewise, reflecting established institutional relations, the reserve banks were unwilling to follow the direction of the board. Thus, in March 1930, changes were made in the composition of the Open Market Investment Committee so that all 12 reserve banks would be represented, albeit without the leadership formerly exercised by Strong. "Open market operations now depended upon a majority of twelve rather than of five governors and the 'twelve came instructed by their directors' rather than ready to follow the leadership of New York as the five had been when Strong was governor."[110] The results were predictable. In the words of Friedman and Schwartz, "that shift stacked the cards heavily in favor of a policy of inaction and drift."[111]

While the origin of the Great Depression remains a source of lively scholarly debate, there are at least two points of agreement. First, the downturn of 1929 might not have turned into the Great Depression absent serious policy errors on the part of the Federal Reserve. The Federal Reserve adopted a restrictive policy precisely when it should have been acting in an expansionary mode. As suggested here, much of this policy failure may be attributed to the loss of Strong's leadership at a time when fiscal and monetary policy tools remained underdeveloped. Secondly, the responses adopted by President Hoover were severely limited by the very features of the associational state he had created. As stressed in this chapter, the combination of the war experience and Herbert Hoover's advocacy resulted in the broad dissemination of a model of state-economy relations that was, in some respects, uniquely American. Prefaced on the fear of large government and bureaucratic structures, the new model placed a great deal of emphasis on corporate self-governance, associationalism, and voluntarism. Hoover believed, incorrectly as it turned out, that such a model could provide the basis for a recovery from (or avoidance of) downturns in the business cycle. This belief would be tested and discarded once tested in the crucible of the Great Depression.

## NOTES

1. Ellis W. Hawley, *The Great War and the Search for a Modern Order* (New York: St. Martin's Press, 1979), p. 19.
2. See Theodore Roosevelt, *The New Nationalism* (Englewood Cliffs, N.J.: Prentice Hall, 1961); and Woodrow Wilson, *The New Freedom: A Call for the Emancipation of the Generous Energies of a People* (New York: Doubleday, Page & Co., 1913).
3. Arthur S. Link, *Woodrow Wilson and the Progressive Era, 1910–1917* (New York: Harper & Brothers, 1954), p. 180.
4. Arthur S. Link, *American Epoch: A History of the United States Since the 1890s* (New York: Alfred A. Knopf, 1958), pp. 177–78
5. See Stephen Skowronek, *Building a New American State: The Expansion of Administrative Capacities, 1877–1920* (Cambridge: Cambridge University Press, 1982), pp. 228–41.
6. Link, *Woodrow Wilson and the Progressive Era*, pp. 187–91.
7. John F. Witte, *The Politics and Development of the Federal Income Tax* (Madison: University of Wisconsin Press, 1985), pp. 195–96.
8. See Edward M. Coffman, "The Battle Against Red Tape: Business Methods of the War Department General Staff, 1917–1918." *Military Affairs* 26,1 (1962):1–10.
9. Grosvenor B. Clarkson, *Industrial America in the World War: The Strategy Behind the Lines, 1917–1918* (Boston: Houghton Mifflin, 1923), p. 111.
10. Bernard M. Baruch, *American Industry in the War: A Report of the War Industries Board, 1921* (New York: Prentice Hall, 1941), p. 17.
11. Ibid., p. 19.
12. Link, *American Epoch*, pp. 207–09.
13. Frederick Palmer, *Newton D. Baker: America at War* (New York: Dodd, Mead & Co., 1931), p. 353.
14. See Clarkson, *Industrial America in the World War*, p. 37.
15. Correspondence of President Woodrow Wilson to Bernard M. Baruch, March 4, 1918. Reproduced in Bernard M. Baruch, *American Industry in the War: A Report of the War Industries Board (March 1921)* (New York: Prentice Hall, 1941), pp. 24–25.

16. George Soule, *Prosperity Decade* (London: Pilot Press, 1947), p. 15.

17. John Maurice Clark, *The Costs of War to the American People* (New Haven, Conn.: Yale University Press, 1931), p. 34.

18. Baruch, *American Industry in the War*, p. 22.

19. Robert D. Cuff, *The War Industries Board: Business-Government Relations During World War I* (Baltimore, Md.: Johns Hopkins University Press, 1973), pp. 158–73.

20. Ibid., p. 174.

21. Clarkson, *Industrial America in the World War*, pp. 116–17.

22. Baruch, *American Industry in the War*, pp. 53–58.

23. Clarkson, *Industrial America in the World War*, p. 172.

24. Baruch, *American Industry in the War*, pp. 65–67.

25. Ibid., pp. 67–71.

26. Soule, *Prosperity Decade*, pp. 20–29.

27. See Simon Litman, *Prices and Price Control in Great Britain and the United States During the World War.* Carnegie Endowment for International Peace, Preliminary Economic Studies of the War, No. 19 (New York: Oxford University Press, 1920), pp. 206–61; Albert N. Merritt, *War Time Control of Distribution of Foods* (New York: Macmillan, 1920), pp. 29–36.

28. Christopher L. Tomlins, *The State and the Unions: Labor Relations, Law, and the Organized Labor Movement in America, 1880–1960* (Cambridge: Cambridge University Press, 1985), pp. 61, 77.

29. See Clark, *The Costs of War to the American People*, p. 47.

30. E. Jay Howenstine, Jr., *The Economics of Demobilization* (Washington, D.C.: American Council on Public Affairs, 1944), p. 147.

31. *Statistical History of the United States*, Series D 589-602, 604.

32. Soule, *Prosperity Decade*, pp. 33–35.

33. Peter Fearon, *War, Prosperity, and Depression: The U.S. Economy 1917–45* (Lawrence: University Press of Kansas, 1987), pp. 15–16.

34. Ibid., pp. 16–18.

35. See Robert Higgs, *Crisis and Leviathan: Critical Episodes in the Growth of the American Government* (New York: Oxford University Press, 1987), pp. 20–34.

36. Baruch, *American Industry in the War*, p. 106.

37. Herbert Hoover, *The Memoirs of Herbert Hoover, vol. 2, 1920–1933* (New York: Macmillan, 1952), p. 36; Ellis W. Hawley, "Herbert Hoover and Economic Stabilization, 1921–22," In *Herbert Hoover as Secretary of Commerce, 1921–28: Studies in New Era Thought and Practice*, ed. Ellis W. Hawley (Iowa City: University of Iowa Press, 1981), pp. 49–50.

38. Quoted in Edwin T. Layton, Jr., *The Revolt of the Engineers: Social Responsibility and the American Engineering Profession* (Baltimore, Md.: Johns Hopkins Press, 1971), pp. 190–91.

39. Herbert Hoover, *American Individualism* (Garden City, N.Y.: Doubleday, Page & Co., 1922), p. 37.

40. Hoover, *American Individualism*, pp. 10–11.

41. Ibid., pp. 17, 19.

42. Herbert Hoover, *The Challenge to Liberty* (New York: Charles Scribner's Sons, 1934), p. 34.

43. Hoover, *American Individualism*, pp. 41–42.

44. Ibid., p. 44.

45. Ibid., pp. 32–33.

46. National Industrial Conference Board, *Trade Associations: Their Economic Significance and Legal Status* (New York: National Industrial Conference Board, 1925), pp. 315–16.

47. Hoover, *The Challenge to Liberty*, p. 41.

48. Ibid., p. 33.

49. See David F. Noble, *America by Design: Science, Technology, and the Rise of Corporate Capitalism* (Oxford: Oxford University Press, 1977), pp. 76–83; Ellis W. Hawley, "Three Facets of Hoover Associationalism: Lumber, Aviation, and Movies, 1921–1930." In *Regulation in Perspective: Historical Essays*, ed. Thomas K. McCraw (Cambridge, Mass.: Harvard University Press, 1981); and Robert F. Himmelberg, *The Origins of the National Recovery Administration: Business, Government, and the Trade Association Issue, 1921–1933* (New York: Fordham University Press, 1976).

50. Hoover, *The Memoirs of Herbert Hoover*, vol. 2, p. 31.

they reduce policy and the state to a reflection of societal forces. Depending on the theory one adopts, one can predict that public policies will benefit capitalists because business is the best organized interest; corporate elites have successfully coopted elected officials; or the state is structurally dependent on the ongoing success of the capital accumulation process. In contradiction with this general prediction, the New Deal unveiled policies that permanently and substantially redefined the power of capitalists vis-à-vis the state and limited the role of the market in the distribution of wealth and economic power and the relationship between labor and capital. The tremendous policy innovations of the New Deal suggest that the state plays a far more autonomous role than any of the society-based theories would have predicted, as shown in a series of articles by Theda Skocpol and others.[9]

One can explain the introduction of policies that militated against the short-term interests of business by acknowledging the role of crisis. As Fred Block has argued, during the Great Depression state managers faced growing popular demands for a recovery program.[10] At the same time, economic decline left business incapacitated, dramatically reducing the threat of a capital strike. This unique set of circumstances created the opportunity to introduce policies that would have been impossible only a few years earlier when business influence was at its peak. Crises undoubtedly create opportunities for autonomous state action and broad departures in policy. However, policymakers can exploit such opportunities in innumerable ways. Crises offer the potential for change but are not, in the end, determinative. Thus, it was critical that the crisis was combined with the formation of a new Democratic party coalition and the consequent demands of coalition maintenance. Crisis along with the formation of the New Deal coalition can provide the elements of a compelling explanation of how some of the New Deal's boldest experiments could have occurred.[11]

The 1932 election brought a realignment of the party system and created the New Deal coalition which would literally recast the American political system, leading ultimately to the creation of a national welfare state. Yet in 1932, there were few indicators that the forthcoming presidential election would bring a fundamental change in policy and the role of the state in society. The Democratic party platform was markedly conservative. While Roosevelt's campaign speeches were energetic and provocative, they failed to present a coherent program. However, some of his statements held the promise that there would be a significant departure from the Republican policies of the previous 12 years. In one campaign speech, he claimed that the growing concentration of capital required "a reappraisal of values," particularly in the midsts of the depression. He went on to note: "A mere builder of more industrial plants, a creator of more railroad systems, an organizer of more corporations, is as likely to be a danger as a help." He called for an "enlightened administration" to engage in "the soberer, less dramatic business of administering resources and plants already in hand . . . of adjusting production to consumption, of distributing wealth and products more equitably, of adapting existing economic organizations to the service of the people." Roosevelt argued that corporations had to "work together to achieve the common end." He was quick to note that the state would have to restrain "the lone wolf, the unethical competitor, the reckless promoter" who "declines to join in achieving an end recognized as being for the public welfare, and threatens to drag the industry back to a state of anarchy." In another speech of 1932, he addressed the "problem of controlling by adequate planning the creation and distribution of those products which our vast economic machine is capable of yielding."[12] Yet, Roosevelt balanced these statements with others that recognized the need for active trustbusting and fiscal conservatism. As Raymond Moley, an original member of the Brain Trust, recalled, Roosevelt "lurch[ed] between the philosophy of controlling bigness and the philosophy of destroying bigness, between the belief in a partnership between government and industry, and the belief in trustbusting. . . . Roosevelt had not the slightest comprehension of the differences between the two sets of beliefs."[13] Such indifference shocked Moley, who recalls: "Not even the realization that he was playing ninepins with the skulls and thighbones of economic orthodoxy seemed to worry him."[14]

If Roosevelt simultaneously embraced the promise of bold experimentation and retained a residual faith in traditional political economic relationships, how can one explain the New Deal innovations? This question can be answered, in part, by considering the demands of coalition building and the administration's opportunity to focus attention on the experiences, expectations, and relationships created in the war. When developing a recovery program, the administration resurrected the procedures and state-corporate relations developed during wartime mobilization. The associationalism of the 1920s, the recovery plans promoted by various corporate leaders and intellectuals, and the experiences of a number of Roosevelt's advisers, themselves veterans of the wartime agencies, gave the model of the WIB great credibility. Indeed, Roosevelt began preparing the nation for the new programs in his inaugural address, when he said that we must treat the task of recovery "as we would treat the emergency of war" and he promised that "the larger purposes will bind upon us all a sacred obligation with a unity of duty hitherto evoked only in a time of armed strife. He explained that under these conditions, he would have to ask Congress for "broad Executive power to wage a war against the enemy, as great as the power that would be given to me if we were in fact invaded by a foreign foe."[15]

Absent the political explanation, the reliance on the model of the WIB is difficult to explain, given the very different nature of the economic tasks at hand. The challenge during the war was one of maximizing production and fighting inflation. Recovery required an end to deflation via restraints on competition and production. While members of Roosevelt's Brain Trust could provide theoretical justification for planning, in the end, theory was not decisive. Rather, one must emphasize the political utility of a program that promised to forge a broad coalition uniting corporations, labor, and farmers, while drawing on preestablished models of state-economy relations. The National Industrial Recovery Act and the Agricultural Adjustment Act provided a means of integrating potential opponents into the policy process and making their economic welfare contingent on the success of the New Deal.[16]

Of course, one might imagine that the administration could have pursued an expansive program of public works rather than structural reform and corporatist planning. Certainly, such a program—in contrast with the limited funds for

backed by the authority of the federal government. Rather than relying on international markets to absorb surpluses—an option considered repeatedly during the 1920s—the Agricultural Adjustment Act provided government payments as an incentive to reduce production. It simultaneously committed the federal government to the goal of parity (i.e., increasing prices until commodities could provide the same purchasing power as that available in the base period of 1909 to 1914). The Agricultural Adjustment Administration (AAA) controlled supply through contracts restricting the acres planted or produced and brought to market. While the program was voluntary, the incentives for participation were impossible to ignore. Participation provided access to benefit payments, nonrecourse loans, marketing orders, export subsidies, and government purchases of surpluses. The Agricultural Adjustment Administration financed the agricultural recovery programs through a processor tax that reflected the difference between the actual price of commodities and the parity price.

Despite the differences between industrial and agricultural production, the basic regulatory model was similar to that adopted in industry. As noted above, there was a focus on cartelization and self-regulation under government supervision, albeit with a greater degree of administrative decentralization. Despite this decentralization, the AAA placed a great emphasis on the largest commodity producers. The U.S. Department of Agriculture's (USDA's) Extension Service had long-standing relationships with large farms that were most active in making use of its technical assistance. Moreover, the larger producers were more familiar with standard business methods, thus facilitating their implementation of production controls. The reliance on the large producers threatened to make permanent the existing distribution of power within the agricultural economy while limiting the use of agricultural policy to address the problem of rural poverty, particularly in the South.[29]

However, one of the key differences between the NRA and the AAA came in the administrative expertise of the latter. Unlike the NRA, the AAA was placed within the Department of Agriculture and thus could draw on a large body of administrators with a wealth of expertise. In the words of Skocpol and Finegold, "At the coming of the Great Depression, the U.S. Department of Agriculture was, so to speak, an island of state strength in an ocean of weakness."[30] The USDA's Bureau of Agricultural Economics employed more social scientists than the rest of the federal government combined. Engaged in ongoing research on production and marketing, USDA bureaucrats could effectively exploit well-established relationships with agricultural associations and, through the extension service, the farmers themselves. The close interplay among academic research, farming, and broader policy issues gave the AAA a great advantage when compared with the NRA which was, in every sense of the word, a temporary agency.[31]

The AAA was successful in organizing farmers and controlling production. As with the NRA, participation rates were impressive: Between 93 and 98 percent of the acreage in top corn-producing states was covered by the agreements along with some 89 percent of the wheat. The AAA contracted over 75 percent of the cotton acreage with similarly impressive sign-up rates in other commodities. However, the AAA engendered a fair amount of controversy. Farmers objected to the levels of support and production controls that were often released too late to affect planting. The production controls also forced the disposal of food at a time when poverty was claiming a growing proportion of the nonfarming population. In addition, a host of internal problems plagued the AAA. Ongoing tensions between the proponents of production controls and surplus marketing schemes were combined with questions over whether the AAA should engage in agricultural planning.[32]

In the end, one must judge the AAA by its impact on farm incomes. Between 1932 and 1935, farm prices increased by 66 percent and farmers' claim on the national income more than doubled. Net incomes increased from $1.9 billion in 1932 to $4.6 billion in 1935. The increase in farm income was a product of transfer payments which reached $573 million by 1935. It was also a result of a drought that eliminated grain surpluses. Despite the growing support of major agricultural groups, processors and distributors strongly opposed the new regulatory system. Their challenge to the AAA came before a sympathetic Court. In *United States* v. *Butler* (1936), the Court invalidated the tax on processors, considered a tax for a special rather than the general interest. The AAA became a casualty of the Court, as had the NRA before it.[33]

## The Elusive Recovery

As noted earlier, Hoover's 1921 Unemployment Conference had resulted in some rather sophisticated conclusions about the best means for managing the business cycle. A system of countercyclical public works and corporate investments, engaged when statistical indicators of economic performance turned negative, would allow for a scientific management of the economy and, hopefully, an end to serious unemployment during recessions and depressions. Although this often overlooked conference predated the New Deal by over a decade, there is little evidence that Roosevelt understood or appreciated its ramifications for the Great Depression and the formulation of a recovery program. Indeed, as Hoover scrambled to promote countercyclical spending through the 1920s and the last years of his presidency, Roosevelt resorted to that old time religion of balanced budgets and fiscal restraint. Fearful of unnecessary deficits, the administration focused on the need for structural reform. The National Industrial Recovery Act, the Agricultural Adjustment Act, and a number of regulatory initiatives were promoted, in part, because they might provide for greater economic stability.

Roosevelt's programs are often and incorrectly associated with Keynesianism due to Keynes's personal interest in the New Deal and the administration's departures from balanced budgets. Fearful of unnecessary deficits, the Roosevelt administration focused on the need for structural reform rather than countercyclical stimulus. The National Industrial Recovery Act and the Agricultural Adjustment Act were promoted, in part, because they would provide greater economic stability. To be certain, Keynes provided a theoretical justification for expansionary fiscal policy as a means of battling aggregate demand failure during a depression. However, two points must be made. First, Keynes only reinforced the decision to spend. As Herbert Stein notes: "Roosevelt did not have to learn about govern-

cessful component of the Roosevelt recovery program. However, the success of the AAA forced an immediate congressional response. Congress passed a number of pieces of legislation restoring key features of the Agricultural Adjustment Act. Thus, the Soil Conservation and Domestic Allotment Act reinstated the production controls through the provision of payments out of general revenues. Farmers were compensated for substituting "soil-building crops" for "soil-depleting crops," a category which included crops such as corn, wheat, cotton, and tobacco that ran persistent surpluses. Congress also passed the Agricultural Marketing Act of 1937 which authorized the formulation of producer committees to formulate marketing agreements regulating production enforced by the USDA Agricultural Marketing Service.[41]

The new legislation did not successfully restrain production. Surpluses in many commodities placed downward pressures on prices and farm incomes. Roosevelt responded to the new agricultural crisis by tying future price-support loans to the passage of legislation to fill the gaps left by *Butler*. Thus, in 1938 Congress passed a second Agricultural Adjustment Act free of the processor tax. Under the act, the Commodity Credit Corporation was authorized to provide nonrecourse loans and control production levels through the denial of loans to farms that exceeded agreed upon acreage allotments. Moreover, it created a mechanism by which the USDA could establish production quotas at the request of the commodity producers. These production controls and support payments were combined with new programs to eliminate surpluses.[42]

The regulatory system created in the period 1933 to 1938 evolved over the course of the next several decades to become highly insulated from external forces and constitute a clear example of government-supervised self-regulation. The USDA's Agricultural Stabilization and Conservation Service which administers price supports and the Agricultural Marketing Service which implements market orders are organized on a commodity-specific basis. This facilitates close relationships with commodity producer groups and agricultural subcommittees from the House and Senate. The leading role of large farmers established by the practices of the AAA have continued through the five decades since the Great Depression. As a result, the majority of benefits are directed toward the large farmers at the expense of small farms that are far more vulnerable to fluctuations in farm prices. By the 1970s, the largest fifth of the farms received more than 62 percent of the benefits from the commodity programs whereas the bottom half received but 9 percent of the subsidies. By the 1990s, the agricultural subsidies approached $30 billion—a level of support that is troublesome given the dramatic decline in the number of farms from approximately 4 million at the time of the depression to some 700,000 in 1993.[43]

The New Deal initiatives in financial regulation were as significant as those in agriculture. The financial collapse of the Great Depression, Senate investigations of investment banking practices, and presidential advocacy of reform forced a series of financial regulatory statutes through Congress. The legislation of 1933 and 1934 completely transformed the structure and regulatory framework of American finance. The Glass-Steagall Act created the Federal Deposit Insurance Corporation and separated commercial banking (i.e., loan making, deposit taking) and investment banking (i.e., securities underwriting and dealing). Henceforth, commercial and investment banking were separate businesses subject to different regulations and regulators. We are concerned here with the New Deal initiatives regulating investment banking. Under the Securities Act of 1933, all public offerings in excess of $100,000 had to be registered with the Federal Trade Commission and accompanied by a prospectus disclosing a host of information on the issuer, the officers, and the terms and purposes of financing. After the filing, the commission had 20 days to examine the contents and, if necessary, bar public sales through the issuance of a stop order. The issuing corporation, its directors, and the investment bankers underwriting the issue could be held liable only if they had failed to exercise "due diligence" in investigating and verifying the sales document. It was believed that the registration process and civil liability would be sufficient to force the release of necessary information.[44]

Following the passage of the Securities Act, the Roosevelt administration introduced new legislation to regulate the stock exchanges. The Securities Exchange Act of 1934 required the New York Stock Exchange and 22 other national exchanges to register with the newly created Securities and Exchange Commission (SEC). The SEC regulation extended the coverage of the Securities Act to new and existing securities issues. The act forced corporations with stocks listed on the exchanges to register and submit to quarterly financial reports. In addition, they had to abide by SEC-established procedures in the solicitation of proxies and report the securities transactions of corporate officers and directors when they involved the stock of the company. To regulate the conduct of the traders, the act mandated dealer registration, established stringent antifraud provisions, and prohibited a number of activities including insider trading and wash sales. Finally, in hopes of limiting speculation, the act set margin loan limits of 55 percent of the current market price of a security, allowing the Federal Reserve Board to change these limits at its discretion.[45]

In addition to direct regulation by the SEC, there was a large measure of industry self-regulation through the activities of trade associations. The SEC vested these associations with quasi-public authority and, in one important case, actually facilitated the creation of a private association that had the authority to regulate its members. Let us explore briefly the SEC's regulation of the exchanges and the over-the-counter market.[46] The first two chairmen of the SEC, Joseph Kennedy and James Landis, urged the New York Stock Exchange to initiate procedural and organizational reforms. However, these requests were denied or met with symbolic gestures. Things changed rapidly, however, after William O. Douglas was appointed chairman of the SEC in 1937. Douglas nurtured close relationships with exchange dissidents and commissioned brokers. He reacted to the exchange's unwillingness to initiate significant reforms by providing an ultimatum: It could initiate a voluntary reorganization and reform program with or accept "an immediate and more persuasive administration by the Commission."[47]

In response to Douglas' threats, exchange president Charles Gay created a committee (including nonexchange members and Adolf Berle, a representative of the Roosevelt administration) to design a reorganization plan. The exchange introduced tough new disclosure requirements, streamlined its organization, and

Like the ICC, the new agency licensed air carriers by providing them with a certificate of necessity acknowledging that "the applicant is fit, willing, and able to
perform such transportation properly, and to conform to the provisions of [the] Act
and the rule of the Authority" and "that such transportation is required by the public convenience and necessity." Beyond the power to approve routes, the act echoed
the earlier railroad legislation by giving the CAA the responsibility of determining
whether the abandonment of a route was in the public interest before giving its approval. The legislation also empowered the CAA to approve consolidations within
the aeronautics industry. Closely following the model of the ICC's railroad and
trucking regulations, the act required that all air carriers file their rate schedules
with the CAA. Rates had to be "just and reasonable" and the CAA had the authority
to reject or adjust rates and rate changes if found unreasonable. The act also prohibited rebates and discrimination. The CAA exercised rate-making authority in
determining compensation for carrying U.S. mail. Finally, the act assigned the
CAA's Air Safety Board responsibility for regulating the safety of air carriers by licensing pilots and aircraft and promulgating air traffic rules.

The Civil Aeronautics Act's goals of restraining competition and promoting industrial development were in keeping with the regulatory focus of the other
New Deal initiatives. The CAA interpreted its mandate to require a prevention of
destabilizing competition. As it explained in its first annual report, it was supposed
to attack "uneconomic, destructive competition and wasteful duplication of services by the statutory requirement that no person or company may engage in air
transportation without first receiving a certificate of public convenience and necessity."[56] The congressional debates repeatedly expressed concerns that competition could undermine stable growth and air safety. The CAA thus sought to manage
competition while guaranteeing a rate of return high enough to allow for orderly
expansion. This entailed the creation of significant regulatory barriers to entry, primarily in the agency's control over certificates of convenience. During the first four
decades of its existence, the Civil Aeronautics Board refused to approve a single
new trunk carrier to begin service on a major route despite tremendous expansion
of air traffic. Indeed, the number of carriers actually fell from 16 to 11 through a series of consolidations. Ultimately, concern over the lack of competition and artificially high fares led to the passage of the Airline Deregulation Act in 1978 which
removed major regulations and eliminated the Civil Aeronautics Board.[57]

The model of government-supervised self-regulation was established in
the National Industrial Recovery Act and disseminated through a host of regulatory initiatives. While this model could be traced back through the War Industries
Board to Theodore Roosevelt's New Nationalism, Franklin Roosevelt also embraced the New Freedom philosophy of deconcentrating corporations through antitrust. This was particularly the case after 1936 when Roosevelt's rhetoric turned
increasingly hostile toward business. Thus, in 1938, Roosevelt appointed Thurman
Arnold to head the Justice Department's Antitrust Division. Arnold reorganized
and expanded the division and began an ambitious campaign of antitrust prosecutions designed to eliminate the "bottlenecks" created by concentrated market
power and various nonmarket mechanisms. By the end of his five-year tenure at
the Antitrust Division, Arnold was responsible for more than half of all the antitrust

cases filed by the Justice Department since the passage of the Sherman Act half a century earlier.[58]

Despite the example of antitrust and others like the Public Utility Holding Companies Act, the New Deal regulations when taken as a whole were designed to promote economic and political stability.[59] On the economic side, many of the regulations reduced competition, provided guaranteed returns, and removed conflicts from the market. On the political side, they integrated economic associations into the policy process and gave the parties a real financial stake in the continued success of policy. Similar features can be discovered in the system of industrial relations created under the New Deal.

## A NEW DEAL FOR AMERICAN LABOR

The Roosevelt administration permanently redefined industrial relations through Section 7(a) of the National Industrial Recovery Act followed by the National Labor Relations Act of 1935. Prior to the New Deal, there were a few significant advances toward greater recognition of, and protection for, organized labor. As noted in Chapter 5, some temporary progress was made during World War I under the supervision of the National War Labor Board which intervened in industrial relations to maintain high levels of wartime production. After the war, the Railway-Labor Act of 1926 facilitated the unionization of railway workers by prohibiting the interference or coercion of employers and establishing a mechanism for the settlement of disputes. In 1932, Congress expanded the legal protections with the Norris-La Guardia Act, affirming association free from employer interference, prohibiting yellow-dog contracts, and limiting the use of labor injunctions. Despite these initiatives, the courts continued to present the employment relationship as subject to freedom of contract.[60]

The New Deal brought unprecedented gains for organized labor. The new regulatory system played a decisive role in stimulating the organization of workers and compelling employers to meet with their representatives to bargain collectively. As noted earlier, the New Deal recovery programs were premised on the belief that industrial stability carried the key to ending deflation and promoting recovery. The administration formulated its labor policy on the conviction that this stability could be promoted through the creation of a system of collective bargaining. As long as such a system was absent, the economy would be prone to industrial disruption. Section 7(a) recognized some of the historical demands of labor and promoted a growth in union membership. The elimination of the NRA created a regulatory vacuum; heightened labor expectations and employer intransigence resulted in a new wave of strikes. As revealed in Figure 6–4, the number of strikes remained at high levels as one of the few means of forcing employer concessions in a period of high unemployment.

Following *Schechter*, Congress moved quickly to pass a labor relations bill proposed by Senator Robert F. Wagner, head of the NRA's National Labor Relations Board. The act created a new National Labor Relations Board (NLRB) comprised of three individuals appointed by the president and confirmed by the Senate. Expanding upon the provisions of National Industrial Recovery Act, the new legislation established the right of workers to elect by majority rule their own exclusive representatives. Three other points deserve mention. The act explicitly prohibited a number of unfair labor practices, including interference with labor unions and employees seeking representation, discrimination against union members or those seeking to protect their rights under the provisions of the act, and refusal to bargain with the chosen representatives of labor. Moreover, the act granted the NLRB independent enforcement powers. It empowered the NLRB to issue cease and desist orders and appeal for court injunctions in response to the violations of these orders. Finally, the act authorized the board to determine the appropriate unit for elections and representation, thus providing the board with significant power over the shape of organized labor in the United States. This would be of great importance as the NLRB had to manage the competition between the AFL and the CIO.

The National Labor Relations Act reduced the conflicts in industrial relations by creating a system of collective bargaining in which representatives of labor and management negotiated over the various dimensions of the employment relationship within distinct legal parameters. Once unions were certified as the authoritative representatives of workers, management had the duty to engage in collective bargaining. This promoted stability in industrial relations by creating a means of regulating the adversarial relationship between labor and management. It is important to note that this system of collective bargaining also minimized direct state intervention and restricted the scope of industrial relations. As Kochan, Katz, and McKersie explain: "The form of collective bargaining . . . fit nicely with the American political and social ethos favoring limited government intervention in substantive decision making, the protection of private property rights, and the freedom to contract."[61] They go on to explain that the system rested on "the philosophy that management had the right to manage, while workers and their union

**Figure 6–4**   Strike Activity, 1920–1940

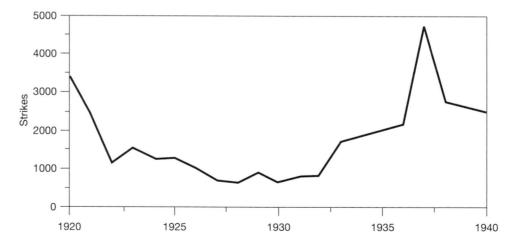

Source: *Statistical History of the United States*, Series D-764.

representatives had the right to negotiate the impacts of those management deci-sions on employment conditions. Since strategic decision making was left exclu-sively to managerial control ... the negotiation and implementation of collectively bargained agreements became the dominant forum for labor man-agement interactions"[62]

By delineating a sphere of corporate autonomy and providing an institu-tional mechanism for the resolution of many labor-management conflicts, the Na-tional Labor Relations Act introduced greater stability into industrial relations. There can be little question that the goal was one of creating industrial stability rather than providing unambiguous support for organized labor. The NLRB and the Roosevelt administration had little patience for workers employing the sit-down strike—an effective tool of forcing the compliance of management by occu-pying key production facilities. This tactic, it was believed, undermined the collective bargaining process particularly when it was used after a union had al-ready by recognized by the board. The goal of promoting stability is also evident in Roosevelt's response to concerns that the NLRB was biased in support of the Congress of Industrial Organizations. Board member Edwin Smith and the board secretary Nathan Witt were believed to be communists and close associates of Lee Pressman, general counsel of the CIO. They envisioned the NLRB as exercising dis-tinct judicial powers and serving on behalf of labor rather than being a neutral in-termediary. In 1939, Roosevelt appointed William M. Leiserson to the board and directed him to "clean up" the situation. Eventually, Leiserson was successful in obtaining the resignation of a number of NLRB officials (including Witt) and bring-ing about procedural changes that would enhance the neutrality of the board.[63]

The neutrality of the NLRB was a critical issue from its inception. The per-ception of neutrality, it was argued, was necessary for the board to be considered a legitimate intermediary in industrial relations and minimize legal challenges that could quickly consume the NLRB's limited resources. The decision to pursue a strategy of legal professionalization was part of this strategy of promoting neu-trality.[64] All professions have distinct professional norms and values. Attorneys value procedural propriety and due process. They seek to resolve conflicts within a neutral system through the application of relatively stable legal rules. It was be-lieved that legal norms could invest the board with a sense of objectivity. Because the law could address a relatively limited set of issues—precisely those issues that did not threaten the existing distribution of economic power—it could contribute to the stability of the industrial relations and set distinct parameters on industrial conflict. As Christopher Tomlins correctly notes, the NLRB's early innovations "en-sured that from the outset its model in both organizational and procedural matters would be one rooted firmly in professional legal practice."[65] This strategy of legal professionalization and strict neutrality was successful: The new labor policy was ruled constitutional in *National Labor Relations Board* v. *Jones and Laughlin Steel Cor-poration* (1937).[66]

The NLRB's performance was truly impressive. By the end of 1939, over 25,000 cases involving nearly 6 million workers had been filed with the board. The NLRB had conducted 2,500 elections for union representation and settled 2,000 strikes. In many instances, the NLRB played a critical role in resolving conflicts bedeed, unions often opposed welfare initiatives out of the concern that the state would assume some of their key functions. Finally, during the early decades of this century, many corporations adopted a paternalistic stance toward their workers, creating a system of welfare capitalism. Companies provided insurance, pensions, and stock-purchase plans, thus limiting the attractiveness of unions and the demand for public sector initiatives.[86] It required the crisis of the Great Depression and the collapse of the state and corporate welfare system to stimulate a movement toward a national system.

The late introduction of social insurance in the United States can be combined with a second important feature: the low levels of funding. Social spending (i.e., transfers and subsidies) has increased as a percentage of Gross Domestic Product from a mere 4.5 percent in the late 1950s to 11.2 percent in the late 1970s. However, in each period the United States devoted a significantly lower portion of national income to social spending than did other industrial nations. Thus, while the United States devoted 11.2 percent of its GDP to social spending in the late 1970s, France, The Netherlands, Norway, and Sweden were spending more than double that amount. Indeed, Japan was the only country that consistently spent at lower levels than the United States, reflecting its well-developed system of firm-based welfare that closely resembles the American Plan of the 1920s.[87]

The comparison of spending levels is interesting for two reasons. First, social welfare spending can play an important role as an automatic economic stabilizer. Declines in economic performance stimulate increases in unemployment and consequent declines in demand. Welfare spending provides fiscal stimulus precisely when it is most needed. As the economy recovers, welfare spending declines, thus preventing excessive fiscal stimulation. It should be no surprise that the nations that engaged in the highest level of public sector spending—much of it in the form of social insurance and transfers—had the best performance during the 1970s when all industrial democracies were forced to address the dual problems of inflation and stagnation. As will be shown in Chapter 8, social spending provided some compensation for workers who exercised restraint in wage decisions, thus making corporatist strategies available to restrain inflation and freeing fiscal and monetary policies to expand employment. Second, despite the low levels of welfare spending, the United States remains among the most hostile to social welfare, reflecting the permanence of some attitudes concerning individual responsibility and self-reliance. As Chapter 10 will reveal, the attack on welfare was a key component of the Reagan administration's opposition to the New Deal state and the expansion of the public sector in the postwar system. For Ronald Reagan, welfare spending, Keynesianism, and regulation were simply different aspects of an interventionist state that provided an insufficient role for market mechanisms.

The New Deal did not result in recovery, despite the high levels of activism and the remarkable record of policy innovation. Roosevelt's efforts were directed toward structural reforms designed to foster industrial stability through an associational system of government-supervised self-regulation. Drawing on the legacy of the New Nationalism, the War Industries Board, and Hooverian associationalism, Roosevelt promoted the creation of administrative agencies to regulate various sectors of the economy by integrating economic associations directly into the policymaking apparatus. The same goal—to promote stability in an environment of extreme instability—animated New Deal initiatives in industrial relations and social welfare. His movement to expansionary fiscal policy came far too late to have much of an impact.

Demand from European nations at war and direct involvement in World War II accomplished what Roosevelt had hoped to do: It created the stimulus necessary to bring the economy to full employment. With government expenditures approaching 50 percent of GNP and deficits approaching 30 percent of GNP, the economy grew by some 70 percent between 1939 and 1945. The unemployment rate fell below 2 percent as the economy ran at levels above full employment. Indeed, as the war reached its peak, policymakers began considering the limits to growth and wondering whether a lack of critical inputs would impede further expansion. The war created expectations of full employment and revealed what active fiscal stimulation could contribute to the realization of this goal. The experience of World War II combined with the innovations of the New Deal to create the basis for the postwar political economic system. We turn now to examine the experience of war mobilization and its effects on the economy.

## NOTES

1. Peter Fearon, *War, Prosperity, and Depression: The U.S. Economy 1917–45* (Lawrence: University Press of Kansas, 1987), pp. 89–95, 102.
2. Ellis W. Hawley, "Herbert Hoover, the Commerce Secretariat, and the Vision of an 'Associative State, 1921–1928.' " *Journal of American History* 6 (1974): 116–40.
3. See William J. Barber, *From New Era to New Deal: Herbert Hoover, the Economists, and American Economic Policy, 1921–1933* (Cambridge: Cambridge University Press, 1985), pp. 104–45; and William E. Leuchtenburg, "The New Deal and the Analogue of War." In *Change and Continuity in Twentieth Century America*, ed. John Braeman, Robert H. Bremner, and Everett Walker (Columbus: Ohio State University Press, 1965), p. 99.
4. Albert U. Romasco, *The Poverty of Abundance: Hoover, the Nation, the Depression* (New York: Oxford University Press, 1965), p. 65.
5. See Thomas Ferguson, "Industrial Conflict and the Coming of the New Deal: The Triumph of Multinational Liberalism in America." In *The Rise and Fall of the New Deal Order, 1930–1980*, ed. Steve Fraser and Gary Gerstle (Princeton, N.J.: Princeton University Press, 1989).
6. Robert M. Collins, *The Business Response to Keynes, 1929–1964* (New York: Columbia University Press, 1981), pp. 23–28; Barber, *From New Era to New Deal*, pp. 121–22; Ellis W. Hawley, *The Great War and the Search for a Modern Order* (New York: St. Martin's Press, 1979), p. 201.
7. Quoted in William Starr Myers and Walter H. Newton, *The Hoover Administration: A Documented Narrative* (New York: Charles Scribners, 1936), p. 155.
8. Kim McQuaid, *Big Business and Presidential Power: From FDR to Reagan* (New York: William Morrow, 1982), p. 24.
9. See Theda Skocpol, "Political Responses to Capitalist Crisis: Neo-Marxist Theories and the Case of the New Deal." *Politics and Society* 10 (1981): 155–201; and Theda Skocpol and Kenneth Finegold, "State Capacity and Economic Intervention in the Early New Deal." *Political Science Quarterly* 97 (1982): 255–78.
10. Fred Block, "The Ruling Class Does Not Rule: Notes on the Marxist Theory of the State." *Socialist Revolution* 33 (May 1977): 6–28.
11. See Kenneth Finegold and Theda Skocpol, "State, Party, and Industry: From Business Recovery to the Wagner Act in America's New Deal." In *Statemaking and Social Movements: Essays in History and Theory*, ed. Charles Bright and Susan Harding (Ann Arbor: University of Michigan Press, 1984).
12. Quoted in Howard Zinn, ed., *New Deal Thought* (Indianapolis, Ind.: Bobbs-Merrill, 1966), pp. 49–50, 52, 81.
13. Raymond Moley, *After Seven Years* (New York: Harper & Row, 1939), pp. 189–90.

68. Badger, *The New Deal*, pp. 118–19.

69. See Theda Skocpol, *Protecting Soldiers and Mothers: The Political Origins of Social Policy in the United States* (Cambridge, Mass.: Harvard University Press, 1992).

70. Edwin Amenta and Theda Skocpol, "Taking Exception: Explaining the Distinctiveness of American Public Policies in the Last Century." In *The Comparative History of Public Policy*, ed. Francis G. Castles (New York: Oxford University Press, 1989).

71. James T. Patterson, *America's Struggle Against Poverty, 1900–1985* (Cambridge, Mass.: Harvard University Press, 1986), p. 57.

72. Leuchtenburg, *Franklin D. Roosevelt and the New Deal*, pp. 121–23.

73. Franklin Roosevelt, "Annual Message to the Congress, January 4, 1935." In *Poverty and Public Policy in Modern America*, ed. Donald T. Critchlow and Ellis W. Hawley (Chicago: Dorsey Press, 1989), pp. 134–35.

74. Leuchtenburg, *Franklin D. Roosevelt and the New Deal*, pp. 63–64.

75. Patterson, *America's Struggle Against Poverty*, p. 64.

76. Ann Shola Orloff, "The Political Origins of America's Belated Welfare State." In *The Politics of Social Policy in the United States*, ed. Margaret Weir, Ann Shola Orloff, and Theda Skocpol (Princeton, N.J.: Princeton University Press, 1988), pp. 65–80.

77. Badger, *The New Deal*, p. 231.

78. Patterson, *America's Struggle Against Poverty*, pp. 68–70.

79. Badger, *The New Deal*, p. 231; Patterson, *America's Struggle Against Poverty*, pp. 68–70.

80. Robert T. Kudrle and Theodore R. Marmor, "The Development of the Welfare State in North America." In *The Development of Welfare States in Europe and America*, ed. Peter Flora and Arnold J. Heidenheimer (New Brunswick, N.J.: Transaction Books, 1981).

81. Patterson, *America's Struggle Against Poverty*, p. 171.

82. See, for example, Charles Murray, *Losing Ground: American Social Policy, 1950–1980* (New York: Basic Books, 1984); Nathan Glazer, *The Limits of Social Policy.* (Cambridge, Mass.: Harvard University Press, 1988).

83. Donald F. Kettl, *Deficit Politics: Public Budgeting in its Institutional and Historical Context* (New York: Macmillan, 1992), p. 55.

84. Christopher Pierson, *Beyond the Welfare State?* (University Park, PA: Pennsylvania State University Press, 1991), p. 108.

85. Stephen Skowronek, *Building a New American State: The Expansion of Administrative Capacities, 1877–1920* (Cambridge: Cambridge University Press, 1982).

86. Edward Berkowitz and Kim McQuaid, *Creating the Welfare State: The Political Economy of Twentieth-Century Reform*, 2nd ed. (New York: Praeger, 1988), Chapter 3.

87. See Rudolf Klein, "Public Expenditures in an Inflationary World." In *The Politics of Inflation and Economic Stagnation*, ed. Leon N. Lindberg and Charles S. Maier (Washington, D.C.: Brookings Institution, 1985), p. 204.

# 7

# FROM THE WELFARE STATE TO THE WARFARE STATE

The Great Depression proved most resistant to the solutions offered by Roosevelt and the New Deal. As shown in Chapter 6, the New Deal brought a host of new regulations and reform initiatives covering many sectors of the economy. The Roosevelt administration introduced the Social Security Act and the National Labor Relations Act, permanently altering the relationship between the state and the citizen and the nature of industrial conflicts. However, this experimentation was combined with a strong strand of fiscal conservatism. Of course, persistent deficits were an inevitable byproduct of the combination of emergency spending and the reduced revenues—both resulting from the Great Depression rather than an expansionary fiscal strategy. While there can be little question that Roosevelt shed a good deal of his fiscal conservatism in the aftermath of the economic collapse of 1937, there is also virtually no question that the fiscal stimulus of World War II came at a most opportune time. The massive outpouring of public spending was unprecedented in U.S. history. It simply dwarfed the spending levels of the New Deal and World War I, as revealed in Figure 7–1. This level of spending combined with the absorption by conscription of a previously unemployed labor force brought full employment and rapid economic expansion. The potential value of expansionary fiscal policy in transforming an economy from depression to full employment was a key lesson of the war that would create new expectations concerning the role of the government in the economy. We shall explore this legacy in greater detail in Chapter 8. Here we focus on World War II economic mobilization.

As noted in Chapter 5, war presents some difficult economic problems for policymakers. Four problems are immediately apparent. First, there is the problem of prices. On the one hand, the shortages of consumer goods, the pressure on la-

**Figure 7–1**  Federal Expenditures and Revenues, 1930–1945

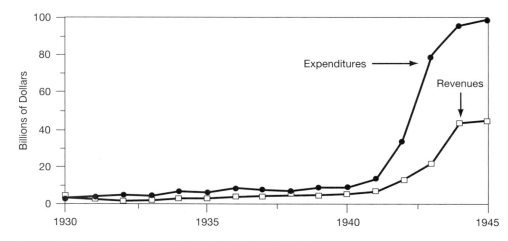

Source: *Statistical History of the United States,* Series Y-254, 255.

bor markets, and the higher levels of money in the economy due to full employment create strong inflationary pressures. On the other hand, the price system plays
an important role in stimulating a movement of resources into the goods necessary
for wartime production. Second, policymakers must address the problem of funding the war effort. Wars are accompanied by an expansion of taxation. Rates are increased; taxes are extended to goods and activities previously untaxed. However,
the financial demands of modern war limit the extent to which taxation can be used
to fulfill the needs. As a result, there has been a great reliance on war debt, incurred
through the issuance of new debt instruments such as war bonds. Third, some
means has to be discovered for funding industrial expansion. Some of the transformation of a peacetime economy to a war posture can be accomplished by converting existing facilities. However, it is also necessary to promote the expansion
of existing facilities and fund the creation of altogether new factories and plants.
Unfortunately, war finance creates shortages of investment capital and thus limits
the extent to which, absent direct government investment, such expansion can take
place. Finally, policymakers must address the impact of war on trade to the extent
that the war effort is dependent on imported inputs. In Chapter 5, we examined
some of these problems as they related to World War I mobilization. In the following pages, we turn to the mobilization for World War II. Moreover, we will also
explore briefly one of the key legacies of World War II: the creation of a strong and
ongoing alliance between the state and the defense industries.

## THE ROAD TO WAR AND RECOVERY

When the war in Europe began in the fall of 1939, the United States was still feeling the effects of the Great Depression. With civilian unemployment rates at 17.2
percent for the year and tremendous unused productive capacity, the economy had

the ability to provide much of the goods needed for the war effort. As with World War I, however, popular sentiment was initially opposed to U.S. involvement in the war. Roosevelt gave expression to this position—a position he did not share—on September 5, 1939, when he called for a munitions embargo against nations involved in the conflict.

In many ways, Roosevelt's political support was remarkably soft due to two factors. First, recent political debacles such as the failed effort to pack the Supreme Court and the fiscal mismanagement leading to the recession of 1937 undermined the president's political support. Conservative Democrats who had gained ground in the 1938 midterm elections could now work in concert with Republicans in Congress to frustrate effectively Roosevelt's legislative initiatives. Second, the Roosevelt administration met with the firm opposition of the business community. Sharp antibusiness rhetoric after 1936, revitalization of antitrust, and the creation of the Temporary National Economic Committee to investigate business organization and conduct under the assumption that business was to blame for the economic maladies of 1937 to 1938 combined to create a deep rift separating the administration and much of the corporate community. The reduction in popular support and conflicts with business combined with isolationist sentiments to limit Roosevelt's discretion in responding to the growing European conflict.

Roosevelt's willingness to remain neutral softened rapidly, however. In November, Congress passed amendments to the neutrality acts of 1935 and 1937 to allow belligerents to buy U.S. war materials if purchased with cash and shipped in the purchaser's own ships. This concession to Roosevelt's desire to help other democracies (especially Britain) against the Nazis could hardly be presented as something resembling neutrality. At the same time, there were few signs that the United States had any intention of entering the war, at least until the May 1940 invasion of France created the strong impression that the United States would be wise to prepare for conflict.[1]

Following the Wehrmacht invasion of France, Roosevelt called on Congress to provide additional funding for the military and procurement. By March 1941, Congress passed the Lend-Lease Act which allowed the president to authorize agencies to sell, transfer, lend, or lease defense materials to the governments of countries whose defense was deemed vital to the United States. This determination was to be made by the president. Initially, Congress appropriated $7 billion for lend-lease and allowed the government to dispose of an addition $1.3 billion of government stocks. In the end, lend-lease would receive some $63.8 billion in appropriations. The net effect (accounting for funds not used and reverse lend-lease from the allies) was approximately $42.9 billion, almost five times the level of support provided through lend-lease in World War I.[2]

The growing economic impact of the war in Europe necessitated the creation of new administrative mechanisms for coordinating production. After a brief and unsuccessful experiment in 1939 with the War Resources Board—a business-dominated board led by U.S. Steel's E.R. Stettinus—Roosevelt established an Office of Emergency Management and a National Defense Advisory Commission. This latter body combined representatives from business and labor to collect information on various aspects of mobilization and to initiate procedures and a system of priorities. In 1940, a new Defense Plant Corporation was created as a sub-sidiary of the Reconstruction Finance Corporation to facilitate plant expansion. Like-wise, the nation's first peacetime draft was introduced in June of 1940. As will be discussed in greater detail, the commission was ultimately replaced by an Office of Production Management in January 1941 and later by additional coordinating agen-cies, including a War Production Board. These efforts suggest that the formal pol-icy of neutrality merely veiled a de facto preparation for war in support of the allies.

The same impression is unavoidable when one considers the support for the Armed Forces. In July 1940, Congress appropriated some $5 billion for the army and navy, more than double the existing level of funding. This was combined with the decision to give the Treasury the authority to issue $4 billion of bonds for na-tional defense purposes. In the same month, export controls were put into place, followed the next month by Roosevelt's decision to provide Britain 50 destroyers in exchange for naval and air bases in Newfoundland and the Caribbean.[3] This flurry of activity is difficult to reconcile with a position of neutrality. As was the case with World War I, neutrality was more political symbol than policy.

With Japan's attack on Pearl Harbor on December 7, 1941, the tentative mo-bilization effort rapidly expanded to create a historically unprecedented set of con-trols imposed by a fragmented array of agencies. Over the course of the next several years, military expenditures would explode, reaching $80.5 billion in 1945, compared with $6.3 billion in 1941. As a result of wartime mobilization, real GNP would in-crease by 70 percent between 1939 and 1940. The dramatic expansion of the economy and state, the new patterns of state-economy relations, and the resulting U.S. domi-nance of the world economy would define the main features of the postwar political economy and provide the basis for a period of significant peacetime growth.[4]

## WAR MOBILIZATION AND ECONOMIC MANAGEMENT

World War II mobilization required the federal government to create administra-tive mechanisms to control prices, channel supply to the services, manage labor shortages and industrial disputes, and finance the war effort. As in the case of World War I, these tasks were addressed through the creation of a complicated net-work of agencies. Although many involved in the effort could draw on their expe-riences of World War I and the emergency of the Great Depression, mobilization nonetheless resulted in the creation of multiple agencies with overlapping juris-diction, unclear mandates, and equally unclear powers. Roosevelt and his advisers groped through the war adopting whatever means appeared expedient to main-tain the necessary supply of materials and limit the impact of war on prices. Al-though Republicans in Congress took the opportunity to oppose Roosevelt's expansion of executive powers on a number of occasions, the existence of a national emergency limited the dissent.

### Mobilizing the Economy for War

The creation of an organizational foundation for mobilization began in earnest in the spring of 1940. Bernard Baruch and some business leaders strongly advocated a return to a single agency like the War Industries Board run by a single administrator. This option was formally presented to Roosevelt in an Industrial Mobilization Plan by a committee he had appointed. However, Roosevelt rejected the creation of a single mobilization agency for several reasons. First, the economy and demands of war were far more complex in 1940 than they had been a generation earlier. This complexity limited what could be accomplished by a single agency. Second, the existence of a single superagency could be a concern to a population still hoping to preserve neutrality. Third and most important, Roosevelt's presidency was devoted in part to concentrating power in the executive. He would not willingly delegate authority to an agency led by a single business leader, thereby creating a coequal power in the administration of the war. As Barry Karl explains: "Roosevelt had no intention of turning such power over to industry or to one of its leaders. It was clear to him that he needed industrial support; but he wanted it to be organized by someone from within his administration, committed to his perception of the nation's needs. He compromised by selecting highly visible figures in industry and giving them an extremely limited managerial authority."[5] This was a model of delegation that Roosevelt has used with some success before. Several entities competing without overlapping mandates would allow for the preservation of presidential power. However, while smaller boards and commissions with multiple fora for representation carried distinct political benefits, they also created troubling problems of coordination that would persist for the duration of the war.

The first significant movement toward mobilization came in May 1940, when Roosevelt resurrected the Advisory Commission of the Council of National Defense under the authority granted 24 years earlier in preparation for World War I. The Defense Commission initially had seven members each assigned responsibility for a specific facet of mobilization (i.e., Consumer Protection, Employment, Farm Products, Industrial Materials, Industrial Production, Prices, and Transportation) and reporting directly to Roosevelt. Afterwards, Donald Nelson was placed in charge of defense purchases and to serve as an eighth member of the Defense Commission. The Defense Commission was created to coordinate war supply, serve as a clearinghouse for information, and develop policies on directing scarce resources toward defense-related priorities. However, as the allies' demands increased, the organization and administrative capacities of the commission proved insufficient.

As an immediate response to the limits of the Defense Commission, Roosevelt created the Office of Production Management (OPM) under the joint direction of Sidney Hillman of the Amalgamated Clothing Workers and William S. Knudsen, a former president of General Motors. During its short life, the Office of Production Management began directing industrial conversion, an expansion of raw materials extraction, shifting resources out of civilian production, and establishing a system of priorities. Although the OPM was initially responsible for defense production, in August 1941 it was assigned responsibility for civilian production as well when the Office of Price Administration and Civilian Supply (see the discussion below) was reformulated as a price control agency. This transfer of authority was accompanied by the creation of a new Supply, Priorities, and Allocations Board with the responsibility of examining economywide production

The fundamental weakness in the present administration of priority ratings by the Army and Navy contracting officers is that it is an attempt to
administer a control system, which must often restrict parts of the program
for the benefits of the whole, through field officers whose primary function
is expediting the particular parts of the program entrusted to them. Accordingly, the War Production Board will immediately undertake supervision over the functions now exercised by contracting and procurement
officers of the armed services with relation to the issuance of priority orders and certificates.[16]

Administrative decentralization and the delegation of priority authority to
the services themselves resulted in fierce competition over resources. Moreover,
the services commonly overstated their needs, thus creating shortages in certain
goods and surpluses in others, not to mention the costs and delays associated with
plant conversions.[17] While there is no question that Nelson was justified in with-
drawing the WPB's support for this system, the remedy was much less than one
might have expected. In practice, this reassertion of WPB authority merely entailed
sending WPB review analysts to work with military procurement field offices
where they would merely approve or reject priority rating proposed by the procurement officer. When the two disagreed, priority decisions could be appealed to
a Priority Appeals Committee, staffed jointly by the WPB and ANMB.

As the established priority system fell into disrepute in the spring of 1942,
WPB Director Nelson announced the mandatory application of the Production Requirements Plan (PRP). The implementing order was issued on June 10, 1942, to
take effect on July 1. Under PRP, scarce metals were allocated to all industrial users
on a quarterly basis. Each metal-consuming firm (exempting those which used less
than $5,000 worth of metal per quarter) were required to provide the WPB with an
application for the upcoming quarter. The application would provide information
on the shipments of the previous quarter, classified by product grouping and pref-
erence/priority status and projected shipments for the upcoming quarter, similarly
classified. The WPB's Requirements Committee would use these applications, filed
on a firm-by-firm basis, to determine the total requirements of metal for each industry. The WPB's material divisions would provide estimates of future supply. In
the end, the Requirements Committee would use this information to allocate resources to each firm within an industry. The goal was to allocate resources in such
a fashion as to remain sensitive to supply constraints and the preference or priority ratings assigned to different goods being produced.[18]

The Production Requirements Plan proved administratively unworkable
and, in the end, contributed to a failure of the WPB to meet the production goals
established by the president and the armed forces. Several factors undermined the
PRP. First, the armed forces were concerned from the onset with the system and
thus proved hesitant to support it. More importantly, the attempts to implement
the system rapidly proved inoperable due to the burdens placed on businesses (e.g.,
need to rework existing contracts and collect data). Finally, the administrative complexity associated with the system was simply daunting. This horizontal control
system required the WPB to work directly with each producing firm. Each firm's

requirements had to be considered in light of past production levels, preference ratings, and projected demand and productive capacity. Allocations then had to take place on a firm-by-firm basis. Thus, in November 1942, WPB Chairman Nelson introduced the Controlled Materials Plan (CMP) to replace the PRP.[19]

Under the Controlled Materials Plan, the claimant agencies (i.e., the War Department, the Navy Department, the Maritime Commission, the Aircraft Scheduling Unit, the Office of Lend-Lease Administration, the Board of Economic Welfare, and the WPB's Office of Civilian Supply) provided the WPB with a quarterly request for steel, copper, and aluminum allocations that reflected program needs. The WPB Requirements Committee examined the requests in light of aggregate supplies and strategic and logistical factors before allocating materials to each of the agencies. The agencies could then determine which programs to reduce or eliminate based on their individual allocation of resources. Each agency subsequently allotted the necessary raw materials to their contractors, subject to the approval of the WPB. The contractors, in turn, were authorized to draw the necessary materials from their suppliers which were prohibited from providing materials without WPB allotment numbers. This system of vertical control had several benefits. First, it was sensitive to the existing productive capacity unlike the earlier priority system which commonly resulted in priorities' inflation. Second, by allocating resources to the claimant agencies rather than the individual firms, the WPB divested itself of the complicated determinations that existed under the Production Requirements Plan. Finally, by delegating authority to the claimant agencies, the WPB would not be as directly responsible for making strategic determinations. Although the CMP was officially inaugurated in November 1942, it was not fully in place until the fall of 1943. In the interim, the CMP gradually replaced the horizontal control system established under PRP.[20]

As mobilization progressed, Nelson and others became far less willing to defer to the armed forces over questions of procurement, believing that the forces would seek maximum supplies regardless of actual need and the broader needs of the civilian population. Thus, in late 1942 and 1943, Nelson began questioning the armed forces' estimates of need, much to the dismay of the forces which questioned a civilian's capacity to critically assess military needs. In late 1942, Nelson created a Production Executive Committee on the WPB and placed it under the direction of General Electric President Charles E. Wilson. Wilson, in turn, proposed to the Joint Chiefs and Roosevelt that the forces be required to present their procurement plans to the Production Executive Committee for clearance so as to avoid scheduling problems. Roosevelt forced the forces to compromise with Nelson and the WPB. However, the dispute over procurement scheduling, when combined with earlier conflicts over bloated estimates of needs, only intensified the military's desire to rid themselves of Nelson.

The efforts to reduce the power of the WPB and, if possible eliminate Nelson, first took form when Roosevelt was convinced by James Byrnes in February 1943 to place the War Industries Board veteran Bernard Baruch in charge of the WPB. Although Roosevelt reversed his decision after Baruch had been asked to fill the position, he nonetheless moved forward in the effort to control the WPB. The persistent problems of coordination, conflicts between the services and Nelson, and pressure from the Senate for the creation of more centralized authority in the mobilization process led Roosevelt to create the Office of War Mobilization (OWM) through an executive order on May 27, 1943. The OWM, placed under the administration of James F. Byrnes, was to exercise overarching powers to supervise the entire mobilization process from the White House and develop policies for "the maximum use of the nation's natural and industrial resources for military and civilian needs."[21] While the OWM's mandate included a broad set of policymaking duties, its most important role was that of a mediator. When conflicts emerged between the War Production Board and other mobilization agencies (such as the War Manpower Commission), or the branches of the services were in conflict over procurement priorities, Byrnes and the OWM intervened in the disputes, thus sheltering Roosevelt from the task. Byrnes exercised his broad mandate over the nation's human and material resources effectively, thereby increasing the power of the OWM and claiming power over policymaking that had been originally assigned to Nelson and the WPB.[22] Ultimately, the armed forces and the OWM were united in their opposition to Nelson and the WPB over what became the most consequential question of the mobilization experience, namely, how and when to lift controls and allow for reconversion to a civilian economy. Before addressing the significance of this conflict, it is necessary to examine three other areas critical for the economic mobilization effort: price stabilization, labor regulation, and finance.

## Managing Inflation

Inflation is an inescapable product of total war. The demands for defense materials create shortages in raw materials and transportation. At the same time, conscription creates acute labor shortages that are translated into higher wage demands. The combined effect is strong inflation that can only be partially attenuated by the increased levels of taxation and savings that also accompany war. This was certainly a factor in World War II. The war period witnessed a significant increase in tax rates, an expression of Roosevelt's commitment to fund as much of the war as possible through direct tax receipts. At the same time, rationing and the conversion of the economy to wartime status limited the opportunities to spend the higher levels of income. In 1940, the nation saved 5.1 percent of disposable income, a figure which would increase to 25 percent by 1943 and 1944.[23] Despite the higher levels of taxation and savings, wartime inflation required the creation of a complex administrative system.

In 1939 and 1940, the U.S. economy started to experience the effects of the war in Europe. As one might expect, the demand for war materials had a stimulative impact on employment and prices. However, little was done initially to manage prices given the decade-long experience with wage and price deflation: By 1941, prices had only increased to the levels of 1929. However, price increases finally forced a response. Leon Henderson, the member of the Defense Commission responsible for price stabilization, initiated a number of efforts to limit inflation. The result was a series of conferences with industry officials, price schedules, and pleas for restraint—various forms of jawboning, none of which was backed with any legal sanctions.

By the spring of 1941, Roosevelt moved to create a more formal system for price controls. Through executive order, Roosevelt established the Office of Price Administration and Civilian Supply. In August, the civilian supply responsibilities were vested in the Office of Production Management, leaving the price control functions in a streamlined Office of Price Administration (OPA). Although the OPA issued 73 price schedules and negotiated over 100 voluntary agreements to restrain prices, prices continued to escalate, thus forcing Roosevelt and Congress to consider new statutory authority for the OPA. The legislation, originally submitted in July, was finally approved by the House just before the bombing of Pearl Harbor. The Emergency Price Control Act of 1942 passed through the Senate in the wake of the bombing and placed the OPA on new statutory footings.

The Emergency Price Control Act authorized the Office of Price Administration to function as an independent agency under the direction of a price administrator. The Emergency Price Control Act directed the OPA to promote price stability through the promulgation of maximum prices on a commodity specific basis. The OPA adopted the price levels of October 1941 as a basis, allowing adjustments to that base in response to increases in costs and a limited number of specified contingencies. It was also given the authority to freeze rents in areas involved in defense production. Although the OPA emerged as the chief economic stabilization agency, Congress did not given it the authority to stabilize wages. Labor advocates were convinced that OPA control over wages could undermine collective bargaining and labor's promise not to strike—a point which will be addressed in greater detail below. In addition to the wage rates, the OPA was prohibited from fixing the prices for agricultural commodities until they exceeded 110 percent of parity (i.e., the purchasing power available for a basket of commodities in the period 1910 to 1914). This provision was designed by agricultural lobbies, including the American Farm Bureau Federation, Agriculture Department bureaucrats, and the congressional farm bloc. All parties agreed that war provided an opportunity to raise farm incomes and argued that attempts to integrate agricultural commodities into the OPA's price stabilization responsibilities would strip away the incentives for an expansion of agricultural production.[24]

Although the OPA imposed price controls on some wholesale prices, the lack of authority over agricultural commodities and wages combined with the fiscal stimulus of extraordinary budget deficits to undermine stabilization efforts. Thus, Roosevelt announced a new stabilization program in April 1942 and the OPA issued its General Maximum Price Regulation expanding control over rents and setting March 1942 prices as a ceiling on consumer prices. This combined with the National War Labor Board's new efforts to restrain wages (see the discussion of the Little Steel formula below) provided some relief on price levels. The OPA regulated prices through a decentralized apparatus of some 8,000 local boards that rationed necessary goods (e.g., butter, petroleum, tires, coffee, shoes) in accordance with an increasingly complex and at times incomprehensible schedule of rationing regulations.[25] However, this once again proved insufficient. Thus, in September Roosevelt called on Congress for new stabilization legislation covering all commodities, wages, and agricultural commodities. The resulting Stabilization Act of 1942 strengthened the system of price controls by authorizing the president to issue a general order stabilizing prices, wages, and salaries at the levels that existed on September 15, 1942. At the same time, farm prices were to be fixed at the maximum for the period between January 1 and September 15, 1942. Subsidies were to be provided to farmers in exchange for lower price levels.

Despite the new authority, the OPA was having difficulties in stabilizing prices, forcing Leon Henderson to resign from the OPA in December 1942. He was replaced by Prentice Brown, a senator from Michigan. Roosevelt used the authority granted under the Stabilization Act to create a new Office of Economic Stabilization (OES). The OES was directed to coordinate the activities of the stabilization agencies while mediating disputes. The importance of the task was reflected in the fact that the office was placed in the White House and placed under the direction of James F. Byrnes, who had resigned as a justice on the Supreme Court to assume the new responsibilities as Economic Stabilization Director. New statutory authority, new leadership at the OPA, and a stabilization superagency seemed to provide clear indications of Roosevelt's resolve to stop inflation. Late 1942 and the early months of 1943 continued to witness price increases deemed unacceptable by all involved in war mobilization. In the war against inflation, the decisive turning point came in April 1943. President Roosevelt issued his executive order demanding that all stabilization agencies "hold the line." This entailed a continuation of price ceilings, the application of the Little Steel formula in wages, and an expansion of rationing efforts. Under this order, the stabilization agencies controlled the impact of inflationary forces. Amazingly, between the issuance of the hold the line order and the end of the war some 28 months later, the cost of living rose a mere 4 percent, compared with 23 percent in the previous 28 months.[26] The performance of prices during the period is presented in Figure 7–2.

## War Work and the Regulation of Industrial Relations

Well before the attack on Pearl Harbor brought a formal declaration of war, labor markets had to accommodate the demands of war production. In September 1940, Congress passed the Selective Training and Service Act to create the nation's first peacetime draft. Under the provisions of the compulsory draft registration act all males between the ages of 21 and 35 were required to register with the draft to produce a large pool of potential conscripts. Roosevelt, in turn, was authorized to draft up to 900,000 for a one-year term of service as long as the nation remained in peace. Between June 30, 1940 and June 30, 1941, the armed forces grew from 458,000 to 1.8 million—a product of the growing recruitment and the draft. By August, Congress had passed the Draft Extension Act, lengthening the term of peacetime service from 12 to 18 months. After the United State declared war, draft eligibility was expanded to males between the ages of 18 and 45. At the same time, the term of service was increased from 18 months to the duration of the war plus 6 months.[27] As the armed forces grew rapidly to 3.9 million men in 1942, 9 million in 1943, 11.5 million in 1944, and 12.1 million in 1945, the impact on the nation's labor pool was significant.[28]

Roosevelt created the War Manpower Commission (WMC) in April 1942 to direct the allocation of labor and relieve shortages in critical areas. The WMC

**Figure 7–2**   Consumer Price Index, 1930–1945

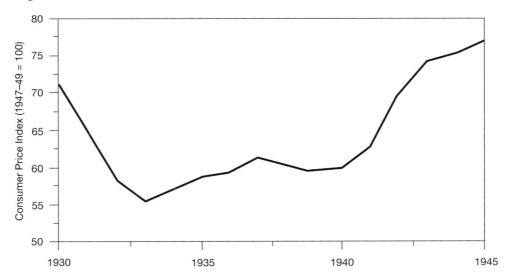

Source: *Economic Report of the President, 1962,* Table B-42.

was placed under the direction of former governor of Indiana Paul McNutt, rather than Sidney Hillman who remained head of the WPB's Labor Division until his resignation from government service soon thereafter. The WMC was officially given authority over labor, both military and civilian, although the formal independence of the Selective Service and its insistence to grant draft deferments on the basis of dependency rather than occupational status compromised the WMC's authority. The WMC, working with the U.S. Employment Service, attempted to identify labor shortages and direct workers to the necessary industries by certificates of availability and the imposition of hiring ceilings on nonessential production facilities. At the same time, the commission sought to direct defense contracts away from firms in areas that had suffered from persistent labor shortages. Although a National Service Act was considered in 1942 and again in 1944 to create a system of industrial conscription, it was defeated when it encountered the resistance of labor and management.[29]

Despite the unprecedented call for members of the armed forces, there were surprisingly few shortages of labor. Indeed, between 1939 and 1945, the total labor force increased from 55.6 million to 65.3 million, despite the expansion of the armed forces.[30] In large part, this can be attributed to three factors: internal migration, increases in workforce participation, and increases in labor exploitation. Let us address them in turn. The wages in war-related manufacturing industries were far greater than those available in agricultural employment. In 1943, when war production was at its peak, the average manufacturing worker earned a *weekly* salary of $43.14, compared with an average agricultural salary of $77 *per month.*[31] As a result of higher wages, between 1939 and 1945 the agricultural workforce fell from 9.6 million to 8.6 million, while the manufacturing workforce increased from 10

come combined with a scarcity of goods would make an increase of taxation relatively painless at present, Roosevelt argued, when compared with the imposition of higher taxes after the war, when goods would be plentiful and thus less expensive. In the end, the Revenue Act of 1944 once again lowered exemptions (to $1000 and $500) and increased tax rates to create a system of marginal rates ranging from 20 to 91 percent. However, this came at the cost of a repeal of the victory tax and a freezing of social security taxes which were slated to increase. Roosevelt quickly vetoed the tax bill—the first tax bill veto in the nation's history—only to have Congress overturn the veto. The Revenue Act of 1944 was the last tax increase of the war. As with the revenue acts passed in previous years, it provided less than the president desired and thus failed to provide the administration with the ability to meet its goal of covering approximately one-half of the war expenses through current revenues.[44]

As John Witte explains, the changes in taxes during World War II left several important legacies. First, during the war, corporate and individual income taxes increased to account for approximately three-quarters of all revenues (compared with less than 40 percent of revenues in the decade prior to the war), thus reducing the reliance on excise taxes and customs. This strong reliance on corporate and individual income taxes would continue throughout the postwar period. Second, the revenue acts passed between 1940 and 1944 dramatically extended the coverage of the tax system. Through the progressive reduction in exemptions and the simultaneous increases in incomes, the percentage of the workforce paying some taxes increased from 7.1 percent to 64.1 percent. Finally, the war taxes increased the progressivity of the tax system. Under earlier tax legislation which set high marginal rates (e.g., the World War I taxes and the Wealth Tax of 1935), only those making fantastically high sums were actually subject to the top rates. Thus, when World War I taxes set a top marginal rate of 77 percent, it applied to those with incomes over $1 million; when Roosevelt's Wealth Tax set the top rate at 81 percent, it applied to those with incomes over $5 million. After 1942, the top rates were imposed on those with incomes over $200,000. Progressivity was transformed from a symbol to reality. These factors, when combined, promised to increase the political salience of tax policy and alter the ways in which tax policy could be used to achieve a host of social objectives.[45]

Of course, the government relied heavily on borrowing during the war through a series of bond drives and funds borrowed directly from financial institutions. As a result of seven war bond drives and a victory bond drive, bonds worth $156.9 billion were purchased by an estimated 85 million bond holders. Some 25 million workers used payroll deductions to purchase the war debt.[46] While bonds were an important source of revenue, Treasury Secretary Henry Morganthau, Jr., argued repeatedly that the bond drives were most important because they could be used to explain the objectives and the importance of the war to the public. In Morganthau's words, the goal was "to use *bonds* to sell the *war*, rather than *vice versa*."[47]

The Treasury placed a priority on maintaining low interest rates to reduce the costs of funding the war debt—a debt that would exceed $260 billion by 1945. To achieve low interest rates, the Federal Reserve was required—over its initial objections—to buy and sell securities to maintain the officially established yields. The Fed also encouraged member banks to hold government debt as reserves by promising to repurchase them at a fixed rate of $\frac{3}{8}$-percent interest. The easy money policy adopted by the Treasury and the Federal Reserve to facilitate low-interest funding for the war debt resulted in a sharp increase of the money supply—an increase of some 150 percent over the course of the war. Because this expansion of the money supply greatly exceeded the rise in GNP, it was a potentially powerful source of inflation. The fact that consumer price increases were restricted to 25 percent of the expansion of the money supply attests to the success of the price control mechanisms discussed earlier.[48]

The Treasury facilitated government borrowing by offering a variety of debt instruments, including three different types of savings bonds, long-term bonds, short-term obligations to corporations and wealthy individuals, as well as interest-bearing tax savings notes that could be turned in to meet tax obligations. By tailoring debt instruments to meet the needs of different groups of potential investors, the Treasury was successful in claiming some 45 percent of all the funds available for investment.[49] However, there were concerns that too little of the debt was being placed with individuals and much of that which was placed with individuals took the form of short-term securities rather than long-term debt. The Treasury was convinced that the ease of cashing in the securities would compensate for the low rates of return and thus attract investors. However, this left open the question of how the government would fund redemptions after the war. As Benjamin Anderson warned government officials in a memorandum in May of 1945: "The so-called war savings bonds, gigantic in volume, are in effect demand deposits. The holders can get their money at any time. These bonds have been sold in a high percentage of cases with the argument that in buying them the purchaser is buying a post-war automobile or a post-war home or a post-war washing machine. . . . The Treasury may have a very grave problem with these demand deposits when the war is over. It is unfunded debt."[50]

The various war bond drives, combined with an expansion of direct government financing, created severe capital shortages in private markets. As in World War I, the government exercised a good deal of capital control. It requested investment bankers to time public offerings so as not to interfere with government bond drives. Moreover, it began direct financing of industrial expansion, funding some two-thirds of the plant expansion through the Defense Plant Corporation (DPC), a subsidiary of the Reconstruction Finance Corporation. Under the pressure of war, new corporate stock and bond issues fell from some $2.6 billion in 1941 to under $1.1 billion a year later. Likewise, the issuance of state and municipal bonds fell from $1.2 billion in 1940 to under $450 million in 1943.[51]

The capital shortages associated with the war were fairly significant, as the above figures suggest. The government attempted to stimulate defense industry expansion through favorable tax provisions allowing corporations to amortize defense plants over a 5-year period rather than the 20- to 30-year amortization schedule that was usually in place. However, the tax provisions could not be sufficient to overcome the pressure the war placed on capital markets. As noted earlier, the government thus directly financed a majority of the war-plant expansions.[52] The

vide peripheral firms with an immediate advantage in meeting new consumer demand and gaining market share in the civilian economy while larger firms were still bound to war production. The impact of reconversion on industrial structure was deemed particularly important. Early reconversion would allow for a greater decentralization of economic power in the postwar period—a goal which fit well with the broader reform instincts of many of the New Dealers who were still active in the federal government while conforming to the post-1937 revitalization of antitrust enforcement. Immediate reconversion could reduce the unemployment problems that could become more intensive in the wake of contract cancellations if efforts were not made to authorize raw materials and transportation for civilian production. If one hoped to preserve some degree of market governance and a decentralized economic structure, early reconversion would appear a necessity.

Despite these arguments, many objected to immediate reconversion. The Joint Chiefs of Staff, James Byrnes of the Office of War Mobilization, Paul McNutt of the War Manpower Commission, and many executives from large corporations who had been administrators in the war mobilization apparatus countered that early reconversion could have terrible consequences. Civilian production, it was argued, would drain resources and manpower away from defense production and the results could be catastrophic should the war escalate to higher levels and the armed forces were left without the necessary material support. Moreover, it was argued that the unemployment resulting from contract cancellation was not necessarily negative. It could force labor into other areas of defense production currently suffering from labor shortages. Employment opportunities in the civilian economy would eliminate this incentive. The military naturally supported this position because it allowed the armed forces uninhibited access to the nation's economic resources. They were very careful to appeal to the need for sacrifice, the uncertainty of the current strategic situation, and the possibility that early reconversion could carry a potentially high cost in lives. Executives from the larger corporations supported the Joint Chiefs and Byrnes, albeit for different reasons. Delaying reconversion until the formal end of the war would essentially force small producers to compete with large corporations that had significant advantages. The result would most certainly be an increase in industrial concentration as oligopolies eliminated their small competitors in many markets. Much in keeping with the elite theories of political economy explored in Chapter 1, such a system would provide distinct benefits for those seeking to promote some form of elite management designed to limit a return to the instability that characterized the 1930s.[58]

Nelson made large movements toward reconversion in November 1943, when he announced that the WPB would start releasing resources for civilian production to take up the slack from an anticipated reduction in defense contracts. However, Nelson was forced to retreat in January 1944, when the army and navy argued publicly that even limited reconversion would be foolhardy prior to the invasion of Europe. Nelson waited until a week after the Allies opened the second front in France before presenting a reconversion program for the WPB's approval. The most important part of the program was a system of "spot authorizations" in which regional WPB's could allow for the release of materials and labor for limited civilian production when it would not interfere with war production which remained an official priority. In addition, Nelson proposed that firms engaged in civilian production be given access to aluminum and magnesium, be allowed to construct prototypes for postwar production, and purchase the machine tools that would be needed in a return from military production.

As one might suspect, these programs drove the Joint Chief to distress, particularly the proposed system of spot authorizations. As in the past, the military made dramatic references to future needs and the boys at the front. They appealed the new WPB policy to James Byrnes at the OWM. Byrnes finally arrived at a compromise between the WPB and the armed forces which was fatal to early reconversion. In August, he announced that spot authorizations could take place subject to the approval of the War Manpower Commission. As noted above, WMC director Paul McNutt was clearly aligned with the military and Byrnes in his opposition to the WPB's plan. Finally, Roosevelt intervened to end the conflict by sending Nelson on a diplomatic mission to China and replacing him at the WPB with Julius Klug.[59]

Absent Nelson's presence, the armed forces, Byrnes, and McNutt continued to prevent any significant efforts toward early reconversion. Claims that reconversion limited supplies to the front resonated with the American public as the Allies encountered new difficulties with Hitler in the Winter of 1944 to 1945. An agreement was reached between the WPB, the OWM, the WMC and the Joint Chiefs to suspend reconversion and the spot authorization program. In essence, early reconversion was no longer politically feasible. Reconversion efforts would not begin again until April 27, 1945, less than two weeks before V-E Day. From Hitler's defeat through the rest of the year, reconversion progressed at a rapid pace, resulting in the wholesale suspension of WPB regulations, a flood of contract cancellations, and the freeing up of rationed resources. The rapidity of reconversion undermined any hopes of using the process as a means of reducing the concentration of market power in the economy. Although some of Nelson's old supporters now called for a selective use of controls to assure that small firms were given priority in their access to materials, there was little enthusiasm for a new system of controls outside of wartime, particularly now that Congress was growing increasingly conservative.[60]

With the end of the war, the economic impact of reconversion would depend in large part on the system for compensating firms for canceled defense contracts and the disposition of government-financed plants and surpluses. As the war drew to a close, the government was forced to cancel 321,068 war contracts worth in excess of $65 billion. Since much of the cost of meeting the contracts had already been incurred by businesses, it was necessary to compensate firms for the cancellations. Following the recommendations made in a report on demobilization written by Bernard Baruch and John Hancock for the OWM, the government adopted the position that contract settlements should be "fair, fast, and final." To this end, the Office of Contract Settlement established uniform payment policies for all procurement agencies in September 1944. Under the system, payment was to be made within 30 days after applications were filed by contractors. Based on contractors' estimates, the agencies were authorized to reimburse firms for between 75 and 90 percent of costs incurred. If the claims were accompanied by evidence of war-related expenditures, the agencies were required to pay 100 percent of the contracted price for goods that had been completed and 90 percent of the costs of raw materials, parts, supplies, labor, and facilities costs. Firms that were bankrupt or threatened with insolvency were granted partial payments to be kept in a bank account and released by the contracting officer to meet the demands of subcontractors. The overriding goal of providing rapid partial payments was to assure that firms engaged in war production would be able to move into civilian production as quickly as possible without suffering from liquidity problems.[61]

A similar logic was applied in eliminating the vast surplus of equipment and raw materials accumulated by the services during the war. Following the publication of the Baruch-Hancock report on demobilization, Roosevelt created the Surplus War Property Administration to represent the various procurement agencies and make regulations concerning the disposal of surpluses. The regulations required agencies to dispose of scrap and raw materials at market prices, allowing for competitive bidding if market prices were unattainable. Used equipment could be discounted between 10 and 50 percent of the original value based on years of use. After V-J Day and the massive contract cancellations that followed, revisions were made in the regulations to promote rapid elimination of surpluses. In many cases, contractors were allowed to retain materials at "fair and reasonable prices." Between September 1, 1945 and December 31, 1946, the government disposed of $2.15 billion dollars of surpluses for $310 million, realizing 14.4 percent of the original cost. The low prices available for surpluses were essentially a large government subsidy that promoted a more rapid return to civilian production.[62]

The disposition of plants was of critical importance. As explained in Chapter 2, the kind of industrial finance system a nation possesses has significant implications for the capacity of the state to direct economic activity. In the United States, a capital market-based system has dramatically limited the role of the state when compared with the credit-based systems that prevail in other advanced industrial states.[63] In a capital market-based system, firms raise funds for expansion through the issuance of stocks and bonds, relying on banks for short-term capital. During the war, this system was virtually suspended as capital markets were swamped with war bonds and restricted by credit controls (see below). Under these conditions, the state became the primary source of capital for corporate expansion. Under the demands of the war, manufacturing corporations devoted some $11.6 billion to build new plants and purchase new equipment. At the same time, the RFC's Defense Plant Corporation spent $16 billion to capitalize private expansion; another $1.7 billion was spent on expanding government production.[64] Much of this investment went to expand capacity in arms, aircrafts, shipyards, aluminum, and synthetic rubbers. As the government became the main source of investment capital, it assumed a far greater responsibility than it had historically for shaping industrial structure and national economic development after the war.

However, the disposition had an important political dimension as well. As noted above, Nelson had encountered strong opposition when calling for early reconversion designed, in large part, to allow for greater competition in the postwar economy. Despite the support of organized labor, small business, and influential Democrats including Senator Harry Truman, he was unsuccessful. The Joint Chiefs, working closely with Byrnes's OWM and executives from the largest corporations that had claimed a lion's share of contracts, were able to derail efforts to promote early reconversion. The winners, it was suspected, would be the largest corporations which would enter the postwar economy with large amounts of capital derived from lucrative defense contracts and would, as a result, easily dispose of the smaller firms. To a great extent, the position of the largest firms during the war shaped their ability to succeed in the postwar and the government disposed of many of its plants. "Big business, by virtue of its contracts for conversion from civilian war production and for expansion thereafter—contracts spread out from 1940 through 1944—already had a first claim to the facilities the government had financed."[65] The profits that accumulated from wartime production allowed the largest firms to purchase the most efficient and profitable plants. They were "turned over to them at such low prices that these prices represented a 'capital subsidy,' making it even more difficult for smaller and newer producers to compete."[66] The new levels of concentration in the postwar period facilitated an expansion into international markets—one which was facilitated, as argued in Chapter 8, by large foreign assistance programs and a liberal trade regime. However, this was not the only legacy of World War II.

## WORLD WAR II AND THE EMERGENCE OF THE MODERN POLITICAL ECONOMY

World War II, as World War I before it, left a number of important legacies. In large part, the remainder of this book addresses the direct and indirect consequences of World War II. The war, more than the depression or any other event, shaped the political economy of the 1950s and 1960s. It provided the basis for a new relationship between the state and corporations, new expectations concerning the role of the state in economic management, and the rise of a large defense sector that would claim a significant amount of national resources. Moreover, the experience of World War II left Americans with a new sense of self-confidence—an important factor given the long struggle with the Great Depression—and a belief in the leadership role that the United States had to fulfill in the new international political economy.

The first and most general legacy of the war is tied to the role of the mobilization process in changing expectations of business elites. As noted in Chapter 6, there was some warming to Roosevelt and the New Deal during the years immediately following the 1932 election. However, growing conflicts with an administration that advocated policies to restrain corporate autonomy and revenues eliminated any desire for cooperation. By the end of the 1930s, business and Republican hostility for the Roosevelt administration had grown dramatically. However, the war once again changed the expectation of business concerning the capacities and proclivities of the national government. As Otis Graham explains:

> Thousands upon thousands of businessmen and lawyers who still harbored a suspicion of government came to Washington to help staff the war mobilization As a social class these Americans had been basically conservative and Republican. During the war they learned of the unique exhilaration of public service, and saw the many potential uses of public agencies

in rationalizing economic patterns and expanding production and consumption. Wartime Washington, they found, was a capital filled with practical people without noticeably radical inclinations. It was an educational experience for the elites of a capitalist society, and in the end a politically moderating one.[67]

In the words of Herbert Stein, "The war provided a breathing spell during which some of the earlier struggles could be forgotten."[68] The impact of the war was immediately evident in the postwar period when business associations increasingly accepted a role for the government in the economy well beyond that which would have been acceptable absent a national emergency.

A second area in which the war left a significant legacy was in the area of macroeconomic management. As noted in Chapter 6, Keynesian ideas rapidly gained support in government and the economics discipline in the wake of the 1937 to 1938 recession. However, at the same time many economists were concerned that secular stagnation would make a return to prosperity impossible. The assumption that government could solve the problem of aggregate demand failure through its spending and taxation policies was a testable proposition that was clearly supported by the experience of the war. In 1938, the last year before war orders began to have an impact on the economy, unemployment stood at 19 percent. The next year it fell to 17.2 percent, falling faster with each year until the economy reached an unemployment rate of 1.2 percent in 1944. This was not only full employment but overemployment. Despite the large outflow of soldiers, total employment increased from 44.6 million in 1938 to 64.3 million by the end of the war. This gain of some 20 million workers was the product of a greater number of women and teens entering the workplace to meet the demand for war labor. At the same time, many southern blacks used the opportunity of war to migrate north into urban areas with higher paying industrial jobs.[69]

To be certain, record deficit spending produced record employment and unemployment rates that would have been unimaginable a few years earlier. However, as noted above, the war also brought innovations in taxation, an increase in the size of government, and new experiences with an expanded role of government in the economy. As Herbert Stein notes: "The war created full employment, deferred the prospect of secular stagnation, provided a respite from the controversies of the New Deal, involved businessmen in the management of government economic policy, and left behind an enormous federal debt, large budgets, and pay-as-you-go taxation. By the end of the war all of the ingredients of the fiscal revolution . . . were present."[70] To be certain, the nation could not depend on another war or series of wars to promote ongoing full employment. However, many contemporary economists believed that a more expansive social spending could provide the necessary stimulus while meeting other goals. Thus, Alvin Hansen explained:

> A positive governmental program looking toward full employment would greatly vitalize and invigorate private enterprise. An expansionist program would permit private enterprise to operate at high output levels.

There is plenty of work to do. We need improved manufacturing equipment to produce more and better goods at lower prices. We need to carry on extensive research in the laboratories of our great private corporations, in our universities, and in our Government bureaus. We need to rehabilitate and modernize our transportation system. . . . We need continued advance in the techniques of production, distribution, and transportation; in short in all those elements that enter into a higher standard of living. We need to rebuild America—urban redevelopment projects, rural rehabilitation, low-cost housing, express highways, terminal facilities, electrification, flood control, reforestation. Many public development programs open fresh outlets for private investment.[71]

The war also had important effects on the role of monetary policy and the power of the Federal Reserve. The heavy reliance on various debt instruments to fund the war, the role of banks in absorbing this debt, and the high levels of personal savings forced changes in the structure of finance. Before the war, finance was concentrated in New York and Chicago. In 1939, 81 banks held deposits in excess of $100 billion. Of this number, 25 were in New York and Chicago. By 1946, 180 banks had deposits in excess of the $100 million mark. Yet only 34 of the 180 were in Federal Reserve cities. Thus, there was a deconcentration of financial power outside the traditional money centers. The war also had implications for the smaller banks. Of the banks with deposits of less than $1 million in 1939, 71 percent realized growth of over 300 percent by 1945.[72] The growing decentralization of financial power and the increase in bank holdings created far greater opportunities for monetary management by the Federal Reserve and meant that monetary policy could play a far more central role in the wake of World War II than it could have in any previous decade in U.S. history.

The nature of the revolution in economic policymaking will be examined in Chapters 8 and 9. For now, we need to consider an additional legacy of the war: the formation of a close relationship between the defense establishment and large defense contractors. During the war, the Reconstruction Finance Corporation funded the expansion of production facilities for defense production. While many of these plants were sold at fire-sale prices to the largest manufacturers, others were turned over to the armed services to allow for guaranteed munitions production in preparation for future wars. Many of these firms (e.g., Ford, Chrysler, Standard Oil) possessed sufficient liquidity and market demand to return to civilian production. Others, however, remained dependent on military purchases for their survival. "The state continued to own the factories they used, and the state still accounted for the majority of their sales. These firms had neither the will nor the resources to escape dependency upon the Pentagon."[73]

During the postwar period, this dependence on military contracts and an escalation of cold war military budgets would be combined with close private-public efforts in defense R&D and the circulation of elites from military positions to defense industry positions, thus giving analysts reason to point to a burgeoning military-industrial complex. In the years following the war, federal funding for defense-related R&D grew dramatically, exceeding $500 million a year by the late

54. Smith, *The Army and Economic Mobilization*, pp. 419–34.

55. Vatter, *The U.S. Economy in World War II*, pp. 84–85.

56. See E. Jay Howenstine, Jr., *The Economics of Demobilization* (Washington, D.C.: American Council on Public Affairs, 1944).

57. James R. Mock and Evangeline Thruber, *Report on Demobilization* (Norman: University of Oklahoma, 1944), p. 244.

58. Hooks, *Forging the Military-Industrial Complex*, p. 99.

59. Polenberg, *War and Society*, pp. 227–33.

60. Ibid., pp. 235–36.

61. Smith, *The Army and Economic Mobilization*, pp. 693, 683–86.

62. Ibid., pp. 686–94.

63. See John Zysman, *Governments, Markets, and Growth: Financial Systems and the Politics of Industrial Change* (Ithaca, N.Y.: Cornell University Press, 1985).

64. Fearon, *War Prosperity, and Depression*, p. 276.

65. Blum, *V Was for Victory*, p. 130.

66. Hooks, *Forging the Military-Industrial Complex*, p. 210.

67. Otis L. Graham, *Toward a Planned Society: From Roosevelt to Nixon* (New York: Oxford University Press, 1976), p. 81.

68. Herbert Stein, *Presidential Economics: The Making of Economic Policy form Roosevelt to Reagan and Beyond* (Washington, D.C.: American Enterprise Institute, 1988), p. 67.

69. See Robert Collins, *The Business Response to Keynes, 1929–1964* (New York: Columbia University Press, 1981), p. 79.

70. Herbert Stein, *The Fiscal Revolution in America*, rev. ed. (Washington, D.C.: American Enterprise Institute, 1990), p. 170.

71. National Resources Planning Board, *After the War—Full Employment* (Washington, D.C.: Government Printing Office, 1943), p. 5.

72. Studenski and Krooss, *Financial History of the United States*, pp. 456–57.

73. Hooks, *Forging the Military-Industrial Complex*, p. 230.

74. See David C. Mowery and Nathan Rosenberg, *Technology and the Pursuit of Economic Growth* (Cambridge: Cambridge University Press, 1989), pp. 161–63.

# 8

# THE POSTWAR POLITICAL ECONOMY AND THE RISE OF THE KEYNESIAN CONSENSUS

The United States entered the postwar period in a position of great strength, particularly when compared to the interwar period when a prolonged depression frustrated policymakers and stagnationists convincingly argued that the U.S. economy had reached the limits of growth. As Chapter 7 revealed, World War II played a decisive role in stimulating the economy. Almost overnight, persistent depression-level unemployment rates were replaced by full employment and in many cases overemployment. The debates over the barriers to growth in a mature economy and the new concerns over structural or technological unemployment were replaced by real concerns that shortages of resources and labor would limit the continued growth of an economy fully mobilized. The nation left the war in a unique position, poised to enjoy a period of prolonged growth and stability.

The success of the postwar political economy can be attributed to at least three factors. First, new international regimes were created for trade and monetary relations. They promoted U.S. interests in a world that offered no significant competition for economic leadership. Second, the postwar period brought a new stability in industrial relations. The conflicts of past decades receded into the distant past as labor enjoyed growing incomes, low unemployment rates, and unions occupied a recognized role in the new political economy. Third, the period witnessed the creation of a new institutional framework for economic management guided by the emerging Keynesian consensus. The importance of fiscal and monetary policies should be largely self-evident. The management of the business cycle affects levels of demand and corporate profitability, thus shaping the capacity of corporations to reinvest to create new productive capacities. It can also guarantee high levels of employment and real income growth, thus bringing far greater stability to industrial relations. A failure to manage the business cycle effectively can, in turn, undermine this process and erode both the living standards of the population and the status of the U.S. economy in the world economy.

## POSTWAR INTERNATIONAL REGIMES

The devastation of World War II left the United States as the lead country in the world economy. The high levels of economic stimulus promoted a dramatic economic expansion. Although the war decimated the capital assets of Europe and Japan, effectively eliminating their immediate presence in international trade, American capital assets were undamaged and, in fact, expanded through the large wartime investments. Driven by the demands of reconstruction and the incapacity of European economies to meet the needs of their populations, the foreign demand for U.S. goods (particularly foodstuffs and capital machinery) further stimulated the growth of the American economy and minimized the severity of the dislocations following the war. American loans to fund European reconstruction stimulated foreign demand for U.S.-made goods; liberal trade and monetary regimes facilitated international trade. Postwar trade and monetary regimes must be recognized as one of the factors that promoted the remarkable growth of the period.

At the end of World War II, the world economy inherited two significant problems from the past: the lack of a stable system of monetary exchange and payments and a system of tariffs and bilateral agreements that impeded the free flow of goods in international markets. The United States, as the new world hegemon, played a crucial role in addressing the two problems through the creation of new monetary and trade regimes. Justified in liberal terms, both provided significant advantages for the United States relative to the rest of the world. Let us address the international monetary and trade regimes in turn.

Prior to the 1930s, the gold standard provided the basis for a relatively stable international payments system. A nation's currency could be used to purchase a particular amount of gold which could be used, in turn, to purchase the currency of another nation. The convertibility of dollars or pounds into gold provided the basis for a relatively stable exchange rate between the two currencies. However, the gold standard began to weaken with the onset of World War I. Nations expanded their money supplies to cover the expenses of the war, creating problems of inflation that forced the temporary abandonment of convertibility. The 1920s brought successive attempts to reestablish a payments system—a feat that was made far more difficult by the high levels of indebtedness to the United States which entered the decade as the world's largest creditor nation. The United States relied on relatively high tariffs to protect domestic industries, thus frustrating the efforts of its trading partners to raise sufficient specie. With the onset of the Great Depression, nations abandoned any efforts to reestablish the gold standard. Britain rejected the gold standard in September 1930 and the United States followed in March 1933. The gold standard was no longer operative once the two major economies ended convertibility. World trade was inhibited by the lack of an international payments system. Following the dramatic dislocations of depression and World War II, attention turned to the creation of a new payments system that would provide a stable basis for currency conversion.

In 1941, the United States and Britain began to hold meetings to consider the potential features of a postwar monetary regime. By 1944, the basic framework for a new system had been established and 44 nations signed an agreement to abide by the new system following a conference in Bretton Woods, New Hampshire. The Bretton Woods system created a new system for international economic affairs and a mechanism for intervening in the event of short-term balance of payments disquilibria. Most important for the United States, the Bretton Woods agreement explicitly acknowledged the dominance of the United States and placed few restraints on national autonomy. Moreover, it provided certain selective benefits for American firms in international markets.

Under Bretton Woods, the dollar became the world's central currency. All currencies could be converted into dollars at a prescribed exchange rate, plus or minus one percent. The dollar, in turn, was convertible into gold at the fixed price of $35 per ounce. All currencies were indirectly convertible into gold, although in practice, the dollar served as the world currency. This created certain benefits for U.S. corporations which could conduct transactions in their home currencies without the transaction costs associated with exchange. However, it also created an obligation, accepted to some extent by most postwar presidents of maintaining domestic price stability.

In addition, Bretton Woods created two important international institutions, both of which were largely funded by the United States and more or less compliant with U.S. wishes. The International Monetary Fund (IMF) was created to manage the system of fixed exchange rates and make whatever adjustments in rates deemed necessary. Moreover, the IMF could provide loans to nations that ran persistent balance of payments deficits. In such cases, the IMF often made loans contingent on a nation's willingness to address long-term balance of payments problems through IMF-proscribed stabilization policies (i.e., the combination of restrictive monetary and fiscal policies) and/or a revaluation of the country's currency. Thus, for example, a nation that ran persistent deficits might receive a devaluation of its currency on the theory that an overvalued currency was limiting the attractiveness of the country's exports in world markets while the buying power associated with the currency stimulated an ongoing influx of imports. In addition, Bretton Woods created the International Bank for Reconstruction and Development (i.e., the World Bank). The World Bank was created to make or underwrite loans to fund postwar reconstruction. As initially conceived, the World Bank would have been capitalized at $10 billion raised through national subscription. It was anticipated that it would be a temporary institution that would cease to exist with the end of reconstruction which, it was hoped, would be concluded within five years. In the end, the World Bank was funded almost entirely by the United States and adopted a very conservative posture with respect to worthy development projects, essentially agreeing to provide funds where they were least needed.

The new monetary regime did not live up to its initial promise. Before examining the problems inherent in the postwar monetary regime, it is important to note that a second major contribution to international economic activity was initiated under the General Agreement on Tariffs and Trade (GATT). At the end of World War II, policymakers looked back to the high tariff barriers and complex network of bilateral agreements that existed prior to the war and helped extinguish trade in the 1920s, thus contributing to the global depression. If such events were to be prevented in the future, it would be necessary to devise new codes of conduct that could limit the various devices that nations used to limit free trade (e.g., tariffs, import quotas, customs unions, and various forms of subsidies and supports). To this end, an Anglo-American committee began meeting in 1943, ultimately arriving in 1947 at a draft agreement for an International Trade Organization. The International Trade Organization would be responsible for managing a liberal trade regime, albeit one which included a number of preferential features to support economic development in poorer nations. A General Agreement on Tariffs and Trade was drafted in Geneva in 1947 to regulate the behavior of members until the signing and ratification of the charter creating the International Trade Organization. In March 1948, the United Nation's Economic and Social Council met in Havana, Cuba, and agreed to the Havana Charter to create the International Trade Organization. Although GATT was to be only a temporary agreement, strong opposition in the Congress forced Truman to withdraw the charter before ratification. As a result, GATT became the de facto foundation for the postwar trade regime.[1]

Three broad and related goals can be associated with GATT. First, GATT aspired to prevent the creation of the preferential trading blocs that had had such onerous political and economic implications in earlier decades. Second, GATT was designed to increase trade and promote growth through the reduction of trade barriers. These goals were pursued through the application of the most favored nation principle. In essence, the most favored nation principle guaranteed that GATT members could export to another member on the same terms as any other nation. Discriminatory duties could not be erected against one nation by another without violating this principle. Formal procedures were established whereby member nations could file grievances against other members who engaged in discriminatory practices. A third goal of GATT was to create a mechanism to reduce existing tariff levels from the prevailing levels on the theory that low tariff levels would facilitate world trade and allow member nations to exploit comparative advantage. The mechanism established through GATT was a series of international meetings or rounds at which member nations could compose agreements reducing their tariff and nontariff barriers.

Several points about the trade regime established under GATT are worth noting. First, GATT was remarkably successful in reducing tariff barriers and facilitating an expansion of international trade. To the extent that this was the driving goal of GATT, it can be deemed a success. After six rounds of GATT negotiations between 1947 and 1967, average tariff levels fell from a high of 40 percent in many nations to approximately one-quarter that level. In 1967, following the Kennedy Round of GATT negotiations, the tariffs on dutiable, nonagricultural goods fell to an average of 9.9 percent in the United States and between 8.6 percent and 10.8 percent in our major industrial trading partners.[2] As shown in Figure 8–1, the volume of international trade expanded dramatically during the decades following GATT.

Second, GATT worked to the distinct benefit of the Untied States relative to other members. Of course, GATT could be justified through an appeal to liberal norms and economic arguments concerning the benefits of free trade. Free and unfettered trade, it was argued, would promote growth on a global scale by allowing each nation to specialize in producing certain goods or commodities and thus exploiting their comparative advantage. Thus, rather than producing a particular good inefficiently, the nation could export those goods which it produced most efficiently and purchase the others in international markets. While the classical notions of trade may have certain merits, there can be little question that by providing open access to all economies, a liberal trade regime provided great advantages for the most developed economies seeking to exploit new markets. The United States, as the largest industrial economy and the only one capable of exporting on a large scale in the immediate postwar period, could take advantage of the liberal rules of trade to use international recovery as an engine of domestic economic growth.

A third point is in some ways a corollary of the second. As the liberal trade regime established under GATT provided distinct benefits to the most powerful economies capable of actively exporting goods in an environment of lowered barriers, it also worked to the detriment of weaker nations. The dominant members of GATT were industrial economies interested in lowering tariffs on industrial goods and more sophisticated products that were not made in less developed countries. At the same time, member nations sought to maintain higher tariffs on agricultural commodities to shelter the market share and income of powerful domestic farm constituencies and provide the basis for higher commodity prices in domestic mar-

**Figure 8–1**   U.S. Merchandise Exports, 1950–1970

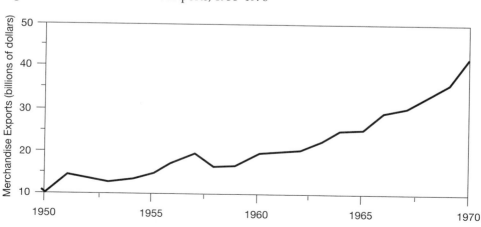

Source: *Economic Report of the President, 1993,* Table B-100.

kets. Moreover, the free flow of more sophisticated goods, it was charged, impeded industrialization in some developing countries. The differential treatment of industrial and nonindustrial nations under the provisions of GATT would become of increasing importance in the 1960s and 1970s, as it was argued by many that the prevailing system reinforced the dependency of developing nations on the first world.[3]

Finally, one must note that the liberal regime that provided one of the foundations for U.S. growth in the postwar period clearly supported U.S. dominance only so long as competing economies were incapable of exploiting the opportunities made available by the progressive reduction of tariffs. By the late 1960s, U.S. hegemony was eroded as the European and Japanese economies grew and claimed an ever greater share of international trade. The same factors that promoted U.S. strength in the early postwar period were now highly disadvantageous. A liberal trade regime provided our partners with greater access to U.S. markets, even after their domestic economies had recovered. Moreover, the fact that U.S. capital stock survived the war—while a distinct benefit initially—would prove disadvantageous as well. Europe and Japan would replace their destroyed capital stock with new machinery and plants. This new capital would embody best practice technology, thus allowing for greater efficiencies than those available in the United States with its aging capital stock. As a result of these factors, economic leadership passed, albeit with some struggle, from a single nation to a collective body of nations. With this passage, the ability of one nation to manage its domestic economy by macroeconomic policy, free from the intrusion of international pressures, diminished rapidly, taking with it the dominant consensus in macroeconomic theory and policymaking.

The promise of Bretton Woods was, to some extent, undermined by the experience of the postwar period. Policymakers in the United States quickly realized that rapid recovery of the world economy would not be forthcoming. Because the war had resulted in the wholesale destruction of the economic infrastructure in much of Europe and Japan, there was very limited capacity to meet domestic demand and to contribute to the maintenance of the international regime. The United States ran large and persistent balance of payments surpluses by the end of the 1940s, creating distinctive problems for an international regime premised on the need to maintain balances of imports and exports. The IMF and the World Bank, both highly undercapitalized, lacked the capacity to drive development at a sufficient pace.

Because the fragility of the international monetary system was combined with the growing threat of the cold war, the United States assumed an even greater role than it had first envisioned. The United States took several measures to promote rapid recovery in Europe and Japan and the development of broader markets for U.S. goods. First, between 1947 and 1958, the United States began exporting dollars. Through the combination of the Truman Plan's assistance for Greece and Turkey and the Marshall Plan promoting European recovery, the United States pushed some $17 billion in grants abroad. The combined effect of these assistance programs and the new military spending in the cold war and the Korean conflict was to make the dollar the world currency. The United States assumed the position of the world's central banker, managing the liquidity of the international system. In addition, the United States tolerated and at times encouraged violations of the fundamental principles of Bretton Woods by allowing Europe and Japan to engage in various forms of protectionism and strategies to discriminate against the dollar. At the same time, the United States promoted an expansion of exports to the United States as part of the effort to drive development.

Unilateral management of the international monetary system provided some benefits to the United States. However, it was not a viable strategy for the long term. By the end of the 1950s, European and Japanese recovery efforts had proceeded to the point that dollars held by America's major trade partners equaled or exceeded the nation's gold reserves. This raised the important question of whether the United States could continue to guarantee convertibility of dollars to gold at the rate of $35 to an ounce. It also raised the threat of a run on the world's banker. This threat became reality in 1960 when speculators moved quickly and in concert to convert dollars into gold with the goal of profiting from minor fluctuations in exchange rates. In the wake of this experience, it became clear that unilateral management had to be exchanged for greater international cooperation.

In 1961, the finance ministers from the world's top industrial powers—the United States, Great Britain, Japan, West Germany, Italy, Canada, France, Belgium, The Netherlands, and Sweden—formed the Group of 10 as a forum for coordinating financial policies and pooling information on monetary management. In the context of the G-10, an attempt was made to increase the stability of the international monetary system. In 1961 the members of the G-10 created a fund separate from the IMF that could lend money to the IMF at their discretion. Similarly, in 1968, the G-10 created Special Drawing Rights—an artificial unit of international reserves that could be used to settle accounts without the actual transfer of resources out of the IMF. Finally, the G-10 promoted the creation of a new two-tiered gold market. In the private markets, gold prices would be set under market conditions whereas gold for public use would still be available at the rate of $35 an ounce. This, it was hoped, would limit the fragility of the system. As Chapter 10 will reveal, any new stability was only temporary. The Bretton Woods regime would become the victim of the growing international economic pluralism and the global inflation of the 1970s. Thus, by the late 1960s and 1970s, the international monetary and trade regimes that provided part of the basis for U.S. growth and success in international markets had become in many ways a detriment, at least under dated assumptions of U.S. hegemony.

## THE STATE, EMPLOYMENT, AND INDUSTRIAL RELATIONS

The debates over the postwar economy were framed, in large part, by the stagnationist thesis which gained a significant audience in the late 1930s. Anticipating the arguments over technological unemployment, the stagnationists argued that the U.S. economy had matured so that capital was increasingly substituted for labor, thereby creating permanent problems of unemployment that explained, in part, the depth and persistence of the depression. The experience of World War II, fresh on the heels of the Great Depression, taught many an important lesson as to the potential role of fiscal stimulation in maintaining full employment. Moreover, it created significant uncertainty. What would become of the American economy with the cessation of hostilities? Would the nation fall back into the high unemployment rates of the depression? A seemingly endless set of studies making recommendations for policy after the war asked these questions and proposed answers. Many seemed to carry a common warning: "If mass unemployment once again engulfs the economy, it may not be easily dissolved. . . . If after the war the volume of employment should return to the early 1940 level . . . not only would there be a great drop in purchasing power, but the expected spending on accumulated savings would hardly be forthcoming in view of the threat of hard times ahead."[4]

In this environment, attention focused quite naturally on the kinds of policies and planning that would be needed to prevent significant postwar dislocations and a return to the economic trauma that engulfed the 1930s. The most important response to these concerns was the Full Employment Bill introduced by Senator James Murray (D-Mont.) in January 1945. The original bill declared that "all Americans . . . have the right to useful, remunerative, regular, and full time employment" and assigned the government the task of assuring "the existence at all times of sufficient employment opportunities." The bill directed the president to employ a "National Production and Employment Budget" that would be drawn up with the assistance of the President's Bureau of the Budget to determine the difference between the levels of Gross National Product necessary for full employment and future GNP. Ultimately, this difference would be filled through expanded public spending through public works. The bill also called for a Joint Committee on the Budget, thereby providing Congress with a central role in the new policy system. The Full Employment bill could have established the basis for a broad Keynesian policy that committed the federal government to an active labor-market policy as a core feature of macroeconomic management.[5]

The Murray bill made it through the Senate largely intact, despite some concerns over the planning processes inherent in the legislation. Oddly enough, objections did not focus on a key assumption underlying the act, namely, that the federal government had the responsibility to define and implement economywide goals. This is clear evidence that the events of the Great Depression and World War II shaped prevailing visions of the public-private interface. Once the bill passed the Senate, the United States Chamber of Commerce, the National Association of Manufacturers, and the American Farm Bureau Federation mobilized their opposition. Southern democrats and midwestern republicans proved to be the greatest source of opposition to the bill.[6] In the end, the House essentially substituted a bill written largely as a response to alternatives proposed by the U.S. Chamber of Commerce. Although President Truman supported the Senate version of the legislation, heavy business lobbying combined with evidence of economic recovery following the war were sufficient to win the passage of the Employment Act of 1946.

In the end, the Employment Act of 1946 adopted the goals of maximum employment, production, and purchasing power, thus diluting the original goal of full employment. The inclusion of goals that could not be realized simultaneously (e.g., high levels of unemployment would threaten to increase inflation rates) meant that the single-minded pursuit of full employment (i.e., regardless of the implications for growth or inflation) would cease to be a significant threat. The focus on spending and public works was replaced with the amorphous statement that the government would use "all practicable means consistent with its needs and obligations and other essential considerations of national policy." The Employment Act replaced the Keynesian National Production and Employment Budget with the *Economic Report of the President*, to be prepared with the assistance of a newly created Council of Economic Advisers (CEA). Since the members of the CEA would be confirmed by the Senate (unlike the Bureau of the Budget which was completely under the control of the president), this provision meant that responsibility for macroeconomic policy would be shared with the Congress. Finally, the act created a Joint Economic Committee to act in the area of economic affairs, once again limiting the concentration of power in the executive. The dream of a full-employment economy guided by planning and public investment would not be a likely possibility under the new legislation.[7]

 The failure to pass the full-employment legislation and the unwillingness of Congress to guarantee an expansive role for the federal government in providing full employment should not lead us to minimize the emphasis placed on growth and the ultimate progress toward full employment. Rather, high employment levels were essential to secure the position of labor relative to corporations and the state. As noted in Chapter 7, the new labor relations system established under the National Industrial Recovery Act and the Wagner Act sought to create industrial stability by integrating corporate management and unions into a system of government-supervised self-regulation. Negotiated settlements between employers and union representatives covering wages, hours, and working conditions were to replace the shop-floor conflicts of the past. In this arrangement, the state was to serve as a neutral intermediary, supervising industrial relations without adopting the priorities of labor or capital. This system was extended during World War II mobilization. To introduce a guarantee of full employment into this context would substantially alter the relationship between corporations and labor and the state.

 World War II brought a short-lived resurgence of labor militancy. Between 1944 and 1946, there were 14,691 strikes involving some 10.2 million workers.[8] Free from the restrictions of the War Labor Board, corporations moved quickly to place additional restrictions on unions. However, because the Wagner Act had successfully altered the institutional context of industrial relations, employers were not free to return to the former pattern of confrontation backed with violence. In the end, the efforts took the limited form of new legislation in the Taft-Hartley Act of 1947.

 In 1946, following strikes in a number of important industries including steel, automobiles, meatpacking, and coal, Congress passed legislation to create a federal mediation board, impose a cooling off period before strikes could be called, and ban secondary boycotts. Truman successfully vetoed the legislation. However, with restrictive labor legislation passing in a majority of states and the 1946 midterm elections which strengthened the anti-union forces in Congress, new legislation was guaranteed. In 1947, Congress finally triumphed in passing the Taft-Hartley Act. The legislation, strongly advocated by trade associations led by the National Association of Manufacturers, had the avowed goal of redressing the imbalance in industrial relations that had been created through New Deal legislation and the NLRB.

Taft-Hartley increased the ability of management to present their views on unions and to call for elections for deciding appropriate bargaining units. At the same time, the act placed a number of new restrictions on labor unions. Unions were prohibited from using jurisdictional strikes, secondary boycotts, or refusing to bargain collectively. They were now required to give a 60-day notice before terminating or changing agreements or be liable for breach of contract. The president was authorized to apply for an 80-day injunction against any strike deemed to threaten national health or safety. More important, Taft–Hartley created a more complicated voting process for the creation of union shops, banned the closed shop, and allowed states to pass legislation to ban union shops altogether, giving rise to the "right to work" laws in many states. At the same time, Taft–Hartley sought to reduce the role of unions in the political process: Unions were now prohibited from directly using their resources in political campaigns and union officials were forced to submit affidavits swearing that they were not members of the Communist party. The role of the NLRB was altered as well. The NLRB was enlarged, thus allowing for the appointment of new board members to moderate the board which was dominated by New Dealers. At the same time, a new Federal Mediation and Conciliation Service was created to intervene directly in labor relations disputes involving interstate commerce.[9]

While unions attacked Taft-Hartley as an assault on the National Labor Relations Act and organized labor, the new legislation is perhaps most significant for what it failed to do. It did not undermine collective bargaining—the core of the New Deal system of industrial relations. As Kochan, Katz, and McKersie explain: "The legislative initiatives of employers and conservatives in Congress did not result in repeal of the national policy favoring collective bargaining but rather in . . . amendments that sought to limit the power of unions and articulate a new set of principles concerning the rights of individual workers in union-management relations." They conclude: "For our purposes the key point concerning the Taft-Hartley act is that it did not alter in any significant fashion the basis NLRA principles governing industrial relations activity. Thus while it undoubtedly produced a shift in bargaining power from unions to employers, Taft-Hartley allowed the basic features of the New Deal to continue to evolve along the path envisioned by the original framers of the system and reinforced by the War Labor Board."[10]

To be certain, Taft-Hartley placed further restrictions on the radicalism of unions and, through a process of elimination, placed far greater emphasis on collective bargaining as the appropriate forum for resolving labor-management disputes. But these tendencies had been in existence since the original New Deal labor legislation. Labor, at least at the elite level, had already become relatively conservative and the collective bargaining system provided no role for the rank-and-file workers who had been a source of militancy in earlier decades. As Tom Kemp notes: "The rank and file was unable to fight back without the leadership, and the unions, of the CIO as well as the AFL, were ruled by a conservative bureaucracy which had no taste for a confrontation with the state. Instead it settled for bargaining within each industry to win wage increases and other concessions which kept their members happy. If necessary the leadership would enforce the contract against recalcitrant members, among whom shop-floor organization was generally weak or non-existent."[11]

The growing conservatism of labor was represented most clearly in what became the underlying logic of the postwar labor-relations system. In a growing economy, workers could trade ongoing productivity increases for increases in wages. In the words of Alan Wolfe: "Workers would produce more for a given unit of time, thereby increasing profit, but in return, the company would protect workers against inflation by guaranteeing wage increases tied to the cost of living. Productivity would generate economic growth, and economic growth would keep labor relations peaceful."[12] This exchange of profitability gains for wage increases provided the basis for postwar labor contracts. Following the example of the agreement reached between the United Auto Workers and General Motors in 1948, new multiyear contracts guaranteed cost-of-living increases and annual increases based on productivity gains. In addition, they provided internal grievance procedures and extended a host of new benefits, particularly insurance and pensions. In terms of internal procedures and expansive benefits, the postwar contracts were reminiscent of the welfare capitalism of the 1920s.

As a continuation of the trend evident since the National Labor Relations Act had been passed in 1935, the power in the unions moved progressively from the shop floor to the leadership of the national unions. This centralization allowed for more careful monitoring of contract compliance and provided greater bargaining power. In addition, the merger of the AFL and the CIO in 1955 eliminated the competition between the two organizations that had been so important in driving unionization efforts in the late 1930s. As a result of this new capital-labor accord, the percentage of the labor force involved in strikes peaked in 1946 at 14.5 percent, declining to an average of 6.2 percent over the next decade. During the same period, average annual wages in manufacturing increased from $2,517 to $4,584—a remarkable increase given the low levels of inflation.[13] The greater centralization of power in the union hierarchies, the depoliticization of labor organizations, and the creation of multiyear contracts with automatic mechanisms for productivity-based wage increases, made labor a stable partner in what Alan Wolfe refers to as a growth coalition.[14] Because the growing welfare of workers and the stability of industrial relations were premised on growth, this coalition would survive only as long as growth-based expectations could be sustained.

## THE KEYNESIAN CONSENSUS AND MACROECONOMIC MANAGEMENT

Political economy is concerned with the interplay of political and economic forces and the ways in which public authority is used to shape patterns of economic activity. As noted in Chapter 1, policy is often a product of the interplay of political coalitions, elite demands, and situational factors (e.g., macroeconomic performance at a given time) as constrained by existing institutional capacities and policy legacies. Economic theory serves an important role in shaping the institutional capacities of the state. It provides models by which officials can understand the economy, design policies, and justify or exclude other policies from consideration. If we wish to understand economic theories as tools applied in politics and policymaking, as means of directing public action and structuring the relationship between the state

component in the costs of production, higher wage rates translate into higher prices unless they are offset by commensurate increases in productivity. As a general rule, the rate of price increases will be equal to the rate of wage increases, minus the rate of labor productivity increases.[21]

Keynesians suggested that the Phillips Curve represented a stable relationship between unemployment and inflation. As a result, the Phillips Curve appeared to provide a clear guide for policymakers. By observing the relationship represented in the curve, one could use policy to move toward an optimal mixture of inflation and unemployment. If the inflation rate were deemed too great, policymakers could exercise fiscal and monetary restraint and reduce it, albeit at the cost of higher unemployment. What would an optimal mixture of inflation and unemployment look like? The answer to that question would depend largely on the ideology of the policymakers. As Douglas Hibbs has shown, nations with labor or leftist governments have historically chosen to promote higher levels of employment at the cost of higher inflation. Conservative governments, in contrast, have promoted price stability at the cost of higher unemployment. Such a trade-off could be considered politically expedient given the natural constituencies of the parties in question.[22]

## A Framework for Economic Management

As noted above, the Employment Act of 1946 established the goal of promoting high levels of employment, price stability, and growth. It simultaneously created new institutions for economic policymaking. Under the system that was created by the Employment Act and that has evolved over subsequent decades, fiscal policy would be formulated and implemented by the three executive branch agencies which would come to be known eventually as the *Troika*. The Council of Economic Advisers, composed of three economists and a staff, would provide the president with analyses of current economic performance and projections of how inflation, employment, and growth rates might respond to different packages of fiscal stimulus. The Treasury would provide estimates of revenues under different assumptions concerning future economic growth. Finally, the Bureau of the Budget (later the Office of Management and Budget) would assist the president in reviewing agency needs and requests and in formulating the budget, the largest and most significant economic policy formed each year. Through the process, presidents could consider what levels of deficit spending would be necessary to promote a target level of employment and, by examining estimates of revenues and government expenditures, arrive at a budget that would deliver the correct amount of fiscal stimulus.

The Employment Act assigned the president primary responsibility for macroeconomic management and provided the basis for a new advisory system with the creation of the Council of Economic Advisers. However, the new macroeconomic policy process did not simultaneously render Congress subservient to the president's determination of fiscal policy goals. As James L. Sundquist observes: "While the authors of the Employment Act assumed a Keynesian approach to economic policy, a pre-Keynesian president would not have to adopt that approach, and the pre-Keynesians who dominated many of the congressional committees were likewise in no way bound. For them, nothing at all had changed—except for what educational effects might accrue from a required annual exercise in Keynesian analysis."[23] In the United States, macroeconomic policies are the product of composite choice. Actors in the executive branch, Congress, and independent bodies like the Federal Reserve all actively engage in policymaking. The products of their separate endeavors may or may not be compatible. Before examining how the mixture of the various policy instruments has functioned during the first two decades after the Employment Act, we must briefly address economic policymaking in Congress and the Federal Reserve.

## Congress and Macroeconomic Policymaking

Despite the president's role in initiating the budgetary process, the budget as any piece of legislation must be passed by the Congress before it can be signed into law. Likewise, tax bills must work their way through the legislative process after having been initiated in the powerful House Ways and Means Committee. As noted in Chapter 1, Congress is characterized by its fragmentation, its local orientation, and its permeability to interest groups—features that have become even more distinct in recent decades as a result of the post-Watergate reforms and changes in campaign finance laws. The distinctive features of Congress as an institution have immediate implications for economic policy. As Lance LeLoup explains: "Congress has become more individualistic, and this may be related to the increased tendency for members to promote their reelection by procuring tangible benefits for their constituencies. But a strong case can be made that members do have other incentives, including economic policy concerns. The problem is that the legislative process tends to facilitate the achievement of individual goals at the expense of collective policy making."[24]

The Joint Economic Committee, a product of the Employment Act, provided a forum for the discussion of economic policy issues and the president's economic program. Composed of seven members from each chamber, it has occupied a largely advisory role. With the passage of the Congressional Budget and Impoundment Act of 1974, the Congressional Budget Office (CBO) and the budget committees in each chamber stripped away what little power the Joint Economic Committee possessed. The CBO and budget committees have better staff resources and clearer mandates, thus serving as alternative (and at times better) sources of advice.[25]

One should not be surprised that the Congress and president are often at odds over macroeconomic objectives and policies. Members of Congress must respond to a far more diverse set of interests and they are far more vulnerable to interest group and constituent lobbying than is the president. The decentralization and lack of institutional mechanisms to force a unification of action were only exacerbated in the 1970s as a series of reforms brought an end to the seniority rule and imposed a new budgetary process with new sources of power within both houses. The 1974 Congressional Budget and Impoundment Act created a new budgetary process and new budgetary institutions which dramatically reduced the role of the president vis-à-vis the Congress. Increasingly, the president's budget requests would be replaced with decisions arrived at in the appropriations and budget committees in the House and the Senate, guided by economic forecasts presented by the Congressional Budget Office. In a fragmented environment with little consensus over the appropriate mix of policy goals, one cannot expect coherent fiscal policy. Indeed, because the president has so little discretionary authority in fiscal policy, coherence may be impossible except on the rare occasions when crises or particular circumstances allow the president to move his program rapidly through Congress.

## The Federal Reserve and Monetary Policy

The Federal Reserve posed a second and equally significant problem in the postwar macroeconomic policymaking system. The Employment Act assigned primary responsibility for fiscal policy to the president. At the same time, it did nothing to address the independence of the Federal Reserve and its use of monetary policy. To be certain, the term *Quadraid* has been coined to refer to the Troika and the Federal Reserve as if they were integrated into a single policy process. However, the Fed has historically protected its political independence and has sought to limit the extent to which it is drawn into political disputes over the goals and timing of policy actions. There is evidence to suggest that the Federal Reserve has respected the general policy goals of the president. However, the history of the postwar period is filled with examples of a Federal Reserve that uses monetary policy to limit the potential inflationary impact of fiscal policy, thereby imposing price stability as a goal that has precedence over employment or growth.

To understand the advantages and biases associated with the Fed's monetary policies, it is critical to examine briefly the structure of the Federal Reserve and the kinds of policy tools the agency can bring to bear in the process. As noted in Chapter 4, the Federal Reserve was created in 1913 as an independent agency. It is, in essence, a quasi-public institution insofar as it is directly integrated into the community of over 5,000 Federal Reserve member banks and a system of 12 district Federal Reserve Banks. The member banks are all of the commercial banks that carry national charters and major state banks. The Federal Reserve Banks are private corporations owned by member banks. They are private, for-profit, institutions. However, each acts as a public agency by making loans to, and holding the deposits of, member banks and issuing Federal Reserve notes. The Federal Reserve's Board of Governors forms the apex of the system. Its seven members serve staggered 14-year terms as presidential appointees; the board is headed by a chairman who is also a presidential appointee, albeit one serving a 4-year term.[26]

The Federal Reserve serves a number of important purposes, not the least of which is its stabilizing role as a lender of last resort to member banks in the financial system. While this function was deemed of the greatest importance when the Fed was created, for present purposes we are more concerned with the ways in which the Fed can manipulate the cost of capital and hence the behavior of banks, businesses, and consumers at various points in the business cycle. Money is like any other commodity: Its price (in this case, the interest rate) is determined through the forces of supply and demand. The Fed uses three key tools to affect the lending activities of banks and hence the supply of capital relative to demand. The Federal Reserve requires member banks to maintain a certain level of reserves to support their loan activity. By increasing the reserve requirement, the Fed reduces the amount of money that the financial system can support. Likewise, reductions in reserve requirements facilitate greater loan activity and thus allow the banking system to support a much larger amount of money. The Fed can also manipulate the discount rate, that is, the rate at which commercial banks can borrow from the Fed when their reserves are too low. By increasing the discount rate, member banks will tend to hold excess reserves, thus minimizing the chance that they will fall short and have to use the discount window.[27]

Open market operations constitute the third and most important tool employed by the Federal Reserve Board. The term open market operations simply refers to the Fed's sale or purchase of securities on the open market. As noted in Chapter 5, the Federal Reserve began executing open market operations in the 1920s. When the Fed sells securities, the buyer pays with cash which is taken out of circulation, thus reducing the amount of money the banking system can support. When the Fed purchases securities from large financial intermediaries, it pushes cash into the economy which subsequently is used to support new levels of loan activity. Because Federal Reserve open market activities take place on a large scale, the impact on the money supply and interest rates can be significant. Policies concerning the purchase and sale of government securities are determined by the Fed's Federal Open Market Committee (FOMC). The FOMC consists of the Federal Reserve Board and the presidents of five Federal Reserve banks, including the powerful president of the New York Federal Reserve, the bank where the majority of open market activity actually takes place. Since changes in the reserve rate can have extreme effects on the money supply, and the discount rate has fairly insignificant effects, open market activities tend to be the policy instruments of choice.[28]

The Federal Reserve is an independent agency. Although the chairman and members of the Federal Reserve Board are appointed by the president and confirmed by the Senate, they do not work under the direct supervision of the president or members of his cabinet. As with other independent agencies, the Fed's Chairman and board appointees cannot be removed over policy disputes. Of course, the president and Congress have the capacity to exercise some control over the Federal Reserve. Congressional oversight is regular and can be, at times, quite lively. However, several factors are particularly important in limiting political control of the Fed. First, the Fed in known for its economic expertise. Its reputation often places its projections beyond question. Given the complexity of monetary economics and the limited analytical resources at the disposal of Congress, effective oversight can be difficult. Second, the Fed is difficult to control politically because its deliberations are conducted in secret. Because there are lags between policy decisions, which are incremental and cumulative, and their ultimate impact on the economy, the performance of the Federal Reserve is most difficult to monitor. Third and related, Congress and the president commonly exercise authority over agencies through the power of the purse. They can manipulate agency appropriations to create the incentives to comply with the wishes of elected officials. However, the Federal Reserve is not dependent on elected institutions for appropriations. Rather, it operates at a profit by holding the reserves of members banks at zero interest. When the scarcity of information and limited budgetary restraints are combined, the difficulties associated with holding the Federal Reserve politically accountable become clear.

Despite the lack of purse strings, presumably the Fed could be restrained by the threat of changes to its organic statute that would reduce or eliminate its much vaunted independence or its discretion in monetary management. At various times, opponents of the Federal Reserve have called for making it part of the Treasury Department or imposing statutory rules for the growth of the money supply and/or permissible levels of inflation. While there is every indication that the Fed takes these threats very seriously, the Federal Reserve remains as a politically independent agency serving an important political function. Elected officials can attribute the blame for poor economic performance to the Fed—a role which it has been quite willing to fulfill. To enact statutory rules for monetary management would transfer responsibility for the performance of the Fed and the economy to Congress—a transfer of authority that Congress is unwilling to accept. As long as the independence of the Federal Reserve serves an important political function, one should expect it to remain a key feature of the system.[29]

In the end, the Federal Reserve is quite distinct from other economic policymaking institutions in the American system. Unlike the president and Congress, it is highly insulated from the demands of those outside of the financial community and the small community of monetary economists. To draw a comparison along the lines suggested in Chapter 1, the Federal Reserve fits well into the elite perspective by virtue of its political insulation and the procedures that virtually prevent democratic participation in monetary policymaking. In contrast, the key actors in fiscal policymaking are highly pluralistic. The budgetary and taxation policymaking processes are open to organized constituencies. As a result, policy is often something of an amalgamation of interest group demands. In contrast, the Fed's natural constituency—financiers and monetary economists—is tightly bound and shares a general consensus that price stability should be emphasized over the competing goal of promoting high levels of employment.

Moreover, because the Federal Reserve is a unitary actor capable of making and implementing policy with a rapidity and sense of purpose that other actors can only imagine, it can exercise great advantages over the president and Congress in setting and pursuing macroeconomic priorities. Although there is some disagreement over whether the Fed can effectively stimulate the economy via low interest rates, there is little question that the Fed has distinct institutional advantages relative to Congress and the presidency. This has become increasingly the case as a large and growing deficit and legislatively imposed rules (e.g., Gramm-Rudman) have limited the discretionary spending of Congress and the president. In this environment, the one agency which retains significant discretionary authority and the capacity to control the economy is the Federal Reserve.

## MACROECONOMIC POLICY AND PERFORMANCE

With the new postwar international environment, a stable system of industrial relations, the Keynesian consensus, and a new institutional framework for macroeconomic policy, the stage was set for a new period of economic management with high rates of employment and relative price stability. As Figures 8–3, and 8–4 suggest, the United States experienced a positive combination of employment and price stability as well as persistent growth. When compared with the previous decades and, of course, the period after 1968, the economic performance of the period would appear ideal.

Three points need to be made before we examine the macroeconomic performance of the period. First, it is very difficult to separate the impact of economic management from the other factors that contributed to growth in the postwar period. The unique features of the immediate postwar period (e.g., American international hegemony, new economic institutions, an enlarged capital stock) all contributed to the strong growth. What is clear from Figure 8–4, however, is that for much of the period in question, the actual gross national product was very close to capacity (i.e., what would have been possible if all factors of production were completely employed).

Second, whether full employment was ever reached is an open question due to the rather hazy and often political definition of the concept. One might define full employment as the level at which all unemployment is voluntary or frictional (i.e., caused by people who are voluntarily moving between jobs). Another useful definition of full employment—and one which would gain great currency among monetarists—was the unemployment rate compatible with price stability. The definition of full employment has changed over time due to changes in the underlying demographics and the labor force participation rates of various groups. Thus, the increase in job participation among women, minorities, and teenagers in the late 1960s and 1970s was commonly cited as one of the factors that forced an increase in the unemployment rate associated with full employment.

**Figure 8–3**  Unemployment and Inflation Rates, 1950–1975

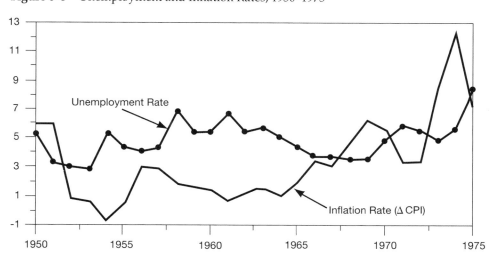

Source: *Economic Report of the President, 1993* Tables B-59, B-38.

and presidential indecision all contributed to the Republican victories in the 1946 midterm elections.[33]

The first Council of Economic Advisers (CEA) was created in August 1946, in the middle of the debates over the potential role of additional price controls. Truman assigned the new CEA a key role in economic decision making—a role which would decline somewhat in subsequent administrations. The CEA participated in Cabinet and National Security Council meetings, where it had the duty of coordinating economic policies throughout the executive branch through a host of interdepartmental committees.[34] Accordingly, Leon Keyserling, a chairman of the CEA during the Truman administration, noted that the President saw the CEA as "an 'independent' agency in the Executive Office of the President" that could be trusted to give recommendations free from the constituent alliances that characterized so many other agencies. Based, in part, on his faith in the expertise of the CEA, Truman looked to the council for direction. Keyserling states that Truman "didn't want alternatives laid out. He wanted a one-armed economist."[35]

Another reason why Truman may have supported the CEA was that its recommendations clearly reinforced his own instincts as to the problems facing the economy. In late 1946, the CEA recommended that the president make price stability his number one priority and argued that this should be achieved through a budget surplus, lower interest rates, vigorous antitrust efforts to limit administered pricing in oligopolistic industries, and an expansion of housing construction to address the housing shortage that was creating ongoing inflationary pressures. The administration pursued a restrictive policy for the next year, albeit without the desired impact on inflation. To this end, Truman successfully vetoed a tax cut bill in June 1947, and another one month later. In November 1947, Truman presented a ten-point economic program to a special session of Congress, calling for Congress to authorize credit controls, regulations on speculative commodity trading, new export controls, various measures to allocate scarce commodities and transportation, efforts to improve agricultural efficiency, consumer rationing, and price, wage, and rent controls. In the end, Congress failed to act on any of the important economic policy requests.[36]

In 1948, Truman combined his concerns with inflation with the upcoming reelection campaign. When Congress convened in January, it moved quickly to pass a significant tax reduction, in part as a response to the record government surplus of $6.8 billion. The legislation was passed in April with large margins, large enough to overturn an expected presidential veto.[37] Following this defeat, Truman called another special session of Congress in July 1948 where he once again requested congressional authorization for a broad anti-inflationary program which would include efforts to reduce excess demand through tax increases and credit controls, controls on the distribution of materials critical for industrial production, and new price and wage controls. The anticipated congressional response provided Truman with an important theme for the campaign trail. He attacked the "rich man's tax bill" and the "unholy alliance of big business and the Republican Party" that had as its primary aim the prevention of new controls on prices. Although Truman's reelection bid was successful and control of both houses returned to the Democrats, the continued battle against inflation was suspended as the nation entered a recession in the beginning of 1949 and unemployment peaked at 5.9 percent. Truman was hesitant to use an expansionary fiscal policy to bring the country out of recession. The recession-induced price stability had been hoped for for too long. In the end, the Korean war (1950 to 1953) provided the way out of the recession. War production once again absorbed excess labor and created the emergency circumstances that could justify price controls.[38]

During the Korean War, Truman and the Congress essentially resurrected the economic policies employed in World War II. Wartime mobilization was addressed in some detail in Chapters 5 and 7. Suffice it to say that an Economic Stabilization Agency, an Office of Price Stabilization, and a Wage Stabilization Board were created to administer controls, largely along the lines of those administered in World War II. In January 1951, the Office of Price Stabilization imposed a regulation freezing prices on goods and services; the Wage Stabilization Board followed suit to freeze wages. These efforts, combined with higher taxes imposed in hopes of limiting the reliance on deficit funding for the war and restrictive monetary policy, created a relatively effective system for controlling inflation. By the fall of 1952, with the end of the war in sight and a Republican presidential candidate promising a removal of controls and a reduction in taxes, the controls began to unravel. In the winter of 1952, Truman's intervention in a coal strike in direct opposition to the decision of the Wage Stabilization Board resulted in the resignation of the board members and an end to wage controls.[39]

## The Eisenhower Administration

The Eisenhower presidency was fiscally conservative, a reflection of the president's own conservatism and his strong distaste for inflation and government controls. Following the Korean War, the economy entered a prolonged period of stabilization, albeit with relatively high levels of unemployment. Nevertheless, President Eisenhower's hatred of inflation expressed itself in the ongoing use of contractionary fiscal and monetary policies to maintain stable prices, whatever the cost in terms of employment. While inflation was reduced to about 1 percent, it was achieved at the cost of high levels of unemployment.

Following a recession in 1954 which was a direct product of reduced defense spending, the economy entered a period of slow growth with extraordinarily low inflation. Despite the lack of inflationary forces, Eisenhower remained very cautious in his use of fiscal policy. Thus, when the economy entered recession in late 1957 and 1958 and the unemployment rate for the year reached 6.8 percent, the administration refused to embark on a stimulative fiscal program. The fear was that any policy changes designed to address short-term problems of unemployment could set the stage for the return of inflation following the recession. The Democrats in Congress responded to the President's inaction by calling for a stimulative program. While some Democrats advocated an expansion of public works programs to restore purchasing power and bring the economy to full employment, their calls were overwhelmed by the demands for tax reductions, which gained growing support as George Meany of the AFL-CIO, the Joint Economic Committee, and Arthur Burns, Eisenhower's former CEA chairman, called for the measure.[40]

Eisenhower had already addressed tax reform early in his first term. In 1953, the administration initiated a complete revision of the tax code—the first time the tax code had been rewritten since 1913! The Internal Revenue Code of 1954 added dramatically to the complexity of the tax code, as it had to account for a far more complex economy and society than that which had existed in 1913. As one might expect, most of the major substantive changes brought tax reductions.[41] Given the employment problems, the Democratically controlled Congress called for additional tax reductions in 1955. However, Eisenhower rejected the proposal and called for a balanced budget in his 1956 State of the Union address—a goal that would be stressed repeatedly over the next several years. However, in 1957 to 1958, increases in transfer payments, housing subsidies, and extended unemployment compensation, when combined with recession-related reductions in revenues, forced higher deficits than the president might otherwise have tolerated. The existence of the deficit was sufficient to derail the Democrats' calls for a new round of tax reductions.[42]

The combination of mild fiscal stimulus resulting from a collection of expenditures that Eisenhower allowed to pass through the legislative process and a rapid increase in the money supply engineered by the Federal Reserve brought the economy out of recession in the early months of 1959. However, the combination of the $12 billion deficit and the resumption of an inflation rate of 2 percent convinced the president and the Federal Reserve that macroeconomic policy must turn restrictive once again. Eisenhower created a Cabinet Committee on Price Stability for Economic Growth in January and sponsored a National Conference on Price Stability in November. Moreover, the Council of Economic Advisers created the Advisory Board on Economic Growth and Stability to facilitate communication among the agencies involved in economic policymaking and to generate quality economic recommendations for the president. The board focused on tax policy, the budget, monetary policy, debt management, and cost-price policy. In each instance, the goal was to stimulate greater public support for a new anti-inflationary policy. In 1960, Eisenhower reduced administration spending to create a budget surplus. When the restrictive fiscal policy was combined with a reduction in the money supply, the result was a return to high unemployment. The recovery was truncated just in time for the presidential election of 1960, a close race between then Vice-President Richard Nixon and John F. Kennedy.[43]

## Kennedy-Johnson: The Triumph of Keynesianism

The Kennedy-Johnson period stands in stark opposition to the conservatism of the previous administrations. Initially Kennedy refused to provide sufficient stimulus to the economy, despite his campaign trail references to the fiscal conservatism of the Eisenhower administration and his belief that the administration had to take the Employment Act more seriously and use macroeconomic policy to achieve rapid growth and full employment. While the Kennedy administration began with a strong streak of conservatism, the economic initiatives of the Kennedy presidency as extended by President Johnson were widely hailed as marking the final triumph of Keynesianism and macroeconomic management.

Kennedy's initial desire to strengthen the role of the Council of Economic Advisers may have been a product of his own personal interest in economics. According to members of Kennedy's CEA, the president had a strong desire to understand the economic rationale for his policies. Although he relied on his economists for policy analysis and recommendations, he developed the capacity to assess critically the options presented him—even when such assessment required a detailed knowledge of economic reasoning. As CEA Chairman Walter Heller noted: "What he was interested in, by God, was getting to the essence, the facts, the analysis, and he really did have a steel-trap mind. We were often amazed at his capacity for understanding a particular set of relationships in economics."[44] Kennedy's desire to be educated in the theories and technical manipulations of data that provided a basis for economic policy recommendations allowed him to appraise the recommendations and question the fiscal impact of the spending proposals presented by his secretaries.

When Kennedy entered office, he shared with his advisers the goal of promoting full employment through demand stimulus. The administration hoped that a combination of expansive fiscal policy (with emphasis placed on the spending side, rather than a reduction of taxation) when combined with tight money policy and tax reform would provide several benefits. Fiscal policy would stimulate demand, thus allowing for rapid expansion and potentially higher levels of investment. The investment effects would be magnified by an investment tax credit (ultimately passed as the Revenue Act of 1962). The high interest rates associated with monetary policy would have the effect of attracting investment and foreign capital, thus allowing for higher levels of capital investment and providing a solution to balance of trade problems. Finally, the high interest rates could be crucial in limiting the return of inflationary forces as the economy was moving out of the recession of 1960. Of course, Kennedy moved with some care out of fear that a mistimed stimulus could force a burst of inflation. Prudence demanded that one wait until the limits of the current recovery became clear.[45]

Clarity was achieved in 1962. By the summer it was evident that the recovery was not going to result in full employment and might actually be truncated by another lapse into recession—one which could potentially threaten success in the 1964 election. Moreover, it was clear that Congress did not share the president's desire for expansive spending. Members of Congress questioned the wisdom of incurring deficits during a period of growth when surpluses were expected to compensate for past debt. This was combined with disagreements over the Kennedy spending proposals. Finally, Kennedy ran into conflicts with business and labor in the spring of 1962 as his CEA announced voluntary wage and price guideposts— a peacetime incomes policy—to limit inflationary forces. The refusal of the steel industry to abide by the guideposts in its pricing decisions led to a direct conflict between Kennedy and the industry in the spring of 1962.[46]

This political and economic environment had an important effect on the Kennedy program. Although Kennedy initially wished to stimulate the economy through expansive spending, this option met with the opposition of Congress and business, suggesting that an expansive spending program could carry high political costs. Yet, with the economy showing new signs of stagnation and the full employment target well out of reach, time could not be devoted to a lengthy struggle with Congress. As the threat of inflation no longer appeared to be significant, Kennedy turned to advocate a large tax cut as a means of stimulating the economy. This conservative Keynesian policy, strongly advocated by CEA Chairman Walter Heller, would cut into business resistance, particularly if combined with cuts in corporate taxes.

In justifying the new policy, Kennedy noted in his economic report: "Tax reduction will remove an obstacle to the full development of the forces of growth in a free economy." Kennedy explained that the tax reduction was justified for two reasons: "First, for the sustained lift it will give to the economy's demand for goods and services, and thus to the expansion of its productive capacity; second, for the added incentive to productive investment, risk-taking, and efficient use of resources that will come from lowering the corporate tax rate and the unrealistic top rates on personal income and eliminating unwarranted tax preferences that undermine the tax base and misdirect energy and resources."[47] The *Economic Report of the President* explained: "If the tax system imposes an excessive drag on the economy—through its effects on purchasing power and on incentives—tax rates may be too high relative to expenditures, even though the budget is in deficit. Thus, tax revision, involving both reduction and reform, can not only provide stimulus for growth and prosperity, but can even, as a result, balance the budget or produce surpluses. . . . prosperity and growth balance budgets."[48]

The administration introduced its proposed changes in the tax code in January 1963. It called for net tax reductions of $11.3 billion for fiscal years 1964 to 1965. The impact of a $11 billion reduction in individual taxes and a $2.6 billion cut in corporate taxes would be partially offset by reforms slated to generate another $2.3 billion in revenues. Reductions in individual and corporate income tax rates and capital gains tax cuts were justified as a means of driving future economic growth and the movement toward full employment. In the end, the 1964 tax act was ushered through the legislative process by Lyndon Johnson. Following the assassination of President Kennedy, congressional resistance dissipated. The tax cut rested heavily on personal income tax reductions of between 20 and 30 percent, depending on the income group. The tax reductions, combined with permissive monetary policy, allowed for the rapid growth in the economy and a movement to full employment.[49]

We shall return to the effects of the tax cut in a moment. Before this , however, it is important to note that the tax cut was combined with the introduction of the full-employment budget as a tool both of meeting the concerns of fiscal conservatives and providing a means of providing the correct amount of fiscal stimulation to bring the economy toward a 4 percent unemployment rate (i.e., full employment). Beginning in the 1962 *Economic Report of the President*, the CEA started employing the full-employment budget to gauge the overall impact of fiscal policy on employment goals and growth. As the CEA's report noted: "Since tax revenues and some expenditures depend on the level of economic activity, there is a whole range of possible surpluses and deficits associated with a given budget program. The particular surpluses or deficits in fact realized will depend on the level of economic activity." The full-employment budget allowed one to "calculate

Johnson was cautious of any advisers who might have a hidden agenda. While he routinely discounted the counsel of his departmental secretaries, he viewed the CEA as being freer of institutional biases, an impression that was reinforced by the professionalism of the staff and the lack of constituencies other than the president. Nevertheless, Johnson would meet only with Chairman Ackley, and oftentimes even required Ackley to work through Joseph Califano, his domestic policy aide. When major policy questions affecting various departments had to be examined, Califano—not the CEA—would bring together the relevant executive branch actors. In this context, the council was often assigned the status of an equal participant.

Because of Johnson's political orientation and the politicization of policy advice, Chairman Ackley found that much of his job consisted of convincing the president that certain policies provided needed tools of economic management. Ackley recalls that Johnson's "pro-farmer, pro-small business, anti-banker, anti-Wall Street" populism led him to reject tools of macroeconomic management that required a reliance on the Federal Reserve. On the occasions when a reliance on monetary policy was recommended, Ackley reports that he had to "fight like the devil to keep him [the President] quiet."[60] In the end, Johnson's dislike of the banking establishment and his personal dislike of Federal Reserve Chairman William McChesney Martin led him to reject policies that would have necessitated a close working relationship between the administration and the Fed. Because Johnson refused consistently to meet with the Quadriad, the CEA had to forge a number of informal ties with the Federal Reserve in hopes of coordinating policies.

The advisory function of the CEA during the Johnson administration was in many ways similar to that which existed during the Kennedy years. The CEA—once again, working exclusively through the chairman or Califano—advised the president as to the general macroeconomic trends, targets, and polices. The role of the CEA in this respect may have been greater than during the Kennedy administration, given the close association of Kennedy and Treasury Secretary Douglas Dillon. The council's position was further enhanced by its capacity to respond to the president's requests with greater rapidity than the other actors within the economic subpresidency. Troika meetings continued as they had in the past. However, Garner Ackley suggests that the role of the Treasury was limited by the overall perception that its constituency interests and its close ties to the financial community affected its ability to provide the president with what he might view as objective policy advice. In contrast, the CEA and the Budget Bureau, both staffed by economists and responsible solely to the president, developed a close relationship with the president. Of course, the relationship between the two agencies was also enhanced by their shared responsibility for the budget and the necessity of operating outside of the Cabinet.[61]

Johnson's slow response to the growing inflation rate can be associated, in part, to his personal biases and style of management. There was, however, a more fundamental problem, namely, the success of the 1964 tax cut. Johnson saw full employment as an important victory for his administration. He did not want to dash this victory to achieve price stability, particularly when the domestic reactions to the war were becoming ever more threatening. Moreover, ongoing economic growth was essential for the success of the administration's War on Poverty. The government could actively seek to eliminate discriminatory barriers and create training and community programs to empower the poor. However, these policies would have the intended impact only if sufficient job opportunities existed. The nation could grow out of poverty if and only if the economy continued to expand. With these concerns in mind, one can only sympathize with Johnson's hesitancy in promoting contractionary policies.

Beginning in 1966, the CEA placed pressure on Johnson for a tax surcharge and the suspension of the investment tax credit to limit inflationary forces, albeit combined with an easy money policy to promote further expansion. CEA Chairman Ackley was joined by Budget Director Charles Schultze in this effort. However, the impending midterm congressional elections—commonly interpreted as a referendum on the president's policies—made the recommendations politically unacceptable. However, the pressure continued until Johnson accepted the need for restraint. In the 1967 *Economic Report of the President*, Johnson called for a 6 percent surcharge on the tax liabilities of individuals and corporations and accelerations of corporate tax payments. This would offset the stimulative effect of $5.8 billion in defense purchases. Combined with "more moderate growth of Federal spending," the surcharge would "increase the freedom of monetary policy to support expansion."[62] However, with the exception of the suspension of the investment tax credit—later rescinded in response to evidence of a softening economy—Johnson's requests went unanswered.

To a great degree, the inability to get Congress to provide the tax surcharge in 1967 reflected Johnson's difficulties in convincing Wilbur Mills, the chairman of the powerful House Ways and Means Committee, to advocate passage of a surcharge without simultaneous reductions in domestic spending. It was feared by Johnson that such cuts would detract from the War on Poverty programs. However, price increases and rising interest rates early in 1968 convinced Congress to push forward on the tax surcharge. In June 1968, Congress passed the Revenue and Expenditure Control Act which provided a 10 percent tax surcharge, continued a number of excise taxes, and accelerated corporate tax payments in exchange for immediate recessions and significant reductions in appropriations for fiscal year 1969.[63]

By the fall of 1968, concerns emerged in the CEA that the combination of the tax surcharge and the reduction in spending was excessive and would result in recession. The CEA recommended a more expansive monetary policy. The Fed complied. However, the dramatic monetary expansion was combined with the continued Vietnam War spending, thereby forcing a return to high inflation rates, albeit with higher levels of unemployment than had existed prior to the surcharge. The combination of inflation and unemployment—the two opposing forces of the Phillips Curve—suggested that the inflation the nation was encountering in the final years of the 1960s was qualitatively different from that which had existed in the past. The stage had been set for a crisis in economic policymaking that would engulf the 1970s and hasten the erosion of the theoretical consensus that had emerged in the postwar decades to guide macroeconomic policymaking.

The U.S. economy enjoyed a period of prolonged growth with relative price stability in the two decades following World War II. The exceptional economic performance and the rapid growth in incomes that it made possible were largely the product of four factors. First, as the only remaining industrial power of note, the United States was in a unique position to shape the recovery of the world economy after the war. A liberal trade regime combined with the creation of a de facto dollar standard placed the nation in a favorable position vis-à-vis the world economy. Moreover, a new growth-based alliance between corporations and organized labor translated into remarkable stability in industrial relations. Finally, the creation of a new macroeconomic policymaking system and the adoption of Keynesian demand management resulted in relatively mild recessions and the achievement of full employment. The unique conditions of the postwar period gave rise to an equally unique record of performance that would shape expectations for decades to come.

By the late 1960s, the recovery of Europe and Japan was complete and the United States's advantages in the world economy began to erode. While the trade regime was promoting ever greater expansions of trade, the monetary regime teetered on the brink of collapse due largely to the persistent outflow of dollars into the world economy. Finally, the inflation that was created by the combination of Vietnam-induced spending and the tax cut of 1964 created a new problem for macroeconomic policymakers, the magnitude of which would become clear only during the 1970s. Despite the predictions of the Phillips Curve, contractionary monetary and fiscal policies did not bring an end to inflation, even though they eroded the growth of the economy and endangered the capital-labor accord of the postwar period. In the end, the war against inflation and unemployment would dominate the 1970s, forcing experimentation with wage-price policy, deep recessions, and the abandonment of the established international monetary regime. In the process, the Keynesian consensus which had unified economists and policymakers thus far in the postwar period would disappear. The resulting theoretical vacuum would leave macroeconomic policy without clear guidance for decades to come.

## NOTES

1. Robert Kuttner, *The End of Laissez-Faire: National Purpose and the Global Economy After the Cold War* (New York: Alfred A. Knopf, 1991), pp. 40–43.
2. Joan Edelman Spero, *The Politics of International Economic Relations* (New York: St. Martin's, 1977), pp. 70–71.
3. See Ian Roxborough, *Theories of Underdevelopment* (London: Macmillan, 1979), pp. 42–69; Celso Furtado, *Economic Development of Latin America: Historical Background and Contemporary Problems*, 2nd ed. (Cambridge: Cambridge University Press, 1976), pp. 194–224.
4. E. Jay Howenstine, Jr., *The Economics of Demobilization* (Washington, D.C.: American Council on Public Affairs, 1944), pp. 46–47.
5. Robert M. Collins, *The Business Response to Keynes, 1929–1964* (New York: Columbia University Press, 1981), pp. 100–101; Lance T. LeLoup, "Congress and the Dilemma of Economic Policy." In *Making Economic Policy in Congress*, ed. Allen Schick (Washington, D.C.: American Enterprise Institute, 1983), pp. 11–12.
6. Margaret Weir, *Politics and Jobs: The Boundaries of Employment Policy in the United States* (Princeton, N.J.: Princeton University Press, 1992), pp. 45–46.
7. Collins, *The Business Response to Keynes*, pp. 107–108; Herbert Stein, *Presidential Economics: The Making of Economic Policy from Roosevelt to Reagan and Beyond* (Washington: American Enterprise Institute, 1988), pp. 76–78.
8. *Statistical History of the United States*, Series D 764-65.

# 9

# STAGFLATION AND THE WAR AGAINST INFLATION

During the first two decades following World War II, the American economy enjoyed relative price stability and, ultimately, full employment. The unique circumstances explored in Chapter 8 contributed to strong economic performance and rising incomes. Active fiscal and monetary policies and the success of the New Deal system of industrial relations and liberal trade and monetary regimes governing international economic activity provided a sound foundation for growth. The late 1960s and 1970s brought an end to this stability. The combined fiscal stimulus of the 1964 tax cut, Great Society spending, and the Vietnam War introduced higher rates of inflation than policymakers were willing to tolerate. Taken by itself, inflation might not have posed a great concern. Policymakers had effectively used monetary and fiscal policy to manage the business cycle in earlier decades. However, the new inflation of the 1970s posed a far greater challenge than anyone might have anticipated for two reasons. First, the inflation rate was remarkably high, matched in this century only by the inflation that accompanied the two world wars. Second, inflation was combined with persistent problems of unemployment, thus undermining a key feature of Keynesianism. Stagflation—the combination of high inflation and unemployment—created a perplexing problem for the Nixon, Ford, and Carter administrations while revealing the frailty of the Keynesian consensus and the inadequacy of existing strategies of macroeconomic management. The dismal performance of the 1970s and the failure of orthodox theory to provide a solution to stagflation set the stage for the policies of the Reagan administration.

Our examination of stagflation and the politics of decline must begin with a brief discussion of the troublesome relationship between inflation and unemployment and competing explanations for the period's unique combination of economic problems. The limits of prevailing theories are clear when one examines the policies of presidents Nixon, Ford and Carter. While the combination of fiscal and monetary policies failed to resolve the problems of the period, other nations realized greater success. A cross-national comparison can reveal the limitations of the American approach to macroeconomic policymaking. Thus, we end with a discussion of how U.S. performance compared with that of other nations and what lessons one might gain from the comparative responses to global inflation.

## EXPLAINING STAGFLATION AND THE 1970s

Economists cherish price stability and for good reason. Prices are an expression of the relationship between supply and demand. They convey a wealth of information and carry signals that direct the allocation of resources. Inflation—the economywide increase in general price levels—can distort these signals and thus affect the functioning of markets. Inflation results from a variety of factors. When demand is greater than potential output, the relative scarcity of key commodities forces price increases. When prices increase for basic inputs (e.g., wages, steel, energy), the effects can be transferred throughout the economy. One can also speak of expectational inflation which occurs when the anticipation of future inflation affects the economic decision making of individuals, groups, and economic organizations. For example, unions may demand higher wages in contract decisions; businesses may set prices higher in the anticipation of future price increases. In the end, the expectation of future price increases creates behavior that make such increases greater than they might otherwise have been.

As shown in Chapter 8, Keynesian economics provided the intellectual framework for economic management in the postwar period, particularly during the Kennedy and Johnson administrations. Keynes's concern was an economy running well below capacity. Thus, he had the luxury of assuming price stability. The need to explain the relationship between employment levels and price levels was exemplified in the economic performance of the postwar period. This theoretical gap was filled by the Phillips Curve, which quickly became a core feature of the Keynesian consensus. The Phillips Curve, as presented in Figure 8–2, posits an inverse relationship between inflation and unemployment. The explanation for this relationship is easily explained. Labor is responsive to the forces of supply and demand. At high levels of unemployment, surplus labor supports low wage rates. As the economy expands, however, unemployment declines. Growing labor scarcity leads to greater labor power which is expressed, ultimately, in higher wage levels. Because labor is a key factor of production, higher wage rates stimulate higher prices unless they are offset by equivalent productivity gains.[1] The Phillips Curve suggested that there was a stable relationship between unemployment and inflation. The mixture of price stability and employment levels could be consciously manipulated by policymakers by engineering a movement along the Phillips Curve in the desired direction. If the inflation rate were deemed too great, policymakers could exercise fiscal and monetary restraint and reduce it, albeit at the cost of higher unemployment. If the economy entered a recession with high levels of unemployment, they could use expansionary policy to return to a higher level of employment and higher prices.

The Phillips Curve seemed to solve an important intellectual puzzle for Keynesians while providing a stable model for policymakers. However, it did not stand without challenges. Indeed, the greatest challenge came from the monetarists who suggested that the relationships presented by the Phillips Curve were unstable and that any movement from the natural rate of unemployment would be short term and result in higher levels of inflation. To understand the critique, it is necessary to consider the constituent elements of inflation. At any given time, the inflation rate reflects the combination of the core inflation rate, demand inflation, and inflation caused by temporary shocks. The core inflation rate is the expected inflation rate. Workers expect a particular rate of inflation and incorporate these expectations into wage demands. Demand inflation is the inflation that exists when demand exceeds supply for key commodities. Inflation can also be a product of shocks to the economic system, such as unanticipated shortages in necessary raw materials or the onset of war.[2]

The monetarist critique and the alleged problems with the Phillips Curve are represented by the Expectations-Augmented Phillips Curve (see Figure 9–1). Unemployment is at its natural level (point A) when the demand for labor exerts no inflationary force. Under these circumstances, the actual inflation rate will equal the core inflation rate (i.e., the expected inflation rate). Most monetarists would prefer to see zero percent inflation. However, the key point is that under these conditions the inflation rate is stable and equal to the expected inflation rate. When policymakers use monetary or fiscal policy to move away from the natural rate of unemployment (e.g., a movement from point A to point B), they create artificially

**Figure 9–1**   The Expectations–Augmented Phillips Curve

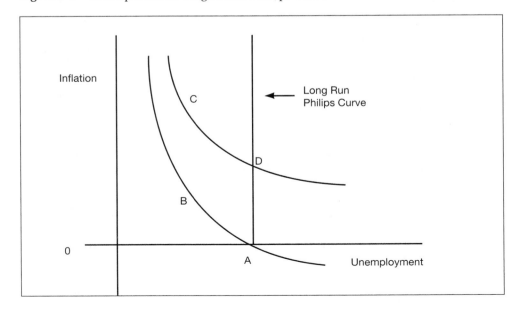

high levels of demand and thus introduce an inflationary force beyond the normal core rate of inflation. As a result, the actual inflation rate exceeds the expected inflation rate, thus undermining some of the incentives that led workers to accept jobs in the first place. When the actual inflation rate is higher than the expected inflation rate, the economy shifts from point B to point C. However, the return to the natural rate of unemployment, point D, is accompanied by a new core rate of inflation since workers incorporate their recent experiences of inflation into their expectations concerning future inflation. In essence, the monetarists argue that any inflation rate is compatible with the natural rate of unemployment. As a result, the long-term Phillips Curve is vertical.

The Expectations-Augmented Phillips Curve carries troublesome implications for Keynesian demand management. While policymakers may successfully engineer a movement along the short-term Phillips Curve to realize lower unemployment rates, any gains will be transitory and may simply result in higher core inflation rates. Since it is much easier to increase inflationary expectations than it is to eliminate them, repetitive movements along the Phillips Curve may result in a ratcheting up of the core inflation rate. Monetarists suggest that monetary policy is ill-suited as a tool of managing the business cycle because of its long and variable lags. It is difficult to predict when changes in the money supply will have their intended impact. The monetarist critique concludes that active countercyclical policy will only result in higher core rates of inflation without long-term reductions in unemployment. Given these restrictions, monetarists argue that the economy should be brought to the natural unemployment rate and then the money supply should be expanded in line with economic growth.

This conservative policy prescription carried little weight in the 1970s because the political demands for macroeconomic stability forced a policy response. Under these circumstances, the mere suggestion that the short-term Phillips Curve could bring short-term gains was sufficient given that the major economic decisions are made by the president who is elected and serves in the short term. It would have taken the complete failure of traditional Keynesian demand management and the rise of free market rhetoric to create an opportunity to create sufficient support for monetarist proposals in the late 1970s and 1980s.[3]

## Explaining Stagflation

The Expectations-Augmented Phillips Curve provided the basis for one explanation of the high inflation rates and persistent unemployment of the 1970s. High inflation rates were considered a product of the persistent attempts to promote artificially low levels of unemployment through expansionary fiscal and monetary policies. Successive movements along the short-term Phillips Curve stimulated an upward ratchet in the core rate of inflation, albeit at unemployment rates that remained too high in an era when politicians of all stripes claimed to support high levels of employment, if not the goal of full employment. Some Keynesians provided complementary explanations based on the steady growth of the previous two decades. It was argued that growth and the full-employment economy of the 1960s created expectations of future growth and the belief that the fruits of this growth would result in higher income levels for all. These expectations were expressed in wage and price decisions, thus creating an inflation prone society.[4]

Monetarist and Keynesian theories tend to discount and in many cases dismiss the institutional factors that may shape economic performance and contribute to inflation. Monetarism, in particular, focuses on how rational actors respond to a disjunction between the expectations of future inflation and actual price increases. This methodological individualism is taken to extremes by the rational expectations school of economics, an intellectual heir of monetarism. According to members of this school, individuals are rational actors functioning on the basis of complete information about the economy. They use this information to project future government activity. With this knowledge and forecasts of future policies, the rational actor can act strategically to avoid the intended effects of policy. The implications are clear: Government management of the economy will be frustrated as long as it is systematic and nonrandom.[5]

While one cannot dismiss the importance of individual action, markets are far less important in the United States than prevailing economic theories would acknowledge. As the past several chapters have shown, during the twentieth century the institutional foundation of the U.S. economy was literally transformed. The creation of collective bargaining and multiyear labor agreements, inflation-indexed social welfare benefits, a regulatory structure created to preserve the profitability and stability of entire industries, and a public commitment to high employment via macroeconomic policy limited the vulnerability to, and power of, the market. Much of economic life was politicized and transformed into an extension of explicit policy decisions. Many group claims on national income were more the products of public policies than the result of rational individual actions and market transactions. The assumptions of individual rational actors interacting within the confines of a free market bears little resemblance to the dense network of political and economic associations, large corporate and government bureaucracies engaged in planning, and public policies designed to insulate selected groups from potential economic dislocations.[6] This fact, when combined with the distinctively conservative policy proposals put forth by monetarism, rational expectations theory, and, later supply-side economics (see Chapter 10), limited the impact of these alternate theoretical frameworks until significant changes had occurred in the political climate.[7]

When a group's claim on national income is determined in a political context by officials subject to the electoral mandate, it is appropriate to conceptualize the economy as a set of institutions with a strong inflationary bias. Under these conditions, inflation becomes more a political-institutional problem than an economic problem, more a problem of governance than a problem of market distortions. The potential implications of this portrayal of inflation will be addressed later in this chapter. For now, it is important to note that whether one examines the economy through the analytical lens of monetarism, Keynesianism, or institutionalism, there is a shared agreement that the economy of the late 1960s and 1970s carried a strong inflationary bias and a vulnerability to exogenous shocks. Ultimately, the OPEC oil price increases and world food shortages in 1973 to 1974 were sufficient to transform an inflationary bias into persistently high levels of inflation.

Of course, inflation was but one-half of the problem facing the American economy in the 1970s. Stagflation constituted a frustrating combination of high inflation and economic stagnation. How does one explain the higher than expected levels of unemployment and the low levels of growth? There is no question that the United States entered a period of declining growth rates after 1968. From 1948 to 1968, Gross National Product grew at an inflation-adjusted average annual rate of 4 percent. Between 1969 and 1980, the average annual growth rate fell to 2.85 percent.[8] The slow growth seems to have several sources which are tied to the disintegration of the unique conditions the United States faced during the 1950s and 1960s. As explained in Chapter 8, the postwar period presented an exceptional environment for growth. Following the war, the United States had the strongest economy in the world due to the dramatic expansion of the economy during the war and the simultaneous destruction of other advanced industrial economies. In addition, the United States strengthened its international position by creating liberal international trade and monetary regimes. The trade regime established under the General Agreement on Tariffs and Trade promoted a reduction of tariff barriers and an elimination of trading blocs to facilitate the free flow of goods and capital. Of course, a liberal trade regime always favors the nations that are strong enough to expand into international trade and grow without the imposition of protectionist barriers.[9] These unique conditions were combined with important domestic factors, including stability in industrial relations through the New Deal system of collective bargaining and the new system of macroeconomic management created under the Employment Act of 1946 and directed by a pro-growth Keynesian consensus.[10]

These factors combined to promote steady expansion and the growth-oriented expectations addressed above. However, by the late 1960s and 1970s, these favorable conditions began to disintegrate. First, strong economic growth in Europe and Japan resulted in greater international economic competition, the integration of the U.S. economy into a world division of labor, and a consequent erosion of America's dominant position in the world economy. Although the United States continued to have the world's largest industrial economy, it could no longer exercise undisputed hegemony. The liberal trade regime which allowed for the growth of the 1950s and 1960s now provided the basis for growing trade imbalances. In 1965, the U.S. trade surplus with Japan turned into a deficit. The trade surplus with the European Economic Community became a deficit in 1972. Indeed, in 1971 the United States experienced a balance-of-trade deficit, something that would become the norm by the end of the decade.[11]

Second, slow growth can be attributed to trends in capital investment in the United States. World War II resulted in economic expansion in the United States and a growth in the capital stock (e.g., machinery, plants). In other industrial nations, the war resulted in a destruction of the capital stock and the consequent need to combine postwar reconstruction with heroic investment in new productive facilities. Growth in the capital stock is critical because it provides the principal means for introducing technical progress into the production process. Technological advances are incorporated into new capital stock, thus increasing the productivity of the workforce. During the period 1950 to 1973, fixed capital stock in the United

pact in other policy areas as well. For example, the goal of promoting price stability and economic expansion led policymakers to introduce a host of regulatory reforms on the theory that the recent growth of regulations had forced businesses to absorb new costs which both contributed to inflation and undermined the incentive to reinvest.

## Nixon and the New Economic Policy

Any discussion of the inflation of the 1970s must begin in the late 1960s. As noted in Chapter 8, the 1964 tax cut was, at first glance, a triumph for Keynesian economics. However, when combined with high levels of social and military spending, the rapid expansion ushered in a new bout of inflation. After considering a host of thorny political questions regarding the impact of various economic policy options on domestic and foreign policy commitments, Johnson imposed a tax surcharge in 1968. It was believed that the surcharge, when combined with restrictive monetary policy, would reduce inflation to acceptable levels without serious consequences for employment. Despite the attempts to slow the economy, when Nixon entered office in 1969, inflation was at 5 percent, the highest since the Korean War. Despite his aversion to inflation, Nixon was unwilling to bring about price stability at the cost of higher unemployment rates. His experience running for President in 1960 at a time of relatively high unemployment and restrictive monetary policy had taught him that economic performance could have great political consequences. In the words of Herbert Stein: "Nixon accepted the priority of the inflation problem, but he was allergic to unemployment."[14] With unemployment rates of 3.3 percent and an inflation rate of 5 percent, a reduction in inflation, it was believed, could be achieved without the creation of high unemployment and long-term political costs.[15]

Nixon's policy of gradualism was an attempt to restrain growth rates and thus introduce greater price stability without simultaneously inducing a recession. The policy entailed monetary and budgetary restraint, an extension of the Johnson administration's income tax surcharge, and the repeal of the investment tax credit. As a result of the policy, the growth rate of GNP declined from 9.1 percent (1968) to 3.3 percent by the fourth quarter of 1969. However, continued gradualism in 1970 had disappointing results: Inflation remained at 5.3 percent while unemployment reached a peak of 6.2 percent by the end of the year. While part of this unemployment rate was a product of a major strike at General Motors, inflation failed to respond as expected to the restrictive fiscal and monetary policies. Simply put, the economy was not behaving in accordance with prevailing Keynesian theories of macroeconomic management, creating something of a puzzle for policymakers.[16]

As the Nixon administration pursued its policy of gradualism, it also attempted to address the microeconomic components of inflation by imposing executive review into the regulatory process.[17] Following the creation of the Environmental Protection Agency, the Commerce Department received numerous complaints from businesses over the potentially high costs of regulatory compliance. These concerns were shared by the Office of Management and Budget. In response, Commerce Secretary Maurice Stans, OMB Director George Schultz, and domestic policy aide John Erlichman, established an interagency quality of life committee in June 1971. In October, an executive order created a Quality of Life review process centralized in the OMB. The review process required agencies formulating significant regulations to submit their rules and supporting analyses for OMB review prior to promulgation. These materials would be provided to other agencies, whose written comments would be forwarded to the OMB and to the agency in question. The review process was limited in impact because it relied on the agencies themselves to determine whether their regulations were "significant" and thus subject to executive review. By all accounts, many agencies simply ignored the process. Moreover, because agencies retained final authority over the issuance of their rules, the OMB was forced to persuade agencies to be more responsive to the inflationary impact of new regulations. The OMB could attempt to introduce additional facts, but it could not prevent the promulgation of new rules. Finally, the review process focused almost exclusively on the EPA, reflecting the concerns with the new clean air legislation.[18]

Nixon's distaste for unemployment led him to adopt a mild Keynesian strategy during his first term in office. Despite an equally strong distaste for direct controls, he gradually adopted a more interventionist stance, resulting ultimately in the application of mandatory wage-price policy. Wage-price or incomes policy is the use of persuasion or direct controls to restrain increases in wages or prices. In the United States, the use of mandatory wage-price policy has been largely limited to war mobilization and demobilization. Absent the emergency of war, presidents have been hesitant to appeal to mandatory controls for three reasons. First, they are difficult to reconcile with liberal values and the American support for voluntarism and market governance. Wages and prices, it is assumed, should be determined in the market. Second, wage-price controls are often unpopular with business and labor. On the business side, controls interfere with the ability of businesses to choose prices that maximize profits. On the labor side, controls may limit labor's ability to secure wage increases in line with inflation; they require the suspension of established collective bargaining relationships. As a result, business and labor commonly join together in their opposition to such policy. Finally, any adequate system of controls embroils officials in the administratively complex task of monitoring costs of basic inputs, a multitude of pricing decisions, and labor contract negotiations. As a result, presidents have appealed to jawboning and voluntary controls, albeit with little effect.[19]

To understand the potential role for wage-price policy, it is useful to consider the limitations of monetary and fiscal policies in addressing the dual problems of the 1970s. Stagflation provided policymakers with two distinct economic problems: inflation and high unemployment. As E. Ray Canterbery explains, this created "the greatest embarrassment for much of orthodox economics . . . because neoclassical and Keynesian economics had concluded that unemployment and inflation could not be coincident events." Fiscal and monetary policies are best used in concert to promote price stability or increase employment through growth. If monetary and fiscal policies are used to address different goals (i.e., price stability *and* economic expansion), they will tend to counteract each other. In practice, they are not independent policy tools. When one recognizes the interdependence of monetary and fiscal policies and the unique conditions of the 1970s, the importance of wage-price policy becomes clear. Policymakers could devote wage-price policy to restraining inflation, thus freeing fiscal and monetary policies for expansion and a reduction in unemployment.[20]

Reflecting Nixon's skepticism concerning wage-price policy—possibly a product of his tenure in the Office of Price Administration during World War II—the movement toward incomes policy was slow to come. At first, the Nixon administration made a number of symbolic gestures suggesting a willingness to adopt a more active stance in fighting inflation. In 1970, Nixon established a tripartite National Commission of Productivity with members from government, labor, and management. While the explicit goal was to address recent declines in productivity, it was hoped that the commission would simultaneously provide a forum for discussing voluntary wage-price agreements. Nixon also created a Government Procurement and Regulations Review Board to examine government actions that placed pressures on costs and prices. The Council of Economic Advisers joined in the act by releasing periodic inflation alerts to draw attention to economic developments (e.g., new contracts, rising prices for key commodities) that threatened to stimulate further inflation. Finally, Nixon suspended the Davis-Bacon Act, requiring the government to pay union scale on government contracts.[21]

These limited efforts failed to restrain inflation and, in the prevailing political climate, they appeared nothing short of anemic. In 1970, Congress passed the Economic Stabilization Act, albeit without the president's support. With the new law, Congress authorized the president to establish wage and price controls backed with fines and injunctions. Nixon could not ignore this new authority. By 1971, business associations were openly questioning the president's economic policy and potential presidential challengers were presenting the ongoing economic difficulties as a sign of presidential incompetence. At the same time, Federal Reserve Chairman Arthur Burns began making public statements concerning the inadequacy of fiscal and monetary policies in addressing the new inflation, directing attention toward some form of incomes policy as an additional tool in the war against inflation. To make matters worse, 1971 witnessed a number of troubling events, including major price increases by U.S. Steel and Bethlehem Steel and inflationary wage settlements in the railroad and steel industries.[22]

On August 15, 1971, President Nixon announced what was unquestionably the boldest macroeconomic policy package in the postwar period. Nixon's New Economic Policy (NEP) was designed to address international and domestic economic problems while reducing the political pressures for action. On the international front, Nixon unilaterally ended the nation's policy of converting foreign-held dollars into gold. This was done without any prior consultation with the International Monetary Fund or the nation's major trading partners. Persistent balance of payments deficits in the postwar period made it impossible for the United States to meet all of its potential obligations, thus requiring a significant change in the international monetary system. However, the move also carried important nationalist implications. By closing the gold window, the United States placed the world on a strict dollar standard. As Block suggests, "the intention of the United States was that its major trade competitors would revalue their currencies upward while the dollar remained fixed to gold at $35 an ounce."[23] Such a realignment of currencies would partially offset the balance of trade problems that the nation had incurred over the previous several years. However, the failure to effectively address inflation in the United States limited the impact of this initiative on the stability of exchange rates, resulting instead in waves of currency speculation and the subsequent need to revalue the dollar and seek a multinational mechanism for stabilizing exchange rate (see Chapter 10).

In hopes of forcing our trading partners to move toward a realignment of currencies to mitigate the negative impact of an overvalued dollar on the American trade deficit, the NEP imposed a 10 percent tariff on imports. This decision could be justified as well as a means of protecting the domestic economy. After four months, central bankers met in Washington and agreed to devalue the dollar against other currencies. As Robert Kuttner notes: "Far from being a cooperative decision, this devaluation was extracted by a unilateral maneuver that other nations roundly resented."[24] Nevertheless, the Nixon administration offered to remove the 10 percent tariff if the other central bankers would actively hold and trade currencies to limit the fluctuation of exchange rates around the newly arrived at levels.[25]

For present purposes, the most important components of the program were tied to the domestic economy and the war against inflation. The Nixon administration announced the combination of a 90-day price freeze and a mildly stimulative fiscal policy. The goal was to combine price and wage stability with growth, thus allowing for an elimination of inflationary expectations and a return to full employment. The initial price freeze was Phase I of the anti-inflation program. During Phase II, lasting from the end of the 90-day freeze through the end of 1972, the administration imposed administrative controls over the price and wage-setting activities of the largest corporations. As part of Phase II, the administration announced the goal of reducing the inflation rate to a range of 2 to 3 percent. The responsibility for implementing the policy was vested in several newly established bodies, including a Price Commission that set standards and heard appeals; a tripartite Pay Board that established wage guidelines, examined wage settlements, and considered union demands for higher wages; and a Cost of Living Council that coordinated the activities of the other bodies. While all firms were required to abide by the price and wage guidelines—subject to fines, injunctions, and criminal penalties—in practice attention focused on larger firms (i.e., those with annual sales in excess of $50 million and over 1,000 employees). The top firms were required to receive prior approval for price and wage increases whereas other large firms were expected to abide by periodic reporting requirements that allowed the various administrative bodies to monitor compliance. The reasoning behind focusing on the largest firms was quite straightforward: These firms, it was believed, set price and wage standards for all firms in their industries and produced goods that could have a significant effect on overall price levels.[26]

With the approach of the 1972 elections, fiscal and monetary policies became more expansionary. Following the election, pressure mounted for a relaxation of wage-price controls in an environment that was increasingly expansionary. Thus, in January 1973, Nixon announced the movement to Phase III of the economic program. Under Phase III, the wage-price guidelines remained in effect. However, with a number of notable exceptions including food, health, and construction, the guidelines were to be self-administered. The justification for the relaxation in wage-price controls—that is, that inflationary expectations had been expunged—was, at best, premature. Poor harvests and a rise in energy prices—a prelude to the OPEC price increases that would come in the fall and winter of 1973—had significant effects on inflation. During the first half of 1973, food costs increased by 20 percent and energy prices increased by 19 percent. Despite the relatively low levels of inflation in nonfood commodities (4.8 percent) and services (4.3 percent), the political response was almost immediate.[27]

In June 1973, the Nixon administration reimposed a price freeze to be followed by a sector-by-sector decontrol to be supervised by the Cost of Living Council. The council made the formal removal of controls contingent on agreements to exercise restraint in pricing and wage agreements. The reimposition of controls— Phase IV of the NEP—was combined with contractionary monetary policy and fiscal policy in hopes of preventing supply shocks from moving through the economy and inducing an inflationary spiral. Inflation could not be restrained, however, following the OPEC price increases. Oil prices increased by some 400 percent, from a level of $3 per barrel in early 1973 to $11.65 a year later.[28] Moreover, a failed harvest in the USSR placed tremendous pressures on food prices. The administration's fiscal and monetary policies only assured that the high rates of inflation would be combined with high levels of unemployment. Congress formally eliminated the option for new wage-price controls when it refused to extend the Economic Stabilization Act beyond April 30, 1974. President Nixon, now battling the accusations of involvement in the Watergate break-in, could harbor no realistic expectation that Congress would allow for another expansion of presidential power.

As noted earlier, wage-price policy offers officials an important economic tool. It can be used to restrain inflation while freeing fiscal and monetary policies to attack unemployment. Although there is no agreement as to what the inflation and unemployment rates might have been absent the Nixon controls, the performance record suggests that the policies were quite successful in the short term. Unemployment fell slightly following the 1970 recession, from a high of 5.9 percent in 1971 to 4.9 percent in 1973. The inflation rate fell as well, hitting 4.3 percent in 1972 and 3.3 percent in 1973, the lowest level of inflation that the nation would experience for a decade. In the end, the lifting of controls, the shock of oil and food prices, and the administration's use of fiscal and monetary policies to limit the impact of these exogenous shocks eliminated any of the gains associated with earlier policy decisions. The subsequent recession, the deepest since the Great Depression, shaped the context for macroeconomic decision making during the brief presidency of Gerald Ford.

## The Ford Presidency: Interregnum of Despair

When Gerald Ford assumed office in August of 1974, he faced a 12 percent inflation rate and an economy entering a third quarter of negative real growth in GNP. The economy had entered a recession but had done so with the worst inflation rate since 1947. In an economic address on August 12, President Ford clearly stated his economic policy priority by stating: "Inflation is domestic enemy number one." In September, the president convened an Inflation Summit with a host of business and labor officials and economists in hopes of developing a coherent anti-inflationary strategy despite the stagnant economy. When his economic program was presented to Congress, it called for a temporary 5 percent tax surcharge on corporations and upper-income taxpayers and reduced expenditures. While this package was combined with extensions in unemployment compensation and minor support for additional antirecessionary programs, it was clearly contractionary in intent. This revealed, more than anything else, the willingness to incur high human costs to fight inflation.[29]

By January 1975, the economy was in the midst of the greatest decline since the Great Depression; the human costs were no longer tolerable, even for one who placed such a priority on price stability. President Ford responded to his "great recession" by accepting the need to move from a contractionary to an expansionary policy.[30] Ford proposed a tax-based stimulus package that took final form as the Tax Reduction Act of 1975. The act included a tax rebate of $8 billion, a personal tax reduction of $12 billion, a one-time increase in social security benefits of $1.7 billion, and a $1 billion earned income tax credit. When Ford signed the tax legislation, he warned that he would not tolerate additional fiscal stimulus because of the strong inflationary biases in the economy. In hopes of reducing inflation, he quickly moved toward the imposition of special import duties on oil and the rapid deregulation of domestic oil prices. The first measure was aborted by the courts, the second by a reluctant Congress and evidence that absent a plan for gradual decontrol the policy would have a significant impact on inflation rates. In January 1976, the economy was clearly in recovery. However, the jobless rate remained high at 7.9 percent. Thus, Ford requested an extension of some $18 billion of tax cuts in 1976 along with an additional tax cut of $10 billion. He hoped to pair this $28 billion tax reduction with an equal amount of budget cuts, albeit without success. Despite the congressional resistance to Ford's policy, the economy had improved greatly since 1974 and 1975. Unemployment remained relatively high in 1976, fluctuating between 7.5 and 7.9 percent. However, inflation was relatively low at an annual rate of 5.8 percent—the lowest since 1972.[31]

Ford's economic policy was conservative and bore little resemblance to the Nixon administration's New Economic Policy. However, greater continuity with the Nixon initiatives was evident in Ford's approach to regulation. As Nixon before him, Gerald Ford attempted to address the costs of regulation, arguing that they were contributing to the inflationary forces while eroding corporate incentives to invest. In August 1974, the Council on Wage and Price Stability (COWPS) was created in the Office of the President to coordinate the anti-inflationary efforts. COWPS was responsible for monitoring events in the private sector that contributed to inflation (e.g., major wage settlements) and assessing the inflationary impact of government policies. To standardize this latter duty, Executive Order 11,821 inaugurated the Inflation Impact Statement. Under the order, all executive branch agencies were required to assess the inflationary impact of major legislative proposals, regulations, and rules subject to review by COWPS and the Office of Management and Budget. Pursuant to this executive order, the OMB recommended a quantified comparison of the costs and benefits of proposed regulations resulting in costs in excess of $100 million and/or had a specified effect on productivity, employment, energy consumption, and the supplies of critical inputs.[32]

Although the executive review process may have increased regulators' recognition of costs and prevented regulatory proposals that could not be justified economically, the program was plagued by problems. Compliance was voluntary and the quality of the agency analyses was often lacking. Moreover, because the analyses were routinely conducted after proposals were formulated, they did not provide a basis for regulatory design. Rather, analyses were conducted to justify the proposed policies before a particular external constituency. Finally, because COWPS lacked the authority to reject regulations that failed to meet cost-benefit criteria, its powers were severely limited.[33] Although the Ford administration made price stability the primary goal in microeconomic and macroeconomic policymaking, this goal remained elusive. The failure of the Ford administration to defeat stagflation and its willingness to tolerate high levels of unemployment set the stage for the 1976 presidential election and the election of a new Democratic president.

## The Carter Presidency: The Phillips Curve Seesaw

Given the poor economic performance of the Ford administration, it should be no surprise that Jimmy Carter stressed the need for competent economic management during the presidential campaign of 1976. His goals were quite straightforward. First, presenting the election as a referendum on fighting inflation with recession, he promised to reduce the jobless rate to 4.5 percent with the ultimate goal of returning the economy to full employment. At the same time, he promised to battle inflation and to maintain a 5.5 percent inflation rate. On the belief that government was a source of inflation, he called for a balanced budget and a reduction of government's claim on Gross National Product. The irreconcilable promises of pursuing price stability and full employment, the consequent movement between expansionary and contractionary policies, sudden downturns in productivity, and exogenous shocks during the second half of his term in office frustrated macroeconomic policymaking throughout the Carter presidency.[34]

Upon assuming office, Carter sought to accelerate the recovery from the recession by unveiling a mild stimulative package which included a one-time $50 tax rebate, $2 billion in new public works, $2 billion of additional public service employment under the Comprehensive Employment and Training Act, and a small permanent tax reduction to be followed by more fundamental tax reform. It was hoped that this fiscal package, combined with growth in the money supply and lower interest rates, would usher in a rapid recovery without inflation. In the spring of 1977, the administration realized that the economy was moving out of the recession without the assistance of the stimulative program. It was feared that any additional stimulation would produce further inflation. Thus, in March, the administration quickly replaced its stimulative package with a number of anti-inflationary measures, including a reduction in federal spending and the introduction of voluntary price-wage guidelines.

This pattern—the movement back and forth between fiscal stimulation and restraint—characterized the remainder of the Carter presidency. Following the contractionary policies of 1977, the administration returned to fiscal stimulation in January 1978 when it presented an expansionary budget to Congress. The decision was based on the CEA's incorrect prediction that the economy would be lurching into recession by the end of 1978. As the economy expanded and inflation grew in the fall of 1978, the administration once again returned to an anti-inflationary stance. Alfred Kahn, an economist who had already realized success in deregulating the airline industry while head of the Civil Aeronautics Board, was selected by the president to chair the Council on Wage and Price Stability. Once again, policymakers turned to fiscal restraint, this time with an emphasis on voluntary wage-price controls.[35]

The decision to employ voluntary wage-price guidelines rather than mandatory controls reflected Carter's skepticism concerning mandatory controls and his tenuous relationship with business and labor. During the summer of 1978, the administration formulated guidelines that were presented to the nation in a presidential speech in October. The guidelines authorized corporations to raise prices to a maximum of 5 percent below the average during the 1976 to 1977 period, up to a ceiling of 9.5 percent. Wages were to be held to a 7 percent annual increase. The administration attempted to attach sanctions to the guidelines, including the denial of large public procurement contracts to companies that exceeded the targets. However, the administration failed to use these sanctions effectively. Thus, the Teamsters revealed the administration's limited commitment to wage-price policy when in 1979 they went on strike and successfully demanded a settlement that exceeded the 7 percent wage target. Even after new advisory bodies were created in the fall of 1979 to provide labor representation in the development of guidelines, the voluntary policy failed to have the desired impact on inflation.[36]

Thus far we have focused primarily on Carter's efforts to address inflation. There is little to suggest that the full employment goal ever carried the same priority as price stability, despite the fact that it did receive the verbal support of the president. There is no better example of Carter's true proclivities in this area than the Full Employment and Balanced Growth Act (or Humphry-Hawkins Act) of 1978. The original legislation took form during the recession of 1975. The bill was, in large part, a resurrected version of the original full employment bill discussion in Chapter 8. In its original version, Humphry-Hawkins created a legal right to employment and established the goal of full employment, albeit with an interim goal of 3 percent unemployment. As it evolved, the legislation jettisoned the legally enforceable right to employment but required the president to achieve a 3 percent unemployment rate within four years of passage. To this end, the president, Congress, and Federal Reserve were directed to work with state and local governments to improve business conditions. However, the government was directed to provide public jobs at the prevailing wage rates, if necessary, to reach the full employment target. The Humphry-Hawkins bill received the strong support of congressional Democrats in 1976, who used it as a means of emphasizing the Ford administration's policy of pursuing price stability through recessionary means.[37]

Although Jimmy Carter gave his support to Humphrey-Hawkins in the 1976 presidential campaign, this support evaporated quickly. In part, this was the product of the opposition of mainstream economists and business, combined with the mixed support of organized labor. It was clear that even if the legislation was a useful political tool in an election year, it did not have sufficient support in its current state to be passed and signed into law. Thus, in late 1977, the Carter administration supported a revised version of the legislation. The goal of full employment and a short-term goal of 3 percent unemployment were replaced with a target of 4 percent unemployment for 1983. The public jobs provisions initially designed as a means of bringing the economy to full employment were eliminated. No alternative mechanism was put place of the public jobs. In a final provision reflecting the president's own ambivalence about the goal of full employment, the new legislation identified price stability as an equally important goal while noting the importance of additional objectives, including increased real income, productivity gains, balanced growth, and balanced budgets. In the end, the largely symbolic piece of legislation was passed into law with a host of additional provisions added by Congress, many (e.g., removing barriers for the handicapped) of which had questionable relevance to the original goal of full employment. With Humphry-Hawkins, any hopes of committing the government to full employment were once again dashed.[38]

As Carter moved between expansionary and contractionary policies, the administration extended the regulatory review initiatives introduced during the Nixon and Ford administrations. In January 1978, Carter established the Regulatory Analysis and Review Group (RARG), consisting of representatives of the CEA, the OMB, the departments of Agriculture, Commerce, Education, Energy, Health and Human Services, Housing and Urban Development, Interior, Justice, Labor, Transportation, Treasury, and the EPA. RARG was directed to focus its efforts on a limited number of select rules and regulations (4 rules per agency per year and a maximum of 10 to 20 rules across agencies) that had an annual cost to industry of $100 million. In March 1978, Carter issued Executive Order 12,044, which required that: "Regulations shall be as simple and clear as possible. They shall achieve legislative goals effectively and efficiently. They shall not impose unnecessary burdens on the economy, on individuals, on public or private organizations, or on State and local governments." Carter required that major rules be justified with a regulatory analysis identifying the problem, alternative responses, and the economic rationale for the agency's decision, preferably presented in accordance with cost-effectiveness criteria.[39]

In October 1978, Carter created a second review body, the Regulatory Council. The Council represented some 35 agencies and was chaired by the EPA Administrator Douglas Costle. Unlike RARG which was designed to review inflationary rules, the council was created to eliminate redundant policies and resolve conflicting regulatory provisions. The goal was to limit corporate compliance costs and reduce the regulatory contribution to stagflation. The Council attempted to prevent regulatory duplication by publishing semiannual regulatory calendars while creating a forum in which regulators could consider the need, compatibility, and cost-effectiveness of their actions.[40]

As in the past, regulatory review was limited by the fact that agencies determined when and if their proposed rules would have a significant inflationary impact and were subject to review. Moreover, RARG's mandate—to examine 10 or 20 regulations per year—automatically limited its impact. Finally, RARG lacked the authority to force agencies to comply with its recommendations. Its chief significance came in its effect on the regulatory process. It introduced new norms and criteria into the regulatory process. In keeping with the efforts of the Nixon and Ford administrations, there was an explicit application of economic analysis to determine whether new regulations were justified.[41] Thus, Susan and Martin Tolchin refer to RARG as "another turning point in presidential management of regulation" characterized by "the ascendancy of economists over lawyers."[42]

If the Carter administration faced trouble walking the line between recession and runaway inflation during 1977 and 1978, this maneuver would prove impossible in 1979. Unexpectedly, productivity growth which had ranged between 2.2 and 2.4 percent during the period 1975 to 1977 fell to 0.6 percent in 1978 and remained low at 1.2 percent in 1979, thus fueling additional inflation and unemployment. More troubling, Carter had to face the unanticipated inflation associated with an explosion in oil prices following the Iranian revolution and a second OPEC embargo. Between early 1978 and mid-1980, OPEC increased oil prices from $14 per barrel to more than $35. As a result, the inflation rate accelerated and reached 13.3 percent for 1979.[43] The impact of rising energy prices is clearly reflected in Figure 9–4 where indexes of oil prices and the consumer price index are presented side-by-side.

While it is convenient to attribute the burst of inflation to oil prices, a host of additional short-term factors were at work. First, government policies contributed directly to inflation through the indexation of entitlement programs, the new social regulatory policies enacted in the early 1970s, and a host of Carter administration policies including the increase in the minimum wage (from $2.30 an hour to $2.90 an hour) and new price supports for dairy and agriculture. A significant expansion of the money supply between 1977 and 1979 also fueled inflation. At the same time, a dramatic drop in the value of the dollar increased the costs of imported goods, despite the active intervention of central bankers attempting to stabilize the dollar in international currency markets.[44]

In the fall of 1979, Carter appointed Paul Volcker to the chairmanship of the Federal Reserve Board. As a conservative economist and a favorite of Wall Street, Volcker's appointment was clearly an attempt to stabilize financial markets in the wake of the new wave of inflation. Moreover, it was hoped that Volcker's distaste for inflation and his adherence to monetarism would place the Federal Reserve at the forefront of the war for price stability. Reflecting his monetarist approach to economic governance, Volcker supported a shift in the Federal Reserve's policy away from the direct manipulation of interest rates to the manipulation of monetary aggregates. It was hoped that the explicit monetarist strategy would provide the missing key to achieving price stability.[45]

Carter's 1981 fiscal year budget proposal accepted a larger than expected deficit. This, combined with upward revisions in the 1980 deficit, led many in the bond market to conclude that the administration had no policy to effectively address inflation even if it now included Paul Volcker at the Fed. The resulting in-

**Figure 9–4**    Inflation and Energy

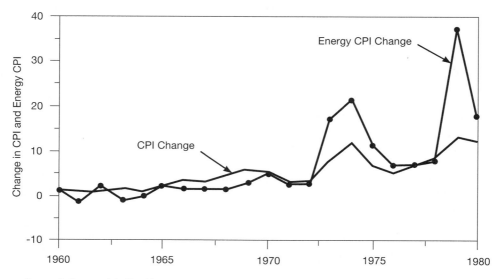

Source: *Economic Report of the President.*

creases in interest rates led the administration to reduce the proposed 1981 budget and to promote a reduction in consumer borrowing through a host of Fed-imposed credit controls and a personal plea by the president. As William Greider notes: "For once, Americans got the message. Within days, consumer spending slowed drastically and so did the borrowing by businesses. The White House mailroom was inundated by cut-up credit cards . . . The President had hoped to capture the average citizen's attention, and he succeeded far too well. If borrowing was suddenly unpatriotic, then so was buying."[46] The resulting recession was deep and poorly timed to coincide with Carter's reelection campaign. Within three months the Gross National Product fell by 10 percent and the economy suffered the steepest decline in any quarter in U.S. history The unemployment rate jumped from a level of 6.3 percent in March to 7.6 percent by May. This level would be maintained for the rest of the year, albeit with little or no impact on inflation. The combination of recession, high inflation, and a historically large budget deficit in 1980 marked the failure of the Carter administration to realize any of its chief economic goals. The stage was set for the election of Ronald Reagan who ran, as had Carter before him, against the stagflation of the 1970s and the failure of economic management.

How does one interpret the apparent vacillation and failure of economic policy during the Carter presidency? Erwin Hargrove suggests: "What appeared to be a policy of zigzag in both microeconomic and macroeconomic affairs was actually a coherent strategy of balancing opposites. This meant splitting the difference in decisions of micro policy between group demands and the requirements of economic sense. It meant waving back and forth in macro policy between expansionary and restraining actions. The difficulty was not the absence of coherence, but absence of a constituency behind the policy."[47] Hargrove raises an important point. The need to promote price stability through fiscal and monetary restraint forced a movement away from the policies demanded by the Democratic party's core constituent groups. At the same time, Carter's desire to balance the two goals and thus periodically sacrifice price stability undermined the support of business and the financial community. However, the real difficulty may not lie with the tensions intrinsic to the Carter presidency or the disintegration of the New Deal coalition. Rather, the real problems may be tied to the unique features of the inflation of the 1970s and the failure of the Phillips Curve and established policy tools to provide an effective solution to stagflation.

## CROSS-NATIONAL RESPONSES TO STAGFLATION

The experience of the United States during the 1970s was not unique, at least with respect to inflation which was a global event. While all advanced industrial democracies had to address inflation during this period, there was a good deal of variation both with respect to performance and adopted strategies of economic management. Some nations experienced high unemployment and inflation. Others maintained full employment and relative price stability. Cross-national comparisons can provide some clues as to why the United States experienced such difficulties. Moreover, it can also reveal a possible means of filling the vacuum left by the failure of the Phillips Curve and the apparent inadequacy of traditional Keynesian policy tools.

Figure 9–5 presents the average rates of inflation and unemployment in several advanced industrial democracies during the period 1973 to 1980. As the figure reveals, there were great differences in performance. Some nations, including Austria, Germany, Norway, Japan, and Sweden were successful in maintaining full employment (4 percent unemployment) and relatively low levels of inflation. At

**Figure 9–5**   Cross-National Performance, 1973–1980

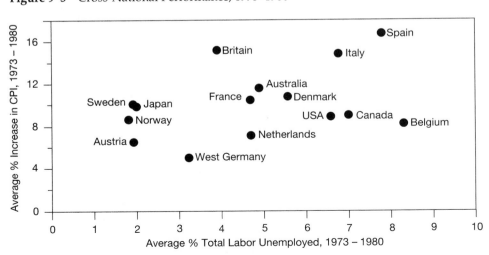

Source: OECD Main Economic Indicators, 1990.

the other end of the continuum, one can identify a second cluster of nations including Spain, the United States, Canada, Britain, Australia, and Italy. For these nations, there was no Phillips Curve tradeoff: They suffered the worst of both worlds with persistent problems of high inflation and high unemployment rates.

Before proposing an explanation for the rather dramatic cross-national variation in economic performance, it is useful to consider once again the relationships central to the Phillips Curve. One of the more interesting aspects of the Phillips Curve is that it grounds the inflation-unemployment trade-off in labor markets that are always in disequilibrium. Inflation grows precisely when employment levels rise to the point that workers can translate market power into higher wages In other words, workers can successfully demand compensation increases that exceed productivity increases. David Cameron urges us to understand "the cyclical movement of an economy, recessions and inflationary booms, and the magnitude of those peaks and troughs as a reflection of the relative power of, and ongoing conflict between, the major economic groups in society—a conflict that centers on a struggle for income."[48] Wage increases that outpace productivity gains can be absorbed by corporations if they are willing to sacrifice profitability. Alternatively, wage increases can be passed on in the form of higher prices, fueling inflation. The failure to meet wage demands can also result in an increase in strike activity as workers use their market power to force compliance. In short, the business cycle is not simply the aggregation of individual market decisions but the expression of a struggle along class lines, much as suggested by the class perspective (see Chapter 1).

We can interpret inflation as a redistribution of national income among producer groups. Policymakers can choose to place limits on this redistribution by slowing the economy or inducing a recession. This creates slack in labor markets and erodes the capacity of workers to force wage demands. As noted earlier, the decision of when to sacrifice employment for price stability is a political determination. Labor or leftist governments will allow for more of this redistribution (i.e., they will tolerate higher levels of inflation) than conservative governments.[49] In the United States, great emphasis has been placed on price stability, producing a greater willingness to induce recessions and absorb the consequent social costs even when the effects on inflation appear to be minimal. The problem faced by many nations during the 1970s was the unresponsiveness of inflation to traditional strategies. Recessions did not bring the long-term reductions in the rate of inflation, thus resulting in the combination of inflation and slow growth that dominated the decade.

If the unemployment-inflation relationship is grounded in labor markets—the fundamental assertion of the Phillips Curve—the correct approach to managing the trade-off may be found in industrial relations rather than the traditional fiscal and monetary instruments of macroeconomic management. Indeed, if one examines the countries that weathered the 1970s with the best performance records, one discovers that they adopted a different approach to industrial relations than those adopted by the high inflation-high unemployment nations like the United States. With the exception of Japan, the nations that had the best performance in the 1970s have corporatist systems. The term corporatism describes a system of organized interest intermediation. Organizations representing business and labor engage in consensual bargaining to arrive at agreements concerning wage levels, employment levels, pricing, and investment. The agreements are typically developed under the supervision of the government which subsequently monitors the implementation of the decisions.[50] In essence, labor unions trade wage stability and industrial peace for promises of stable employment levels and, at times, limits on price increases. Governments typically facilitate these agreements by providing a higher social wage (i.e., welfare benefits) for labor and support for business adjustment in the form of selective investments, export subsidies, or state-financed labor training. The key point is that the conflict between labor and business is removed from the market through the creation of consensual wage-price policies developed and implemented by business and labor peak associations.[51]

The key distinction between corporatist and noncorporatist systems is captured by a typology presented by Leon N. Lindberg.[52] According to Lindberg, in systems with muted confrontation and structured bargaining (i.e., corporatist systems), organized economic groups are integrated into the policy process and engage in explicit bargaining to construct agreements that will preserve their share of national income. In such systems, strong trade associations and unions exercise authority over their members and are thus capable of authoritative decision making in the formation of policy. Lindberg contrasts these corporatist systems with systems with statist or controlled management and those with open and unstructured confrontation. In systems with statist or controlled management (e.g., Japan and France), business associations work closely with state bureaucracies to coordinate government investment, trade barriers, and export subsidies to maintain high levels of growth. While tripartite decision making is impossible due to the fragmentation of labor associations, employment levels are maintained through the pro-business industrial policies implemented by the government and backed with administratively directed flows of capital.[53]

In terms of performance, the poorest records are associated with nations that have open and unstructured confrontation. In such systems (e.g., the United States, Britain, Canada, Australia, and Italy), the competition between labor and business over their relative share of national income takes place in the market. With firm autonomy, weak economic associations, and higher levels of bureaucratic fragmentation, the kinds of structured bargaining that are essential to economic management in corporatist nations are impossible. The kinds of class conflicts inherent in the business cycle cannot be effectively managed through the introduction of new institutions. Because wage-price policies and sectoral investment are not available, officials must rely on fiscal and monetary policies. As noted earlier, fiscal and monetary instruments are too closely linked to be used to address independent economic goals. As a result, nations without wage-price policies commonly move back and forth between contractionary and expansionary policies as the attention turns from inflation to unemployment as key policy problems. The records of the Ford and Carter presidencies provide good example of such stop-go policymaking.

While corporatist arrangements may appear to violate prevailing norms of economic governance, they have existed at certain points in U.S. history, albeit as temporary responses to emergency situations. One can identify the experiences of the two world wars and the National Recovery Administration as periods in which corporatist arrangements were used as a means of reducing economic instability. If corporatist arrangements enhanced the capacity of many nations to manage stagflation in the 1970s, one must ask why such an approach was deemed impossible in the United States. The reasons are many. As noted in Chapter 1, the United States is characterized by strong liberal norms which recognize little role for the state in managing economic relations. Beyond the question of ideology, however, one must examine the institutional and organizational features that preclude corporatist policymaking. In the United States, low levels of unionization and weak labor unions are combined with weak trade associations that are incapable of limiting the autonomy of their members. As a result, workers and employers cannot be bound by the decisions of the major economic associations and will comply with agreements only as long as they prove profitable. As shown in Chapter 5, defections from the NRA were common as the economy began to show signs of recovery. Of course the Nixon administration revealed that wage-price policy was possible without the heavy reliance on economic interest groups. However, the NEP embroiled the administration in a host of complex tasks and proved highly unstable when extended beyond a limited period.

Two other factors are worth noting when discussing the possibility of corporatist policymaking in the United States. First, as shown in Chapter 5, the New Deal system of industrial relations incorporated an adversarial relationship at the core of collective bargaining. It was not designed to promote consensual decision making such as that which occurs in corporatist systems. Finally, in corporatist systems the state facilitates the creation of business-labor agreements through the provision of benefits. On the labor side, high levels of welfare spending provides a social wage that compensates for some of the reduction in private wages. On the business side, the state provides selective investments to ease adjustment and subsidize exports. In the United States, low levels of welfare spending and the stigma attached to various social programs effectively limit the provision of a social wage. Moreover, because the United States has a capital–market-based financial system, the state lacks the capacity to channel significant amounts of capital into particular industries.[54]

Policymakers do not have a free choice of policy instruments. In the United States, economic policy and policymaking institutions evolved with the Keynesian goal of restoring self-equilibrating markets that were temporarily plagued by a deficit of aggregate demand. In the end, because of the organization of the American economy and the legacy of past policy decisions, a political-institutional response to a political-institutional problem was impossible. Officials had to rely on blunt macroeconomic policy tools and market-based economic theories that did not recognize the importance of nonmarket arenas of decision making. Because there was no capacity to manage inflation and unemployment by addressing the structural relationship between economic interest groups, officials had to pursue competing objectives through the use of indirect policy instruments.

The stagflation of the 1970s provided a great challenge to the Keynesian consensus and established strategies of macroeconomic management. Absent a more statist solution, officials had to pursue price stability through recessionary policies and restrictions on regulatory policymaking. To address the problem of unemployment, they had to rely on fiscal and monetary stimulation which exacerbated underlying inflationary trends. Policymakers were trapped by a Phillips Curve that no longer provided a stable foundation for policymaking. Continued stagflation set the stage for a new approach to economic management and opened the debate over the long-term viability of the New Deal system.

In the presidential campaign of 1980, Ronald Reagan attacked the system that had evolved in the decades following the New Deal. He attacked Keynesianism and the attempts of social engineers to manage a market system. He indicted the welfare state for eradicating work incentives and undermining growth. He pointed to the economic performance of the previous few years as evidence of a failure of the New Deal system and called for a return to a market and a reduction of state intervention in the economy and society. If the cross-national experience reveals anything, it is that the market provided one of the greatest impediments to successful economic management. Nevertheless, the Reagan administration pursued price stability with great vigor, turning to the antistatist doctrines of monetarism and new supply-side doctrines. In the end, the war against inflation was won, albeit at the cost of the greatest recession since the Great Depression and looming budget deficits that threaten to restrain the scope and scale of future government programs. We turn now to an examination of this period.

# NOTES

1. See Edwin Mansfield and Nariman Behravesh. *Economics USA* (New York: W.W. Norton., 1986), pp. 154–55.
2. See James E. Alt and K. Alec Chrystal, *Political Economics* (Berkeley: University of California Press, 1983), pp. 59–69; E. Ray Canterbery, *The Making of Economics*, 3rd ed. (Belmont, Calif.: Wadsworth, 1987), pp. 238–46.
3. See Howard R. Vane and John L. Thompson, *Monetarism: Theory, Evidence, and Policy* (Oxford: Martin Robertson, 1979).
4. See, for example, Arthur M. Okun, *Equality and Efficiency: The Big Tradeoff* (Washington, D.C.: Brookings Institution, 1975).
5. See Thomas J. Sargent and Neil Wallace, "Rational Expectations and the Theory of Economic Policy." *Journal of Monetary Economics* 2 (April 1976): 169–84.
6. Compare Charles S. Maier, "Inflation and Stagnation as Politics and History." In *The Politics of Inflation and Economic Stagnation*, ed. Leon N. Lindberg and Charles S. Maier (Washington, D.C.: Brookings Institution, 1985); and Mancur Olson, *The Rise and Decline of Nations: Economic Growth, Stagflation, and Social Rigidities* (New Haven, Conn.: Yale University Press, 1982).
7. See Kenneth Hoover and Raymond Plant, *Conservative Capitalism in Britain and the United States* (London: Routledge, 1989).
8. Calculated from percentage change in real GNP from the previous year. Data from *Economic Report of the President, 1981*.
9. See Robert Kuttner, *The End of Laissez-Faire: National Purpose and the Global Economy After the Cold War* (New York: Alfred A. Knopf, 1991), Chapter 2.
10. See Alan Wolfe, *America's Impasse: The Rise and Fall of the Politics of Growth* (New York: Pantheon Books, 1981).
11. See Joan Edelman Spero, *The Politics of International Economic Relations* (New York: St. Martin's, 1977), p. 73.
12. Angus Maddison, *Phases of Capitalist Development* (Oxford: Oxford University Press, 1982), pp. 96, 109.
13. Barry Bluestone and Bennet Harrison, *The Deindustrialization of America: Plant Closings, Community Abandonment, and the Dismantling of Basic Industry* (New York: Basic Books, 1982), Appendix 1.

14. Herbert Stein, *Presidential Economics: The Making of Economic Policy from Roosevelt to Reagan and Beyond* (Washington, D.C.: American Enterprise Institute, 1988), p. 135.

15. Stein, *Presidential Economics,* pp. 148–50.

16. Charles E. McLure, Jr., "Fiscal Failure: Lessons of the Sixties." In *Economic Policy and Inflation in the Sixties,* ed. William Fellner (Washington, D.C.: American Enterprise Institute, 1972), pp. 63–66.

17. See Marc Allen Eisner, *Regulatory Politics in Transition* (Baltimore, Md.: Johns Hopkins University Press, 1993), Chapter 8.

18. George C. Eads and Michael Fix, *Relief or Reform? Reagan's Regulatory Dilemma* (Washington, D.C.: Urban Institute Press, 1984), pp. 46–48; Larry N. Gerston, Cynthia Fraleigh, and Robert Schwab, *The Deregulated Society* (Pacific Grove, Calif.: Brooks/Cole, 1988), pp. 42–50; Alfred A. Marcus, *Promise and Performance: Choosing and Implementing an Environmental Policy* (Westport, Conn.: Greenwood Press, 1980), pp. 125–27.

19. See Craufurd D. Goodwin, ed., *Exhortation and Controls* (Washington, D.C.: Brookings Institution, 1975).

20. E. Ray Canterbery, *The Making of Economics,* 3rd ed. (Belmont, CA: Wadsworth Publishing Co., 1987), p. 239. See Fritz W. Scharpf, "Economic and Institutional Constraints of Full-Employment Strategies: Sweden, Austria, and Western Germany, 1973–1982." In *Order and Conflict in Contemporary Capitalism: Studies in the Political Economy of Western European Nations,* ed. John H. Goldthorpe (Oxford: Oxford University Press, 1984), pp. 271–72.

21. Stein, *Presidential Economics,* pp. 158–60.

22. See Leonard Silk, *Nixonomics,* 2nd ed. (New York: Praeger, 1973), pp. 53–69.

23. Fred Block, *The Origins of International Economic Disorder: A Study of United States International Monetary Policy from World War II to the Present* (Berkeley: University of California Press, 1977), p. 197.

24. Robert Kuttner, *The End of Laissez-Faire: National Purpose and the Global Economy after the Cold War* (New York: Alfred A. Knopf, 1991), p. 66.

25. Ibid., Chapter 2.

26. See Silk, *Nixonomics,* pp. 75–79; Arnold Weber, "The Continuing Courtship: Wage-Price Policy through Five Administrations." In *Exhortation and Controls,* ed. Craufurd D. Goodwin (Washington, D.C.: Brookings Institution, 1975).

27. George P. Shultz and Kenneth W. Dam, *Economic Policy Beyond the Headlines* (New York: W.W. Norton, 1977), p. 74.

28. Spero, *The Politics of International Economic Relations,* pp. 225–26.

29. Alan S. Blinder, *Economic Policy and the Great Stagflation* (New York: Academic Press, 1979), pp. 209–16.

30. See Otto Eckstein, *The Great Recession* (Amsterdam: North-Holland, 1978).

31. Blinder, *Economic Policy and the Great Stagflation,* pp. 209–16.

32. Howard Ball, *Controlling Regulatory Sprawl: Presidential Strategies from Nixon to Reagan* (Westport, Conn.: Greenwood Press, 1984), pp. 51–54; Eads and Fix, *Relief or Reform?* pp. 50–54; Thomas O. McGarity, *Reinventing Rationality: The Role of Regulatory Analysis in the Federal Bureaucracy* (Cambridge: Cambridge University Press, 1991), pp. 18–19.

33. See James C. Miller III, "Lessons of the Economic Impact Statement Program." *Regulation* vol. 1, (July-August 1977), pp. 16–18.

34. Stephen Woolcock, "The Economic Policies of the Carter Administration." In *The Carter Years: The President and Policy Making,* ed. M. Glenn Abernathy, Dilys M. Hill, and Phil Williams (New York: St. Martin's Press, 1984), pp. 37–38.

35. Erwin C. Hargrove, *Jimmy Carter as President: Leadership and the Politics of the Public Good* (Baton Rouge: Louisiana State University Press, 1988), Chapter 4.

36. Ibid., pp. 85–86.

37. Margaret Weir, *Politics and Jobs: The Boundaries of Employment Policy in the United States* (Princeton, N.J.: Princeton University Press, 1992), pp. 134–36.

38. Ibid., pp. 136–41; Lance T. LeLoup, "Congress and the Dilemma of Economic Policy." In *Making Economic Policy in Congress,* ed. Allen Schick (Washington, D.C.: American Enterprise Institute, 1983), pp. 17–21.

39. See Gerston, Fraleigh, and Schwab, *The Deregulated Society,* pp. 44–48; Eisner, *Regulatory Politics in Transition,* pp. 184–87; McGarity, *Reinventing Rationality,* p. 19.

40. Eisner, *Regulatory Politics in Transition,* pp. 184–87; Eads and Fix, *Relief or Reform?* pp. 61–62.

41. Ball, *Controlling Regulatory Sprawl,* pp. 58–60; Susan Tolchin, "Presidential Power and the Politics of RARG." *Regulation,* (July-August 1979): 44–49; Gary C. Bryner, *Bureaucratic Discretion: Law and Policy in Federal Regulatory Agencies* (New York: Pergamon Press, 1987), pp. 134–40.

42. Susan and Martin Tolchin, *Dismantling America: The Rush to Deregulate* (Boston: Houghton Mifflin, 1983), p. 49.

43. Stein, *Presidential Economics,* p. 219; Charles E. Jacob, "Macroeconomic Policy Choices of Postwar Presidents." In *The President and Economic Policy,* ed. James P. Pfiffner (Philadelphia: Institute for the Study of Human Issues, 1986), p. 75.

44. Hargrove, *Jimmy Carter as President,* pp. 95–96.

45. See John T. Woolley, *Monetary Politics: The Federal Reserve and the Politics of Monetary Policy* (Cambridge: Cambridge University Press, 1984), pp. 103–104, 111–114.

46. William Greider, *Secrets of the Temple: How the Federal Reserve Runs the Country* (New York: Simon and Schuster, 1987), pp. 184–85; Andrew H. Bartels, "Volcker's Revolution at the Fed." *Challenge* 28, 4 (September-October 1985): 35–42.

47. Hargrove, *Jimmy Carter as President,* p. 107.

48. David Cameron, "The Politics and Economics of the Business Cycle." In *The Political Economy,* ed., Thomas Ferguson and Joel Rogers (Armonk, N.Y.: M.E. Sharpe, 1984), p. 239.

49. See Douglas Hibbs, "Political Parties and Macroeconomic Policy." *American Political Science Review* 71 (1977): 1467–87.

50. See Phillipe Schmitter, "Modes of Interest Intermediation and Models of Societal Change in Western Europe." *Comparative Political Studies* 10 (1977): 7–38; and "Interest Intermediation and Regime Governability in Western Europe and North America." In *Organizing Interests in Western Europe,* ed. Susan Berger (New York: Cambridge University Press, 1981).

51. See David R. Cameron, "Social Democracy, Corporatism, Labour Quiescence and the Representation of Economic Interest in Advanced Capitalist Society." In *Order and Conflict in Contemporary Capitalism: Studies in the Political Economy of Western European Nations,* ed. John H. Goldthorpe (Oxford: Oxford University Press, 1984).

52. Leon N. Lindberg, "Models of the Inflation-Disinflation Process." In *The Politics of Inflation and Economic Stagnation,* ed. Leon N. Lindberg and Charles S. Maier (Washington, D.C.: Brookings Institution, 1985).

53. See John Zysman, *Governments, Markets, and Growth: Financial Systems and the Politics of Industrial Change* (Ithaca, N.Y.: Cornell University Press, 1983).

54. See Graham K. Wilson, "Why Is There No Corporatism in the United States?" In Gerhard Lehmbruch and Phillipe C. Schmitter, eds. *Patterns of Corporatist Policy-Making* (Beverly Hills, Calif.: Sage, 1982).

government is at the root of economic decline, and (2) the assumption that tax reductions and significant reductions in taxation could be reconciled with the movement toward a balanced budget.

## The Excesses of Government

Both as candidate and president, Ronald Reagan attributed most of the nation's economic and social woes to big government. As Reagan explained in his inaugural address: "In this present crisis, government is not the solution to our problem; government is the problem. From time to time we've been tempted to believe that society has become too complex to be managed by self-rule, that government by an elite group is superior to government for, by, and of the people. Well, if no one among us is capable of governing himself, then who among us has the capacity to govern someone else?"[2] The theme of big government versus individual empowerment permeated the Reagan policy statements. Take, for example, the broad justification for the *Program for Economic Recovery*:

> The new policy is based on the premise that the people who make up the economy—workers, managers, savers, investors, buyers, and sellers—do not need the government to make reasoned and intelligent decisions about how best to organize and run their own lives. . . . The most appropriate role for government economic policy is to provide a stable and unfettered environment in which private individuals can confidently plan and make appropriate decisions. . . . Decisions to work, save, spend, and invest depend crucially on expectations regarding future government policies.[3]

With the assumed impact of the government on economic and social life, one might suppose that nations with large governments were also nations with lower growth rates and higher inflation rates than nations that have more restrained public sectors. A quick examination of the evidence is suggestive. In 1980, the U.S. government claimed 30.8 percent of the GDP, compared with 40.1 percent in the United Kingdom, 44.5 percent in France, and 44.7 percent in West Germany. Yet, as argued in Chapter 9, during the 1970s nations with larger public sectors seemed to perform better that the United States on a number of indicators, including unemployment, inflation, and productivity gains.[4] This record suggests that the assumption that big government undermines economic prosperity was, in large part, a rhetorical device rather than an accurate account of past economic performance.[5] While the performance of the European nations would prove less favorable a decade later when U.S. growth, unemployment, and inflation rates would look relatively favorable, at the time when Ronald Reagan was articulating his *Program for Economic Recovery*, the core assumption that large governments were plagued by serious problems rested on relatively weak empirical evidence.

## Taxation and Economic Performance: The Logic of the Laffer Curve

When Ronald Reagan entered office, he encountered budget deficits that were widely deemed to be unacceptable for a nation at peace. For decades, Republicans had argued the importance of balanced budgets. They constituted an important symbol of governmental responsibility and competent management. Outside of periods of deep recessions or wars, deficits were understood to be hazardous to the economy and to the moral fiber of the nation. With Reagan's sharp criticism of President Carter's budget deficits fresh in the minds of the population and the strong popular demand for tax cuts, the president had to find some means of approaching balanced budgets. Tax increases were neither politically viable nor philosophically justifiable, given the strong antitax sentiments of the population and the Reagan indictment of high marginal tax rates as a factor undermining economic incentives and individual liberty. This left the option of spending cuts. To be certain, the administration proposed large reductions in a host of domestic programs. However, there were limits to the overall impact of domestic budget cuts on spending levels given the promise of increased defense spending.

In this context, supply-side economics and the Laffer Curve fulfilled an important political function. They provided a means of reconciling the seemingly irreconcilable promises of increased defense spending and balanced budgets via tax cuts. The Laffer Curve did not arrive in Washington with the Reagan administration. For much of the 1970s, economist Arthur Laffer's account of the relationship between taxes and revenues found support in the policy community. Jude Wanniski of the *Wall Street Journal* popularized Laffer's ideas in editorials and in his book *The Way the World Works*. By 1977, the Republican National Committee had embraced the Laffer Curve. Simultaneously, the Laffer Curve provided the core assumption for new tax legislation promoted by Representative Jack Kemp and Senator William Roth.[6]

The Laffer Curve (presented in Figure 10–1) describes the relationship between taxation rates and revenues. The key assertion of the Laffer Curve is that the same level of revenue is available at two tax rates. At a tax rate of zero percent, revenues are zero. As tax rates approach 100 percent, revenues will also approach zero. If workers are required to give up their entire wage in the form of taxation, they will either loose their work incentive or they will invest in the underground economy to escape the tax collectors. With the two end points of the curve in place, it becomes clear that a given level of revenues could be generated via a lower *and* a higher tax rate. The central idea is that as marginal rates increase beyond a certain threshold, the economy and revenues shrink. By lowering the tax rate from A to C, for example, the economy grows thus providing higher levels of revenue. This reduction of tax rates will continue to yield higher levels of revenue via growth until the economy moves to point E, at which both growth and revenues are maximized. A movement in either direction on the Laffer Curve will produce a reduction in revenues, although a movement to points D or B will bring economic expansion at the same time.[7]

The Laffer Curve was appealing for at least two reasons. First, the key relationship between tax rates and revenues was both intuitive and simple. As noted in Chapter 1, discourse in complex policy areas like macroeconomic policy is typically dominated by those with the requisite expertise. The complexity of the debates can exclude nonexperts from participating, thus creating a gap between the political and technical discourses surrounding a given policy. Because the core insight of the Laf-

## The Spending Record

Ronald Reagan viewed the growing budget deficit and high levels of domestic spending as indicative of a large and undisciplined state committed to social engineering and the excesses of Keynesian management. In a news conference early in his presidency, Reagan proclaimed: "What we create we ought to be able to control. I do not intend to make wildly skyrocketing deficits and runaway Government simple facts of life in this administration."[10] Ronald Reagan promised spending reductions in virtually every area save defense, where a growth in spending would be necessary to compensate for a Soviet military buildup that had provided "significant numerical advantage in strategic nuclear delivery systems, tactical aircraft, submarines, artillery, and anti-aircraft defense."[11]

Despite Ronald Reagan's constant indictment of the high levels of government spending, the largest reductions in domestic spending were restricted to the first year when President Reagan recommended large cuts in the budget proposed by the Carter administration. The proposed 1982 fiscal year budget called for $7.2 billion in additional defense spending and a record $41.4 billion reduction in nondefense spending. Although congressional Democrats and moderate Republicans were stunned by the recommended cuts, President Reagan built upon high levels of popularity and mobilized popular support behind the budget by giving a nationally televised address in which he warned of the economic problems that would emerge if the budget were not passed. In the end, Congress accepted the vast majority of defense spending increases while limiting the domestic spending cuts to $35 billion.[12]

Welfare policies were targeted by the Reagan administration because of their alleged role in extending rather than ameliorating poverty and because of the critical role of entitlement policies in driving budgetary growth. Due to the popularity of Social Security, it was largely excluded from the reductions. Attention focused, instead, on policies that were for the most part, means tested: Aid for Families with Dependent Children, Medicaid, Supplemental Security Income, and Food Stamps were hit much harder than the broad social insurance schemes. Additional grant programs designed to alleviate poverty such as the Comprehensive Employment Training Act and Head Start, also suffered, with the former being eliminated altogether and replaced later with the Job Training Partnership Act (see Chapter 11). Although the debates over welfare reform were lively and extended throughout the 1980s, the vast majority of changes in the above-mentioned programs occurred during the first year as part of the Omnibus Budget Reconciliation Act of 1981. Thereafter, Congress resisted further reductions in welfare spending and usually funded programs at higher levels than requested by the administration, reducing defense appropriations to offset these changes. Second, the reductions in many of the welfare and education programs were deep, even if they were far less than what the administration had requested. Thus, the requested AFDC reduction of 28.6 percent was revised to 14.3 percent. A requested 51.3 percent cut in Food Stamps was rejected by Congress for a reduction of 13.8 percent. Because the changes were implemented during the deepest recession since the Great Depression (see the following discussion of inflation), their impact on poverty was magnified. The combination of domestic budgetary changes resulting from the Omnibus Budget Reconciliation Act and the recession resulted in as much as a 7.6 percent increase in the poverty population.[13] While the administration did not receive all it requested and indeed often had to accept continued growth in key programs, by tightening eligibility requirements it changed the trajectory of growth in social spending. Thus, while real increases in welfare spending occurred during the Reagan presidency, they were lower than would have occurred under the programs as they had existed in the last year of the Carter presidency.[14]

The goal of reducing the growth in domestic spending was combined with a firm commitment to expansive defense spending. While the Reagan administration met mixed success in affecting domestic programs due to the power of Congress in the budgetary process, its success in defense was almost unquestionable. Following the U.S. experience in the Vietnam war, support for military spending declined dramatically. A period of relative isolationism was combined with real declines in levels of defense spending, reinforced by the hopes of lasting detente with the Soviet Union. In 1980, defense claimed a mere 5 percent of GNP. Ronald Reagan criticized the policy of reducing military strength, arguing that the United States could not maintain peace, democracy, and market economies without a strong, revitalized military. The existing hostage crisis in Iran, the Soviet invasion of Afghanistan, and the recent victory of the Sandanistas in Nicaragua could be identified as signs of American weakness and the high costs of complacency.

Once in office, Ronald Reagan made good on his campaign promises and promoted the largest peacetime military expansion in U.S. history. The goal of creating a 600-ship navy, restoration of the B-1 bomber, the development of the B-2 Stealth, and the Strategic Defense Initiative fueled expansion in the defense budget. In 1981 alone, real defense spending increased by some 17 percent. By 1985, defense budget authority had increased by almost 53 percent, adjusted for inflation, including more than a doubling in funds for procurement which had increased at an annual rate of 13.5 percent. The increases in procurement and R&D relative to military personnel (which increased at an annual rate of 4.1 percent) reveal that the defense buildup was driven by the goal of weapon modernization.[15]

Increases in defense spending continued in subsequent years, albeit at levels below what the president had requested. As noted above, after 1981, Congress compensated for increases in domestic programs above what the president requested by reducing the appropriation for defense. The result was a shift in resources between policy priorities without significant departures from the final levels of spending recommended by the administration. Nevertheless, by the end of the Reagan presidency, defense spending had increased to 7 percent of GNP. In inflation-adjusted dollars, defense claimed more resources at the end of the Reagan presidency than it had at the height of the Vietnam war. This heavy expenditure for military procurement and R&D was a tremendous economic stimulus that led to rapid growth and high levels of profitability in the defense industries.[16]

While significant spending reductions took place in some areas, the cuts were simply trivial in comparison with the simultaneous reductions in taxes. Reserving a discussion of the deficit for later in the chapter, it is important to note that the common argument—Congress created the deficit by its unwillingness to abide by administration requests—is difficult to substantiate. In the period 1982 to 1987, the government spent some $90 billion dollars over what had been requested by the Reagan administration. However, this sum fades from significance when we note that during this same period, the federal deficit exceeded $1.1 trillion. Even strict obedience to presidential budget requests would not have been sufficient to address the budgetary imbalance. In the end, one must address changes in tax policy rather than congressional spending decisions to explain the budget deficit.[17]

## The Laffer Curve and Beyond: The Politics of Taxation

Tax policy was of critical importance for the Reagan administration. High marginal tax rates were interpreted as a clear indicator of runaway governmental growth. In a presidential address to the nation, President Reagan noted that "we've reached, indeed surpassed, the limits of our people's tolerance or ability to bear an increase in the tax burden."[18] Reagan's observation was largely correct, at least in political terms. The 1970s witnessed something of a tax revolt, particularly at the state and local levels. Frustration with stagnant incomes and growing taxes (a result of "bracket creep," or the tendency of inflation to push taxpayers into higher brackets), was combined with a decline in the trust in the government. Ronald Reagan rode this tide of discontent and exploited the political salience of high taxation, promising lower taxes throughout the 1980 campaign.

Reagan's opposition to high taxes did not rest simply on their unpopularity (a constant feature of U.S. politics) or the antitax sentiment that emerged over the course of the past several years. Rather, he was concerned with the consequences of high taxes for industrial growth and American competitiveness. He explained: "We invented the assembly line and mass production, but punitive tax policies and excessive and unnecessary regulations plus government borrowing have stifled our ability to update plant and equipment. . . . Excessive taxation of individuals has robbed us of incentives and made overtime unprofitable."[19] This understanding of the high costs of taxation fit well with the central message of the Laffer Curve: Tax reductions would result in productive investment, additional workplace effort, and economic growth.

The centerpiece of the Reagan tax policy was the Economic Recovery Tax Act (ERTA) of 1981. Initially a version of the tax legislation proposed by Representatives Jack Kemp and William Roth in the final years of the Carter administration, ERTA took form only after a rapid exchange between the administration, congressional Democrats, and Republicans which resulted in the incorporation of additional reductions and tax expenditures. As David Stockman, Reagan's OMB Director would later note, "Due to all the 'backloaded' congressional ornaments, the size of the tax cut just kept growing beyond 1984. It was like a fiscal volcano, rising steadily against the distant horizon."[20] The willingness of Congress to accept and even promote tax reductions was not surprising given the strong antitax sentiment and the strong popular support for President Reagan. "What *was* surprising and in fact somewhat bizarre," John Witte explains, "was the frenzy with which both parties rushed to increase the bounty and their disregard for the fiscal consequences, which have since become so troublesome in the American economy. In short, the bill got out of hand as the damn broke."[21] Although Ronald Reagan would be given blame for the growing fiscal problems that followed the passage of ERTA, the new tax legislation was clearly a composite of provisions provided by the president, the House, the Senate, and members of both political parties.

In its final form, ERTA included a 23 percent reduction in personal income taxes (with the highest marginal rate reduced from 70 percent to 50 percent), a reduction in the capital gains tax (from 28 percent to 20 percent), accelerated depreciation for businesses, oil tax reductions, and a host of additional tax expenditures ranging from the reasonable (e.g., deductions for Individual Retirement Accounts) to the bizarre (e.g., provisions allowing businesses to sell excess losses to other firms for tax purposes). Although about one-third of the 1981 tax cut was later revoked, this $162 billion tax cut was the largest in U.S. history, easily exceeding the $22.8 billion tax cut of the Ford administration. This unprecedented tax reduction was combined with a provision that threatened permanently to alter tax politics. To prevent a repeat of the events that stimulated such grave dissatisfaction with taxation in the 1970s, ERTA indexed tax brackets thus eliminating the inflation-driven bracket creep that provided a ready source of revenues without tax legislation increasing marginal rates.[22]

Under the logic of the Laffer Curve, a tax reduction like that found in ERTA should have had a strong stimulative effect of the economy. This growth, in turn, should have brought higher levels of revenues than higher marginal rates in a smaller and more stagnant economy. Indeed, the Reagan administration projected inflation-adjusted growth rates of 4.4 percent for the period 1982 to 1986, much improved from the stagnant growth of the 1970s. In reality, these growth rates never materialized. A 2.2 percent growth rate brought lower levels of revenues than expected, particularly when considered in light of the monumental ERTA reductions. Because of ERTA in 1981, taxes on individuals fell by $32 billion in 1982, $75 billion in 1983, $113 billion in 1984, $135 billion in 1985, and $160 billion in 1986. This large and growing loss of revenues was not sustainable.[23] It was forcing a growing gap between spending and revenues that threatened and delivered significant increases in the national debt.

The real consequences for the federal deficit began to materialize quickly following the passage of ERTA. In this context, additional tax reductions were impossible. Indeed, new tax legislation eliminating some of the "back-loaded" provisions and loopholes was passed with the Tax Equity and Fiscal Responsibility Act of 1982 and the Deficit Reduction Act of 1984. However, with the Democrats back in control in the Senate and with a strengthened majority in the House, the focus shifted in 1985 and 1986 to some of the more striking provisions of ERTA that provided benefits to corporations and high income taxpayers. The result was the Tax Reform Act of 1986.

The Tax Reform Act eliminated a variety of tax loopholes and shelters with the goal of taxing all income uniformly and thus simplifying the tax code. The complicated schedule of 14 individual income tax rates ranging from 11 percent to 50 percent was replaced, in effect, by three rates of 15 percent, 28 percent, and 33 percent. At the same time, by almost doubling the personal exemption (from $1,080 to $2,000) and the standard deduction for married couples (from $3,670 to $5,000), it was possible to remove 4.3 million families from the tax system, thus creating greater incentives for the so-called working poor to continue their work effort. While low-income families benefited from the Tax Reform Act, the tax burden was transferred to corporations that claimed such substantial gains after ERTA. The rates on corporate income were increased to a top rate of 34 percent, with reductions in the depreciation allowances and the R&D credit. The top rate on long-term capital gains was increased from 20 percent to 33 percent.[24]

The new relief for the working poor and the elimination of pro-business tax expenditures can be attributed, in part, to the changes in political circumstances. The resurgence of the Democrats and the growing menace of the deficit-framed tax politics. However, as Paul E. Peterson and Mark Rom explain, one must also acknowledge the importance of Ronald Reagan's populism: "The President appreciated the political appeal of lower marginal rates; like many others, he felt that high marginal rates were a major infringement on individual liberties as well as a deterrent to economic growth. With the issue posed in these terms, he was willing to sacrifice a lot: business tax preferences, favorable treatment of capital gains, and tax shelters for the rich. Nothing justifies Reagan's claim to populist conservatism as clearly as does the 1986 tax reform."[25] Thus, even though the Tax Reform Act did not have a significant impact on revenues—it was, from its inception, designed to be revenue neutral—it brought much needed reform to the tax system.

## Regulatory Relief and Reform

Ronald Reagan assumed the presidency with a firm commitment to reducing regulation. On the campaign trail, he freely linked regulation to the economic decline of the previous decade. As he noted in a 1980 speech: "When the real take-home pay of the average American worker is declining steadily and eight million Americans are out of work, we must carefully re-examine our regulatory structure to assess to what degree regulations have contributed to this situation."[26] David Stockman, Reagan's OMB director, made the connection ever more striking in his "Economic Dunkirk" memo, an early statement of Reagan administration economic policy. In this memo, he warned of "a ticking regulatory timebomb" and predicted that the regulations of the 1970s would "sweep through the industrial economy with near gale force" unless there was "a series of unilateral administrative actions to reduce the regulatory burden."[27] As the administration would later suggest, the large regulatory state imposed great costs on the economy by shaping investment decisions: "When capital investment is made it's too often for some unproductive alterations demanded by government to meet various of its regulations."[28] The administration promised regulatory relief and reform by expanding regulatory review and establishing stringent criteria for the justification of new policies.

In January 1981, Reagan created the Presidential Task Force on Regulatory Relief, chaired by Vice-President George Bush. The task force was charged with reviewing proposed rules and existing regulations and to cut through "the thicket of irrational and senseless regulations."[29] The task force was to recommend changes and compile a list of those regulations that were most burdensome for business. Under executive order, the President placed a freeze on pending executive branch regulations and called on regulatory agencies to cease issuing final rules for the next 60 days as the task force examined their impact. In the end, the vast majority of the pending regulations were put into effect. However, from January 1981 to August of 1983 when the task force was disbanded, it identified 119 regulations for review. Of this number, 76 were revised or vacated.[30]

Less than a month after the creation of the Task Force on Regulatory Relief, Reagan issued Executive Order 12,291, the centerpiece of the administration's regulatory reform effort. As noted in Chapter 9, regulatory reform efforts had been promoted as a means of restraining prices in the 1970s, albeit with mixed success. James C. Miller III, a member of the task force and chief architect of the executive order, drew on his experiences in the Ford administration to avoid some of the pitfalls of earlier efforts. The executive order proclaimed that "regulatory action shall not be taken unless the potential benefits to society for the regulation outweigh the potential costs to society." The order mandated that all executive branch agencies submit Regulatory Impact Analyses (RIA) with major rules. In stark contrast with past efforts, Executive Order 12,291 authorized the OMB to mark any rule as a major rule subject to review. Agencies were required to conduct a cost-benefit analysis to determine "the potential net benefits of the rule, including an evaluation of effects that cannot be quantified in monetary terms." The RIA was to be presented, along with the proposed rule-making package, to the OMB 60 days before the publication of the proposed notice and a final RIA was to be submitted along with a draft of the final rule 30 days before its publication in the *Federal Register*.[31]

Earlier review processes were relatively hollow due to the lack of executive enforcement powers. With Executive Order 12,291, the Reagan administration assigned the OMB the power to delay the rule-making process. Agencies could be kept from publishing the notice of proposed rule making until the review and necessary consultation were completed. Agencies were ordered to refrain from publishing a final RIA or rule "until the agency has responded to the [OMB] Director's views, and incorporated those views and the agency's response in the rulemaking file." Compliance with the conditions established by the OMB was no longer optional. The Task Force played the role of mediating conflicts between recalcitrant agencies and the OMB. To facilitate the regulatory review process, OMB guidelines suggested that all costs and benefits be monetized and expressed in constant dollar terms, and that agencies apply a 10 percent discount rate. The OMB promptly imposed the new review procedures. In 1981, 95 regulations were returned by the OMB or withdrawn by the agencies under OMB pressure for failure to meet the criteria. An additional 87 were returned or withdrawn the next year with similar rates for the remainder of the Reagan presidency.[32]

The regulatory review process carried serious implications for some agencies. The technical demands of cost-benefit analysis exceeded the capacity of agency staff and forced regulators to devote resources to outside contractors. Depending on a number of factors—for example, the complexity of the regulation, the kinds of primary research required, the heterogeneity of the industry in question—the

presidency. Most important for those who wished to claim credit for economic policy in the 1980s, inflation remained low, moving between a low of 1.1 percent in 1986 and a high of 4.4 percent for 1987 and 1988. Economic growth, price stability, and a falling unemployment rate replaced the stagflation of the 1970s, setting the context for the election of George Bush in 1988.[41]

While the dramatic actions of the Federal Reserve were critical in promoting a stabilization of prices, it is important to note that other factors were at work as well. First, one must consider the factors that drove inflation in the Carter administration. In 1979 and 1980, energy and food prices outpaced inflation in other goods and services. The elimination of these pressures in the 1980s was critical in reducing inflationary pressures. The virtual collapse of OPEC resulted in a two-thirds reduction in oil prices between 1980 to 1985. Moreover, food surpluses contributed to price stabilization, even if they created additional budgetary problems through the expansion of farm subsidies. In addition, the expansionary fiscal policy had an indirect but important impact on inflation. At first glance, this appears counterintuitive since expansionary fiscal policy was assigned much of the blame for the inflationary problems of the late 1960s and 1970s. However, the great reliance in deficit spending—the deficit exceeded the $200 billion threshold in 1983—inflated the value of the dollar since foreigners wishing to purchase government bonds had to do so in dollars. The resulting strong dollar reduced costs of imports, albeit at the cost of American jobs. Trade surpluses turned into a deficit of $6.1 billion in 1983, exceeding $100 billion by 1986. According to Isabel V. Sawhill and Charles F. Stone, the collapse of OPEC, food surpluses, the debt-inflated dollar, and measurement corrections in the role of home ownership costs in calculating the Consumer Price Index accounted for 52.3 percent of the reduction in inflation, with the remainder attributable to the recession-induced unemployment rates.[42]

It is stunning to note the high price that the Federal Reserve was willing to pay to achieve price stability. The induced recession resulted in a loss of output and high unemployment rates. Overall, some 1.6 million manufacturing jobs and another 212,000 mining jobs disappeared during the course of the Reagan administration.[43] When considered on a per-family basis, the recession's cost per family was significant. In 1979, median family income was $33,454 (1989 dollars). At the depths of the recession, income fell to $30,111 and did not exceed the 1979 level until 1987. Indeed, by 1989, median family income was only $759 above the level reached a decade earlier.[44] Of course, as Sawhill and Stone remind us,

> Recessions are not equal opportunity disemployers. The odds of being drafted into the fight against inflation increase steadily the lower an individual's earnings and family income to begin with. The relative income losses suffered by the working heads of poor families, for example, are four to five times as great as the losses for those heading high-income families, even after adjusting for the cushioning effect of taxes and transfers; and the 1981–1982 recession drove 4.3 million more people into poverty. At every income level, male heads of families experience greater income losses than female heads of families, and black men suffer the most of all.[45]

To be certain, inflation imposes costs on society. Highly variable inflation rates can create a good deal of uncertainty, thus discouraging investment. It also undermines the real incomes of some individuals on fixed incomes, assuming that their incomes are not indexed for inflation. However, the widespread belief that inflation is a major economic problem is in many ways curious given the extent to which middle-class families—holders of low-interest fixed mortgages—benefited from the inflation of the 1970s. Between 1973 and 1980, real inflation rates averaged 0.1 percent, compared with an average real interest rate of 6 percent during the period 1981 to 1988.[46] With the advent of inflation-indexed benefits, most people on fixed incomes were not hurt significantly by inflation. Indeed, as Paul Peretz has shown, despite the popular concerns over inflation, it has "few aggregate effects and rather minor long-term distributional effects."[47] One should exercise skepticism when evaluating claims concerning the long-term impact of inflation. In the end, it would appear that the costs of inflation are more symbolic than they are real. Inflation suggests a loss of economic control and, due to the money illusion, a loss of purchasing power. What, then, is most striking is that the costs of recession are real and immediate: unemployment, lost income, and all of the attendant social ills. A war against inflation claims high casualties whether policymakers are victorious or not. If they are successful, the benefits are simply much smaller than usually assumed. When one considers the costs of the 1981 to 1982 recession, one cannot help but conclude that the greatest costs of inflation are incurred through the policies designed to achieve price stability.

## DEFICITS AND THE AMERICAN POLITICAL ECONOMY

By the end of 1982, inflation was at a low that could not have been imagined at any time since the imposition of wage-price controls under Nixon's New Economic Policy. Moreover, the economy had entered an expansionary stage that would continue well into the Bush presidency. However, the greatest long-term legacy may be the large budget deficit and debt. The record deficits during the Reagan presidency that continued during the Bush Presidency surpassed those of any president since Franklin Roosevelt—a president who accumulated debt as a product of the Great Depression and World War II. The growth in the deficit and debt are presented graphically in Figures 10–3 and 10–4. As the figures reveal, the deficit and debts have become the lasting products of the economic policy of the 1980s. In part, this is because the debt feeds itself. By 1990, the costs of financing the debt were 14.7 percent of the budget or $184.2 billion in net interest payments, compared with 8.9 percent of the budget or $52.5 billion in 1980.

It is somewhat shocking to note that these increases in the deficit and debt have occurred despite a high level of public attention and a number of attempts to introduce greater discipline into the budgetary process. The most important effort to address the process was the Gramm-Rudman-Hollings Balanced Budget and Emergency Deficit Control Act of 1985. The goal of the act was to establish declining deficit targets that would result in a balanced budget within five years. Failure to achieve the targets would result in automatic cuts by the General Accounting Office drawn equally from defense and domestic spending. In 1987, following the

**Figure 10–3**   Federal Deficits, 1970–1992

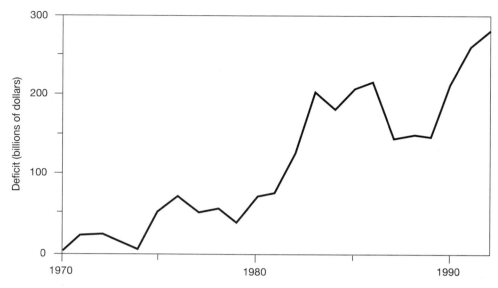

Source: *Economic Report of the President.*

**Figure 10–4**   Federal Debt, 1970–1992

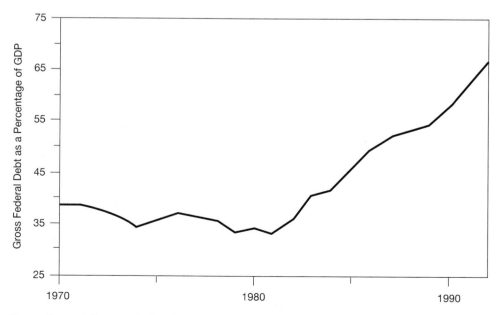

Source: *Economic Report of the President.*

Supreme Court's decision that the GAO's role in the new process was unconstitutional, the Reagan administration and Congress negotiated changes to Gramm-Rudman. New deficit targets were created with the target of reaching a balanced budget by fiscal year 1993, albeit with exceptional reliance on draconian cuts after the 1988 presidential election. To meet the constitutional objections, the OMB was assigned responsibility for enforcing the deficit targets. While Gramm-Rudman did result in some modest deficit reductions, it was plagued by the large portions of the budget exempted from the process and the frequent reliance on optimistic economic projections that allowed Congress to meet the provisions of the process while avoiding the pain associated with genuine progress.[48]

As Figures 10–3 and 10–4 reveal, the new procedural constraints had little long-term impact on the deficit. While the growth in the deficit and debt levels is clearly evident, there remains some debate over whether the levels have reached a crisis point. Is there some threshold of debt beyond which an economy suffers irreparable damage? Is there a debt ceiling that forecloses the possibility of further growth?

While it is true that the economy grew during the 1980s, the rate of growth was outpaced by the growth in the debt. As Benjamin Friedman explains in his fine book *Day of Reckoning*, the history of debt in the United States was relatively easy to understand prior to the 1980s.[49] The nation incurred large debts largely as a result of wars and the Great Depression. Outside of those rare events, the norm was either the explicit attempt to buy down the debt via budget surpluses or sustained growth resulting in a reduction of the debt relative to national income. Thus, large World War II spending created debts which amounted to 70 cents per dollar of income by 1950. Due to growth in the following decades, the debt had fallen to 26 cents per dollar of national income by 1980. This level of indebtedness was approximately the same as that of 1920. However, by the end of 1987, the debt was 44 cents per dollar, despite the lack of national emergency. This change in the nation's debt position was largely a product of fiscal policy. Friedman explains:

> The substantial rise in federal debt in relation to income that our new fiscal policy has brought about is unprecedented in our history. Apart from the wars that every schoolchild recognizes and the Depression that every grandparent remembers, we have always experienced declining government indebtedness. But with a fiscal policy centered on large across-the-board tax cuts, and no real desire in any quarter to cut the core programs like defense and Social Security and Medicare that dominate the government's spending, increasing indebtedness through both peace and prosperity has now become our national policy. In the 1980s, the federal debt ratio . . . [was] rising just as fast as it had fallen in the previous three and a half decades after World War II.[50]

The deficit and the debt carry the potential for serious long-term damage to the American economy. Even if it is impossible to paint the situation as one of immediate crisis, the trajectory initiated in the 1980s is unsustainable. Of course, one can indict the current deficit and debt as symbols of fiscal impudence and a failure of governance. Balanced budgets tend to carry support because they represent a sense of control over the fiscal affairs of state and responsible leadership. While these are not trivial issues insofar as they may affect the citizenry's sense of governmental legitimacy, we are concerned primarily with the economic impact of the current budgetary difficulties. Let us address them in turn.

To understand why the deficit should be a source of concern, it is important to consider five points: the impact of the deficit and debt on capital markets; the costs of financing to the government; the debt's impact on trade; the limits the debt places on economic policymaking; and the role of the debt as an instrument of wealth redistribution.

## The Debt, Capital Markets, and Investment

When the government seeks to fund its deficits (thus converting it into debt), it relies primarily on capital markets. It sells U.S. government bonds at auction. Given the security of the investment and the high rates of return, the government is first in line in the competition for capital. What happens when the government extracts hundreds of billions of dollars per year from the pool of national savings? Quite simply, it reduces the amount of capital available for other uses. When one considers the relatively low national savings rate in the United States, the pool of available capital is already relatively small. The combined effects of low levels of savings and the draw of the national government in funding the deficit have had a serious downward impact on the net national savings rate (i.e., the pool of private savings, expressed as a percentage of GNP, minus government borrowing). The net national savings rate stood as 8.4 percent of GNP during the 1950s and 1960s, declining slightly to 7.8 percent of GNP during the 1970s. However, due to a decline in personal and business savings and the growing pressures of servicing the national debt, the net national saving rate fell to 3.8 percent of GNP by 1986, and 2.4 percent by 1988.[51]

The debt-induced reduction in the net national savings rate translates into a smaller pool of capital available for corporations seeking to fund expansion and the purchase of new equipment. Money, like any other commodity, is responsive to the forces of supply and demand. As the supply of capital falls as a result of debt, the costs of capital increase, thus creating disincentives for replacing aging equipment and increasing the overall costs of production. The impact of such decisions in an integrated global economy can be quite significant. Decisions to withhold reinvestment can translate into a loss of competitiveness, a reduction in sales, and a reduction in profits available for reinvestment. Alternatively, corporations may replace domestic capital with a reliance on less expensive foreign capital, opening the door for additional problems of corporate buyouts and the wholesale purchase of the American industrial base by foreign-based corporations—a trend that was clearly exhibited in the 1980s.

## The Costs of Financing the Debt: A Question of Policy Priorities

When one addresses the costs of financing the debt, one must go beyond the impact on capital markets and the rise in the costs of capital. To be certain, bonds are purchased with funds that might otherwise be lent to industrial borrowers through loans, commercial debt, or equities. However, the costs of servicing the debt (i.e., making the interest payments) comes out of the annual federal budget. As a portion of this budget, it has increased along with the debt. In 1990, 14.7 percent of the federal budget was absorbed by net interest payments on the debt, a sum of $182.2 billion. This can be compared with interest payments of 10 percent of the budget in the last year of the Carter presidency. Between 1980 and 1990, the total net interest payments well exceeded $1 trillion. It is important to note that these figures represent net interest payments. Surpluses in a host of government trust funds (e.g., the Social Security Trust Fund) are also used to buy government debt. When interest payments to these funds are included, the federal government's 1990 interest paid on the national debt was $264.8 billion.[52]

The importance of these figures is clear when one places the debt service in the broader context. When total interest payments are taken into account, interest on the national debt becomes the second largest category in the federal budget. In 1990, it was second behind national defense which cost a total of $299.3 billion and more expensive than Social Security which paid out $248.6 billion. In contrast, Food Stamps, AFDC, and Supplemental Security Income—the worrisome welfare state policies that were often presented as the major drag on the economy—cost a total of $38.7 billion, or 14.6 percent of the interest paid on the debt. Another comparison is even more enlightening. It is commonly argued that improvements in education and training are necessary if the United States is to succeed in the new world economy (see Chapter 11). When all 1990 federal expenditures on elementary, secondary, vocational, and higher education are combined with the expenditures on training and employment programs, the total is approximately $27 billion, only slightly more than one-tenth of the 1990 interest payments.[53] These comparisons are illustrative of the size of the interest payments versus other activities deemed important by the federal government and the American electorate. They provide a clear testament to how the resources that are devoted to interest payments could be used absent the debt. In essence, one major cost of the debt is the opportunity cost associated with devoting over one-quarter trillion dollars to expenses that have no positive impact on economic growth or the welfare of the population.

Of course, some have suggested that the impact of the deficit and debt on budgetary priorities was more than a negative but unintended by-product of the Reagan agenda. If Ronald Reagan and the Republican party could identify an expansionary logic inherent in the American welfare state, this logic no longer prevailed in the wake of the 1980s. New entitlement programs would be impossible without new taxes or reductions in existing programs. Budgetary politics became a zero-sum game, thus transforming the rules of the American political system.

## The Debt and the Dollar: The International Dimension

With the deficit and debt, the U.S. government cannot and should not rely solely on domestic capital markets as a source of funds. It has been necessary to sell the debt to foreign investors. The availability of foreign capital has been important in

tion."[61] The combination of new taxes and regulatory expansion would be cited by conservative critics of the Bush administration as the proximate causes of the recession which dominated the second half of the Bush presidency and set much of the stage for the 1992 elections.

The economic slowdown began in the second quarter of 1989, when the GDP growth rate fell from 3.2 percent to 1.8 percent. The growth rate remained slow, fluctuating from the 0 percent during the third quarter of 1989 to 1 percent in the second quarter of 1990, before the growth rate became negative for three quarters. The recession was relatively mild, as explained in the *Economic Report of the President*, which noted that the recession "was shorter (8 months, compared with a postwar average of 11) and slightly less severe (output declined 2.2 percent relative to a postwar average of 2.8 percent; unemployment rose 2.8 percent, less than the postwar average of 3.4 percent) than other recessions." The report went on to note that "more troubling was the anemic pace of the recovery that began in March 1991. . . . Growth was so sluggish, in fact, that job creation was insufficient to prevent unemployment from rising even months after the recovery had begun."[62] Indeed, the slow recovery skillfully avoided the attention of consumers, employers, and ultimately voters.[63]

The Council of Economic Advisers understates the reality. Despite the resumption of growth in the second quarter of 1991, unemployment actually increased from a level of 6.7 percent for 1991 to 7.4 percent by the end of 1992.[64] In short, "recovery" brought further increases in unemployment, elevating the jobless rate above that which existed in the depth of the recession. The failure of the jobless rate to improve is not in itself remarkable. The unemployment rate is commonly understood as lagging behind other indicators for a host of reasons. What is remarkable is that a jobless rate of 7.4 percent was the best that could be accomplished with a budget deficit of $290.2 billion, well above the $221.2 billion deficit record set by the Reagan administration in 1986, and a prime interest rate of 6.25 percent, the lowest in 20 years.[65] If an unprecedented level of economic stimulus could not propel the economy to anything resembling full employment, one was forced to ask whether expansionary fiscal and monetary policies were sufficient. Of course, this was not a question new to the 1990s. For more than a decade, policymakers and analysts had questioned whether existing macroeconomic policy tools had to be combined with some form of industrial policy to nurture the kinds of high-wage, growth-oriented industries that provided a foundation for economic prosperity in the postwar period. With the erosion of the industrial base—a result of a debt-induced inflation in the value of the dollar, a growing level of international economic integration, and a loss of American comparative advantage in mass production industries—many argued that what was needed were new policies targeted to development. We turn now to an examination of these debates.

## NOTES

1. "Program for Economic Recovery, White House Report, February 18, 1981." *Weekly Compilation of Presidential Documents* 17, 8 (1981), p. 141.
2. "Inaugural Address of President Ronald Reagan, January 20, 1981." *Weekly Compilation of Presidential Documents* 17, 4 (1981), p. 2.

3. "Program for Economic Recovery," p. 155.

4. OECD, *Historical Statistics, 1960–1988* (Paris: OECD, 1990), pp. 48, 51, 68.

5. See David R. Cameron, "Does Government Cause Inflation? Taxes, Spending, and Deficits." In *The Politics of Inflation and Economic Stagnation*, ed. Leon N. Lindberg and Charles S. Maier (Washington, D.C.: Brookings Institution, 1985).

6. Herbert Stein, *Presidential Economics: The Making of Economic Policy from Roosevelt to Reagan and Beyond* (Washington, D.C.: American Enterprise Institute, 1988), pp. 245–46.

7. See Jude Wanniski, "Taxes, Revenues, and the 'Laffer Curve.' " *The Public Interest* 50 (Winter 1978): 3–16.

8. Murray Weidenbaum, *Rendezvous with Reality: The American Economy After Reagan* (New York: Basic Books, 1988), p. 19.

9. Stein, *Presidential Economics*, p. 248. See pp. 246–49.

10. "President's News Conference of January 29, 1981." *Weekly Compilation of Presidential Documents* 15,5 (1981), p. 65.

11. "Program for Economic Recovery. Address before a Joint Session of the Congress, February 18, 1981." *Weekly Compilation of Presidential Documents* 17,7 (1981): 134.

12. Paul E. Peterson and Mark Rom. "Lower Taxes, More Spending, and Budget Deficits." In *The Reagan Legacy: Promise and Performance*, ed. Charles O. Jones (Chatham, N.J.: Chatham House, 1988), pp. 222–23.

13. Kenneth Hoover and Raymond Plant, *Conservative Capitalism in Britain and the United States* (London: Routledge, 1989), p. 113.

14. John A. Ferejohn, "Changes in Welfare Policy in the 1980s." In *Politics and Economics in the Eighties*, ed. Alberto Alesina and Geoffrey Carliner (Chicago: University of Chicago Press, 1991), pp. 123–26, 135–36; Lee D. Baldwin and John L. Palmer, "Social Policy: Challenging the Welfare State." In *The Reagan Record*, ed. John L. Palmer and Isabel V. Sawhill (Cambridge: Ballinger, 1984).

15. Phil Williams, "The Reagan Administration and Defence Policy." In *The Reagan Presidency: An Incomplete Revolution?* ed. Dilys M. Hill, Raymond A. Moore, and Phil Williams (New York: St. Martin's Press, 1990), pp. 201–05; Peterson and Rom, "Lower Taxes, More Spending, and Budget Deficits," pp. 28–35.

16. Williams, "The Reagan Administration and Defence Policy." pp. 201–05.

17. Benjamin Friedman, *Day of Reckoning: The Consequences of American Economic Policy* (New York: Random House, 1989), pp. 131–32.

18. "The Nation's Economy: Address to the Nation, February 5, 1981." *Weekly Compilation of Presidential Documents* 17,6 (1981): 95.

19. Ibid.

20. David A. Stockman, *The Triumph of Politics: The Insider Story of the Reagan Revolution* (New York: Harper & Row, 1986), p. 289.

21. John F. Witte, *The Politics and Development of the Federal Income Tax* (Madison: University of Wisconsin Press, 1985), p. 211.

22. Peterson and Rom, "Lower Taxes, More Spending, and Budget Deficits," pp. 218–20.

23. Friedman, *Day of Reckoning*, pp. 128–29.

24. Jeffrey H. Birnbaum and Alan S. Murray, *Showdown at Gucci Gulch: Lawmakers, Lobbyists, and the Unlikely Triumph of Tax Reform* (New York: Random House, 1987), Appendix A; William A. Niskanen, Jr. *Reaganomics: An Insider's Account of the Policies and the People* (New York: Oxford University Press, 1988), pp. 99–101.

25. Peterson and Rom, "Lower Taxes, More Spending, and Budget Deficits," p. 221.

26. Quoted in Dick Kirschten, "President Reagan After Two Years—Bold Actions but Uncertain Results." *National Journal* 15,1 (January 1, 1983), p. 7. See the discussion of the administration's deregulatory initiatives in Marc Allen Eisner, *Regulatory Politics in Transition* (Baltimore, Md.: Johns Hopkins University Press, 1993), pp. 182–91.

27. Timothy B. Clark, "OMB to Keep Its Regulatory Powers in Reserve in Case Agencies Lag." *National Journal* 13,11 (March 14, 1981), p. 426.

28. "The Nation's Economy," p. 95.

29. "Remarks Announcing the Establishment of the President's Task Force on Regulatory Relief, January 22, 1981." *Weekly Compilation of Presidential Documents* 17,4 (1981), p. 34.

30. Richard Andrews, "Economics and Environmental Decisions, Past and Present." In *Environmental Policy Under Reagan's Executive Order: The Role of Benefit-Cost Analysis*, ed. V. Kerry Smith (Chapel Hill: University of North Carolina Press, 1984), pp. 73–74; Timothy B. Clark, "If Reagan Wants to Trump the Regulators, Here's OMB's Target List for Openers." *National Journal* 13, 3 (January 17, 1981): 94-98.

31. Timothy B. Clark, "Do the Benefits Justify the Costs? Prove It, Says the Administration." *National Journal* 13, 31 (August 1, 1981), p. 1382.

32. Office of Management and Budget, *Interim Regulatory Impact Analysis Guidance*, June 12, 1981; Thomas O. McGarity, *Reinventing Rationality: The Role of Regulatory Analysis in the Federal Bureaucracy* (Cambridge: Cambridge University Press, 1991), p. 22.

33. Paul R. Portney, "The Benefits and Costs of Regulatory Analysis." In *Environmental Policy Under Reagan's Executive Order: The Role of Benefit-Cost Analysis*, ed. V. Kerry Smith (Chapel Hill: University of North Carolina Press, 1984), pp. 229, 231.

34. Murray L. Weidenbaum, "Regulatory Reform Under the Reagan Administration." In *The Reagan Regulatory Strategy: An Assessment*, ed. George C. Eads and Michael Fix (Washington, D.C.: Urban Institute Press, 1984), pp. 33–53.

35. Lawrence Mosher, "Will EPA's Budget Make It More Efficient or Less Effective." *National Journal* 13, 33 (August 15, 1981): 1466–69.; Niskanen, *Reaganomics*, p. 131.

36. Howard Ball, *Controlling Regulatory Sprawl: Presidential Strategies from Nixon to Reagan* (Westport, Conn.: Greenwood Press, 1984), pp. 93–97.

37. Weidenbaum, *Rendezvous with Reality*, p. 9.

38. Paul Volcker and Toyoo Gyohten, *Changing Fortunes: The World's Money and the Threat to American Leadership* (New York: Times Books, 1992), p. 167.

39. Andrew H. Bartels, "Volcker's Revolution at the Fed." *Challenge* 28, 4 (September-October 1985), p. 38.

40. Friedman, *Day of Reckoning*, pp. 147–49. Figures from *Economic Report of the President, 1991* (Washington D.C.: Government Printing Office, 1991), p. 356.

41. Figures from *Economic Report of the President, 1991.*

42. Isabel V. Sawhill and Charles F. Stone, "The Economy: The Key to Success." In *The Reagan Record: An Assessment of America's Changing Domestic Priorities* (Cambridge, Mass.: Ballinger, 1984), p. 80.

43. Charles K. Wilber and Kenneth P. Jameson, *Beyond Reaganomics: A Further Inquiry into the Poverty of Economics* (Notre Dame, Ind.: University of Notre Dame Press, 1990), p. 108.

44. David P. Calleo, *The Bankrupting of America: How the Federal Budget is Impoverishing the Nation* (New York: William Morrow, 1992), pp. 93–94.

45. Sawhill and Stone, "The Economy," p. 83.

46. Calleo, *The Bankrupting of America*, p. 198.

47. Paul Peretz, *The Political Economy of Inflation in the United States* (Chicago: University of Chicago Press, 1983), p. 69.

48. Donald F. Kettl, *Deficit Politics: Public Budgeting in its Institutional and Historical Context* (New York: Macmillan, 1992), pp. 95–100.

49. Friedman, *Day of Reckoning*, pp. 115–16.

50. Ibid., p. 116.

51. William D. Nordhaus, "What's Wrong with a Declining National Savings Rate?" *Challenge* 32, 4 (1989): 22–26.; Paul A. Volcker, "Facing Up to the Twin Deficits." *Challenge* 27, 2 (1984): 4–9.

52. David Brashear, *Government in Crisis* (Alexandria, Va.: Chesapeake River Press, 1991), pp. 56, 81; Niskanen, *Reaganomics*, p. 25.

53. Brashear, *Government in Crisis*, pp. 53, 138.

54. See Bartels, "Volcker's Revolution at the Fed."

55. See John T. Woolley, *Monetary Politics: The Federal Reserve and the Politics of Monetary Policy* (Cambridge: Cambridge University Press, 1984).

56. See Paul Starbonin, "Trouble in the Temple." *National Journal* 25, 22 (1993): 1278–81.

57. See Kettl, *Deficit Politics*, pp. 26–28.

58. Samuel Bowles, David M. Gordon, and Thomas E. Weisskopf, *After the Wasteland: A Democratic Economics for the Year 2000* (Armonk, N.Y.: M.E. Sharpe, 1990), p. 203.

59. Barbara Sinclair, "Governing Unheroically (and Sometimes Unappetizingly): Bush and the 101st Congress." In *The Bush Presidency: First Appraisals*, ed. Colin Campbell and Bert A. Rockman (Chatham, N.J.,: Chatham House Publishers, 1991).

60. Aaron Wildavsky, *The New Politics of the Budgetary Process*, 2nd ed. (New York: HarperCollins, 1992), pp. 482–526.

61. Jonathan Rauch, "The Regulatory President." *National Journal* 23, 48 (1991): 2902–06.

62. *Economic Report of the President, 1993* (Washington, D.C.: Government Printing Office, 1993), p. 21. Figures on growth from Table B-4, p. 324.

63. See Paul Starobin, "Confusing Signals." *National Journal* 23, 48 (1991): 2907–2911.

64. *Economic Report of the President, 1993*, Table B-38, p. 391.

65. Ibid., Table B-74, p. 435; Table B-69, p. 429.

# 11

# THE DECLINE AND RENEWAL OF THE AMERICAN ECONOMY

In recent years, the American economy has been beset by a host of problems including stagnant growth in real incomes and a related growth in the poverty rate, a fall in the rate of productivity growth, and a wave of bank failures. Unprecedented peacetime budget deficits and debt have been combined with a high trade deficit and the transformation of the United States from the position of the largest world creditor nation to the largest international debtor. With these changes in the economic circumstances, it is not surprising that many have presented the current situation as part of a long-term trend in national economic decline. These stories of decline have been accompanied by the call for new industrial policies or, more recently, industrial strategies. In each case, the goal is to foster new high-growth industries that can guarantee income growth and a reversal of national economic fortunes.

The unique features of the postwar economy that provided a basis for rapid economic growth have largely disappeared in the past two decades. Anticipated occupational trajectories and expectations of growing real incomes have been some of the casualties of these changes. This stagnancy—and for many, downward mobility—has broad implications. As Katherine S. Newman explains:

> The meaning of "being American" has been inextricably embedded in expectations for upward mobility and domination in international trade. The 1970s and 1980s have reshaped this self-perception in ways that we have yet to fully articulate. This change is evident in our fears for the country's economic future and our frustrations over the impact of change on our standard of living, a resurgent conservatism over the responsibilities of the fortunate toward the fate of the poor, a heightened sense of compe-

tition between and within generations for the resources needed to raise a family or retire in comfort, and increasing worries over the long-term impact of inner-city decay and minority poverty.[1]

Newman correctly notes that "American culture has always celebrated forward motion, progress, upward mobility. . . . When reality fails to provide what we think we are owed, we seldom readjust our expectations. Instead, we stew in frustration or search for a target for our anger, pointing fingers at more fortunate generations, incompetent presidents, disloyal corporations."[2] In short, individual situations are easily translated into political demands or, as important, alienation from the political system. Hence, economic decline cannot be ignored by policymakers.

Contemporary analyses of the American economy present similar stories of economic decline, albeit stories that identify somewhat different factors. While the accounts vary, they acknowledge the importance of a limited set of causal factors including levels of technological innovation, capital formation and investment, short-term managerial incentives, corporate rigidity, labor training, and trade policy. What kinds of policies should officials formulate to retard or reverse the decline of American industry? This question has been a constant feature of the economic policy debates since the late 1970s. The answer will depend on which of the above-mentioned factors are granted the greatest importance in explaining the performance of the American economy relative to that of foreign competitors.

In this chapter, we begin with a brief review of the economic record of the last few decades. Is it in fact true that the economy has entered a period of deindustrialization and decline? The second task is to address the industrial policy debates of the past several years along with the political and philosophical objections to industrial policy. Third, the chapter turns to examine the key problems addressed by analysts along with the kinds of proposals that have been offered in response. The chapter closes with a discussion of the practical limitations to creating and administering an industrial policy. As with other policy questions, past decisions and institutional structures set definite limits on the capacity of policymakers to formulate coherent and effective responses to the competitiveness question.

## THE RISE AND DECLINE OF THE AMERICAN ECONOMY

As the past several chapters have revealed, the postwar period began with a period of steady growth and, by the mid-1960s, the attainment of full employment. By any measure, the economic performance of the two decades following the war was impressive. By the 1960s, extremely low levels of unemployment and steady growth, both products of the tax cut of 1964, were combined with relative price stability. However, this idyllic situation was quickly compromised by the growing problem of inflation—a direct consequence of the high levels of fiscal stimulation resulting from the 1964 tax cut, Vietnam War spending, and growing domestic spending. When taken by itself, inflation was not the origin of the economic malaise that would consume the following decade. Rather, poor economic performance was a product of the efforts to eliminate inflation through the application of restrictive

teristic of all highly developed economies."[9] While advocates of the deindustrialization thesis dismissed such explanations as largely the product of erroneous measures of growth and productivity gains, the common ground shared by the participants in the deindustrialization debate was more critical than the disagreements.[10] Whether or not one adopts the deindustrialization thesis or the productivity thesis, the net result is a loss of many high-wage jobs that were the mainstay of the postwar American economy. Indeed, the stagnation of real incomes from the early 1970s to present is in part a product of this job loss. As Americans have been forced to ponder a future of stagnant incomes, the demands for some response have grown in number and intensity.

One must address the impact of deindustrialization with some care. While it is true that goods-producing jobs (that is, jobs in manufacturing and construction) have declined while service-sector jobs have grown in number, the typical characterization of service jobs as low-wage "hamburger flipping" positions is woefully inadequate. As Max Dupuy and Mark E. Schweitzer of the Federal Reserve Bank of Cleveland explain: "It is unreasonable to describe service-producing employment, which accounts for nearly 80 percent of U.S. nonfarm jobs, as 'lower paying.' In 1992, the average weekly wage for full time workers in this sector was only 3.9 percent below the average goods-producing wage."[11] Indeed, the median weekly wages for goods- and service-producing jobs are quickly converging, as service-sector positions increasingly demand higher levels of education and skills for entry. When seen in this light, the transformation from a goods-producing economy to a service-producing economy may not be as tragic as many proponents of the deindustrialization thesis suggest. There is, however, one very important exception. Wage levels in the service sector closely track levels of educational achievement. As a result, among workers with only high school degrees, goods-producing jobs offer a median wage that is 20 percent higher than comparable service-sector jobs.[12] However, as Dupuy and Schweitzer note, the fact that less educated workers benefit from goods-producing jobs does not necessarily lead one to call for reindustrialization: "this is not an adequate argument for designing a policy that would shift the distribution of employment opportunities toward goods production. Instead, it suggests once again the importance of educating Americans to meet employers' needs."[13] Despite this cautionary note, the industrial policy debates have focused on developing strategies to strengthen and expand the nation's industrial base and reverse the movement toward a service-based economy.

## THE INDUSTRIAL POLICY DEBATE

Since the late 1970s, a number of analysts have called for policies to renew the American economy and replace declining industries and lower-level service sector jobs with high-wage, high-growth industries that would be able to flourish in an increasingly competitive world economy. In the early 1980s, the federal response to the fluctuating fortunes of the American economy was, at the very best, incoherent. A network of subsidies, tax expenditures, training programs, and loans and loan guarantees created over the course of the century in response to industry lobbying and a variety of policy initiatives such as the War on Poverty were combined with a set of ad hoc voluntary trade agreements backed with the threat of anti-dumping procedures to protect selective industries. The odd collection of policies and selective protectionist measures was combined with a defense-oriented industrial policy designed to promote innovation in defense technologies. The Reagan administration, with its strong bias against excessive state intervention and social engineering, objected to industrial policy except when connected to the rebuilding of the American military capacity and the Strategic Defense Initiative.

Against this context of declining performance and policy incoherence, a legion of analysts and policymakers introduced proposals for an industrial policy of one type or another designed to rebuild the American economy. In 1983 alone, "at least 17 bills proposed an armada of national development boards, commissions on competitiveness, and the like, 9 of which would reestablish the RFC in one form or another."[14] Take the example of the House Banking, Finance, and Urban Affairs Committee. Its subcommittee on Economic Stabilization proposed the creation of a Bank for Industrial Competitiveness to fund industrial revitalization, an Advanced Technology Foundation to make grants to fund applied research and development, and a Council on Industrial Competitiveness to coordinate a broad based industrial policy.[15] Likewise in 1983, Representatives Stan Ludine, Dave Bonior, Dick Gephardt, and Tim Wirth cosponsored a National Industrial Strategy bill that would have created a National Industrial Development Bank to provide "patient capital" for long-term investments and an Economic Cooperation Council with representatives of business, labor, the government, and public interest groups to oversee a broad industrial strategy and a variety of policies that impact on competitiveness.[16] These proposals, like the other overtures aimed at creating a comprehensive industrial policy, failed to attract sufficient support. For many, industrial policy appeared to be something that was far too difficult to reconcile with American political traditions, particularly in a period when policymakers were too busy calling for a reaffirmation of markets and decrying excessive government regulation.

The United States had something resembling an industrial policy during World War I, the New Deal, and World War II. In fact, many of the contemporary proponents of industrial policy either explicitly or implicitly model their proposals on a positive reading of these past experiences.[17] As shown in earlier chapters, during these national emergencies, new institutions were created to coordinate the use of resources on an economywide basis, to shift production priorities, to allocate capital, and to circumvent the market with negotiated agreements covering prices and production levels. Although the historical record hardly provides unambiguous support for the adopted models, critics of industrial policy are quick to identify the near failure of the War Industries Board, the National Industrial Recovery Act, and the Reconstruction Finance Corporation. While it might be difficult to reconcile these planning institutions with American political traditions, the existence of a national emergency did reduce the need for such reconciliation. The question for many was whether the economic problems of the 1970s and 1980s constituted a crisis of sufficient magnitude to warrant an industrial policy.

Of course, every nation has public policies that affect industry. As previous chapters have shown, despite the attraction to laissez-faire principles of state-economy relations, the United States has a seemingly endless number of policies that shape economic activity even outside the emergence of a war or depression. This is the case in the 1990s; it was the case in the 1790s. However, as John Zysman cautions, one must not confuse policies impacting on industry with *industrial policy*.

> Market competition, price-driven adjustment, and government limited to regulatory functions would best describe the ideological principles behind the policy, but at all levels of jurisdiction, the reality is an extensive web of ad hoc government policies that promote and control industry. . . . Americans allow a multitude of industrial policies to compete with each other while denying that they have any policies at all. But if industrial policy is understood as a conscious federal strategy linked to tactics for the particular sectors, then it is indeed true that America has no policy.[18]

In a most minimalist sense, every nation has "industrial policies." However, industrial policy is best understood as an integrated set of policies designed to facilitate the adjustment of capital and labor out of industries in decline and into new industries that offer high wages and a significant potential for growth. This may entail the promotion of research and development (R&D), the financing of new innovations, labor training and relocation, and the creation of specialized export and import regimes.

One can find different models of industrial policy in the United States' major competitors. However, the model that did the most to stimulate the industrial policy debates in the United States was that of Japan. The Ministry of International Trade and Industry (MITI) has been central to Japan's industrial policy. Based on long-term economic forecasts, MITI promotes the allocation of capital through the Industrial Bank of Japan and the Japanese Development Bank to industries deemed strategic to future development. Financing carries with it the direct supervision of MITI and the Ministry of Finance. Financing is combined with additional policies including, at one time or another, protective tariffs, import quotas, and controls on foreign investment and technology. The Japanese economy is a dense network of organizations linked into the formation and execution of industrial policy. Export cartels, organized by MITI, allow for the development of long-term export strategies and link corporations in the development of research and development. At the same time, government-business councils (213 in 1987) are organized to provide a context for ongoing consultation and to define future policies and industrial policy goals. "Rationalization" or "recession" cartels are created by MITI to protect declining industries and allow for an orderly and equitable disinvestment of capital. Although Japan formerly eschewed protectionist policies for a variety of incentives (e.g., additional financial assistance, tax and regulatory relief) in the early 1980s, there have been ongoing complaints that structural impediments limit the ability of other nations to export to Japan. These impediments are tied, in large part, to Japanese *keiretsu*, or industrial groups that link firms across sectors of the economy and adopt purchasing policies designed with an eye to long-term development and foreign market penetration.[19]

While the United States has industrial policies in the minimalist sense of the term, it has not had an industrial policy that even comes close to resembling that of Japan. The reasons are many. Let us address the distinctive ideological impediments, reserving a discussion of the institutional and political impediments for later in the chapter. There is a strong ideological aversion to industrial policy insofar as it violates accepted norms of state-economy relations. To be certain, the United States has not been faithful in its observation of the principles of laissez faire. As has been shown throughout the preceding chapters, public policies have played and continue to play a significant role in shaping economic activity. However, there is a logical problem that supercedes the historical record. The faith in free market governance is difficult to sustain if one seriously considers the legal and institutional foundations of market transactions. Transactions (and so much more) depend on the way in which property rights are defined. Yoram Barzel defines property rights in the following way: "Property rights of individuals over assets consist of the rights, or the powers, to consume, obtain income from, and alienate these assets. Obtaining income from and alienating assets require exchange . . . The rights people have over assets (including themselves and other people) are not constant; they are a function of their own direct efforts at protection, of other people's capture attempts, and of government protection."[20] As this suggests, efficient market exchanges are possible only after law has defined property rights, standards (e.g., weights and measures), and appropriate currencies. Additional laws addressing the limits of exchange (e.g., what can and cannot be exchanged), liability, and intellectual property rights are necessary as well as a set of institutions designed to adjudicate property disputes.

The popular notion that property rights and markets are essentially prepolitical neglects the fact that property and exchange rest on a complicated network of laws, policies, and institutions. When the market is understood in this manner, the discussion of whether or not the state should intervene in the market is meaningless. As Stephen Cohen and John Zysman correctly remark: "The thing policy is least able to do is have *no* impact on a nation's competitive position. And that, of course, is what conventional economics sternly prescribes for it."[21] There are, quite simply, qualitatively different patterns of state-economy relations. Nevertheless, classic market liberal notions concerning the limits of public authority and the self-sufficiency of the market shape the discourse over industrial policy. Thus, some critics of contemporary industrial policy debates suggest that the best industrial policy is to reduce the impact of policy on investment and production decisions by simplifying taxation, reducing regulations, lowering deficit spending, and eliminate government loans. These factors, it is argued, will minimize market distortions thus facilitating corporate decision making.[22]

Of course, the ideological concerns go beyond the question of whether or not the state should intervene. One can also address the problem of fairness. It is commonly argued that the state cannot involve itself in industrial policy because it would entail the task of selecting winners and forcing other firms to be losers. By deciding to support one industry over another, one is violating norms of equity or fairness. While this argument proves to be a common objection to industrial policy proposals, it assumes that existing policies do not create biases. In actuality, policy impacts differently on different lines of business and on different size enterprises. Policy already selects winners and losers. However, the determination is, quite often, the unintended product of multiple and conflicting policies established over the course of the century through the lobbying of numerous economic groups often seeking relief from one crisis or another or simply hoping to claim special benefits. The key question is thus not whether policies favor one form of economic activity over another—this is largely unavoidable. Rather, the key question is whether policy should explicitly select winners and losers, in accordance with some larger vision of what kinds of industries would contribute to long-term growth. While some industrial policy advocates have attempted to sidestep this issue by focusing on key technologies, the effect is virtually the same given the fact that firms are situated differently with respect to their ability to exploit the decision to promote a given technology.

This raises another important problem, however. Policymakers in several nations have attempted to identify and promote particular industries. However, they have done so with mixed success, even in nations such as France which are famous for their administrative expertise. The key point is this: By selecting one industry or set of technologies over another, policymakers may be assuming greater knowledge than actually exists. As Don Lavoie notes: "Relations between the health of different sectors of a modern economy are so intricate and complex that it is the height of pretense to claim that any single agency could take them all into account in its decisions to reallocate credit to certain sectors. . . . In a free credit market entrepreneurs have to compete with one another to discover profitable projects in order to secure future command over such funds. To the extent that government agencies disperse favors in the form of cheap credits, the competitive discovery process is subverted and politically favored projects succeed at the expense of others that may have been more economically efficient." Lavoie concludes on a somber note: "Since the case for any particular use of the planning power lies beyond the capacity of human reason to establish, that power will instead be wielded in response to political clout rather than careful debate."[23] In sum, the movement toward industrial planning could simultaneously distort price signals and thus eliminate the best source of information on economic activity while providing policymakers with another means of responding to interest group pressures.

While the "knowledge problem" may not be as debilitating as Lavoie suggests, one must not lose sight of the tremendous administrative capacities necessary for industrial policymaking. The desirability of industrial policy may be great, particularly in an era of structural change when the old sources of high-wage employment are in a most precarious position. However, the practical problems of feasibility may be far too great. Existing institutional structures and modes of political action may not be capable of accommodating a broad industrial policy. A discussion of feasibility will be reserved for later. For now, it is critical that we turn to some of the core components of the various plans for industrial policy.

## COMPETING RESPONSES TO DECLINE IN THE UNITED STATES

Analysts and proponents of industrial policy have identified a number of factors that have contributed in one fashion or another to past competitiveness and could, by implication, be part of an industrial policy. Each industrial policy proposal has relied on a combination of several of these factors to develop a plan for industrial revitalization. In this section, we review the key factors and survey the debate. In particular, we address technological innovation, capital formation and investment, changes in corporate structure, labor training, and trade policy.

## Technological Innovation

Technological innovations are critical to economic dynamism and growth. The relationship between technology and production is an intimate one. As David F. Noble correctly notes, "Modern technology in America . . . was characterized from the outset by the overriding imperative of manufacturers: profitable utility. From the start, modern technology was nothing more nor less than the transformation of science into a means of capital accumulation, through the application of discoveries . . . to the process of commodity production."[24] Given the key role of technological innovation in economic growth and profitability, one should not be surprised that a popular response to the decline of the American economy has been a call for expanded public spending in research and development (R&D).

Total R&D spending in the United States is largely on par with that in Germany and Japan. Much of the R&D is supported through provisions in the tax code. For example, tax deductions for research and development placed in the Economic Recovery Tax Act of 1981 provided approximately $1.3 billion worth of support for corporate R&D in 1982 and 1983.[25] However, one can doubt that these tax expenditures have the desired results. As Robert S. McIntyre and Dean C. Tipps concluded after studying the R&D investment decisions of a large sample of firms: "Evidence is overwhelming that the billions of dollars the federal government spends each year on tax incentives to encourage investment have failed to achieve their purpose."[26] While R&D spending in the United States is largely equivalent to that in our major competitors, the picture changes when one looks at civilian R&D that is not defense related. Indeed, when R&D is subtracted, "spending has been flat at 1.8 percent of the GNP, for most of a decade, while German and Japanese spending is rising and now stands at 2.6 and 2.8 percent of GNP respectively."[27]

What is seldom appreciated is the extent to which the U.S. federal government funds R&D relative to other advanced industrial nations. As Gary Saxonhouse explained: "In the late 1970s the Japanese government funded no more than 1.9 percent of all research and development undertaken by private sector industry. This contrasts with West Germany funding 15.8 percent of private sector R&D, France funding 25.3 percent, the United Kingdom funding 30.9 percent and with the United States so actively involved in private sector R&D as to fund fully 35.3 percent of all research and development undertaken by the private sector of the American economy."[28]

Of course, these figures represent government contribution to R&D prior to the defense buildup of the 1980s. Between 1979 and 1988, federal R&D spending increased by 42 percent. Not only did the overall levels of government R&D expenditures increase, but the role of the Pentagon increased its share of national R&D from approximately one-quarter to one-third. Thus, during this same period, mil-

bility question looms large in the area of R&D spending, however, due to a number of complications. As noted earlier, the decision to engage in direct state investment in R&D raises important equity concerns. Such a policy would place the federal government in the position of choosing winning technologies and thus commercial winners and losers since particular corporations are situated due to past investments to make immediate profits from particular technologies.

There is, however, a more fundamental problem. Richard R. Nelson and Sidney G. Winter argue that the decision to vest responsibility in the state contradicts a basic fact: "In an economy that relies basically on profit-seeking private enterprise to provide goods and services, it is virtually inevitable that much R&D decision making will be decentralized to private business firms, with return to R&D internalized through secrecy, patent protection, or market domination."[36] While there are problems associated with capturing the returns (e.g., firms may copy innovations or engage in overlapping R&D spending), there are even greater problems associated with the direct government R&D policy. As Nelson and Winter explain, government may be forced "to explore alternatives that no private firms think are worthwhile funding themselves."[37]

Without expanding existing R&D funding levels (which are already high), policymakers can create R&D consortia to pool industry resources and allow for concerted efforts at addressing problems common to an industry. Congress made progress in this direction by passing the National Cooperative Research Act of 1984. The act extended an antitrust exemption for joint R&D projects. By the end of 1988, some four years after the passage of the act, more than 200 applications had been registered with the Justice Department. The best known initiative authorized under the act is Sematech, a research consortium of computer chip and equipment producers based in Austin, Texas. Sematech is a joint industry-government venture, run under the supervision of DARPA. As one might suppose, the justification for the creation of Sematech was defense related, stemming from the realization that many key defense systems relied on foreign-produced computer components. With this justification in place, Sematech was subsidized by the government with a $250 million annual budget. Sematech focuses on fabrication technology, production techniques, quality control, and test equipment in hopes of improving the productive capacities necessary for a new generation of integrated circuits.[38] The promotion of R&D consortia with partial public funding may provide one means of circumventing some of the equity concerns, particularly if the consortia focus on sectoral R&D and remain open to all industry actors.

## Capital Formation and Investment

The importance of technological innovations is clear: Corporations require the ongoing generation of technological innovations if they are to remain viable in a dynamic economy. However, innovations are nothing more than intellectual solutions to particular problems faced in the production process. They do not have an impact on economic activity until they are paired with capital investment and thus integrated into the production process. Capital investment is "the major vehicle of economic growth because it embodies technical progress."[39] Through capital investment, dated technology and an aging capital stock can be replaced with best practice technology. It is possible that an economy could be characterized by high levels of R&D and ongoing technical innovation and yet fail to have the innovations incorporated into the productive process. In such a case, the critical bridge between theory and practice—that is, capital investment—may be simply insufficient.

There are a few key questions that must be addressed when examining capital investment. First, one must address the availability of capital for investment. One of the great problems that emerged in the 1980s was a reduction in the pool of capital. As noted in Chapter 10, the needs of funding the growing deficit and national debt placed significant pressure on the pool of capital. The net national savings rate (i.e., national savings, less the government's demand on the available capital for funding the deficit) was 8.4 percent of GNP during the 1950s and 1960s, slipping to 7.8 percent of GNP during the 1970s. However, falling personal and business savings and the growing demands of funding the national debt undermined the net national saving rate, which fell to 3.8 percent of GNP by 1986, and 2.4 percent by 1988. The resulting growth in the cost of capital translated into a reduction in investments and a subsequent reduction in output, wages, and living standards as a consequence of the failure to incorporate new technological innovations into the production process. While part of the reduction in domestic capital could be offset by foreign investment, this carried negative long-term consequences for American firms.[40]

Part of the solution to the reduction in the pool of available capital rests with fiscal management and deficit reduction. According to Nordhaus, every $1 reduction in the deficit would result in an additional 90¢ in savings.[41] However, "while many people emphasize the importance of increasing business investment . . . high saving is likely to flow primarily into housing and foreign investment."[42] The problem, therefore, is not simply the pool of available capital, but the lack of any means of effectively directing capital into those uses which would result in future growth. John Zysman provides an important framework for understanding the nature and significance of this second portion of the investment equation.[43]

In *Governments, Markets, and Growth*, John Zysman argues that a nation's capacity to engage in effective industrial policy is strongly linked to its system of industrial finance or, more precisely, officials' capacity to direct the allocation of capital. As explained in Chapter 2, corporations may fund expansion through profits that are retained for that purpose. However, given the scale of investment necessary for many strategies of expansion, corporations rely on external sources of funding. It is in this connection that states may possess the capacity to direct growth by favoring certain forms of investment. Zysman shows that there are three different systems of industrial finance. Some nations, including France and Japan, have credit-based systems with administered prices. The costs of capital (i.e., interest rates) are set by public policymakers on sectoral levels. Differential interests rates may also be combined with more direct determination of which firm should receive funding at low rates. The key point is this: Since corporations rely primarily on credit to fund industrial expansion, the state plays a great role in determining which industries will be favored. In addition to credit-based systems with administered prices, one may find credit-based systems dominated by banks. The clearest example is West Germany. Bankers sit on the boards of the corporations that receive long-term loans. The banks possess voting stock and thus combine the access to capital with some voice in defining long-term growth strategies. Since banks are concerned with the long-term integrity of an industry, rather than the short-term profitability of a particular firm, they can favor investments that may provide benefits in future decades.

In contrast to the credit-based systems, the United States has a capital market-based system of industrial finance. Corporations do rely on bank loans for short-term expenses. However, capital markets provide the primary source of investment funds. They issue stocks and bonds to raise capital for expansion. In this system, industrial decision making does not rest with state policymakers but with individual, privately owned firms responding to immediate market stimuli. Policymakers cannot use access to commercial finance as a means of directing industrial development.

There are additional implications for industrial performance. Those who extend credit to a firm have the opportunity to exercise a voice or exit in response to declining rates of return. The decision to affect long-term investment decisions or exit from the relationship will depend, in part, on the costs associated with the two options. Because the United States has well-developed secondary stock and bond markets, investors—and particularly large institutional investors such as mutual funds that manage a large basket of securities—can divest themselves of poorly performing securities in at a minimal cost. Indeed, such behavior has become routine: "Although some fund managers invest for the long term, most turn over their stock holdings rapidly in an effort to maximize the current value of their investment portfolio, since this is the main criterion against which their own performance is judged."[44] This decision, if adopted on a broad scale, would result in the rapid decline in the value of a firm's securities. This creates a strong bias toward short-term profitability and militates against the long-term investments that might bring growth at the cost of short-term losses.

Of course, while the United States has a capital market-based system, there are exceptions. The prevailing system of financing differs by sector and historically. In some sectors of the economy such as electric utilities and defense, the government has played a relatively greater role in shaping production decisions, prices, and access to capital. Moreover, in the early stages of some technologies (e.g., computers) the state has constituted an important source of capital and an automatic market for prototypes. However, these exceptions do not undermine Zysman's general prediction: Systems which tend toward a higher level of state control (i.e., credit-based systems) will have a greater capacity to pursue long-term goals with respect to industrial planning than will systems which rely heavily on capital markets in which investment decisions are made and executed at the level of the firm.

The implications of Zysman's analysis are clear and explain, in part, why so many industrial policy advocates have called for the creation of a development bank of some sort capable of directing capital into productive investments. As noted above, many of the bills circulating in Congress in the early 1970s called for a new version of the Reconstruction Finance Corporation to fund industrial expansion. Others, noting the RFC's role in bailing out failing enterprises and its mixed performance record, focused instead on some form of development bank Thus, Magaziner and Reich called for the creation of a "government-subsidized lending institution" to provide partial funding for the purchase of capital goods and the implementation of high-risk manufacturing processes.[45] Similarly, Lester Thurow concluded that the United States should create a public investment bank capitalized at $5 billion and chartered under a ten-year sunset provision.[46] As Thurow correctly noted, given the heavy involvement of the federal government in capital markets (with over $1 trillion in outstanding loans and loan guarantees and an additional $100 billion a year in lending), "such a bank would neither constitute a noticeable extension of current government banking activities nor threaten the credit markets with its size."[47]

While any attempts to create a new RFC or development bank would confront a host of political problems, one must not lose sight of what are perhaps the two most important difficulties: insulation and diffusion. For a development bank to function effectively, it must be insulated from the demands of members of Congress and a plethora of organized interests who might see in the loans another means of bringing home the bacon—the genesis of much of the $1 trillion plus in federal loans and loan guarantes. Moreover, given the uncertainty over which technological innovations will successfully make the transition to meeting a significant demand, a bank would have to be prepared to make a tremendous diffusion of loans, backing innumerable horses in an uncertain race. This, in turn, would require a large amount of capital to prevent each individual loan from being trivial in impact. In an era in which the pool of capital is shrinking as a percentage of GNP, the availability of such a sum of capital would appear to be highly doubtful absent concerted attempts to reduce the deficit or a period of sustained growth which would undermine the arguments in support for such a bank.

## The Organization and Management of the Firm

As explained in Chapters 2 and 3, some of the key innovations that promoted growth in the late nineteenth and early twentieth centuries were organizational. The modern corporation, with its hierarchical governance and multiple layers of administration, was well suited to managing the complexities associated with producing diverse products and serving geographically dispersed markets. Moreover, it allowed for a scale of production that allowed for the realization of significant economies of scale. These factors translated into cost reductions that allowed for a more expansive market and competitive advantages when U.S. firms came into direct competition with foreign-based producers. The key question posed by many contemporary analysts is whether the organizational innovations that facilitated economic growth have become an impediment.

American firms are renown for their short-term calculations. As explained above, this is partially a product of the existing system of industrial finance. Because U.S. firms rely heavily on capital markets and large institutional

tle III programs for dislocated workers. It is administered by the states through federal-state matching funds. It is important to note that fewer than half of the Title III participants are enrolled in classroom or on-the-job training. For the remainder, JTPA is largely involved with facilitating job searches. Although the various evaluations of CETA and JTPA are spotty, there is a fair amount of agreement on two points. First, the programs failed to service a significant part of the eligible population due largely to low levels of funding. Moreover, the impact of training was minimal, with low levels of skill retention and a minimal impact on post-training wage levels. As Burt Barnow notes: "Training programs are clearly not going to end poverty in the United States—the average wage at placement of $4.53 per hour does not provide sufficient income from year-round full-time employment for a family of four to exceed the poverty level. Ironically . . . such a person would still be eligible for the program under the definition of economically disadvantaged."[65]

The lack of success of employment policy is difficult to explain. On an ideological level, one might expect training programs to be broadly acceptable. As Margaret Weir admits, the "pattern of policy is puzzling." She continues: "For a nation that claims the work ethic as a central feature of its political identity, the United States has been remarkably lax in introducing and sustaining policies that actively promote employment."[66] As Gary Mucciaroni argues, one can attribute the failure of employment policy to multiple sources. In part, one must acknowledge the lack of a clear mission or mandate.[67] Mucciaroni explains: "As a result of the adoption of a less-than-full employment, social-welfare-oriented mission, the policy played a residual role in efforts to combat unemployment. A commitment to full employment would have given employment and training programs the legally mandated, overarching purpose these programs have always lacked."[68] As a result of the blurred mission and the poverty orientation, training programs like CETA failed to attract the support of strong interest coalitions, thus making them vulnerable to budget cuts.

Beyond the obvious proposal to enhance the quality of primary and secondary education, many have suggested that the United States adopt a policy to address the postsecondary training of the noncollege bound through an enhanced system of vocational education or mandatory corporate-based training. Lester Thurow, for example, has suggested that training be promoted in one of two ways. Following the example of France, corporations could be taxed 1 percent of sales from which firms could deduct their internal training costs. Since they would be paying for training in any event, it would be in their best interest to implement on-job programs. In the absence of such a system, Thurow suggests that the Social Security system be expanded to create a training account for each citizen. The funds could be drawn on for university, vocational, or on-site training and then repaid through payroll deductions.[69] Michael Porter arrives at similar conclusions, arguing that the United States must upgrade its vocational training.[70] "What is required for competitive advantage is specialized skills tailored to particular industries." To this end, Porter suggests that firms direct more resources toward continually upgrading their labor forces while forging closer relationships with educational institutions to promote the specialized education most relevant to their productive processes.

Of course, labor training is not, when taken by itself, sufficient to retain or create high-wage manufacturing positions. As Reich correctly notes: "Since millions of other production workers around the world are seeking to learn these same advanced production techniques, America's production workers would still face formidable competition from foreigners willing to labor for a fraction of even the minimum American wage. Extra training may retard the loss of these production jobs or the decline in their real wages, but it is far from a solution to the problems faced by unskilled and semiskilled American workers competing worldwide."[71] The key point to be noted here is that the problem of industrial decline in the United States has not been primarily a result of a poorly trained labor pool. As a result, human capital investments can be, at the very most, one component in a larger package. Most industrial policy proponents clearly recognize this fact.

## Trade Policy

Trade policy provides a key feature of most industrial policy proposals. The reasoning for this is rather clear. As noted above, the growing international economic pluralism has forced the United States to compete with foreign-based firms. During the 1970s, more jobs were created by exports than were lost to imports. Indeed, by 1976, exports created 6.6 million jobs, compared with the 5.6 million lost to imports. However, this situation was reversed in the 1980s due, in part, to the debt-induced appreciation of the dollar.[72] However, the reversal was also a product of the strategies adopted by more aggressive competitors. Many foreign nations had relatively well-orchestrated mercantilist trade policies designed to provide selective benefits for exports and impede the importation of goods produced in other nations. Thus, the U.S. firms have increasingly lost market share in domestic markets to foreign-based producers while experiencing some difficulties in gaining entrance to foreign markets due to the existence of tariff and nontariff barriers.

Critics of Japan and the European Union cite trade as one of the key issues that shape the decline in U.S. competitiveness. The claim is that our competitors routinely contradict the principles of free trade. A return to a liberal trade regime—such as that envisioned by the framers of the General Agreement of Tariffs and Trade—would result in a free flow of goods and a realization of comparative advantage. While the adherence to the idea of free trade has been a central dogma in the United States, it has had little impact on policy. Indeed, the calls for free trade have been combined with a combination of protectionist measures and export promotions. As previous chapters suggest, this is nothing new. Rather, the reliance on tariffs to protect domestic industries and cement partisan coalitions is as old as the Republic.

One should not be surprised that the reliance on protectionist measures in the United States increased during the 1970s and 1980s as U.S.-based firms came under ever-greater challenges. To reduce the impact of foreign imports into domestic markets, the United States has negotiated voluntary export restraints (VERs) with its major trade partners. VERs are quotas that are voluntary only in the narrowest of senses: Mandatory quotas would undoubtedly come into play should negotiations break down. Thus, protectionist measures were created or strengthened

"defensive strategic-trade policy" that combines investment in training, domestic infrastructure, and R&D with a strategic posture in trade in which the United States adopts a position of strict reciprocity. Thurow explains:

> The United States should announce that it will duplicate any policies put in place in the rest of the world. Foreign industrial policies in wealthy countries will be matched dollar for dollar. Any subsidy going to Airbus Industries in Europe will be matched by an equivalent subsidy to the American airframe-manufacturing industry. Any delay in permitting an American telecommunications device to be used abroad, such as the delays Motorola experienced in Japan with its cellular telephones, will be matched with delays for advanced Japanese equipment in the United States. Americans are no longer in a position to force the rest of the world to play the economic game by its rules, but Americans can play the game by their rules.[82]

In a world in which the United States has numerous trade partners each with its own industrial policy, export subsidies, and network of import restrictions, the practical problems with such an approach are obvious. Rather than acting strategically, the United States would essentially become committed to subsidizing every industry that received support elsewhere and restricting imports in a far more extensive manner than we do at present. One of the results of such a policy might be to force our competitors to abandon policies that they have implemented in reference to their own economic development. The results might well be the opposite. Strict reciprocity is a reactive policy that is high in retribution and lacking in strategic value. It may, in the end, prove far more destabilizing than the current mixture of policies.

A more coherent approach may be to promote continued liberalization through GATT while allowing for managed trade for some products. Liberal trade assumes an elimination of government intervention such as tariffs and nontariff barriers. However, for many products that are the objects of industrial policies, managed trade may be far more appropriate. Under managed trade, it is assumed that government policies are used to create comparative advantage in a given product. In hopes of managing the process and avoiding trade wars and a glut of goods in international markets, nations negotiate quantitative targets for trade flows. VERs constitute an ad hoc quantitative target. A managed trade regime would create distinct rules for governing international competition in certain products. Nations could establish minimum targets for the portion of their markets that would be open to imports under the understanding that imports and exports would be in balance over the long run.[83]

Robert Kuttner, a strong advocate of a managed trade regime, notes that such an approach could yield great benefits for the United States. He writes:

> By recognizing that managed trade is sometimes the best available option, the United States would be able to better differentiate short-term tactical maneuvers from long-term strategic economic goals. Because of its

devotion to the GATT, the United States typically regards all departures from liberal trade as short-term tactical expedients, to be given up unilaterally as soon as possible. But if managed trade in key industries is legitimate, we become much freer to press out trading partners—not simply to practice laissez-faire in their own economies (our traditional diplomatic goal) but to bring a balance of obligations and benefits to the trading system. We are also freed to define industrial goals for our own domestic economy and strategies for carrying them out.[84]

Through a managed trade regime, the stability of a multilateral regime would replace the dense network of bilateral agreements while freeing the United States to pursue different strategies for different sectors of the economy. At present, "the government continues to treat trade in the same laissez-faire manner that it would like to treat the domestic economy" while "none of the countries in the rest of the world wish to—or feel they can afford to—leave trade to the unfettered marketplace"[85] While a managed trade regime would allow the United States to exercise far greater discretion in designing strategies, U.S. policymakers have expressed opposition to managed trade in recent GATT negotiations, arguing instead for further liberalization.[86]

## THE FEASIBILITY OF INDUSTRIAL POLICY

The various components of an industrial policy may be desirable or not, depending on one's interpretation of the economic performance of recent decades and one's sensitivity to norms of market governance and a limited state presence. Undoubtedly, many of the policies addressing R&D, capital investment, labor training, and trade could have a positive impact on U.S. industry if effectively implemented. This final clause, however, is crucial. Desirability and feasibility are two distinct factors. The existing muddle of public policies is the product of a high decentralized governmental system. High levels of horizontal fragmentation frustrate attempts to coordinate public policies and force a great deal of compromise in policy design. Moreover, the unfettered access to sites of policymaking creates a situation of hyperpluralism. In this context, the possibility that policymakers could formulate a coherent industrial policy and implement it effectively is, at best, remote. As Lester Thurow correctly notes: "To be successful, industrial policies require that government participants have some ability to exercise discretion and judgment. These participants have to have some freedom from the geographical constraints that so often are built into American legislation."[87] As the history of policymaking in this century suggests, this freedom is quite rare outside of those limited circumstances of national emergency.

Due to the ongoing power of localism and problems of horizontal fragmentation, the national government has found it particularly difficult to promote a coherent industrial policy outside the defense-related industrial policy described above. Questions of desirability aside, the fragmented institutional structure combined with high levels of interest group access have created ongoing concerns about the practicality of industrial policy. In this policy vacuum, state and local govern-

17. See Don Lavoie, *National Economic Planning: What is Left?* (Washington, D.C.: CATO Institute, 1985), pp. 212–31.

18. John Zysman, *Governments, Markets, and Growth: Financial Systems and the Politics of Industrial Change* (Ithaca, N.Y.: Cornell University Press, 1983), pp. 266–67.

19. Chalmers Johnson, "The Institutional Foundations of Japanese Industrial Policy." In *The Politics of Industrial Policy,* ed. Claude E. Barfield and William A. Schambra (Washington, D.C.: American Enterprise Institute, 1986); George C. Lodge, *Perestroika for America: Restructuring U.S. Business Government Relations for Competitiveness in the World Economy* (Boston: Harvard Business School Press, 1990), pp. 50–53.

20. Yoram Barzel, *Economic Analysis of Property Rights* (Cambridge: Cambridge University Press, 1989), p. 2.

21. Stephen S. Cohen and John Zysman, "Can America Compete?" *Challenge* 29, 3 (1986), p. 63.

22. See Murray L. Weidenbaum, "Industrial Policy Is Not the Answer." *Challenge,* 26, 3 (1983): 22–25.

23. Lavoie, *National Economic Planning,* pp. 180, 181.

24. David F. Noble, *America by Design: Science, Technology, and the Rise of Corporate Capitalism* (Oxford: Oxford University Press, 1977), p. 4.

25. John F. Witte, *The Politics and Development of the Federal Income Tax* (Madison: University of Wisconsin Press, 1985), p. 232.

26. Robert S. McIntyre and Dean C. Tipps, "Exploding the Investment-Incentive Myth." *Challenge* 29, 3 (1985): 47–52.

27. Lester C. Thurow, *Head to Head: The Coming Economic Battle among Japan, Europe, and America* (New York: William Morrow, 1992), p. 157.

28. Quoted in Walter Adams and James W. Brock, *The Bigness Complex: Industry, Labor, and Government in the American Economy* (New York: Pantheon Books, 1986), p. 354.

29. Glenn R. Pascall and Robert D. Lamson, *Beyond Guns and Butter* (Washington, D.C.: Brassey's, 1991), p. 65; Michael E. Porter, *The Competitive Advantage of Nations* (New York: Free Press, 1990), p. 726. See Lloyd J. Dumas, "National Security and Economic Delusion." *Challenge* 30, 2 (1987): 28–33.

30. Laura D'Andrea Tyson, *Who's Bashing Whom?: Trade Conflict in High-Technology Industries* (Washington, D.C.: Institute for International Economics, 1992), p. 289.

31. Graham, *Losing Time,* pp. 185–86, 227–32.

32. Ibid., pp. 185–86, 227–32; see Bruce Edelson and Robert L. Stern, *The Operations of DARPA and Its Utility as a Model for a Civilian ARPA* (Baltimore, Md.: Johns Hopkins Foreign Policy Institute, 1989).

33. See Angus Maddison, *Phases of Capitalist Development* (Oxford: Oxford University Press, 1982), pp. 19–21.

34. William J. Abernathy, Kim B. Clark, and Alan M. Kantrow, *Industrial Renaissance: Producing a Competitive Future for America* (New York: Basic Books, 1983), p. 107.

35. Richard Florida and Martin Kenney, *The Breakthrough Illusion: Corporate America's Failure to Move from Innovation to Mass Production* (New York: Basic Books, 1990), p. 27.

36. Richard R. Nelson and Sidney G. Winter, *An Evolutionary Theory of Economic Change* (Cambridge, Mass.: Harvard University Press, 1982), p. 387.

37. Ibid., p. 393.

38. Michael L. Dertouzos, Richard L. Lester, Robert M. Solow, and MIT Commission on Industrial Productivity, *Made in America: Regaining the Productive Edge* (Cambridge, Mass.: The MIT Press, 1989), pp. 106, 261, 309.

39. Maddison, *Phases of Capitalist Development,* p. 22.

40. William D. Nordhaus, "What's Wrong with a Declining National Savings Rate?" *Challenge* 32, 4 (1989): 22–26; Paul A. Volcker, "Facing up to the Twin Deficits." *Challenge* 29, 2 (March-April 1984): 4–9.

41. Nordhaus, "What's Wrong with a Declining National Savings Rate?" p. 24.

42. Ibid.

43. See Zysman, *Governments, Markets, and Growth.*

44. Dertouzos, Lester, and Solow, *Made in America,* p. 62.

45. Ira C. Magaziner and Robert B. Reich, *Minding America's Business: The Decline and Rise of the American Economy* (New York: Harcourt Brace Javanovich, 1982), p. 353.

46. Lester C. Thurow, *The Zero-Sum Solution: Building a World-Class American Economy* (New York: Simon & Schuster, 1985), p. 280.

47. Ibid.

48. Porter, *The Competitive Advantage of Nations*, p. 529.

49. Ibid.

50. Robert B. Reich, *The Next American Frontier* (New York: Times Books, 1983), p. 141.

51. Michael J. Piore and Charles F. Sabel, *The Second Industrial Divide: Possibilities for Prosperity* (New York: Basic Books, 1984).

52. Mark H. Lazerson, "Organizational Growth of Small Firms: An Outcome of Markets and Hierarchies?" *American Sociological Review* 53 (1988): 330–42; Craig Littler, "Taylorism, Fordism and Job Design." In *Job Redesign: Critical Perspectives on the Labor Process*, ed. David Knights, Hugh Willmott, and David Collinson (Aldershot, England: Gower, 1985); and Mark Granovetter, "Small Is Bountiful: Labor Markets and Establishment Size." *American Sociological Review* 49 (1984): 303–34.

53. Piore and Sabel, *The Second Industrial Divide*, p. 282.

54. Roy B. Helfgott, "America's Third Industrial Revolution." *Challenge* 29, 5 (1986): 41–46.

55. Ibid., p. 43.

56. See Douglas Hibbs, *The American Political Economy: Macroeconomics and Electoral Politics* (Cambridge, Mass.: Harvard University Press, 1987).

57. See Robert B. Reich, *The Work of Nations: Preparing Ourselves for 21st Century Capitalism* (New York: Alfred A. Knopf, 1991).

58. Thurow, *Head to Head*, p. 51.

59. Cohen and Zysman, "Can America Compete?" p. 63.

60. Dertouzos, Lester, and Solow, *Made in America*, p. 80.

61. Ibid.

62. Ibid., p. 91.

63. See Charles F. Stone and Isabell V. Sawhill, "Trade's Impact on U.S. Jobs." *Challenge* 30, 4 (1987): 12–18.

64. Burt S. Barnow, "Government Training as a Means of Reducing Unemployment." In *Rethinking Employment Policy*, ed. D. Lee Bawden and Felicity Skidmore (Washington, D.C.: Urban Institute Press, 1989); Margaret Weir, *Politics and Jobs: The Boundaries of Employment Policy in the United States* (Princeton, N.J.: Princeton University Press, 1992), pp. 126–28.

65. Barnow, "Government Training as a Means of Reducing Unemployment," p. 127.

66. Weir, *Politics and Jobs*, p. 4.

67. Gary Mucciaroni, *The Political Failure of Employment Policy, 1945–1982* (Pittsburgh: University of Pittsburgh Press, 1990), p. 258.

68. Ibid.

69. Thurow, *Head to Head*, p. 279.

70. Porter, *The Competitive Advantage of Nations*, p. 725.

71. Reich, *The Work of Nations*, p. 248.

72. See Stone and Sawhill, "Trade's Impact on U.S. Jobs."

73. Graham, *Losing Time*, pp. 177, 78.

74. Magaziner and Reich, *Minding America's Business*, pp. 159–163, 208.

75. See Robert Kuttner, *The End of Laissez-Faire: National Purpose and the Global Economy After the Cold War* (New York: Alfred A. Knopf, 1991), pp. 144–49; Paul R. Lawrence and Davis Dyer, *Renewing American Industry* (New York: Free Press, 1983), pp. 72–83; Christoph Scherrer, "Governance of the Steel Industry: What Caused the Disintegration of the Oligopoly?" In *Governance of the American Economy*, ed. John L. Campbell, J. Rogers Hollingsworth, and Leon N. Lindberg (Cambridge: Cambridge University Press, 1991); and Louis Schorsch, "The Abdication of Big Steel." *Challenge* 27, 3 (1984): 34–40.

76. Tyson, *Who's Bashing Whom?* p. 272.

77. See Robert Z. Lawrence, "Innovation and Trade: Meeting the Foreign Challenge." In *Setting National Priorities: Policy For the Nineties*, ed. Henry J. Aaron (Washington, D.C.: Brookings Institution., 1990), pp. 181–82.

78. C. Fred Bergsten, *America in the World Economy: A Strategy for the 1990s* (Washington, D.C.: Institute for International Economics, 1988), pp. 137, 136.

79. Dertouzos, Lester, and Solow, *Made in America*, p. 142.

80. Porter, *The Competitive Advantage of Nations*, p. 669.

81. Thurow, *Head to Head*, p. 293.

82. Ibid., p. 296.

83. See Tyson, *Who's Bashing Whom?* pp. 133–36.

84. Kuttner, *End of Laissez-Faire*, p. 156.

85. Bennett Harrison and Barry Bluestone, *The Great U-Turn: Corporate Restructuring and the Polarizing of America* (New York: Basic Books, 1988), p. 190.

86. Kuttner, *The End of Laissez-Faire*, pp. 152–57.

87. Thurow, *The Zero-Sum Solution*, p. 21.

88. Alice M. Rivlin, *Reviving the American Dream: The Economy, the States and the Federal Government* (Washington, D.C.: Brookings Institution, 1992), p. 211.

89. Peter K. Eisinger, *The Rise of the Entrepreneurial State: State and Local Economic Development Policy in the United States* (Madison: University of Wisconsin Press, 1988).

90. Ibid., pp. 341–42.

91. Ibid., p. 342.

# 12

# LOOKING FORWARD, LOOKING BACK

With the presidential election of 1992, 12 years of Republican rule came to a close and Bill Clinton was elected president of the United States. Economic conditions in 1992 go far in explaining the change in leadership. Although inflation was low at 3.1 percent, the nation was experiencing a 7.4 percent unemployment rate, a falling per capita income, a record budget deficit of $340.3 billion, a federal debt that was 68.2 percent of Gross Domestic Product, and persistent trade deficits that had fluctuated between $65 billion and $109 billion over the course of the previous four years.[1] Moreover, one of the fundamental promises of the Reagan and Bush administrations—to reduce the role of the state in society—had been forgotten. Despite the fact that Ronald Reagan and George Bush had indicted the Carter administration's supposed love of large government, after 12 years of Republican presidents the federal government claimed 23.5 percent of GDP, compared with an average of 21.4 percent GDP during the Carter presidency. And this was after a prolonged period of growth. Thus, in 1980, the federal government spent $613 billion, compared with $1.5 trillion in 1992.[2]

Bill Clinton's campaign promises were numerous and changed as the campaign season progressed. However, a number of important political economic goals were consistently articulated. Clinton stressed the need for economic growth and job creation—a salient overture given the slow recovery from the 1990 to 1991 recession. This was to be accomplished through an ambitious spending program on public works, additional investment tax credits, and a middle-class tax cut. At the same time, he called for serious deficit reduction to free up domestic capital for productive investment. Given the central role of entitlements in driving budgetary growth, Clinton promised welfare reform, a system of national health care, and expansive training programs combined with some national service requirements. On the side of trade, Clinton pledged to force a future reduction of tariffs and various structural impediments that limit the access of U.S.-produced goods to foreign markets. To this end, he proclaimed his support for a revised version of the North American Free Trade Agreement (NAFTA), the completion of additional improvements in GATT, and the active use of trade policy to force nations to allow U.S. exports into their markets on the same terms as their goods enter the U.S. market.[3]

This policy agenda was ambitious, particularly when compared with those of the Reagan and Bush presidencies which were directed, in large, to eliminating the excesses of the past and forcing a return to the private sector and a greater reliance on market mechanisms. Clinton's choice of economic advisers reflected his broad policy agenda. The free marketers of the Reagan-Bush years were replaced with industrial policy and strategic trade advocates, including Council of Economic Advisers chair Laura D'Andrea Tyson, Labor Secretary Robert B. Reich, and Domestic Policy Council Senior Adviser Ira Magaziner. Robert Rubin of Goldman Sachs & Co. was named to head a new National Economic Council, a body analogous to the National Security Council, albeit for coordinating the economic policies of the Office of Management and Budget, the Treasury, the Council of Economic Advisers, and other executive agencies with economic policymaking powers.[4] Whether supportive advisers and a democratically controlled Congress will be sufficient to assure the successful implementation of the president's program remains to be seen. What became immediately clear, however, was the conflict between the competing policy promises made by candidate Clinton. An expansionary fiscal policy focusing on infrastructural investments fell victim to the deficit which also turned vague promises of middle-class tax reductions into across-the-board tax increases. While NAFTA narrowly passed through both houses of Congress, debates over the proposed national health insurance—clearly the largest welfare state policy since the New Deal—promise to continue for some time to come. As in the past, broad programs and committed advisers do not success make.

## LOOKING BACKWARD ONCE AGAIN

In *Looking Backward, 2000-1887*, a utopian novel written a century ago, Edward Bellamy presented a provocative vision of a future society. Bellamy's protagonist, Julian West, had fallen into a trance only to awaken a century later. In his Boston of 2000, want and scarcity had been eliminated along with class divisions, economic competition, and administrative irrationality. Social harmony, myriad technological innovations, and a new communal order had replaced the conflicts and urban squalor of the late nineteenth century. Bellamy extrapolated from the growing power of science, the changes in economic organization, and the new doctrines of administration to arrive at one possible future.[5] The chief failure of Bellamy was to look forward without taking more than a momentary glance back. He appreciated the potential implications and promise of the new without appreciating the power of the past.

Marx correctly noted in *The Eighteenth Brumaire of Louis Bonaparte*, that "men make their own history, but they do not make it just as they please; they do not make it under circumstances chosen by themselves, but under circumstances directly encountered, given and transmitted from the past. The tradition of all the dead generations weights like a nightmare on the brain of the living."[6] The Clinton administration must rule under the same circumstances that facilitated a Republican defeat in the 1992 elections. The "circumstances directly encountered, given and transmitted" include the problems detailed in the past several chapters. At the same time, they include the host of institutional, political, and intellectual factors inherited from the past

As noted in Chapter 1, the American political system is characterized by extreme degrees of horizontal and vertical fragmentation that impede policy integration. Multiple agencies, congressional committees, subcommittees, and elites define policies addressing common problems and yet they do so without coordinating their actions. In the end, the economy is forced to evolve within a complex network of public policies and institutions that commonly aim at irreconcilable and competing ends. High levels of fragmentation, in the absence of strong programmatic political parties, allow for high levels of interest group access. The resulting hyperpluralism allows any affecting interest to place a claim on policymakers and the Treasury, further frustrating the creation of coherent policy and creating high political costs for elected officials wishing to change the trajectory of existing policies in hopes of fundamentally reorienting prevailing patterns of state-economy relations. Some analysts express their fear of class domination or elite management of society. A more realistic fear is that the very coherence required for any sense of management is an impossibility given the existing institutional framework.

To make things more frustrating, one must make policy within an ideological context that places sharp limits on public debate. Markets play such a central role in the prevailing understanding of economics and political organization in the United States that it is often difficult for policymakers to conceptualize problems without reference to the market. Thus, the *Economic Report of the President* proclaimed that "All nations which have broad-based representative governments and civil liberties have most of their economic activity organized by the market." The report went on to explain: "All nations in which the government has dominant control of the economy are run by a narrow oligarchy and in most economic conditions are relatively poor. In the absence of limits on the economic role of the government, the erosion of economic freedom destroys both political freedom and economic performance."[7] Markets, it would seem, are necessary and sufficient for democracy, broad civil liberties, and economic wealth whereas planning—commonly defined as any politically unpopular departure from the market—is a prescription for failure.

As the past chapters have detailed, markets are not natural and prepolitical institutions. Rather, markets are the products of public decisions concerning the assignment, limits, and transfer of property rights. They are political artifacts. As economic and political circumstances change and new policies are enacted, the market is reconstructed on new foundations, redefined to reflect new values and popular concerns. Nevertheless, the market stands as an important symbol in the American political-economy debates. As Robert Reich correctly notes: "Many of the most important choices have nothing to do with the grand mythic division between free markets and control. When almost every discussion about the unwanted or the desirable side effects of corporate activity becomes shoehorned into a debate

sizes price stability over competing policy goals such as full employment and growth. Moreover, its capacity to promote growth and full employment via monetary policy appears quite limited compared with its capacity to dampen inflationary pressures. As shown in Chapter 10, the Federal Reserve was willing and able to inflict incredible human costs during the 1981 to 1982 recession in hopes of taming inflation, even if inflation imposed relatively few costs on those who were sacrificed in the war for price stability. The loss of jobs and family income and the escalation of the deficit, debt, and exchange rates were seen as acceptable costs in the war against inflation. Whether such decisions can be vested in elites who are highly insulated from democratic restraints and participatory norms is a question with implications that are more than trivial. What is beyond question is that the Federal Reserve is strongly inflation-adverse and one can expect policy to trade-off employment for price stability as long as the Fed is playing the central role in economic management. Once macroeconomic policy is freed from the tasks of debt and deficit management, policymakers will have greater discretion to pursue economic goals including full employment. However, the experiences of recent years suggest that an increase in income, when taken by itself, may not be sufficient to increase employment levels. Dollars may simply flow abroad to foreign competitors. It thus becomes necessary to combine macroeconomic policy with growth-oriented microeconomic policies.

## The Promotion of Manufacturing

There is no question that the United States has suffered a reduction in manufacturing jobs in the past several decades—particularly since the early 1980s. There is a great debate over the question of causality. Did the loss of jobs represent a process of deindustrialization or was it, instead, a result of productivity gains that allowed corporations to produce at constant levels with a smaller labor component? Undoubtedly, the correct answer cannot be discovered on an economywide basis; it is industry specific. Whether deindustrialization or productivity gains are cited as the source of a loss of manufacturing jobs is in some ways of lesser importance for, in either event, the result is a growing portion of the population lacking access to the kinds of high-wage jobs that were routinely available in the postwar period and provided a basis for a large middle class with expectations of growing incomes. Compensating for this loss must be a key goal for policymakers. Falling incomes can have dramatic implications for the political system, particularly in a nation in which upward mobility has been understood as something of a birthright.

Since the early 1980s, the promotion of business expansion has focused heavily on the supply side through efforts to limit the costs of regulatory compliance and provide a host of tax reductions designed to create greater incentives to invest. These efforts have proven insufficient and have carried a number of negative externalities. Nevertheless, the need for additional investment credits has become the mainstay of Democrats and Republicans, as exhibited in the 1992 presidential campaigns where virtually all major candidates strongly supported some form of support for investment.

Experience with industrial policies implemented in other nations can offer important information as to the kinds of policies that can play an important role in promoting growth. As shown in Chapter 11, much of what we mean when we address industrial policy is, in fact, social policy. Primary, secondary, and vocational education are all important factors in economic growth and productivity. We cannot expect a nation with poor educational resources to quickly adapt to new production techniques and technologies that require a basic competence in mathematics and computer science. In a world where capital is highly mobile and production facilities can be moved from one location to another in response to the quality of the labor pool or infrastructure, strong social policies can play an important role in attracting new industries. In the end, it makes little difference whether American workers are employed by firms based in New York, Tokyo, or Bonn as long as facilities are located in the United States. Since the United States has effectively lost its comparative advantage in many mass production industries in which low wages are of the greatest importance, much is to be gained through social policies designed to invest in human capital and thus develop (or attract) high-wage high-growth industries with true export potential.[12]

Undoubtedly, additional policies designed to fund research in a civilian version of DARPA, to facilitate the creation of additional research and development consortia, and to direct capital to potential growth industries would facilitate growth. The specter of the market will undoubtedly be called forth to cast any attempts to guide growth as movements toward planning that are, by definition, lacking in legitimacy. Policymakers would be wise to counter such claims with a frank accounting of the other periods in the nation's history when selective promotion and public investment were deemed in the national interest. From the provision of capital and land for transportation in the nineteenth century (see Chapter 3) to the high levels of defense-related R&D during World War II and the postwar period, the nation's history is replete with examples of successful strategies of investment. While there are notable examples of failed investments in the United States and abroad, these do not outweigh the examples of success. However, if selective microeconomic policies designed to promote growth are to have the intended impact, they must be coupled with efforts to address the status of the United States in the world economy and to rethink the logic of the current international regimes.

## Status of the United States in the World Economy

As shown in Chapter 8, the United States exerted a leadership role in the immediate postwar period in helping to design new international regimes and accepting unilaterally the costs of managing those regimes. To be certain, GATT and Bretton Woods were in the distinct interest of the United States. A liberal trade regime facilitated the growth of the strongest economy; the new monetary system established the U.S. dollar as a de facto international currency. With the growth of other industrialized economies and the emergence of greater international economic pluralism, the existing trade and monetary regimes became difficult to maintain. The disintegration of the monetary regime occurred gradually over the 1960s, culminating in the unilateral actions of the Nixon administration to close the gold window as part of the New Economic Policy.

The deterioration of GATT has been more gradual. Although GATT was premised on the assumption that a global movement toward free trade and an elimination on tariff and nontariff barriers was in the interest of all nations, many of the United States's key competitors have adopted industrial policies with subsidies for exports, export cartels, and selective tariff and nontariff barriers. Ricardian theory suggests that free trade will benefit all parties by allowing each to exploit its comparative advantage. However, industrial policies with strong strategic trade components are enacted precisely in the hope of creating (rather than discovering) comparative advantage in internationally competitive, growth-oriented high-wage industries.

Serious discussion of trade policy in the United States has too often been derailed by the sterile debates over the virtues of "free trade" versus "protectionism," as if this simple dichotomy captures the sophisticated strategies and experiences of other advanced industrial nations. As with the market-planning dichotomy that has framed the industrial policy debates, the free trade–protectionism comparison undermines the possibility of a systematic approach to trade—one that is oriented toward broad national objectives. Such simplifications cannot account for the fact that "an immense amount of trade expansion and efficient wealth-creation has taken place in nations that, by Ricardian lights, are appallingly mercantilist."[13] In the absence of a systematic approach to trade and a realistic assessment of the comparative experiments with various trade strategies, U.S. policymakers will continue to proclaim the principles of laissez faire and to denounce the mercantilist strategies of their competitors. At the same time, due to the high levels of institutional fragmentation and interest group access, declining industries will continue to receive selective trade benefits. As Chapter 11 explained, our experience with voluntary export restraints negotiated on a case-by-case basis in response to industry lobbying has not been a positive one. In a fragmented institutional system with unlimited group access, all interests affected by changing patterns of trade have the opportunity to seek selective benefits. At the same time, market norms impede attempts to pair such benefits with intrusion into the realm of corporate decision making.

Unless trade policy is integrated into a broader slate of policies oriented toward growth and future competitiveness, the de facto policy will continue to be one of selective protectionism combined with vociferous objections to departures from norms of laissez faire on the part of our major trade partners. The political, institutional, and ideological obstacles to meaningful alterations in state-economy relations are great. However, they have been great in the past and yet have yielded to skillful political leadership and inventive designs for institutional and policy change. The regulatory initiatives of the Progressive Era, the associationalism of the 1920s, the government-supervised self-regulation of the New Deal, the new fiscal and monetary policies of the postwar period, and the market-oriented initiatives of the past decade constitute a testament to the assertion that significant changes in patterns of state-economy relations are possible. While the past shapes

the future, it is not determinative. This is, in the end, one of the great lessons offered by the history of the American political economy.

## NOTES

1. *Economic Report of the President, 1993* (Washington, D.C.: Government Printing Office, 1993), Tables B-37, 59, 74, 76, and 103.
2. Ibid., Tables B-76, 77.
3. See Paul Starobin, "Time to Get Real." *National Journal* 24, 51–52 (1992): 2878–82.
4. See Paul Starobin, James A. Barnes, Julie Kosterlitz, Margaret Kriz, and Kirk Victor, "Clinton's A-Team." *National Journal* 24, 51–52 (1992): 2892–96.
5. See Edward Bellamy, *Looking Backward, 2000–1887* (New York: Penguin, 1982).
6. Karl Marx, *The Eighteenth Brumaire of Louis Bonaparte* (New York: International Publishers, 1963), p. 15.
7. *Economic Report of the President, 1982* (Washington, D.C.: Government Printing Office, 1982), pp. 27, 28.
8. Robert B, Reich, *Tales of a New America: The Anxious Liberal's Guide to the Future* (New York: Random House, 1987), p. 232.
9. *Economic Report of the President, 1993*, Tables B-74, 79.
10. Ibid., Table B-84.
11. See Donald F. Kettl, *Deficit Politics: Public Budgeting in its Institutional and Historical Context* (New York: Macmillan, 1992).
12. See Robert B. Reich, *The Work of Nations: Preparing Ourselves for 21st Century Capitalism* (New York: Alfred A. Knopf, 1991).
13. Robert Kuttner, *The End of Laissez-Faire: National Purpose and the Global Economy After the Cold War* (New York: Alfred A. Knopf, 1991), p. 157.

# INDEX